SLAVE SYSTEMS

This is a ground-breaking edited collection charting the rise and fall of forms of unfree labour in the ancient Mediterranean and the modern Atlantic, employing the methodology of comparative history. The eleven chapters in the book deal with conceptual issues and different approaches to historical comparison, and include specific case-studies ranging from the ancient forms of slavery of classical Greece and of the Roman empire to the modern examples of slavery that characterized the Caribbean, Latin America, and the United States. The results demonstrate both how much the modern world has inherited from the ancient in regard to the ideology and practice of slavery, and also how many of the issues and problems related to the latter seem to have been fundamentally comparable across time and space.

ENRICO DAL LAGO is Lecturer in American History at the National University of Ireland, Galway. His books include *The American South and the Italian Mezzogiorno* (co-editor, 2001), *Slavery and Emancipation* (co-editor, 2002), and *Agrarian Elites: American Slaveholders and Southern Italian Landowners, 1815–1861* (author, 2005).

CONSTANTINA KATSARI is Lecturer in Ancient History at the University of Leicester. She is co-editor of *Patterns in the Economy of Roman Asia Minor* (2005) and is completing a monograph on the Roman monetary economy. Her articles on Roman economy and ideology have appeared in edited collections and internationally acknowledged periodicals.

SLAVE SYSTEMS

Ancient and Modern

EDITED BY

ENRICO DAL LAGO

AND

CONSTANTINA KATSARI

CAMBRIDGE UNIVERSITY PRESS
Cambridge, New York, Melbourne, Madrid, Cape Town, Singapore, São Paulo, Delhi

Cambridge University Press
The Edinburgh Building, Cambridge CB2 8RU, UK

Published in the United States of America by Cambridge University Press, New York

www.cambridge.org
Information on this title: www.cambridge.org/9780521881838

First published 2008

Printed in the United Kingdom at the University Press, Cambridge

A catalogue record for this publication is available from the British Library

ISBN 978-0-521-88183-8 hardback

Contents

Figures

Tables

Contributors

ENRICO DAL LAGO is Lecturer in American History at the National University of Ireland, Galway. He is the author of *Agrarian Elites: American Slaveholders and Southern Italian Landowners, 1815–1861* (2005) and co-editor (with Rick Halpern) of *The American South and the Italian Mezzogiorno: Essays in Comparative History* (2001), and *Slavery & Emancipation* (2002). He is currently working on a comparative study of American Abolitionist William Lloyd Garrison and Italian Democrat Giuseppe Mazzini.

STANLEY ENGERMAN is John H. Munro Professor of Economics and Professor of History at the University of Rochester. He is either co-author or co-editor of several books, among them *Time on the Cross: The Economics of American Negro Slavery* (co-author with Robert Fogel, 1974), *British Capitalism and Caribbean Slavery* (co-editor with Barbara Solow, 1987), and *A Historical Guide to World Slavery* (co-editor with Seymour Drescher, 1998). His more recent publication is *Slavery, Emancipation, and Freedom: Comparative Perspectives* (2007).

STEPHEN HODKINSON is Professor of Ancient History at the University of Nottingham, where he directs the AHRC-funded research project 'Sparta in Comparative Perspective', and is Co-Director of the *Institute for the Study of Slavery* and the *Centre for Spartan and Peloponnesian Studies.* He is the author of *Property and Wealth in Classical Sparta* (2000) and co-editor (with Anton Powell) of *Sparta: New Perspectives* (1999), *Sparta: Beyond the Mirage* (2002), and *Sparta and War* (2006). His current research focuses on cross-cultural approaches to ancient Sparta and on her role as a comparative model in modern thought.

FÁBIO DUARTE JOLY is Adjunct Professor in Ancient and Medieval History at the Universidade Federal do Recôncavo da Bahia. He took his Ph.D. in Economic History from the University of São Paulo, Brazil. He is the author of *Tácito e a metáfora da escravidão: um estudo de cultura política romana* (2004) and *A escravidão na Roma antiga: política, economia e cultura* (2005). He also wrote entries on Roman slavery for the *Encyclopedia of Antislavery and Abolition* (2007), edited by Peter Hinks and John McKivigan.

CONSTANTINA KATSARI is Lecturer in Roman History at the University of Leicester. She is the author of several articles in journals and edited collections and co-editor (with Stephen Mitchell) of *Patterns in the Economy of Roman Asia Minor* (2006). She is currently working on her monograph on the monetary economy of the Roman empire.

RAFAEL DE BIVAR MARQUESE is Professor of History at the University of São Paulo. He is author of *Administração & Escravidão: Ideias sobre a gestão da agricultura escravista brasileira* (1999) and *Feitores do corpo, missionarios da mente. Senhores, letrados e o controle dos ecravos nas Americas, 1660–1860* (2004), and editor of *Manual do agricultor brasileiro – Carlos Augusto Taunay* (2001). His current interests are in projects that deal with both slaveholders' ideologies and slave management in Brazil and in the Americas.

JOSEPH C. MILLER is Thomas Cary Johnston Professor of History at the University of Virginia. He is author of *Way of Death: Merchant Capitalism and the Angolan Slave Trade, 1730–1830* (1988), the editor of *Slavery and Slaving in World History: A Bibliography*, 2 vols. (1999, 2nd edn, web version in preparation, Virginia Center for Digital History), and co-editor (with Paul Finkelman) of *The MacMillan Encyclopedia of World Slavery* (1999). He is currently working on a world history of slavery and slaving from the earliest times to the recent slaveries and contemporary slaving-like practices.

ORLANDO PATTERSON is John Cowles Professor of Sociology at Harvard University. He is the author of many books on slavery and related subjects, among them *Slavery and Social Death: A Comparative Study* (1982), *Freedom: Freedom in the Making of the Western Culture* (1991), and the first two volumes of a trilogy on race, immigration, and multiculturalism: *The Ordeal of Integration: Progress and Resentment in America's 'Racial Crisis'* (1998), and *Rituals of Blood: The Consequences of Slavery in Two American Centuries* (1999).

OLIVIER PÉTRÉ-GRENOUILLEAU is Professor of History at the University of Lorient and a former member of the Institut Universitaire de France. He is the author of several books, among them *L'argent de la Traite. Milieu négrier, capitalisme et développement: Un modèle* (1996) and *Les Traites Négrières: Essai d'histoire globale* (2004), and editor of *From Slave Trade to Empire: Europe and the Colonization of Black Africa, 1780s–1880s* (2004).

TRACEY RIHLL is Lecturer in Classics and Ancient History at the University of Wales, Swansea. She is the author of *Greek Science* (1999) and *The Catapult: A History* (2007), and editor (with C. J. Tuplin) of *Science and Mathematics in Ancient Greek Culture* (2002). Her papers on ancient slavery include 'The origin and establishment of ancient Greek slavery', in *Serfdom and Slavery*, ed. M. Bush (1996), and 'War, slavery and settlement in early Greece', in *War and Society*, ed. J. Rich and G. Shipley (1993). Her current interests are in both ancient science and technology and ancient slavery.

WALTER SCHEIDEL is Professor of Classics at Stanford University. He is the author of *Measuring Sex, Age and Death in the Roman Empire: Explorations in Ancient Demography* (1996) and *Death on the Nile: Disease and the Demography of Roman Egypt* (2001), editor of *Debating Roman Demography* (2001), co-editor (with Sitta von Reden) of *The Ancient Economy* (2002), and (with Ian Morris and Richard Saller) of *The Cambridge Economic History of the Greco-Roman World* (2007).

MICHAEL ZEUSKE is Professor of Iberian and Latin American History at the University of Cologne. He is the author of several books, among them *Insel der Extreme. Kuba im 20. Jahrhundert* (2000), *Sklavereien, Emanzipationen und atlantische Weltgeschichte. Essays über Mikrogeschichten, Sklaven, Globalisierungen und Rassismus* (2002), *Schwarze Karibik. Sklaven, Sklavereikultur und Emanzipation* (2004), and *Sklaven und Sklaverei in den Welten des Atlantik, 1400–1940. Umrisse, Anfänge, Akteure, Vergleichsfelder und Bibliografien* (2005).

Acknowledgments

We wish to thank all those who contributed to the international conference on 'Slave Systems, Ancient and Modern', held at the Moore Institute for Research in the Humanities and Social Studies (then Centre for the Study of Human Settlement and Historical Change), National University of Ireland, Galway, on 24–26 November 2004, at which several of the chapters in this book were presented in an early form. The conference lasted three days and saw for the first time scholars of slavery in the ancient Mediterranean and in the modern Atlantic present explicitly comparative historical papers and engage together in discussions over the concrete possibilities of comparative research in the two regions. The conference benefited from the help of a number of people and we are very grateful to all of them.

In particular, we wish to thank the Director of the Moore Institute, Nicholas Canny, and the Centre's Secretary, Marta Shaughnessy, for their help and availability. Also, the conference would not have been possible without the financial help of the President's Office at the National University of Ireland and of the university's History Department; we wish to thank wholeheartedly both the President, Iognaid O'Muircheartaigh and Professor Stephen Ellis, Head of the History Department. Work towards the publication of the present edited collection has benefited from the financial contribution of the *Millennium Research Fund*, National University of Ireland, Galway. Particular thanks go to the Center for Hellenic Studies, Washington DC, for allowing us to publish an updated version of Stephen Hodkinson, 'Spartiates, helots, and the direction of the agrarian economy: toward an understanding of helotage in comparative perspective', in *Helots and their Masters in Laconia and Messenia: Histories, Ideologies, Structures*, ed. N. Luraghi and S. E. Alcock. Washington, DC: Center for Hellenic Studies, 2003, pp. 248–86. We also wish to thank those who contributed in different ways, offering their enthusiastic help at difficult junctures in the enterprise of organizing the conference, and especially Professor Gearoid O'Tuathaigh, Reverend Patrick Towers and Sonia Guilhe. Finally, we wish to thank Michael Sharp, an extremely competent and patient editor with whom we had the luck to publish our book at Cambridge University Press.

PART I

Slavery, slave systems, world history, and comparative history

CHAPTER 1

The study of ancient and modern slave systems: setting an agenda for comparison

Enrico Dal Lago and Constantina Katsari

Historical studies of slavery are, by definition, both global and comparative. Slavery, in fact, is an institution whose practice has covered most of the documented history of the world and has spread across many different countries and regions around the globe. Thus, very few societies have remained historically untouched by it, while, at different times and in different degrees, most have seen a more or less strong presence of slaves employed for a variety of different purposes within them. Throughout history and in many societies, masters have utilized their slaves for tasks as diverse as working on landed estates or even on industrial complexes, or, more commonly, serving in households and other domestic settings, and, more rarely, for specific military or religious purposes.

The chapters gathered in this collection represent the variety of experiences associated with slavery, while they focus particularly on the scholarly study of its influence on the economy and society of those cultures that made extensive use of it. Though the dimensions of the scholarly study of slavery, much as slavery itself, are truly global in their breadth – and the authors of each chapter are aware of this – the declared scope of the present book is to focus on the comparative analysis of two specific regions of the world where slavery flourished at different times: the ancient Mediterranean and the modern Atlantic. What justifies the choice of these two particular areas is the fact that, in the course of their history, both regions saw the rise, heyday, and eventual end of self-contained, self-sustaining, highly developed and profitable systems of slavery, or 'slave systems'.

Historians and historical sociologists have commonly used the term 'system' to describe a complex set of factors that allowed the economy and society of a particular historical culture to operate. Depending on the time and place, a 'system' would be defined by the existence of specific sets of relationships between different economic operators – such as elites, labourers, or merchants – and between them and different types of institutions – such as the state, the king or emperor, the banks, etc. The 'system' operated in such a way that the particular types of social relationship that characterized it mirrored the economic relationships, which in turn defined its very structure. The organic integration among its different parts, which created an economic mechanism that was both self-contained and self-sustaining, allowed a specific 'system' to operate efficiently. The well-defined economic mechanism aimed at dealing with the effective production, distribution, and consumption of goods within a specific social scene or across societies and states. Despite the fact that the term 'system' has been connected with the economy, we should not forget that such socio-economic systems have also a cultural dimension that plays a definite role in their formation.

A much studied case is that of the feudal system, first described by Marc Bloch for medieval western Europe and then by Witold Kula for early modern eastern Europe.[1] In its simplest definition, the term 'feudal system' refers both to the social ties that bound a nobility to perform military duties for a king in exchange for grants given in land, and also the particular type of labour arrangements that bound the serfs to their lords on the latter's landed estates. More recently, scholars have used the term 'system' also to indicate particular types of organic sets of economic and social relationships that have historically encompassed large areas of the world, with different countries and regions included within them. Arguably, the most famous example is in Immanuel Wallerstein's 'world-system' analysis, at the heart of which is the process of historical formation, from the sixteenth century on, of the particular economic relationships that characterized the different components of a capitalist system spread over the entire globe and centred upon western Europe.[2] In Wallerstein's view, these economic relationships arose together with strong social inequalities associated with them and also in relation to different types of labour – among them slavery – that characterized the different areas within the system.

The expression 'slave system' refers to the scholarship cited above in that it describes a self-contained, self-sustaining set of organic relationships, both at the economic and at the social level. In this case, though, at the heart of this set of relationships was the institution of slavery, whose influence pervaded nearly every aspect of at least some of the cultures that were integrant parts of the few historically known 'slave systems' – especially the ones flourishing in the ancient Mediterranean and the modern Atlantic. Much like feudalism defined the feudal system, therefore, slavery

[1] See Bloch 1975 (1932); and Kula 1976 (1962). [2] See Wallerstein 1974–89.

defined a 'slave system' by providing the foundation of an economy in which (a) elite wealth and slave ownership were two notions inextricably connected to each other, (b) a large part of the trade revolved around buying and selling slaves, (c) a high percentage of the workers were enslaved labourers, and/or (d) states and other types of institutions relied on the profits made with slavery for their prosperity. Also, within a 'slave system', the social hierarchy mirrored the economic one based on slave ownership, while slavery influenced relationships equally within the family and in society at large in some particular cultures.[3]

By using the term 'slave system', we intend to refer explicitly to the pervasiveness of the institution of slavery – an institution based on the 'slave mode of production' and system of labour – in the economy and society of those regions, countries, and states that were interconnected parts of a unified market area. In some respects, then, the concept of 'slave system' relies on the definition of 'slave society', first advanced by Moses Finley and then utilized also by Keith Hopkins and Ira Berlin.[4] According to this definition, unlike in a 'society with slaves', in a 'slave society' slavery was at the heart of the economic and social life of a particular culture and it influenced it in such a way to create a large class of slaveholders, who effectively held a great deal of power and exercised it over the non-slaveholding population. Significantly, according to both Finley and Hopkins, genuine 'slave societies' were historically only a few[5] and, among them, the best-known cases are classical Athens and imperial Rome in the ancient Mediterranean and the nineteenth-century United States and Brazil in the modern Atlantic. Both the ancient Mediterranean and the modern Atlantic represent two major 'slave systems', which, in turn, include areas representing specific socio-economic 'subsystems'. Such 'subsystems' were, for example, the Athenian or the Brazilian ones. The wider 'slave systems' of the Mediterranean and the Atlantic consisted ultimately of a collection of different cultures interrelated in an organic way, as a result of the influence of slavery on their economy and society. Eventually, these systems provided the opportunity for the development of genuine 'slave societies' at the centre of their trade networks.

If one decided to study 'slave systems' such as those of the ancient Mediterranean and the modern Atlantic within the framework of a

[3] The classic study of 'slave systems' in antiquity is Westermann 1955.

[4] See Finley 1998; Hopkins 1978; and Berlin 1998.

[5] Notice also that Orlando Patterson supports a view opposite from Hopkins; see Chapter 2 note 5 in this volume.

chronological sequence of phenomena on a global scale, undoubtedly the methodological approach of world historical analysis would be the most appropriate. World history, intended as a discipline that studies the global past of human societies, is consistently on the rise nowadays. Scholars who have chosen this approach have either attempted exceptionally broad ranging surveys or, more interestingly, they have focused on finding common patterns of historical development among societies located in particular areas of the world. Among the latter types of studies, the most acclaimed have treated patterns of historical spread and influence of either a particular economic feature, such as trade, or else of a particular socio-political institution, such as Islam.[6] Yet, while slavery *per se* could easily be researched as either of the two, the study of 'slave systems' would require, because of its nature, a more specific type of world historical approach.

Recently, historians and historical sociologists have become increasingly aware of the importance of seas and oceans for the study of world history, focusing, above all, on the unifying influences that the latter have exercised in economic and social terms on the cultures that have flourished around them.[7] In particular, scholarship on the Mediterranean and the Atlantic has steadily increased in size, thus acknowledging the importance of these regions as historically integrated socio-economic areas within a global context. Specifically, recent studies such as Peregrine Horden and Nicholas Purcell's *The Corrupting Sea* and John Elliott's *Empires of the Atlantic* not only followed the established historiographic tradition by considering the two seas as unifying entities but they opened new paths by providing invaluable suggestions for researchers of the ancient Mediterranean and the modern Atlantic within the context of world history.[8] Moreover, important suggestions in this sense have come also from the few studies that belong to the recent field of research of 'historical globalization'.[9]

To be sure, the suggestions coming from the studies mentioned above would prove particularly useful, if one wished to proceed to identify patterns of historical development by employing a comparative method, when researching on two specific 'slave systems' such as the ancient Mediterranean and the modern Atlantic. In this case, the methodological approach would focus specifically on sustained and combined analysis of

[6] On the state of the art of world history, see Hodgson and Burke III 1993.

[7] See Wigen 2006; Horden and Purcell 2006; Games 2006; and Matsuda 2006.

[8] See Horden and Purcell 2000; and Elliott 2006. The few studies on the Mediterranean, including Harris 2005, refer invariably to Braudel 1975 (1949). On the ever-growing scholarship on the 'Atlantic world', see Armitage and Braddick 2002.

[9] See Hopkins 2002.

the two 'slave systems', so to identify important similarities and differences between them and to understand their meaning in comparative historical perspective. Ever since March Bloch published his pioneering article on the comparative history of European societies in 1928, comparative historians have debated on the correct approach and aim of historical comparisons.[10] In the end, it is fair to say that most of them have agreed on the fact that, broadly speaking, the features he had originally outlined – a certain similarity between the facts observed and certain differences between their contexts – are still the indispensable requirements for a comparative study of the type that, according to Peter Kolchin, employs a 'rigorous' approach to historical comparison.[11]

There are, of course, other ways of doing historical comparison, and several of the studies that employ them would probably fall under another category described by Kolchin as employing a 'soft' approach to historical comparison, for the reason that, rather than developing into full-blown comparative analyses, they either simply hint at the possibility of doing this or provide brief comparative treatments of significant themes they treat.[12] Most likely, though, the majority of comparative studies would fall somewhere in between these two extremes of 'rigorous' and 'soft' approaches to historical comparisons. The chapters collected in this book are a proof of the validity of different comparative approaches to the history of the 'slave systems' of the ancient Mediterranean and the modern Atlantic, and these approaches cover the entire spectrum contained within the two definitions of 'rigorous' and 'soft' comparisons. At the same time, the essays also provide a critically informed approach to comparative history that does not refrain from identifying the latter's limitations in regard to the study of particular historical problems.

When researching 'slave systems', whether from a global or a comparative historical perspective, one should first acknowledge the importance of studies written by a number of scholars who have analysed slavery in all its different aspects. Particularly significant, for the purpose of the present book, are those studies that have attempted to treat the development of slavery as an institution through subsequent historical periods and also those that have provided treatments encompassing all the varieties of slavery that have characterized different historical societies. Among the former types of studies, the most significant are those written by David

[10] See Bloch 1928; see also Skocpol and Somers 1980.
[11] See Kolchin 2003a: 4. On the debate over comparative history, see Cohen and O'Connor 2004.
[12] See Kolchin 2003a.

Brion Davis, who has provided – in his trilogy *The Problem of Slavery in Western Culture*, *The Problem of Slavery in the Age of Revolutions*, and *Slavery and Human Progress* – the most comprehensive treatment of the history of slavery as both a social institution and a cultural feature of the western world from antiquity to the nineteenth century.[13] Davis' is, in many ways, a model of world historical analysis with invaluable suggestions for the study of 'slave systems', for it shows, through the development of the institution of slavery, the similarities and differences in the types of contexts in which it operated at different historical times in the West. Among those studies that have, instead, provided a broad treatment of slavery covering different parts of the world in different historical periods, the most acclaimed has been Orlando Patterson's *Slavery and Social Death*, a model study of both world history and comparative history at the same time.[14] On one hand, in fact, it is fair to say that Patterson's book is the one study that has succeeded more than any other to show the importance and pervasiveness of slavery as a global institution in the entire history of the world. On the other hand, the suggestions for comparative studies of 'slave systems' are also innumerable in Patterson's work, since at its heart lies comparison on a grand scale between all the known slaveholding historical societies; the author's purpose to arrive at a working definition of the most likely constant characteristics of slavery and of its variants has been amply fulfilled.

Inspired by Davis' and Patterson's works, scholars of slavery have gathered in impressive collaborative projects that, for the first time, have attempted to catalogue and detail the varieties of experiences related to slavery and the issues attached to it across historical eras and places. From these efforts, encyclopaedias, chronologies, and guides to both the actual phenomenon of world slavery and the massive and intricate scholarship attached to it have recently arisen.[15] At the same time, a monumental attempt by Joseph C. Miller to systematically keep track of and divide into categories the ever-increasing number of scholarly studies on world slavery has produced a comprehensive bibliography, recently updated as a supplement of the journal *Slavery & Abolition*, which represents the state of the art of scholarship in the field.[16] Furthermore, the projected edited multi-volume *World History of Slavery* by Cambridge University Press

[13] Davis 1966, 1975, 1984. See also Davis 2006. [14] Patterson 1982.

[15] See Rodriguez 1997; Finkelman and Miller 1998; Drescher and Engerman 1998; and Rodriguez 1999.

[16] See Miller 1999b; and Thurston and Miller 2005.

promises to encompass all areas of the world and to span from antiquity to the present.

Parallel to broad studies of slavery in world and comparative historical context, another type of research has produced more specific comparative studies, aiming at providing a combined analysis of one or two particular slave societies. The archetype of these studies is Frank Tannenbaum's 1946 book *Slave and Citizen*, which compared the institution of slavery in the United States and Latin America. This book subsequently led to the publication of a number of specific comparative studies – such as the ones by Herbert Klein and Carl Degler – between the slave society of the American South and those of Latin American countries such as Cuba and Brazil.[17] This tradition of comparative historical studies is the one that most appropriately fits Peter Kolchin's idea of 'rigorous' approach to comparative history. This type of comparison, while for a long time restricted to studies on the slave societies of the New World, has recently broadened its scope and included the comparative research between the nineteenth-century American South and contemporary African and European societies characterized by different degrees of unfree labour.[18] From this particular type of scholarship have come particularly valuable suggestions for a 'rigorous' comparative historical approach to the study of 'slave systems', especially from the methodological point of view.

Aside from the few studies that belong to this tradition of scholarship, for the most part comparative research on slavery has employed in different terms and degrees a 'soft' approach to historical comparison. This is especially true in regard to comparison between ancient and modern types of slavery, about which there is no specific and sustained comparative study to date, even though a number of ancient and modern historians have hinted at the possibility. Among ancient historians (aside from the already mentioned Moses Finley and Keith Hopkins) Keith Bradley, Walter Scheidel, Stephen Hodkinson, Brent Shaw, Alan Watson, and Geoffrey de Ste Croix have also provided a number of interesting comparative points with the modern world – and particularly often with the ante-bellum American South – in their treatments of different aspects of ancient slavery. Thomas Wiedemann, specifically, attempted with the foundation of the Institute for the Study of Slavery at the University of Nottingham the promotion of the comparative study of slavery through a series of edited volumes that would have included studies of individual slave societies across time and space. Sadly,

[17] Tannenbaum 1946. See also Klein 1967; and Degler 1971.
[18] See Fredrickson 1981; Kolchin 1987; Bowman 1993; and Dal Lago 2005.

his untimely death prevented him from seeing the completion of this project.[19]

Among modern historians, instead, the most effective at providing comparative treatments referring to aspects of ancient slavery have been specifically, besides David Brion Davis and Orlando Patterson, Elizabeth Fox-Genovese and Eugene Genovese and Michael O' Brien, who have also investigated the effects of the legacy of ancient slavery on the society and intellectual culture of slave societies in the New World, and specifically of the American South.[20] Aside from these individual efforts, some ancient and modern historians have also participated in collaborative enterprises of collective volumes either on the history of slavery or on the history of both slavery and serfdom, providing juxtaposed treatments of ancient and modern topics. Even though not explicitly comparative, these collections of papers have hinted at important parallels and connections not only between different types of slavery but also between different systems of unfree labour.[21]

On the basis of the suggestions coming from all the works we have mentioned above and from the methodological developments that we have previously discussed, we wish to start with the publication of the present book a project of diachronic comparative study of 'slave systems', focusing specifically on the ancient Mediterranean and the modern Atlantic. In regards to the comparative approach, our preference goes to the 'rigorous' method described by Kolchin; however, as the chapters in the book show, we recognize the validity of all the studies that have hinted at possible comparisons between the ancient and modern worlds and we refer to them for the justification of our project. The general objective of our comparative project is the analysis of the 'slave systems' that flourished in the ancient Mediterranean and the modern Atlantic in their wholeness. Several of the chapters in this book look at the systems from a rather general point of view, placing them firmly in the context of world history and relating them to the scholarship on both world slavery and comparative slavery. At the same time, we think that the specific focus of particular comparative studies needs to address themes of combined analysis between two or more particular 'slave societies' – whether these are the ante-bellum

[19] See Bradley 1987, 1994; Hodkinson 2003: 245–85; Chapter 4 in this volume; Shaw 1998a; Watson 1987, 1989; Ste Croix 1983; and Wiedemann and Gardner 2002.
[20] See Davis 2006; Patterson 1982; Fox-Genovese and Genovese 2005; and O'Brien 2004.
[21] See especially Bush 1996a; Engerman 1999; and Brown and Morgan 2006.

American South and the Roman empire, or colonial Brazil and ancient Greece, etc. – as some of the chapters in this book do.

Ultimately, the unifying theme behind all the chapters, whether explicitly or implicitly comparative and whether relying on a world history or comparative history approach, is the fact that they are all based on a 'diachronic' view of the ancient and modern past. By this, we mean a view that looks as much at comparisons as at connections between the ancient and the modern worlds, depending on the methodological approach taken by the author of the chapter. In particular, unlike most sustained comparative studies, which focus on 'synchronic' comparisons between specific features of two or more contemporary societies, the examples of 'rigorous' method present in this book have a clear 'diachronic' thrust, which allows them to compare and contrast ancient and modern 'slave systems' as independent units of research and identify both common and different features across time and space. The ultimate aim of this enterprise is to start to identify the defining features, both at the methodological level and in terms of application, of a model for the 'diachronic' comparative study of 'slave systems' – one specifically focusing on the ancient Mediterranean and the modern Atlantic – that might be helpful to other studies of the same type in the future.

The best way to start an actual 'diachronic' comparative study of 'slave systems' is to discuss the methodological issues specifically related to it. Part I in the present book – entitled 'Slavery, slave systems, world history, and comparative history' – is, therefore, dedicated to presenting the research methods of ancient and modern slavery, with a particular focus on the ancient Mediterranean and the modern Atlantic. Referring back to the general points we made previously on world history and comparative history and on world slavery and comparative slavery, this part includes – besides our own methodological introduction – two chapters that represent two radically different approaches regarding the study of 'slave systems'. The first chapter, in fact, upholds the validity of historical comparison to the point of even setting up an agenda for future research on comparative slavery, while the second chapter questions the very validity of the definition of 'slavery' – and thus the possibility of comparing different types of slavery – preferring, instead, to focus on the analysis of 'slaving' in world history.

The two chapters are representatives of the ongoing debate between, on one hand, comparative historians and historical sociologists, and, on the other hand, world historians and historians of globalization over the pre-eminence given either to the study of slavery as a collection of experiences that took place at specific times and in specific places or to the study of slavery as an overall dynamic process. The difference between the two approaches is of paramount importance for the study of ancient and modern 'slave systems'. In one case, 'slave systems' can be taken and studied as relatively fixed and somewhat self-contained units of analysis – thus leading to insightful findings on the meaning of similarities and differences between them – while, in the other case, they are 'deconstructed' and stripped of their 'systemic' aspects, so to emphasize the dynamic components of the process of 'slaving' that has generated them; a process which is the actual object of the analysis. Thus, depending on which approach one takes – whether it focuses on actually comparing ancient and modern 'slave systems' or on analysing the development of the process of 'slaving' from the ancient to the modern worlds – he/she will ask different questions, will find different results, equally valid, and will have to rely on different sets of scholarship altogether.[22]

In his chapter, Orlando Patterson argues that historical comparison between ancient and pre-modern societies, both 'slaveholding societies'[23] and 'slave societies', is the only empirical method that allows scholars to reconstruct how slavery worked in the ancient world, given the notorious scarcity of data available.[24] In order to demonstrate his methodology, his own specific comparative study focuses on the understanding of the relationship between sexual division of labour and slavery in pre-modern societies. At the same time, he identifies broad themes of comparative analysis, such as the identification of the distinctive features of slavery as a 'relation of domination', the explanation of the reasons of its rooting in 'slaveholding societies' – and, more specifically, of its pervasiveness in genuine 'slave societies' – and the analysis of the consequences of the centuries-long reliance on slavery for human, specifically western, culture. In doing this, Patterson sets a preliminary agenda filled with crucial suggestions for the comparative study of ancient and modern 'slave systems', while identifying, at the same time, specific reasons for the need of such a comparative project.

[22] Important works that have influenced the development of comparative methodology of 'slave systems' are especially Davis 1966; Patterson 1982; Finley 1998; Hopkins 1978; Nieboer 1971 (1910); and Engerman and Genovese 1975. Important works that have influenced the development of world historical methodology on 'slaving' are especially Miller 1999a; Phillips 1985; Curtin 1990; Lovejoy 2000; and Blackburn 1997.

[23] This definition is akin to Finley's and Hopkins' 'societies with slaves'.

[24] See Chapter 2 in this volume.

Patterson, then, proceeds to provide an initial answer to his preliminary question by setting up a statistical analysis of the 186 types of societies classified by anthropologist George P. Murdock.[25] The results of Patterson's analysis show, first of all, that, in societies with extensive farming, polygyny is strongly associated with female participation in the 'dominant mode of subsistence'; yet, while in such societies there is a causal link between the interaction of polygyny and warfare on one hand and slavery on the other – and between bridewealth, or bride price, and slavery in societies with intensive farming – there is no evidence of a direct association between female participation and slavery; rather, we encounter a negative relationship between the two. Patterson concludes that, 'in the long run then, increased slavery would eventually lead to growing numbers of men in the labour force, even if the initial effect was to increase the number of women, hence the negative association we observe between slavery and female participation'.[26] Then, in an enlightening case-study in historical comparison, Patterson turns his attention to the 'slave societies' of Dark Age Greece. He proves the validity of the comparative method by finding crucial similarities between the early Greek societies and some of the premodern 'agro-pastoral slave systems' (all of them objects of his statistical analysis), taking into consideration both the strong link between slavery and warfare and the status and labour tasks of male and female slaves.

If Patterson's chapter is a model of comparative historical analysis, Joseph C. Miller's chapter presents an altogether different approach, concerned, instead, with the large issues of continuity and change in world history. Thus, in his chapter, Miller constructs a world history with a particular focus on the ancient Mediterranean and the modern Atlantic, in which the dynamic process of 'slaving' – rather than the static concept of 'slavery' – provides the element of continuity, seen from the point of view of both the enslavers and the enslaved, while change relates to the differences in modes and strategies employed in different historical epochs. Placing at the heart of his analysis the fundamental questions of how and why some people resorted to slaving from time to time and from place to place throughout human history, Miller proceeds to sketch out elements of a 'global history of slaving'. His initial aim is to provide a basic definition of 'slaving' as 'a strategy focused specifically on mobilizing directly controlled *human* resources'.[27] Such a strategy was employed by opportunistic individuals who enslaved outsiders for personal ends, thus

[25] See Murdock and Provost 1973a and 1973b. [26] See Chapter 2 in this volume.
[27] See Chapter 3 in this volume.

challenging the prevailing ethos of the community. For Miller, then, the entire world history of 'slaving' unfolded as a series of such challenges brought to the prevailing community ethos by different categories of enslavers at different times and in different places.

Thus, in the ancient Mediterranean, mercantile interests provided the enslaving with the means to challenge the prevailing aristocratic ethos, while, later on, 'generals in Rome's sweeping military campaigns on the frontiers ... used their captives to displace previous and less market-oriented landowners'.[28] Miller, then, provides a crucial comparative point by claiming that 'Old World practices of slavery were essentially female, private and broadly incorporative and assimilative within the strongly hierarchical, patriarchal, households within which the great majority of the enslaved lived'; in contrast, the particular type of economic expansion that characterized the modern Atlantic from the fifteenth century onwards took place in entirely novel contexts, in which 'slaving' was a highly commercialized activity and much more strictly regulated in legal terms.[29] Tracing the origins of these developments to the medieval Mediterranean, Miller shows how they eventually ended up affecting the native populations of both Africa and the Americas and benefiting the Iberian, Dutch, French, and English colonies in the New World.

Miller concludes with a plea for 'historicizing slaving', a type of analysis that 'allows us to describe processes of commercialization unique to the Atlantic in language developed from analysis of earlier processes' such as the ones that occurred in the ancient Mediterranean.[30] In doing this, he sets the tone for a type of historical comparison that integrates the dimension of historical change within it – thus, leaving us with the suggestion, in the context of the study of ancient and modern 'slave systems', to take into account the dynamic characteristics of the phenomenon of slavery in world history. And to be sure, in an ideal study of ancient and modern 'slave systems', the type of comparative historical analysis represented by Orlando Patterson's chapter – an analysis which takes equally into account ancient sources and modern ethnographic data – could be combined with the type of world historical analysis represented by Joseph C. Miller's chapter – an analysis in which comparison between ancient and modern must be developed within a historical framework emphasizing both

[28] See Chapter 3 in this volume.

[29] In his claim, Miller is joined by scholars such as David Brion Davis, Immanuel Wallerstein, Eric Wolf, Robin Blackburn, Philip Curtin and others, who have argued about the 'novel' character of modern Atlantic slavery.

[30] See Chapter 3 in this volume.

continuity and change. Ultimately, the integration of these two methods, we believe, could yield insights into the nature of ancient and modern 'slavery' and 'slaving' that would not be possible to grasp otherwise, especially if we think about all the elements of the complexity of the task at hand.

An essential part of the study of both slavery and 'slave systems' is economics, especially since the very notion of 'system' has a strong economic dimension. In order to study the 'slave systems' that flourished specifically in the ancient Mediterranean and modern Atlantic in comparative perspective, one must first focus on the identification of their economic features, whether from a more structural or more dynamic point of view. In this sense, the three chapters of Part II on 'Economics and technology of ancient and modern slave systems' not only provide an accurate picture of scholarly research on these features but also complement each other in treating different economic components and in providing both ancient and modern perspectives. In fact, while the first chapter in the section consists in a genuine comparative effort at answering the fundamental question of the economic conditions conducive to the rise of slave systems in the ancient and modern worlds, the remaining two chapters focus on specific aspects of the economy of the ancient Mediterranean and the modern Atlantic – one treating the relationship between slavery and ancient technology in the Greek and the Roman worlds and the other focusing on both early nineteenth-century and contemporary perceptions of the economics of plantation slavery in the Americas.

Each of these three chapters in its own way deals, ultimately, with two crucial issues that scholars of ancient and modern slavery have addressed when focusing on economics: whether, in 'slave systems', slavery – though pervasive at all levels – was particularly associated with one or more specific economic activities, and whether, either as a result of this association or regardless of it, the economic system at the heart of genuine 'slave societies' was particularly profitable. Regarding the first point, there is no doubt that a superficial comparison would lead someone to believe that the slave systems of the ancient Mediterranean and of the modern Atlantic differed enormously, given the fact that, while slaves in the Greco-Roman world were employed in an enormous variety of economic activities, slaves in the Caribbean and in the American mainland supplied, first and foremost, forced labour in plantation agriculture. Yet, this would be an oversimplification of a sort, since a more accurate comparative study would show that large numbers of slaves were employed in agriculture in both ancient and modern 'slave societies'. On the other hand, while we might well discover that in the ancient Mediterranean slavery and pre-industrial technological production were not irreconcilable, by the same token in different areas of the modern Atlantic there were a number of agricultural activities in which slavery was associated with what was, at least, incipient industrial production.[31]

Ultimately, this shift in scholarly perspective reflects also on our notions on the overall profitability of ancient and modern 'slave systems'. On these issues, both ancient and modern historians have argued for decades on either side of a divide that has opposed supporters of either a 'pre-modern' view, or a more 'modern' view of the economic functioning of slavery.[32] It is hard to see that conciliation among these two opposite views will happen any time soon, simply because the premises from which they build their assumptions and according to which they treat their evidence are fundamentally different. Yet, it is at least possible to say that, on the basis of ever mounting evidence in favour of a combination of both 'pre-modern' and 'modern' features in both ancient and modern 'slave systems', supporters of the two views are likely to increasingly soften their now still rigid stance.[33]

In his chapter, Walter Scheidel applies the comparative method as a heuristic tool to the combined study of ancient and modern 'slave systems', setting as his primary goal that of understanding the nature of the constitutive elements of slavery and 'slave societies' in economic terms. In particular, Scheidel seeks to answer the question of 'why would individuals who relied primarily or exclusively on the labour of others choose to employ slaves for a particular type of activity'.[34] In order to achieve his aim, he first criticizes Stefano Fenoaltea's model, according to which 'effort-intensive activities' were harsh and closely supervised, while 'care-intensive activities' were 'benign and unsupervised', eventually leading to

[31] Key studies on the whole economy of the ancient Mediterranean include Finley 1973; and Scheidel and Von Reden 2002. On the Roman empire, see Rostovtzeff 1957; and Garnsey and Saller 1987. For the modern Atlantic, see Eltis *et al.* 2004; and Berlin and Morgan 1993. On the United States, see Fogel and Engerman 1974; Smith 1998; and, with specific reference to manufacturing, Carlton and Coclanis 2003; and Delfino and Gillespie 2005.

[32] For the ancient world, studies emphasizing 'pre-modern' aspects have been headed by Finley 1973. Among the studies by 'modernists', see Rostovtzeff 1957; and Mattingly and Salmon 2001. For the modern world, important studies supporting the 'backwardness' of the American South include Genovese 1965 and Wright 1978. Important studies supporting the modern, 'capitalist', view include Fogel and Engerman 1974; and Oakes 1982.

[33] Studies on modern slavery that have argued for a combination of 'pre-modern' and modern features in the economy of the American South include Smith 1998; Young 1999; and Follett 2005.

[34] See Chapter 4 in this volume.

manumission.[35] This model, as indicated by Scheidel, only explains the omnipresence of slavery in domestic service, animal husbandry, manufacturing, and commerce in the ancient Mediterranean, all activities highly rewarded, but cannot explain the function of the 'slave systems' of the modern Atlantic. Scheidel, then, goes on to construct his own, composite model, relying partly on Christopher Hanes' research on the incidence of 'turnover costs' – meaning costs related to workers' replacement – on slave economies and on the type of labour markets, 'thin' or 'thick', on which they relied. He also partly relies on James Watson's classification of open 'slave systems' – with full assimilation of ex-slaves into society – and closed 'slave systems' – with social confinement of ex-slaves even after manumission.[36]

Through his own model, Scheidel shows that 'socio-cultural conventions and expectations' also played a major part in influencing the link between slavery and either effort-intensive or care-intensive activities, in both ancient and modern times. Scheidel, then, ties his findings to a discussion on the factors conducive to the rise of 'slave systems', the most important of which being shortage of labour and access to slaves, and, secondarily, demand for slave-produced goods and accumulation of capital. In a particularly insightful comparative analysis, Scheidel not only shows that, in different modes and degrees, these factors were present both in the slave systems of classical Greece and Republican Rome and in the modern New World 'slave systems', but also that an equally important factor to take into account was the increase in 'commitments among the free population that conflict[ed] with economic activities'[37] – as happened, for example, in both ancient Rome and fifteenth-century Portugal. Ultimately, though, according to Scheidel, the combination of all these factors could end in the formation of 'slave systems' of either of two types: '"peripheral" systems with favourable land/labour ratios, and "core" systems in which a combination of high commitment levels, capital inflows, and overseas expansion raises demand for labour'[38] – a further, important suggestion to keep in mind in building our own model for the comparative study of 'slave systems'.

Tying in with Walter Scheidel's discussion on the type of economic activities most likely to be connected with slavery and 'slave systems', Tracey Rihll's chapter focuses on the relationship between slavery and technology in the Greco-Roman world, but with plenty of possible

[35] See Fenoaltea 1984: 635–68. [36] See Hanes 1996: 307–29; and Watson 1980.
[37] See Chapter 4 in this volume. [38] See Chapter 4 in this volume.

comparative points with modern pre-industrial societies. To begin with, Rihll argues that, while it is true that in the ancient Mediterranean there were plenty of slaves involved in high skill occupations, it is also true that in ancient manufacturing it was fairly difficult to gather a permanent staff of free workers, primarily because of the prejudice attached by free men to a permanent employment of that type. Hence, they constantly used skilled slaves in manufacturing activities in both Greece and Rome; slaves who, because of a number of factors, ended up living in a semi-free status (sometimes even leading to manumission), not unlike skilled slaves in the few industries of the ante-bellum American South. As in the ante-bellum American South, in antiquity also this status was a major incentive for slaves who wished to be employed.[39] In general, skilled slaves employed in manufacturing were either trained *in loco* by the artisan himself or bought already in possession of specific skills, in which case their value was, naturally, much higher.

This, then, raises the issue of capital investment, also because, theoretically, technological innovation[40] in manufacturing was so expensive that only the wealthy and kings could undertake it. Against this conventional wisdom, though, Rihll argues that most technological innovations in antiquity occurred in ordinary workshops with little expenditure 'of materials or cash either in their development or in their adoption'.[41] These innovations, similarly to the modern ones, tended to save capital, rather than labour – or neither, in the case of the famous 'automata'. And yet, there were also cases of labour-saving devices, such as the mechanical flour mills, whose adoption was possibly encouraged by mass production of bread for the population of ancient cities. Nevertheless, risk was always involved in technological innovation, and, even in the case of success by the inventors, the degree of improvement of ancient mechanization over manual labour was often fairly small. Still, the connection of manufacturing production, and thus technology, with slavery – despite the high costs of skilled slaves – has certainly not been properly analysed in all its implications. In particular, Rihll alerts us to the fact that 'slavery forced people with diverse technical skills and education across linguistic and cultural boundaries' and thus 'was perhaps the main agent of technology transfer and innovation' in the ancient Mediterranean[42] – a point that, incidentally, could be equally made

[39] On skilled slaves in ante-bellum southern manufacturing, see Dew 1994.

[40] Technological innovation in antiquity seems to have been a common phenomenon according to recent archaeological evidence. For more information see also Green 2000: 29–59.

[41] See Chapter 5 in this volume. [42] See Chapter 5 in this volume.

regarding technological diffusion among the 'slave societies' of the modern Atlantic.

Providing an ideal counterpart to Rihll's treatment of technology and slavery in antiquity, Michael Zeuske's chapter looks at reception and 'transfer' of economic and technological issues among the slaveholding elites of the Caribbean in the early nineteenth century.[43] Zeuske takes the lead from works written by Alexander von Humboldt and by Cuban economic reformer Francisco de Arango y Parreño to claim that the crisis slavery went through in the modern Atlantic at the beginning of the nineteenth century – mainly due to the successful slave revolution in Haiti and the temporary fall in sugar prices – prompted the slaveholding and intellectual elites of the Americas to modify and improve the economic systems of the 'slave societies' that they headed. In doing this, they provided an early example of political and anthropological comparison, while, at the same time, their efforts showed a high degree of connection and common conceptual development. Hence, the methodological question of whether we should study slavery in the New World in comparative perspective or as *histoire croisée* – the term, used in French historiography, referring to an analysis focused on historical connections and ideological 'transfers'.[44] Though Zeuske tends to lean toward the latter in his judgment, in his chapter he manages to integrate both approaches, in the process providing an important model for a comparative and interlinked study of 'slave systems'.

Early nineteenth-century Cuba – where Humboldt and Arango met – was at the centre of debates among planters and intellectuals about technological improvement and modernization of the 'slave systems'. While residing in Cuba, Humboldt became aware of these debates and elaborated a comparison between the slave economies of the Americas, in which he took into account different issues, among them sugar production and race relations, and arrived at Arango's conclusion that, without changing their practice of slavery with radical reforms, the Cuban elite faced the threat of a slave revolution as in Haiti. Humboldt's comparative treatment of the sugar economies – and especially of issues such as 'the internal organization of the plantations, the techniques utilized to process sugar, and in general the yields of the soil and the sugarcane' – highlights the degree of interlinking and conceptual transfer between the slaveholding elites of the Americas.[45] Eventually, these debates and 'transfers' led to a renewed strength of the slave

[43] See Chapter 6 in this volume.

[44] On *histoire croisée*, see Werner and Zimmermann 2003: 7–36.

[45] See Chapter 6 in this volume.

economies of both the Caribbean and the American mainland. In both, the planter elites combined information from England's scientific practice of agriculture with a shrewd knowledge and exploitation of the new market opportunities in the world economy to reaffirm their power on the 'slave system' of the modern Atlantic for several decades, despite the demise of empires and the threats of slave revolutions and also of possible emancipations.

In the end, much like in the ancient Mediterranean, in the modern Atlantic also 'slavery functioned as an agent of transfer of an economic culture' and, where there were the right conditions, also of technological innovation.[46] In the process, it changed the economics of 'slave systems' in both cases, as elites established a dialogue between each other over improvement and modernization of the agricultural and manufacturing production and in connection with parallel developments in the market economy. At the same time, slavery's role as a connecting agent also resulted in an ever increasing awareness by the slaves of the existence of millions of their brethren toiling in different agricultural and manufacturing regions and in the spread of knowledge among them of the attempted revolts against the system. Thus, in a study that seeks to compare ancient and modern 'slave systems', slavery has to be taken not only as the social and economic foundation of them, but also as the very structural factor that, due to its pervasiveness, provided the chance to both slaveholding elites and slaves to establish and maintain communication with their peers, although in different ways and degrees.

Focus on the broad economic features of 'slave systems' can be useful especially at the very beginning of a large project of comparison between the ancient Mediterranean and the modern Atlantic. However, when one moves from this initial stage to a more specific type of comparison – thus, between specific 'slave societies' – he/she needs to identify particular themes around which to construct a sub-project of a more particular nature. One such theme is the object of Part III, which focuses specifically on ideologies and practices of slave management in the Greco-Roman world and in the Americas. Also in this case, the two chapters that form it represent two different methodological approaches to the comparison of ancient and modern 'slave systems'; both valid, though for different reasons. One of the chapters is a case-study in the vein of 'rigorous' approach to historical comparison advocated by Peter Kolchin and applied to ancient and modern theories of slave management; the other chapter,

46 See Chapter 6 in this volume.

instead, looks at the same theme showing the extent to which there were connections between the ancient and modern worlds and, thus, it is closer to the idea of *histoire croisée* –though a diachronic version of it.

To be sure, a narrow assessment of these two methods of historical investigation could see them as mutually exclusive, especially because historians tend to ask very different questions by employing them, and, ultimately, this is the main reason why they rely on completely different types of scholarship. As we have noted above, the 'rigorous' method of historical comparison is well established among historians of modern slavery, who have constructed a number of 'synchronic' comparisons between 'slave societies';[47] it is, though, utterly under-represented in scholarship on ancient slavery, where broad sweeping studies on the slavery experience in antiquity or more specific studies on aspects of either Greek or Roman slavery, but never in comparative perspective, continue to dominate the field.[48] One of the consequences of this is that 'rigorous' historical comparison, in 'diachronic' mode, between ancient and modern 'slave societies', or between aspects of ancient and modern 'slave systems', is virtually unknown.[49] The reason for this is tightly linked to the sort of questions customarily asked in 'rigorous' comparative studies; difficult questions to answer, given the difference of the available sources and the continuous focus primarily on similarities and differences. The attempt to make sense of complex issues such as the slaveholding elites' ideologies, the practices of management, the treatment of the slave labour force, the slaves' life and culture, the aims and objectives of slave rebellions, and other themes could present additional difficulties.

An altogether different type of study is, instead, the attempt to find actual connections between the ancient and modern worlds, with a particular focus on the practices of slavery. This type of study is, in fact, part of a well-established and very large body of scholarship on the influence of ancient Mediterranean cultures on the modern western mind; that is, the way the 'classical tradition' influenced numerous aspects of western civilization and formed new fields of research, such as philosophy, politics, religion, law, to cite but a few, particularly from the Renaissance onwards.[50] In nearly every enterprise they embarked upon, the very same

[47] See Tannenbaum 1946; Klein 1967; and Degler 1971. See also Foner and Genovese 1969; Hall 1971; Mullin 1992; McDonald 1993; Drescher 1999; and Marquese 2004.

[48] See Finley 1998; Hopkins 1978; Garnsey 1996; and Wiedemann 1981 – the latter a sourcebook. For more specific studies, see, instead, Garlan 1988; Bradley 1987, 1994; and Kirschenbaum 1987.

[49] The exception is Patterson 1982.

[50] For examples, see Pocock 1975; Skinner 1978; and Rahe 1992.

merchant and intellectual elites who played such a large role in the creation of the modern Atlantic world kept the accomplishments of their ancestors in the ancient Mediterranean as their models, they read and often followed what they had written, and in many cases they strove to achieve what they had achieved.[51] It is no wonder, then, that, in the practice of slavery also, the models of classical antiquity loomed high in the cultural background of the educated planter elites of the Americas; thus, the investigation of this influence is a particularly promising effort that has the potential of shedding much light on issues not usually investigated in a 'rigorous' type of historical comparison between ancient and modern 'slave systems'.[52]

Relying on both Kolchin's 'rigorous' approach and Theda Skocpol and Margaret Somers' method of 'contrast of contexts',[53] in their chapter, Enrico Dal Lago and Constantina Katsari attempt an experimental study of two particular 'slave societies' of the ancient Mediterranean and the modern Atlantic – the Roman world and the ante-bellum American South – in 'diachronic' comparative perspective.[54] Aware of the enormous difference in available evidence between the two case-studies, they focus on a specific theme for which it is possible to treat comparatively two particular sets of sources: the ideal model of slave management. Not surprisingly, this is a theme widely discussed by both ancient Roman and ante-bellum southern agronomists and agricultural reformers, who both saw it as a key to enhancing the productivity of the landed estates on which slaves formed the bulk of the labour force. In their chapter, Dal Lago and Katsari treat different aspects of slave management, keeping a firm focus, though, on the model of master–slave relationship and treatment of the workforce that agricultural reformers in both cases thought possible to achieve following certain sets of rules. Remarkably, comparison shows that there were several similarities regarding the advice on the treatment of slaves in the works of both the ancient Roman and the ante-bellum southern agronomists; yet, there were also specific differences, mainly because of the different types of Roman and American slavery and agricultural systems.

Similarities related particularly to the importance of the slaves' well-being in the ideal model of slave management; a feature that may suggest, among other things, a comparable concern by Roman and American masters for their capital investments. Other similarities show in the employment of comparable systems of punishment and rewards as a

[51] On the United States, see Gunmere 1963; Reinhold 1984; and Richard 1994.

[52] See Davis 1966, 2006; O'Brien 2004; and Fox-Genovese and Genovese 2005.

[53] See Kolchin 2003a; and Skocpol and Somers 1980.

[54] See Chapter 7 in this volume.

means to reinforce the masters' grip over their workforce – though, in this case, the specific types of rewards and punishments differed strongly between the two case-studies. Ultimately, for Dal Lago and Katsari, these similarities point to the existence of a comparable paternalistic ideal in the model of slave management – one tightly linked, in both cases, to the way relationships within the master's family were structured around the *pater familias*.[55] Yet, while for American masters 'it is very likely that paternalistic attitudes were related to a capitalist concern for the maximization of production', the same cannot be said for Roman masters.[56] Also, the difference between the racial exploitation of African-American slaves and the absence of racial issues in Roman slavery is of critical importance not only in the context of ideals of slave management, but also for the overall comparative study of 'slave systems' in the ancient Mediterranean and the modern Atlantic.[57]

Though dealing with very similar issues related to slave management and to the master–slave relationship in the ancient and modern worlds, with their chapter, Rafael de Bivar Marquese and Fabio Joly construct an altogether different type of study, at the heart of which, rather than historical comparison, is the influence of classical authors on modern practices of slavery.[58] Their focus is on colonial Brazil, where, at the beginning of the eighteenth century, a group of Jesuit authors relied heavily on the classical tradition in order to uphold the validity of an idea of society that had at its centre the patriarchal Christian master, from whose authority subject categories such as children, women, and slaves were supposed to be utterly dependent. As they did so, these Jesuit authors utilized excerpts from both Greek economists on household management and Roman agronomists on slavery and agriculture, thus providing an ideological justification for the rule of the Christian *pater familias* and master over his subjects that ideally linked in a sort of historical continuum the 'slave systems' of the ancient Mediterranean and the modern Atlantic. By the early eighteenth century, in fact, slavery was firmly rooted in the socio-economic structure of Portuguese Brazil and inextricably linked with the gigantic expansion of sugar production that had taken place in a number of European colonies located in the Atlantic Ocean.[59]

[55] On paternalism in the ante-bellum American South, see Smith 1998; and Genovese 1974. On ancient Rome, about which the concept is hardly used, the best match is possibly Saller 1982.

[56] See Chapter 7 in this volume.

[57] On the difference race made between ancient and modern types of slavery, see Patterson 1982; and Davis 2006.

[58] See Chapter 8 in this volume.

[59] On sugar-based slavery in the Atlantic, see Curtin 1990; Blackburn 1997; Mintz 1985; and Schwartz 1985.

In their chapter, Marquese and Joly show that, even though the Society of Jesus had long owned slave-based sugar plantations, the Jesuit authors of the eighteenth-century treaties sought specifically to address the increasingly unmanageable problem of slave revolts, by 'showing the faults committed by Luso-Brazilian masters in the control of their slaves'; significantly all faults related to having 'moved away from the precepts of Catholic morality'.[60] Thus, in their treaties, these Jesuit authors utilized excerpts from both Biblical and ancient Greek writings to uphold the idea of reciprocal duties in the master–slave relationship as a model for patriarchal relationships within the household, or else they utilized ideas and information from ancient Roman agronomists to address issues such as the proper exercise of power and distribution of rewards and punishments to the slaves on sugar plantations and, in general, the proper treatment of slaves by their masters. Ultimately, for Marquese and Joly, despite the great differences between ancient and modern slavery, the reliance of eighteenth-century Jesuit authors on Greek and Roman writings found its justification in the existence of several elements of continuity – such as the legal codes and also the very sources of the patriarchal, household-centred, ideology of the master classes of the New World – between the 'slave systems' of the ancient Mediterranean and the modern Atlantic, elements that, however, soon became at odds with the increasingly commercial character of Atlantic slavery from the eighteenth century onwards.

Whether one agrees or not with the fact that the 'commercialization of slavery' that took place at some point in the early modern period (different authors place it either in the sixteenth, the seventeenth, or in the eighteenth centuries) constituted a sharp break with a tradition that stretched back all the way to the classical past, there is no doubt that, until then, the elements of continuity with the ancient Mediterranean identified by Marquese and Joly had played an important part in the story of the making of the 'slave system' of the modern Atlantic. Thus, even if one embarks on an exercise of 'rigorous' historical comparison between specific features of particular ancient and modern 'slave societies' – as Dal Lago and Katsari have done – he/she cannot ignore the fact that, at the very least as a powerful background to the modern practices of slavery, stood an awareness by articulated masters and intellectuals of walking in the footsteps of individuals who had trodden that path before, or at least some of it, and who had left important clues on how to negotiate it for those who came after them. Yet, to us, awareness of this crucial connection, whether explicit

[60] See Chapter 8 in this volume.

or not, can only further enrich the appreciation and understanding of the enormous complexities of a proper comparative study of ancient and modern 'slave systems', while it also stands as an important reminder of the need of collaboration between experts of both antiquity and the modern world – as the examples of the two chapters in this section testify – for a more effective approach to such a project.

One of the most important issues to take into account in a comparative study of ancient and modern 'slave systems' is whether they were 'open' or 'closed' with regard to the social mobility of the slaves.[61] This is, in fact, a crucial issue, since the difference in rates of manumission and in the subsequent assimilation of ex-slaves into the society implies the existence of a much wider set of differences between the economic and social systems and the types of slavery, on which they relied. In this respect, the difference between the 'slave systems' of the ancient Mediterranean and of the modern Atlantic was truly remarkable, since in the former manumission was certainly a great deal more frequent than in the latter, while – even though variations from case to case do exist – there is no doubt that social assimilation was much easier for ex-slaves in classical antiquity than in the New World. In other words, in an ideal scale going from 'open' to 'closed', the 'slave societies' of the ancient Mediterranean would be closer to the 'open' end of the scale, while the 'slave societies' of the modern Atlantic would be closer to the other end of the scale.[62]

There are several explanations for this and one of the most important has to do with race. The absence of racial discrimination in the ancient world, doubtless, was a major factor that facilitated social fluidity to such an extent that ex-slaves (*liberti*) could reach some of the higher positions in ancient Roman society; on the other hand, the pervasiveness of racial discrimination in the modern world led to a constant prejudice against individuals of African descent, which they bore as a stigma even after being freed.[63] Yet, manumission is only part of the story of the different ways of 'exiting slave systems' – the subject of Part IV. The two chapters in this section complement each other in addressing a host of other types of 'exits', aside from manumission. In fact, the first chapter is a broad comparative study, which attempts a classification of the different ways of achieving freedom that slaves had at their disposal – whether with the help of the master or by themselves – in a number of ancient and modern societies. The second

[61] These terms are in Watson 1980.

[62] On some of these issues in relation to manumission, see Patterson 1982; Phillips 1985, and 1996.

[63] On some of these issues, see Watson 1987.

chapter, by contrast, confines its analysis firmly within the modern period, as it ought to, given the fact that its focus is on the variety of processes that led to the emancipation of entire slave populations in the Americas.

In fact, emancipation on a mass scale was a wholly modern phenomenon; no such thing ever happened in the ancient world. And again, even though there is a number of reasons for this striking difference – and one that we need to keep constantly in mind in our comparative project on 'slave systems' of the ancient Mediterranean and modern Atlantic – it is not difficult to see that some of the necessary preconditions, among them the increasing democratization of public opinion and the making of a radical abolitionist movement, simply never had a chance to occur in the ancient world. By the same token, it would be even more unlikely to imagine an enforced emancipation of all the slaves of one of the most productive 'slave societies' in the ancient world resulting from a major war fought over slavery and won by a declared antislavery government – as, however, happened only in the case of the American Civil War, even in modern times.[64]

In his chapter, Olivier Pétré-Grenouilleau shows how both manumission and emancipation are part of a typology of ways of 'exiting slave systems', which he sets up in order to identify the reasons for their occurrence and to investigate their actual effects on different 'slave societies', both ancient and modern. Relying heavily on the work of Claude Meillassoux on Africa[65] and citing examples spanning from the Greco-Roman world to colonial and ante-bellum America, Pétré-Grenouillau begins his typology analysing 'systemic exits' from slavery – acts that led to the masters' liberation of slaves, without affecting negatively the nature of the system, but rather strengthening it. He discusses Meillassoux's distinction, in relation to Africa, between two terms often used as synonyms: 'enfranchisement', as a systemic exit authorized [by the master] and/or with the master's *consent*, which could bring a complete obliteration of the past enslaved status of the individual, even though it rarely did, and 'manumission', as a similar 'systemic exit', which might have had a more restrictive meaning.[66] Pétré-Grenouillau, then, focuses on the different types of actions brought by the slaves against ancient and modern 'slave systems', with particular attention to the ante-bellum American South and ancient Rome. He argues, thus, that 'passive' slave resistance – based on minor acts of

[64] Several scholars have pointed out the significance of the uniqueness of the American path to emancipation in the modern world. See above all, Kolchin 2003a; Freehling 1994; and Foner 1983.

[65] See Claude Meillassoux 1991. [66] See Chapter 9 in this volume.

interruption of day-to-day labour activities – could just be as devastating as 'active', or violent, resistance, simply by harming the productivity of the system.

Unlike the numerous acts of resistance, which never actually gained slaves an exit from the system, the less-frequent slave rebellions focused precisely on this target and, whether in the ancient or the modern worlds, their occurrence seems 'to have corresponded to the moments either following the establishment of a "slave system" or its quick expansion', or to those times in which a system seemed to be threatened.[67] Although they all failed but one (the one in Haiti) slave revolts usually led to changes in the 'slave system' – such as a hardening or a diffusion of tensions – though not necessarily in 'anti-systemic' ways. The same goes also for the 'maroon' communities of fugitive slaves, who, after exiting the system, did not fundamentally threaten it by living outside it. Finally, Pétré-Grenouillau looks first at the processes of 'natural exits' from 'slave systems', with the decline and disappearance of slavery, which – he argues – was rarely definitive and often led to different forms of 'unfreedom', and then at the processes of 'enforced exits', which – as a result of the spread of abolitionism, from the eighteenth century onwards – constituted a novelty in world history and led, ultimately, to state-based enforcements of slave emancipation, whether originating from inside or outside the systems.

Picking up where Pétré-Grenouilleau's chapter finishes, Stanley Engerman's chapter focuses on the different paths followed by 'slave societies' across the Americas toward emancipation. Treating emancipation as an economic issue leading to legal action, Engerman shows how only in very few cases – at times of crisis of the 'slave systems' – it resulted from agreement among slaveowners; in such cases, emancipation was both un-legislated and uncompensated, and thus entirely voluntary. One such scenario could have very well developed in the United States in the aftermath of the abolition of the Atlantic slave trade, at the beginning of the nineteenth century, but the reinvigoration of the slave system brought by the expansion of cotton production prevented this from happening.[68] As it happened, in most cases, 'emancipations occurred as a result of ... laws passed against the wishes of slaveowners ... economic debates and arguments between slaveowners and others'.[69] The debates revolved around the two main questions of whether emancipation should be

[67] See Chapter 9 in this volume.
[68] On this particular point, see both Kolchin 2003b; and Berlin 2004.
[69] See Chapter 10 in this volume.

immediate or gradual and whether there should be any compensation either for the slaveowners or for the slaves. Here, emancipation schemes differed widely and all types of arrangements were implemented across the Americas, but only in two cases – the United States and Haiti – was emancipation both immediate and uncompensated, as a result of war and revolution, respectively.

As Engerman shows, in most cases, the main issue addressed in the debates over emancipation was its cost for the slaveowners, given that slaves were considered a legitimate form of property. As a consequence, gradual schemes involving transitional periods of unpaid labour or 'apprenticeship', before the achievement of full freedom, proved to be particularly popular, especially when accompanied by ideas about the need to 'educate' the slaves to the habits of freedom. Nearly all these schemes, thus, provided some form of compensation for the slaveowners, either in the form of additional labour provided by the slaves or by postponing the date of emancipation as far as to another generation – as in the case of Brazil's 'free womb' law. Not surprisingly, 'in no case of slave emancipation, immediate or gradual, were the slaves offered any compensation'.[70] Particularly important were also the labour arrangements in the period of transition from slavery to freedom. Depending on the conditions of their access to the land, the ex-slaves could either end up working for landowners under some type of rent scheme, or buy land and start their own agricultural business. Ultimately, though, the void left by the absence of slave labour had to be filled somehow, and this was done by replacing it either with indentured labour or with white labour.

The long-term perspective on types of 'exits' from the 'slave systems' employed by Olivier Pétré-Grenouilleau, spanning the entire course of the centuries-long history of slavery, highlights how much of a break from accepted tradition, customs, and habits were the emancipation schemes described by Stanley Engerman, however conservative they might seem to us today. The dimensions of this break appear in all their magnitude when one pauses to think about the fact that, even as the abolitionist movement rose to the fore in Britain and America, slaves continued to be considered by the overwhelming majority of public opinion as little more than the legal property of the slaveowners. Thus, in investigating 'slave systems' – especially those of the ancient Mediterranean and the modern Atlantic – we need to keep constantly in mind that forced emancipation of slavery, whether compensated or uncompensated, was one of the main novel

[70] See Chapter 10 in this volume.

factors that sharply distinguished antiquity from the modern world by leading to the end of modern slavery in a way that would have been impossible in the ancient world.

The above discussion on the modern features of emancipation leads us to the last section in the present volume: Part V, on 'Slavery and unfree labour, ancient and modern'. Emancipation was a phenomenon that, in the modern world, affected not only slavery, but also serfdom in ways that constituted sharp breaks with the past, as several recent studies have pointed out; one needs only to think about the almost contemporaneous decrees releasing Russian serfs in 1861 and American slaves in 1863 to realize it.[71] This consideration has important bearings on a comparative study of ancient and modern 'slave systems'. In fact, just as one, in doing such a study, has to keep constantly in mind the distinguishing characteristics of slavery as a socio-economic institution, or of 'slaving' as a process, for that matter, he/she needs also to be aware of the fact that, at the most basic level, slavery was but the most extreme of a whole range of systems of 'unfree labour', among which was also serfdom. Awareness of this larger context in which to place the comparative studies of 'slave systems' not only helps to identify the peculiarities of slavery in comparison with other types of 'unfree labour', but also helps to provide a more accurate picture of the past, both ancient and modern.

If we focus specifically – as we have done so far – on the ancient Mediterranean and the modern Atlantic, there is no doubt that other forms of 'unfree labour' played important roles in both, vis-à-vis the correct functioning of the economy, if not also the profitability of the entire system. This was certainly the case of several regions in the ancient Mediterranean, where, during the Roman period, slavery was one of several types of labour, both free and unfree, associated with agricultural activities.[72] This was also the case in several regions of the modern Atlantic, where, until the nineteenth century, different forms of free and coerced agricultural labour coexisted, mostly outside the regions with the highest slave populations.[73] Recognizing the importance of these broader contexts, scholars have started analysing historical forms of labour, as if they were placed in a sort of continuum going from slavery to freedom, looking at connections between them and between the different societies that employed them and, in the process, setting the guidelines for an ideal

[71] See Kolchin 1990: 351–67.
[72] See especially Garnsey and Saller 1987; and Foxhall 1990: 97–114.
[73] See especially Wolf 1982; and Stern 1988: 829–72.

comparative analysis that should as much include 'slave systems' as 'serf systems', and so on.[74]

Stephen Hodkinson's final chapter is very much a representative of this recent trend of scholarship that places slavery in a broader context and looks at connections and comparison between different historical forms of 'unfree labour'. His focus is on ancient Sparta in comparative perspective and, in particular, on the insights that comparison with other systems of 'unfree labour' might offer to the understanding of the relationship between the Spartiate masters and the helots in relation to the agrarian economy. As Hodkinson shows, helotage is a particularly significant case-study precisely because helots have been variously, and erroneously, classified as the equivalent of either modern slaves or modern serfs, lacking a more accurate description of their actual servile status. While comparison based on these broad classifications is hardly useful in this case, Hodkinson argues that more specific types of comparison, focusing on particular themes – as in the case of Paul Cartledge's article on 'rebels and *sambos*' in ancient Greece[75] – are far more productive and, in this vein, he seeks to enlighten specifically 'the social relations of production between Spartiates and helots, especially the degree of Spartiate direction of helot farming, and the implications for the helots' experience of servitude'.[76]

Relying on the methodological treatment provided by Skocpol and Somers and on specific comparisons with American slavery, Russian serfdom, and pre-colonial African slavery, Hodkinson proceeds to address issues such as the degree of helot control by the Spartiates, the relation of the farming population to the land, and in general the pattern of formation of the Spartan agrarian economy. He points out that comparison with the three agrarian systems of unfree labour he has chosen shows that 'the extent of the masters' or landowners' intervention to control the location and disposition of their dependent labour force is often related to the degree to which they themselves were responsible for forming the fundamental elements of the agrarian economy';[77] this seems, to a certain extent, to have been the case also in Lakonia. Hodkinson draws important insights on the character of the Spartiate masters' residence in or at a distance from the landed estates and on the effects that either had on the helot population and on the strength of local helot communities, when seen in comparison specifically with the master–bondsmen relationship in

[74] See Wallerstein 1974–89; Bush 1996a; Engerman 1999; and Bush 2002.
[75] Cartledge 1985; see also Genovese 1979, the work that inspired Cartledge.
[76] See Chapter 11 in this volume. [77] See Chapter 11 in this volume.

the ante-bellum American South and Tsarist Russia. He concludes with a plea to engage in other specific comparative studies between other aspects of helotage and modern types of 'unfree labour' and with a consideration of how – as Orlando Patterson also remarks in his chapter – we may be able to fill part of the void left by the lack of available evidence for the ancient world through the comparative method.

Stephen Hodkinson's plea and, even more, his comparative study of systems of 'unfree labour' in ancient Sparta and in three other societies provide a fitting conclusion for a comparative study of ancient and modern 'slave systems' for different reasons. First of all, his study proves the validity of the comparative method, when applied to specific themes, while, at the same time, it highlights crucial elements of continuity and change between the ancient and modern worlds – both themes that the authors of the other chapters have treated at length. Moreover, Hodkinson's study succeeds in contextualizing the study of 'slave systems' in the ancient Mediterranean and the modern Atlantic, by showing, through a specific comparison between four particular societies, the connection and interdependence between slavery and other forms of 'unfree labour'. We can say, then, that, ultimately, this is the road to follow in future comparative studies of the ancient Mediterranean and the modern Atlantic not just as 'slave systems', but as complex economies and societies including within themselves – in different forms and degrees and within different regions – different 'systems of labour', free and unfree.[78] Thus, a future study that might go beyond the suggestions of our own project on 'slave systems' would be one that fruitfully compares, in similar vein, 'systems of labour: ancient and modern'.

[78] For valuable suggestions in this sense, see Davis 2000; and Kolchin 2000.

CHAPTER 2

Slavery, gender, and work in the pre-modern world and early Greece: a cross-cultural analysis

Orlando Patterson

Historians of western antiquity have increasingly come to rely on the comparative method in their attempts to gain a better understanding of slavery in the ancient Mediterranean.[1] There are good reasons for this. Slavery was widespread in western antiquity and rose to great importance in the two ancient societies we know most about – Athens and Rome – but there is a tantalizing shortage of data on the subject. Clio has been especially cruel to classical historians, giving them just enough information to confirm that slavery was important in many ancient states but not enough to go beyond informed guesses.

In situations such as this, the comparative method is the only recourse after having exhausted what we can learn from the available evidence. By comparing what we know about ancient slavery with other kinds of slave-holding societies, we might be able to situate both the institution and its social context within broader classificatory frameworks that might shed light on the ancient cases.[2] In many ways, this is no different from what archaeologists do. Indeed, given the importance and long acceptance of archaeology – an inherent comparative discipline – in the study of the ancient world, it is puzzling that it took so long for social and economic historians of antiquity to turn to the comparative approach as a method of supplementing and helping to make sense of their subject.

My main substantive objective in this essay is to explore the relationship between the sexual division of labour and the occurrence of slavery in pre-modern societies. A secondary objective is to comment on the comparative method, and to further demonstrate the validity of the quantitative exploration of cross-cultural data. Finally, I hope to show that this approach may be of some help in the study of aspects of the social history of the ancient West.

[1] See Scheidel, Chapter 4, this volume. See also, Hodkinson 2003: 248–85; and Patterson 2003: 289–309.

[2] Fine 1983: 29. See also Garnsey 1988.

THE GOALS OF COMPARATIVE SLAVE STUDIES

There are at least four major objectives in the comparative study of slavery. A first objective is to understand the elementary structure of slavery as an institutionalized relation of domination. The analytic level here is micro-sociological. We are concerned with understanding what is distinctive about this mode of coercive interaction across cultures and time.

A second objective is to understand the factors that explain the presence or absence of slavery, especially in its institutionalized form. Here, we wish to know why it is that the institution became rooted in one society or one type of societies – what may be called 'slaveholding societies' – but not in others. This chapter will be mainly concerned with this problem.

A third objective shifts our analytic focus from the micro-sociological to the macroscopic. Slavery as an institutionalized micro-sociological relation of domination has existed throughout the world. However, only in a small minority of societies has slavery acquired crucial structural significance, meaning that its removal would have entailed critical dislocations in the society at large and major disruptions in the status and power of important groups that had come to depend on slaves as a power base. These are what Sir Moses Finley has called 'genuine slave societies'.[3] While the relative size of the slave population is important in defining these societies other factors may be of equal or greater significance. This was true, for example, of many Islamic societies that were structurally dependent on relatively small populations of slaves who performed vital military and administrative roles.[4] The goals here are to understand the circumstances under which such 'slave societies' – as distinct from mere 'slaveholding societies' – emerged; the nature and variations of such societies; the dynamics of change within each class of them; and the factors accounting for their decline.[5]

The fourth objective turns our attention to the consequences of slavery for human cultures. Slavery has been called the 'peculiar institution'. I have suggested elsewhere that its universal distribution makes this adjective inappropriate and anachronistic.[6] It may, indeed, have been peculiar to nineteenth-century liberals, especially those in America, who found

[3] Finley 1968: 307–13. [4] Ayalon 1951; Crone 1980.

[5] Keith Hopkins' dogmatic assertion that there were only five large-scale slave societies in world history is too absurd to be taken seriously; see Hopkins 1978: 99–102. In pre-colonial and nineteenth-century West Africa and the Sudan alone there were more than a dozen large-scale slave societies.

[6] Patterson 1982: vii–x.

themselves living in a society that, on one hand, thrived on large-scale plantation slavery, while, on the other hand, celebrated a revolution and constitution that extolled liberty and universal equality. However, within the broad arc of western history, there was nothing peculiar about slavery. Indeed, it is precisely in the West that slavery rose to greatest importance. Not only did the West's two source civilizations – ancient Greece and Rome – depend heavily on it, but it persisted with varying levels of significance throughout the Middle Ages, rose again in the sugar plantations of the Mediterranean islands of Renaissance Europe and was a major factor in the emergence of capitalism and of the post-Columbian Americas.[7]

The questions for the comparative historian of slavery here are: what were the long-term consequences of this pervasive *doulotic* presence for western culture? How did it influence its legal systems, its ideas about labour, equality and rights? What awesome consequences flowed from the fact that Christianity, the formative institution in western culture, emerged in a large-scale slave society, it was strongly dependent on freedmen in its critical early years, and drew heavily upon the metaphor of slavery and redemption for its defining theological doctrine? I have explored these issues at great length elsewhere and will therefore not be discussing them in this chapter.[8] Similarly, we may enquire into the consequences for Islamic and West African cultures of the strong dependence on slavery in many of them. How did the preoccupation of the Koran with slavery influence its notions of justice? What were the long-term consequences of the fact that so many major Islamic states relied heavily on slaves for military and executive functions? How did slavery influence Islamic notions of marriage and sex? How did it influence the development of Islamic notions of 'race' and colour?

THE NATURE OF SLAVERY

In *Slavery and Social Death*[9] I attempted to address the first set of issues. There, I argued that slavery is best seen as a relation of domination distinguished from other related forms of domination and bondage in three respects. The first one was the totality of the master's power over the slave. For all practical purposes, this power amounted to life and death, for, while it is correct that many slaveholding societies had laws punishing the

[7] Phillips, Jr 1985; Bonnassie 1991; Pelteret 2001; Blackburn 1997; Solow 1991.
[8] See Patterson 1991. See also Davis 1966, 2006; and Glancey 2002. [9] See Patterson 1982.

willing murder of slaves, in practice such laws amounted to dead letters because of the nearly insurmountable obstacles usually placed in the prosecution of murderous masters. In all but a few slave societies slaves could not give evidence against their masters and in the USA they could not even give evidence against a Euro-American who was not their master. Hence, no action could be taken against a master who brutally murdered a slave in front of several hundreds of them.

Second, the slave was always considered not to belong to the community in which he was inserted or born. He belonged to his master and his master's household and, as such, he was a non-person in the eyes of the community. The slave, as I have shown, was viewed everywhere as a genealogical isolate, a deracinated person without history or future. In lineage-based societies, he/she was considered kinless; in more advanced politico-legal systems such as Rome, he was considered legally dead. In post-Revolutionary America, he was defined legally as half a person, but even that half did not belong to him but to his master, who had the right to vote. I have introduced the term 'natal alienation' to describe this condition. 'Natal alienation' does not mean that the slave did not have a natural community, or relatives. What it does mean, however, is that he/she and his/her children had no legal or socially recognized status in their communities. Slaves loved their children and kinsmen dearly, but they had no custodial claims on their children or spouses. They were people who truly did not belong.

The third distinguishing feature of slavery is that, in all societies where it existed, the slave was considered a person without honour. Having no honour meant that slaves had no honour to defend. They were mere surrogates of their masters and, to the degree that they were insulted, it was their master's honour that was impugned; not their own. In medieval Germanic lands, for example, the honour price of the slave, relatively small as it was, went to the master.[10] The honourlessness of the slave – the fact that he was a mere surrogate of another – had a number of important consequences for masters. In many societies, where trading was considered dishonourable but was nonetheless profitable, masters used their slaves to perform this role for them; Cicero being the most famous case. Slaves and freedmen also helped to solve the problem of the lack of a law of agency in the commercial life of Rome.[11] Apart from a man's son, these were the only persons who could act as 'non-contractual agents' for him.

[10] Wergeland 1916: 36. [11] See Kirschenbaum 1987.

A second consequence of the honourlessness of the slave was the parasitic enhancement of the master's honour. Indeed, in many slaveholding societies the ego and honour enhancement that slaveownership brought was the sole gain of the institution, since slaves were of little economic significance and, as often as not, an economic burden on the master. The slave, as a human surrogate, projected the honour and *dignitas* of the master for the entire world to see. Daily life in ancient Rome gave constant and noisy exhibitions of this: the Roman *pater familias* never left his house without a grand retinue of slaves and freedmen preceding him. Hegel was acutely aware of the honorific dimension of slavery and, as is well known, tried to make philosophical sense of it in *The Phenomenology of Spirit*.[12]

However, as I have pointed out elsewhere, he got it all wrong with his tortured Teutonic speculations about the existential impasse, which was created by the fact that the master sought honour from someone whom he had profoundly dishonoured.[13] So too, did a long line of French and German intellectuals, including Karl Marx, who found this section of the *Phenomenology* irresistible.[14] It takes only the most cursory empirical investigation of the comparative data on slavery, especially western slavery, to realize that masters rarely faced such an honorific impasse: not Cato, not Cicero, not Thomas Jefferson, and certainly not any of the English slaveholders of the Caribbean with whose biographies I am familiar.

ATTEMPTS TO EXPLAIN THE PRESENCE OR ABSENCE OF SLAVERY AS AN INSTITUTION

There is now a vast and growing body of literature on slavery.[15] Few of these works, however, are genuinely comparative in the senses defined above. The great majority are on modern slave systems, in which specific aspects of slavery are treated in particular societies – the slave family, slave mortality, the profitability of slavery, manumission, and so on. Otherwise, they tend to be regional studies which compare and contrast different societies in a given area, but rarely attempt to explain either slavery or slave society in general terms.

The evolutionists of the nineteenth and early twentieth centuries were the first to offer explanations of what they liked to call the 'origins' of slavery. Many of them, even if in highly speculative ways, did advance theories which more modern studies have shown to be of some value. All of

[12] Hegel 1961 (1807): 228–40. [13] Patterson 1982: 97–101.
[14] See, for example, Kojeve 1969. [15] See Miller 1999b.

them emphasized warfare and the demand for labour at certain crucial points in the scale of development as the crucial factors.[16] Westermarck's views were typical in this respect.[17] He found that among most primitive tribes, slavery was unnecessary because women usually did most of the work; war captives were either sacrificed or eaten. However, with more complex societies, he argued, and a 'cooler perception of permanent advantage', prisoners were spared and enslaved; first women, then men.

Since they were nearly all evolutionist in orientation, a popular argument of these early comparative scholars was that a causal link existed between stages of socio-economic development and slavery. Modern studies and statistical tests have found no empirical support for this view.[18]

One factor given special prominence by earlier scholars which has stood the test of time is the relationship between slavery and the socio-economic role of women. The subjection of women, it was argued, provided both a social and economic model for the enslavement of men. As early as 1840, E. Biot was writing that 'la femme est la première esclave'.[19] Forty years later, A. Tourmagne[20] offered a more sophisticated version of this view in his suggestion that the husband–wife relationship was the model for slavery.

The most important early twentieth-century theorist, and someone whose work is still widely cited, was H. J. Nieboer,[21] who broke with the evolutionists in propounding his open-resource theory. His work was unusual, too, in its reliance on statistical methods and a more rigorous comparative database. His central hypothesis was that slavery was found as an important institution only where land or some other crucial resource existed in abundance relative to labour. In such situations, free persons could not be induced by wages or other means to work for others, so they ought to be forced to do so. The theory has had a lasting appeal, especially to economic historians, since it is both testable and consistent with neoclassical economic theory. Decades later, it was revived by C. J. Baks[22] and by the MIT economist Domar[23] who seemed, or pretended, to be unaware of the fact that he was re-inventing a sixty-year old theoretical wheel. However appealing, the theory has been shown by me[24] and other scholars[25] to have no empirical support in the cross-cultural data on slavery, and Engerman[26] has sharply questioned its theoretical consistency.

[16] See Spencer 1893; Biot 1840; and Hobhouse 1992. [17] Westermarck 1906–8.
[18] Pryor 1977: 81–102. [19] Biot 1840. [20] Tourmagne 1880. [21] Nieboer 1971 (1910).
[22] Baks, Breman and Noolj 1966: 90–109. [23] Domar 1970: 18–32. [24] Patterson 1977: 12–34.
[25] See Pryor 1977: 81–102. [26] Engerman 1973: 43–65.

Three modern scholars have gone beyond Nieboer in attempting to explain the presence of institutionalized slavery in the pre-capitalist world. Drawing on Baks,[27] anthropologist Jack Goody has begun arguing that 'slavery involves external as well as internal inequality, an unequal balance of power between peoples'.[28] From this somewhat unpromising start, Goody soon has enriched his analysis with both the ethno-historical data on Africa and the statistical data from George P. Murdock's ethnographic sample of world societies.[29] Unlike earlier analysts in this tradition, Goody has taken account of the role of slaves and, to a limited degree, the extent of their presence. He also has paid special attention to the role of women in the emergence of slaveholding. We cannot explain the complex facts of slavery, he argues, 'except by seeing the role of slaves as related to sex and reproduction as well as to farm and production, and in the case of eunuchs, to power and its non-proliferation'.[30] He has tried to revive the Nieboer thesis in his argument that slavery was one solution where hired labour was unavailable due to abundance of resources and limited technology.

However valuable, Goody's contribution is hardly complete. It is confined to Africa, and it only acknowledges the varying degrees of slavery and the complex role of slaves. Little attempt is made to explain, even within Africa, why some societies came to rely so heavily on slavery while others with very similar social systems did not.

Though not directly addressing the subject of slavery, the related work of Ester Boserup on bridewealth, polygyny, and female participation in the labour force is very important. According to Boserup there are two basic kinds of pre-modern societies: 'the first is found in regions where shifting cultivation prevails and the major part of agricultural work is done by women. In such communities we can expect to find a high incidence of polygyny and bridewealth being paid by the future husband or his family'.[31] The second group is characterized by the predominance of plough cultivation. Men do most of the agricultural work and wives are entirely dependent on their husbands for economic support. Polygyny is rare in such societies and the dowry payments typical upon marriage. Goody, while generally sympathetic to Boserup's arguments, finds a major difficulty with it in regard to Africa, where he claims that polygyny rates are highest in those parts of the continent where women do relatively less work.[32]

[27] Baks, Breman and Noolj 1966. [28] Goody 1980: 16–42. [29] Murdock and White 1969: 329–69.
[30] Goody 1980: 40. [31] Boserup 1997: 515. [32] Goody 1980.

But there are problems with Goody's own critique, since they are based on regional data which need not be typical and, as such, inimical to Boserup's argument. There are other reasons behind polygyny. One of these is warfare which, by creating an unbalanced sex ratio and generating captives, both creates and supplies the need for polygyny, a hypothesis that goes back to Herbert Spencer and which was tested and supported more recently by M. Ember.[33]

The question of the productive and reproductive role of women and its relation to slavery has been a major source of controversy in the modern literature on slavery, as Robertson and Klein have noted in their introduction to a collection of works they edited on the subject.[34] They emphasize the fact that most slaves were women in sub-Saharan Africa and that they were preferred mainly because of their role in production. They take issue with scholars who emphasize the reproductive and sexual role of women in explaining their higher market value and greater rate of assimilation than male slaves. But there are problems with Robertson and Klein's arguments. Posing the issue as one between whether women are valued as slaves more because of their economic than non-economic roles is not very useful. The interesting difference between male and female slaves is that women were potentially useful both as workers *and* as multi-functional reproducers as well as sexual partners, whereas men were rarely of value in reproduction and only occasionally used as sexual partners. Ironically, this is made clear by most of the case studies in the very volume introduced by Robertson and Klein who found themselves in the odd position of contradicting the findings of several of the works they had commissioned.[35]

The Robertson and Klein volume raises another issue of central importance to slave studies. It is the fact that most of the best works on pre-modern slavery are based on African cases, and a disproportionate number from the Sudanic region. Generalizing from these studies immediately poses one of the critical problems in comparative and historical sociology, the so-called 'Galton problem', which we come to in the next section.

The economist Pryor has come closest to formulating a theory of the occurrence of institutionalized slavery combining modern statistical

[33] Ember 1974: 197–206. [34] Robertson and Klein 1983: 3–25.

[35] See, for example, Strobel 1983: 111–29; Sardan 1983: 130–43; Broadhead 1983: 160–81.

techniques with cross-cultural data. He distinguishes between social slavery and economic slavery and argues that different factors explain the presence of one or the other form. Central to his argument, though, is the nineteenth-century idea that there is a correspondence, or 'homologism', between male domination of women and men's domination of their slaves. In Pryor's own words, 'the key to my proposed theory of the determinants of slavery resides in the societal parallels which one finds between dominant husband and an exploited wife, on the one hand, and a master and his slave, on the other hand. The exploited wife and slave (either male or female) fulfil the same role, namely, to exercise power'.[36]

While I agree with the importance attributed to female participation and social status, I strongly disagree with the main causal direction claimed in Pryor's theory. Where women dominate the labour force, there is no need for men to acquire slaves for economic purposes. To the contrary, it is precisely in such societies that slaves, when used at all, are acquired for social purposes. Just the opposite is true where free women are dominated by men in mainly social terms. I also question how far one can take the view that slaves and women are socially interchangeable. A major point I made in *Slavery and Social Death* is that, however many the parallels between the condition of non-slave women, especially wives, and slaves, there is nonetheless a profound difference between them. Wives everywhere belonged to their communities, were intimately kin-bound, while slaves were nearly always deracinated and kinless; wives everywhere had some rights and could seek the protection of their kinsmen, while slaves were powerless in relation to their masters.

Perhaps the biggest problem with Pryor's theory is that of causal direction. He assumes that 'the family and social-structure variables – posited as determinants of slavery – seem much more basic than the institution of slavery'.[37] However, it is not clear that one can always assume that the causal link flows in this direction. In some societies the dominance of women in the workforce partly accounts for absence of slavery; in others, it is the dominance of slavery that accounts for women in the workforce. The most cursory view of the modern slave systems, especially those of the Caribbean, makes this clear. Much the same holds also for the ancient and medieval societies we know most about.

[36] Pryor 1977: 81–102. [37] Pryor 1977: 81–102.

SOME METHODOLOGICAL ISSUES

How does one go about explaining the presence of slavery? It is tempting to confine oneself to the societies and regions one knows most about and attempt to generalize from them. As I noted earlier, this is typical of many regional specialists, especially those who work on Africa.[38] However, all such attempts face one formidable problem, first prominently identified by Francis Galton, who gave it his name.[39] Galton's problem consists in the fact that, unless one is careful about the way cases are selected, one can never be sure whether the causes one isolates in comparatively explaining slavery – or any other social phenomenon – are genuinely independent or are due to diffusion. This danger is most evident in regional studies, where there are known, as well as unknown but presumable, historical links between societies. As we noted earlier, the numerous studies of slavery in West Africa and the Sahel constitute the classic instances of this danger. Another area is the ancient Mediterranean. However different the slave-holding societies of these regions, the known interactions between them make it difficult to generalize about the factors accounting for the varying presence of slavery in them.

In my view, the strategy that works best, especially if the goal is to understand the factors explaining the presence of slavery as an institutionalized relation of domination – as distinct from those accounting for the rise of large-scale slavery – is the multivariate, cross-cultural approach. Critical for the success of this method – and the only way to get around Galton's problem – is the use of a sample of societies that are, to the greatest degree possible, historically independent of each other. The late Yale anthropologist, George Peter Murdock, spent a lifetime developing just such a sample. His basic strategy was to identify all the major cultural provinces of the pre-modern world, and then select representative societies – as historically far removed from each other as possible – for each province. Many scholars, myself included, have found Murdock's sample invaluable. The final version of it, with 186 societies (see Appendix), was developed with Douglas White and has the added advantage that a vast body of coded data, contributed by scholars who have used it, is now available for anyone using the sample.[40]

[38] See especially Lovejoy 2000b; and Manning 1990.

[39] See Naroll 1965: 428–51; and Naroll 1968.

[40] See Murdock and White 1969: 329–69; Murdock and Morrow 1970: 302–30; and Murdock and Provost 1973b: 203–25.

I have added my own codes to this data set[41] and the most important variables with which I have coded the different societies in my analysis are the following: slavery absent (0) vs slavery present (1). 'Slavery absent' includes the Murdock and White code 'incipient slavery'; i.e. slavelike conditions that are non- hereditary. 'Slavery present' includes slavery, as defined earlier; that is hereditary and institutionalized.

The other important variable we will be considering concerns the relative participation of women in the labour force.[42] I have used a reformulated three-category code to assess women's economic role. According to it, societies are divided between those where (1) there were fewer women than men in the labour force; (2) women and men were about equal in numbers in the labour force; (3) women were greater in numbers than men in the labour force. A complicating factor is that, in any given society, women may have been dominant or equal in some respects, but not others. Several attempts have been made to deal with this problem and I have relied primarily on Douglas White's code, 'female contribution to subsistence', which was reconstructed from the three most reliable previous codes on the subject.[43] This code takes into account the dominant mode of subsistence in evaluating women's economic contribution. The code on warfare is constructed from the codes of Valerie Wheeler's study of warfare.[44] It is partly based on Keith Otterbein's study of the subject[45] and now to be found in codes 891–916 of the *Standard Cross Cultural Sample* codebook.

This is not the place to go into the details of one's statistical methods. I will here only briefly note that, in what follows, I have relied mainly on two kinds of statistical techniques. One is traditional cross-tabulation analysis, in which simple tests of independence are conducted to ascertain whether observed frequencies and proportions are indicative of some relationship between the variables or are due to chance. However, even if we have established that there is a statistically significant relationship between two variables, we are still faced with the problem of whether the relationship is spurious, due to the fact that they are related to a third, unexamined variable. Additional variables may be examined by the traditional methods but the question of spuriousness is not easily resolved and more variables create their own problems. To get beyond these problems I employ a family of statistical techniques that have been specially developed for the

[41] See Patterson 2000: Codes 917–20. Note, however, that I have revised these codes for this chapter, adding seven societies to the list of societies with slavery.

[42] Murdock and Provost 1973a. [43] Code 890 of the *Standard Cross-Cultural Sample*.

[44] Wheeler 1974. [45] Otterbein 1970.

analysis of categorical data, just the sort of data that historians and qualitative social scientists work with: these are loglinear as well as logistic and ordered logistic modelling.[46]

The logic is easily comprehended, even if the statistical and computational techniques are complex. We simply ask a series of 'what if' questions of the data, each such question being, in statistical jargon, a model. For example, we may ask, what if there is no relationship whatsoever between the variables we are examining, what would the original table look like? Or what if there is only a relationship between, say, female participation and agriculture, but not between agriculture and slavery, what would the figures in the table look like? Our statistical program takes these questions, transforms the figures in our tables into logs, rearranges the data to look exactly as they would if our 'what if' questions were the case. We then compare the 'what if' (or modelled) results with the observed data in our original tables and see how much they differ or how close a fit there is between them. If our tests show that there is little difference between the observed, original data and that resulting from the data rearranged in answer to our 'what if' question or model, then we say the model is a good fit and accept it, or more properly, we say that there are no statistically valid grounds for rejecting it, given the set of variables we modelled; otherwise, we reject it.

Modelling is not a methodological panacea and a respectful scepticism is recommended. In the first place, the old statistical adage applies: garbage in, garbage out. The most powerful statistical technique is worthless, if the data being manipulated are questionable. Secondly, there is no guarantee that all the relevant variables have been incorporated in a given model. What is left out may be as, or more, important than what is actually examined. Third, modelling may clear up the nature, direction, and strength of the associations that exist in the data but we are still left with the task of interpreting the results that our fitted models present us with. In the end we have to come up with a story; a theory, that accounts for our results. Finally, and closely related to the last point, is the fact that statistical modelling always leaves unsettled the question of causality. Contrary to the impression sometimes given by social scientists, no statistical technique can identify causal relations. For several years it was thought that a technique known as path-analysis had finally mechanized the processes of causality, but statisticians have recently come to agree that this was an intellectual fantasy. In the final analysis, it is the analyst who has to make causal sense of the resulting associations by means of the theory, causal model, or story he

[46] For a non-technical and readable introduction, see Agresti 1996.

tells about the associations his statistical analysis dishes up. I will attempt one such causal story following the data analysis in this chapter.

SLAVERY AND FEMALE PARTICIPATION IN THE DOMINANT MODE OF SUBSISTENCE

Let us begin by asking the most basic and pertinent question: what is the association between slavery and female participation in the sample at large, making no adjustments for other variables (the so-called zero-order association). Figure 2.1 reports the results and they are, at first sight, not very promising.

It shows that, globally, there is no significant association between the two. At this most basic level we cannot reject the contrary claim that slavery is equally likely to be present, or equally likely to be absent, at any level of female participation, which is another way of saying that the two are not related. While this raises important questions, it is no more decisive than would be a table showing a strongly significant association between slavery and female participation at this level of aggregation. The latter, on further scrutiny, may turn out to be spurious once we control for other variables, while Figure 2.1, after controls, may be seen to have concealed important associations. Even so, this nearly complete lack of significance at the zero

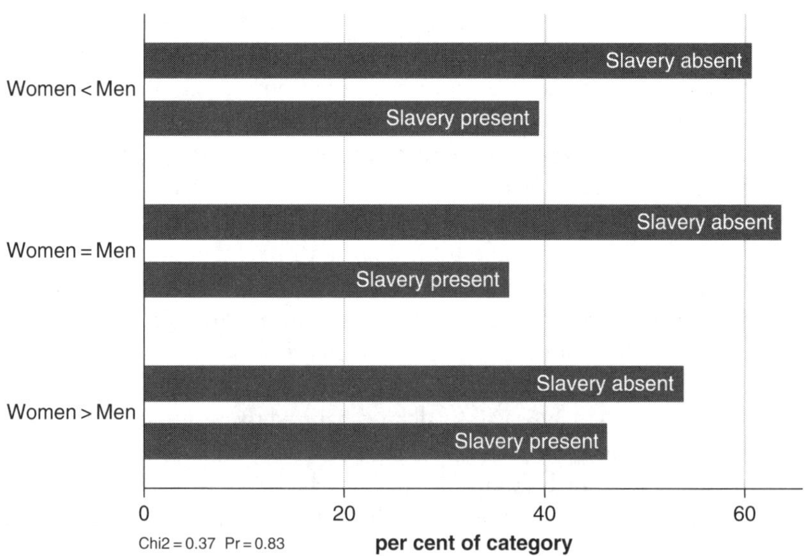

Figure 2.1. Per cent slavery by female participation

order level does indicate that, if there are any relationships to be found behind this most composite level, they will be complex and highly qualified.

To begin the process of uncovering these hidden associations, let us first look at the broad distinction between types of societies, referred to in the *Standard Sample* as modes of subsistence. Societies are classified according to their dominant or primary means of procuring their livelihood as follows: hunter-gathering, fishing, pastoralism or animal husbandry and agriculture. Figure 2.2 shows the association between slavery (present/absent) and the mode of subsistence.

Very few hunter-gathering communities have slaves. The evolutionists were at least right on this point. When prisoners of war were taken, they were held mainly, if at all, for honorific and sacrificial purposes, as was true, for example, of the Tupinamba of north-eastern Brazil. Alternatively, they were absorbed as wives; the Caribs of the pre-Columbian Caribbean being a notable case. Sacrificed slaves were also sometimes eaten and, in this regard, it is worth noting that, of the eleven societies in the sample that practised some form of cannibalism (6.6 per cent of the total), a little over a half was slaveholding. Of the four exceptional cases involving institutionalized slavery among hunter-gatherers in our sample – the nineteenth-century

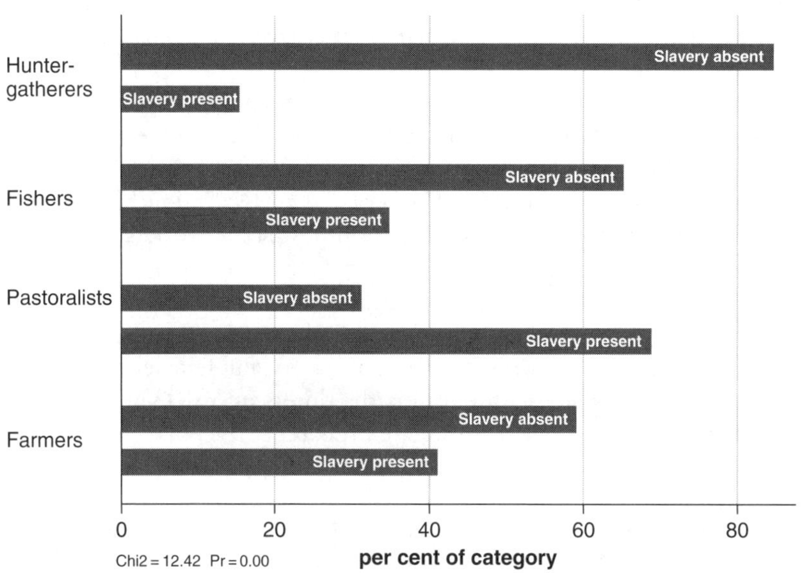

Figure 2.2. Per cent slavery by subsistence mode

Comanche of Texas, the Tehuelche of Patagonia, the Cayua of southwestern Brazil and the Abipon of Argentina – only the Cayua was not characterized by endemic warfare.

While Figure 2.2 is, overall, statistically significant, we do not know which of the two-way relationships really holds. It clearly suggests that hunter-gathering and slavery do not go together but it is not at all clear whether each of the other main types of subsistence is non-spuriously related to slavery. In fact, at the bivariate level, neither agriculture nor fishing are significantly related to slavery. Pastoralism is the only dominant subsistence mode that has a direct and positive relationship with slavery: fully 69 per cent of all predominantly pastoral societies are slaveholding, compared with only 35 per cent of predominant fishing groups and 41 per cent of agriculturalists. This, however, does not mean that these subsistence modes do not relate to slavery in important ways when we control for other variables. What accounts for the high propensity of pastoral societies to have institutional slavery? Warfare is one factor. As Figure 2.3 shows, 61 per cent of societies with endemic warfare in our sample have institutionalized slavery.[47] Examples in our sample of such societies run the full range of pre-modern societies, from the Babylonians, *c.* 1750 BC, the Romans of the second century AD and pre-Columbian Aztecs, through the Pastoral Fulani, Tuaregs, and Ashanti of pre-colonial Africa to the pre-contact Haidi of the north-west coast of North America. Further, all twelve of the societies classified as having large-scale slavery were characterized by frequent warring.

Pastoral societies are more prone to warfare than any of the other types: 80 per cent in our sample.[48] The best fitting loglinear model allows for a three-way interaction between warfare, the existence of pastoralism as the dominant subsistence mode, and slavery.[49] The association between pastoralism, slavery, and female participation in pastoral work is more complicated. Among non-pastoral societies (the vast majority) female participation in pastoral work is strongly related to slavery. As Figure 2.4 shows, this is more the case where men and women participate equally. However, there is no association between slavery and female participation in pastoral work where pastoralism is the dominant mode of subsistence (the table, not shown, has a chi square probability level of 0.71).

[47] On warfare and slavery in Africa, see Meillassoux 1991. For a tragic contemporary case see Jok 2001; on pre-historic Europe, see Pearson and Thorpe 2005; on ancient Rome, see Hopkins 1978.

[48] See Goldschmidt 1979: 15–27; and Salzman 1979: 429–46.

[49] Likelihood ratio statistic $G^2 = 1.17$; p-value $= 0.88$; df $= 4$.

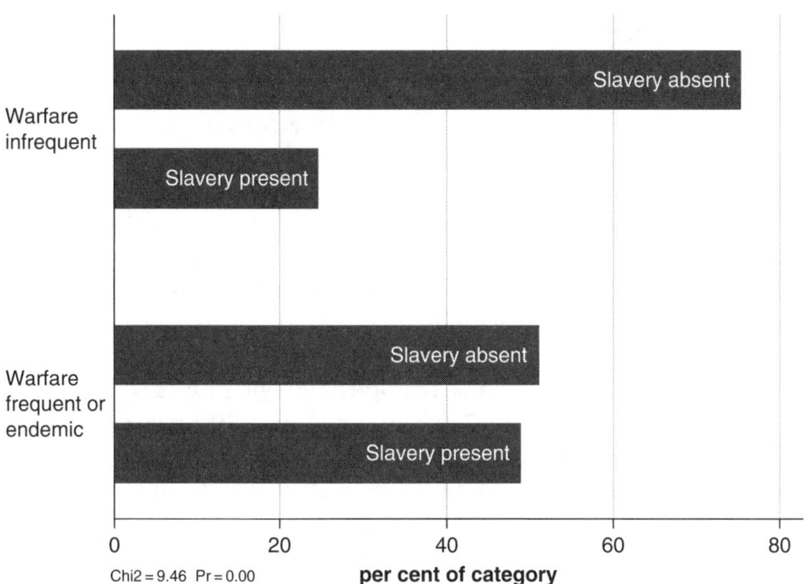

Figure 2.3. Per cent slavery by warfare

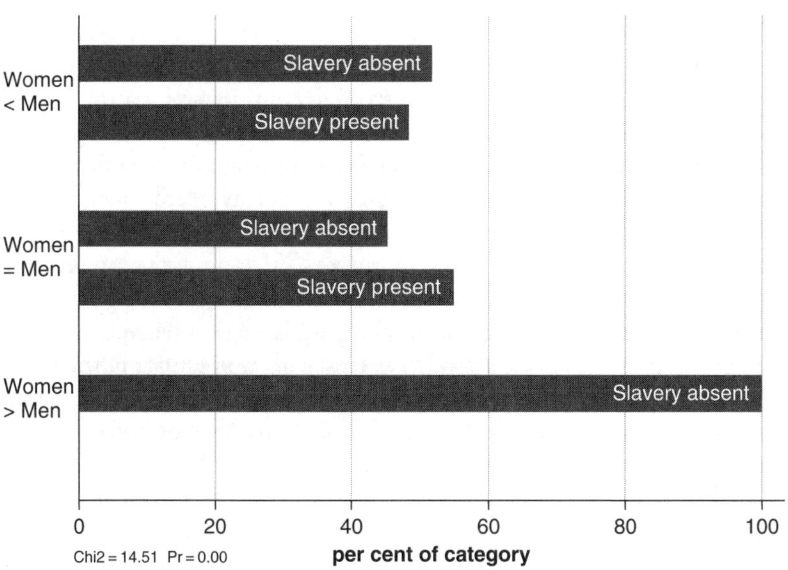

Figure 2.4. Slavery by female participation in animal husbandry: all societies

Indeed, as Figure 2.4 indicates, there is not a single case of a pastoral society in which women are the dominant producers. At the same time, every pastoral society in which women participate in farming has institutional slavery (the table, not shown, has only the 'Slavery present' column). The high prestige of animal husbandry among pastoralists accounts for this outcome. Where women are incorporated as slaves they tend to do the most menial kinds of pastoral tasks and/or engage in agriculture. I also found that there is a more marked tendency for slavery to exist where the livestock involved were sheep and goats. Most of the pastoral and agro-pastoral societies of the Sahel fully exemplify this pattern, especially the Fulani and Tuareg.

Fishing communities stand at the other extreme from pastoralists. As indicated earlier, there is no bivariate association between slavery and societies where fishing is the dominant mode of subsistence. Secondly, while the relationship between fishers and warfare is highly significant, it is the opposite of what we found among pastoralists: the great majority of fishers (73 per cent) rarely engage in warfare. We found that all but one of the minority of cases, where fishers engage in warfare, were slaveholding and were therefore tempted to think that, while fishers are generally pacific, those that do engage in warfare are more than normally inclined to have slavery. However, our loglinear analysis did not support this hunch. The most appropriate model is one that permits a relationship between slavery and warfare, on the one hand, and fishing and warfare (negatively), on the other, but in which fishing as a dominant mode and slavery remained independent.[50] Finally, and again in striking contrast with pastoralists, in none of the fishing communities, where women engage in farming, do we find slavery. Farming does not have the same low status among fishers as it does among pastoralists and is an occupation worthy of free persons.

The great majority of pre-modern societies were predominantly agricultural, and several of the main hypotheses concerning the presence of slavery, which we came across in our literature review, involved the sexual division of labour in them. Recall Boserup's distinction between societies in which shifting agriculture predominates, with women doing the major part of agricultural work, and plough-based agricultural systems, where men do most of the agricultural work. In the Murdock sample, these are referred to as extensive and intensive agricultural systems. Boserup also claimed to have found that polygyny and bridewealth payments at marriage prevailed in extensive systems, while the dowry and only small

[50] Likelihood ratio $G^2 = 2.04$; p-value = 0.92; df = 6.

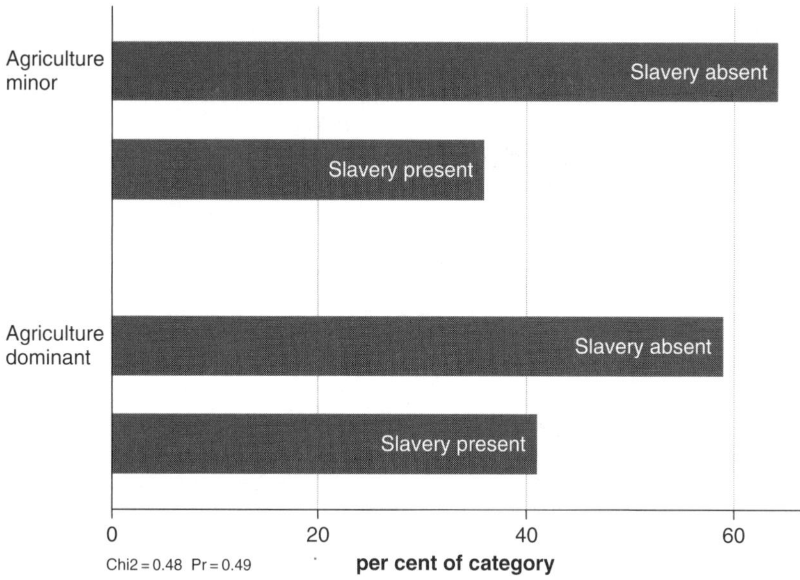

Figure 2.5. Slavery by agricultural level

minorities of polygynous marriages were to be found in intensive agricultural societies. It would seem reasonable to speculate that slavery would be more frequently found in societies with extensive agriculture.

Figures 2.5 and 2.6 appear not to support this speculation. At the bivariate level, there is no association between slavery and female participation in agricultural societies, as Figure 2.5 shows. And the same holds even when we distinguish between extensive and intensive agricultural systems. Indeed, Figure 2.6 indicates, somewhat surprisingly, that slavery is found more frequently among intensive agriculturalists in our sample, although the association is not significant. Again, this does not necessarily mean that the distinction between intensive and extensive farming is not important. The question, however, is, under what circumstances (or controls) might it be significant and important?

In addition to their participation in the dominant subsistence mode, two other variables figure prominently in evaluating the socio-economic position of women: the existence of bridewealth in marriages, and polygyny. Bridewealth or bride price is usually the payment of property and/or services by the kin of the groom-to-be to the family of the betrothed.[51]

[51] See Goody and Tambiah 1973: 1–3; for a detailed case study, see Harris 1972: 55–87.

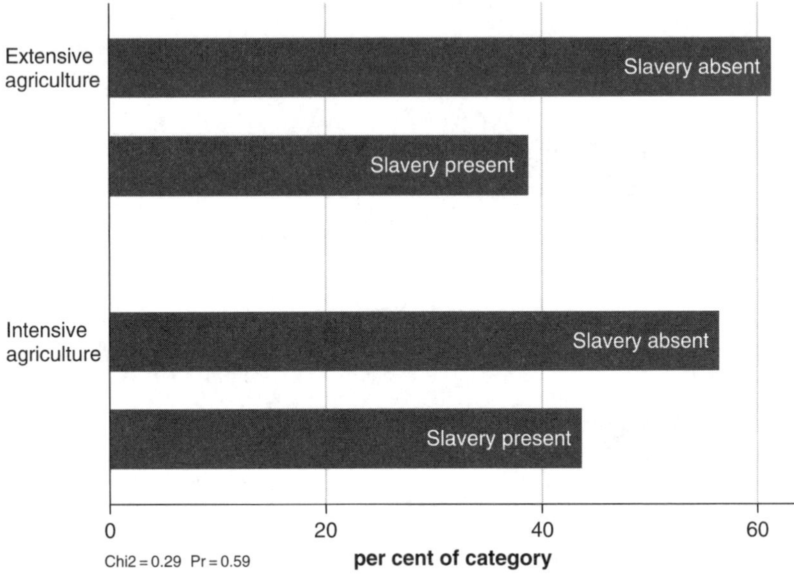

Figure 2.6. Slavery by agricultural type

Goody has pointed out that with true bridewealth the property goes to the bride's kinsmen, usually her father, who often uses it to acquire wives for her brothers. In such cases it functions largely as a means of regulating marriages and legitimizing the children of the bride. Where the bridewealth goes directly to the bride and her husband, as is often the case in Eurasia, Goody suggests that it is a form of 'indirect dowry'.[52] Bridewealth payments vary across cultures. Whatever its symbolic and regulatory role, however, it invariably has an important economic dimension and is closely related to female participation in production. Bride payments tend to be high where women's economic and social roles are highly valued. They are a measure of a woman's value 'determined by the qualities of physical appearance, character and social standing which she possesses'.[53] And it is also closely related to polygyny. 'The two institutions', writes Goody, 'appear to reinforce one another.'[54]

The bridewealth variable in the standard sample was recoded as a simple dichotomy: societies in which it is the norm and those in which it is not. In saying that it is normative, we mean that it is the prevailing mode, although this allows for a number of cases where other considerations may apply to a

[52] Goody and Tambiah 1973: 2–3. [53] La Fontaine 1972: 99. [54] Goody and Tambiah 1973: 10–11.

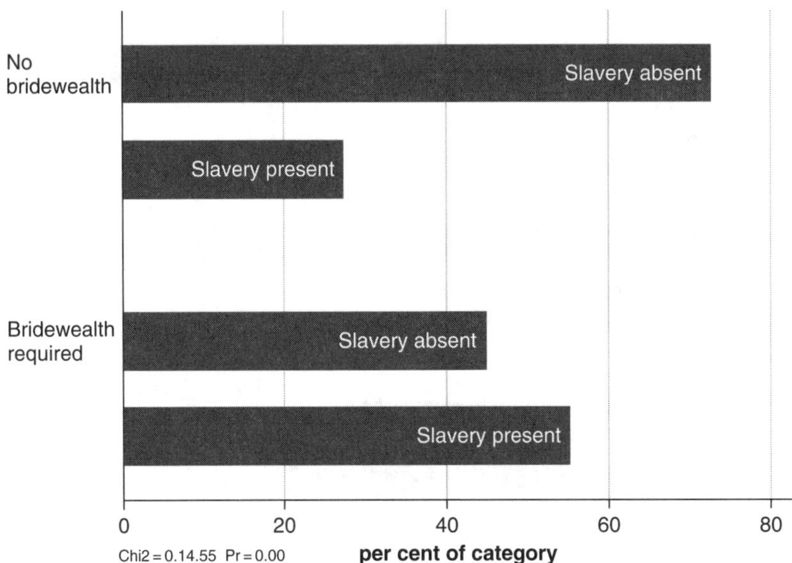

Figure 2.7. Slavery by bridewealth

small minority of marital exchanges. From Figure 2.7 we see that there is a strong and highly significant relationship between this variable and slavery. Over a half of all societies with bridewealth have slaves, compared with 27 per cent of those using other considerations (mainly the dowry) or no consideration. Using the language of odds, the presence of bridewealth more than triples the odds of finding institutional slavery.

We consider, next, the role of polygyny, which all the scholars reviewed emphasized as a critical variable in any attempt to understand both the presence of slavery and the sexual division of labour, as well as their relationship. Figure 2.8a confirms what several studies have established:[55] that the level of women's participation in the dominant mode of subsistence is strongly associated with the existence of full polygyny (meaning that more than 20 per cent of marriages are polygynous). Further, as Figure 2.8b shows, there is an equally strong association between the existence of polygyny and slavery: over a half of societies with full polygyny are slaveholding, compared with a third of those that practise monogamy or very limited polygyny.

[55] Burton, Brudner and White 1977: 227–51; Burton and White 1984: 568–83.

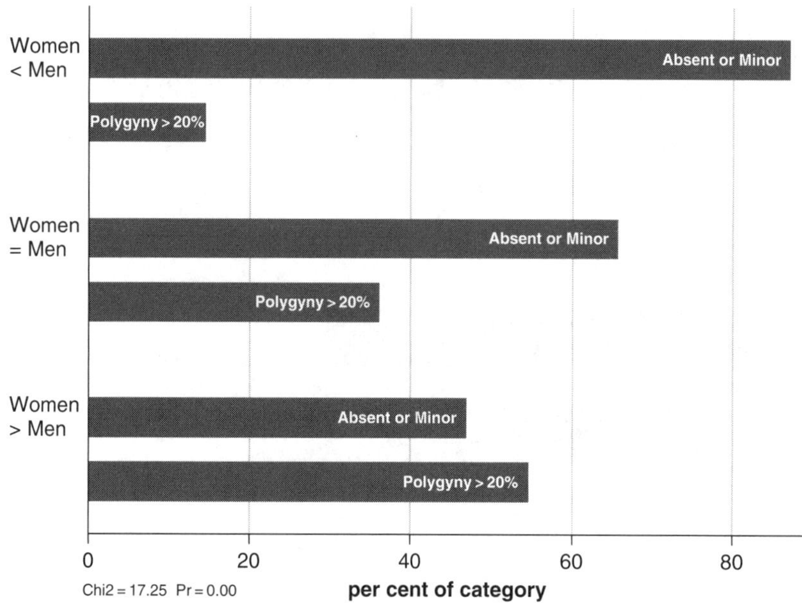

Figure 2.8a. Polygyny by female participation

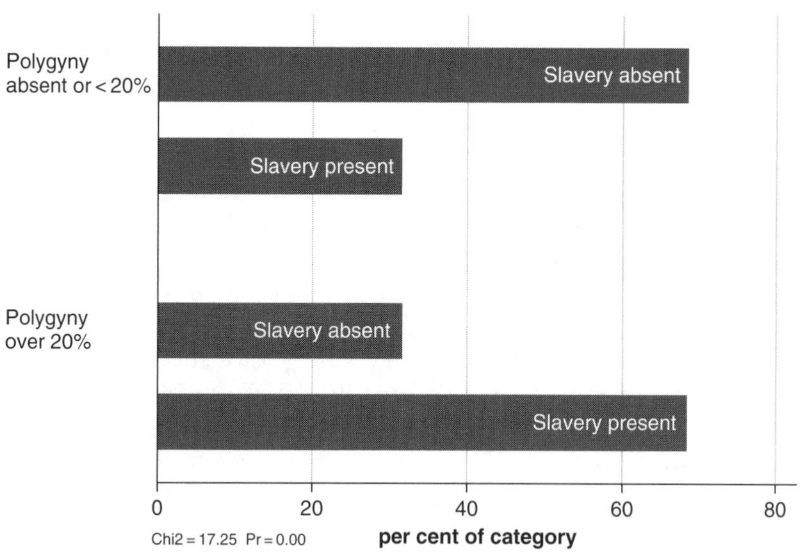

Figure 2.8b. Slavery by polygyny

Table 2.1a *Ordered logistic regressions of female participation on selected variables for extensive agriculturalists*

	Model 1		Model 2		Model 3		Model 4	
	OR	P > |z|	OR	P > |z|	OR	P > |z|	OR	P > |z|
Slavery	1.31	0.60	0.72	0.59	0.40	0.17	0.15	0.05
bride			6.65	0.00	5.05	0.01	4.38	0.06
polygyny					4.96	0.01	9.36	0.01
War01X							0.76	0.73
#Obs	61		61		61		46	
LL	−55.23		−49.65		−46.74		−28.97	
LR chi2	0.27		11.43		17.26		15.15	
Prob > 2	0.60		0.00		0.00		0.00	
Pseudo R2	0.00		0.10		0.15		0.20	

It will be recalled that we earlier found no association between extensive (often hoe-based) and intensive (often plough-based) agriculture and slavery. We must now examine the distinction more closely because it is common knowledge among anthropologists and other social scientists that it is closely associated with polygyny and female participation. As the Russian anthropologist, Andrey Korotayeve, recently observed, 'an average intensive plough agriculturalist in a culture with a very low female contribution to subsistence would never even consider seriously the possibility of having five wives (as he would not be able to feed all of them). Yet, this would not constitute a serious problem for a hoe horticulturalist within a culture with a very high female contribution to subsistence' because 'getting five wives, first of all acquires 10 hands which may feed the horticulturalist himself.'[56] In our sample, extensive agriculturalists were, in fact, more than twice as likely as intensive farmers to have women participating equally or more than men in subsistence ($p = 0.006$), and while nearly half (48 per cent) of extensive agriculturalist practised full polygyny, this was the case among only 27 per cent of intensive farmers.($p = 0.006$).

Table 2.1a reports results of four nested, ordered-logistic models regressing female participation (here the response or dependent variable) on four predictor variables: slavery, the existence of bridewealth in marriage transactions, polygyny and warfare. These models are restricted to societies

[56] Korotayev 2001: 179–203. For an informative case-study see Jacoby 1995: 938–71.

Table 2.1b *Ordered logistic regressions of female participation on selected variables for intensive agriculturalists*

	Model 1		Model 2		Model 3		Model 4	
	OR	P > |z|	OR	P > |z|	OR	P > |z|	OR	P > |z|
Slavery	0.85	0.74	0.54	0.24	0.48	0.18	0.47	0.19
bride			4.36	0.00	4.04	0.01	3.70	0.02
polygyny					2.12	0.20	2.73	0.11
War01X							0.81	0.69
#Obs	**122**		**122**		**122**		**110**	
LL	**− 70.40**		**− 65.49**		**− 64.71**		**− 57.53**	
LR chi2	**0.11**		**9.94**		**11.49**		**11.73**	
Prob > 2	0.74		0.00		0.00		0.02	
Pseudo R2	0.00		0.07		0.08		0.09	

where extensive agriculture is the dominant norm. Table 2.1b shows results for societies where intensive agriculture is the norm. Consistent with our earlier analysis, we see that in only one of the eight models (model 4, Table 2.1a) is female participation significantly predicted by slavery. Among intensive farmers it is not. Among extensive farmers, however, the relationship is more interesting. Controlling for bride and polygyny improves the prediction of female participation but it is only with the introduction of the variable of frequent warfare (Table 2.1a, model 4) that it becomes significant at the 0.05 level.

This pattern is counter-intuitive in two respects. First, just looking at the odds ratios we find the coefficients reversing in size as we add our controls. Second, and more substantively, it appears as if slavery considerably *reduces* the odds of women in the labour force. Expressed more precisely, in slaveholding societies, the odds of women outnumbering men in the dominant mode of production decline by a factor of 0.15 when compared with non-slave societies, holding bride price, polygyny and war constant, which is the same as saying that there is an 85 per cent decline in the odds of women outnumbering men. Further, the odds of women outnumbering men and/or working equally with men, as opposed to participating less than men, are 85 per cent less than would be found in non-slave societies.

It is interesting that the association only becomes significant where there is frequent warfare and it is not unreasonable to infer that slavery strongly reduces the odds of women outnumbering or being equal to men, in contrast with men outnumbering women, primarily in societies with extensive farming, where there is frequent warfare.

Note that, where bridewealth is the prevailing marital norm, female participation is strongly and positively predicted. The effect declines somewhat with the polygyny control added but still remains strong in the final model (model 4, Table 2.1a). In such societies, the odds of women outnumbering men or of outnumbering and/or being equal to men, in contrast with men outnumbering women, are over four times greater than for societies where there is no bridewealth. Note that this positive effect holds also for intensive farming communities. In fact, bridewealth is the only variable that is indifferent to the intensive-extensive distinction.

In sharp contrast, the existence of polygyny is powerfully associated with the dominance or equality of women in the labour force, holding other variables constant. As with slavery, there is a strong interactive effect with warfare. In the full model, restricted to extensive societies, we find that the existence of polygyny increases the odds of more women in production by a factor of 9.36 when compared with non-polygynous, extensive farming societies, other variables being held constant. At the same time, polygyny has no significant effect in plough-based and other intensive farming communities.

We observe that warfare, by itself, does not have a significant effect in either type of farming communities, in spite of the fact that adding it to the model does result in important parameter changes in the other independent variables among societies with extensive agriculture. This suggests a strongly interactive effect and, indeed, when we regress female participation with a war–slavery interactive term added to the model, the odds ratio of the interaction is 8.0, meaning that it increases the odds of more women in the dominant mode of subsistence by a factor of 8 when compared with societies with no slavery *and* little or no warfare.

We next made slavery the response or dependent variable and ran similar models, reported in Tables 2.2a and 2.2b. The results are largely similar with a few important exceptions. In the full model, (model 4, 2.2a) bridewealth is significant only at the 0.10 probability level where there is extensive farming although the effect is much larger than among intensive farmers. Warfare is important in both kinds of societies but its effect on the odds of slavery is twice as great among intensive farmers, where it is also significant at under 0.05 probability.

Polygyny seems to be the pivotal variable in these models and we were led to examine the interactive effect of warfare with it. The results were striking. Our most parsimonious model and (to the degree that the Pseudo

Table 2.2a *Logistic regressions of slavery on selected variables for extensive agriculturalists*

	Model 1		Model 2		Model 3		Model 4	
	OR	P > chi2	OR	P > chi2	OR	P > chi2	OR	P > chi2
fempartX	1.3	0.45	0.83	0.67	0.53	0.20	0.24	0.05
bride			4.13	0.01	3.0	0.09	4.05	0.09
polygyny					6.23	0.00	5.50	0.05
war01X							4.89	0.04
#Obs	**61**		**61**		**61**		**46**	
LL	**− 40.65**		**− 37.85**		**− 34.34**		**− 23.03**	
LR chi2	**0.46**		**6.07**		**13.09**		**15.52**	
Prob > 2	0.50		0.05		0.00		0.00	
Pseudo R2	0.00		0.07		0.16		25.20	

Table 2.2b *Logistic regressions of slavery on selected variables for intensive agriculturalists*

	Model 1		Model 2		Model 3		Model 4	
	OR	P > chi2	OR	P > chi2	OR	P > chi2	OR	P > chi2
fempartX	0.88	0.72	0.64	0.26	0.58	0.18	0.49	0.12
bride			3.64	0.00	3.89	0.01	2.62	0.04
polygyny					3.11	0.04	2.68	0.10
war01X							2.17	0.07
#Obs	**122**		**122**		**122**		**110**	
LL	**− 81.70**		**− 76.40**		**− 74.36**		**− 66.14**	
LR chi2	**0.13**		**10.74**		**14.83**		**14.93**	
Prob > 2	0.72		0.00		0.00		0.00	
Pseudo R2	0.00		0.06		0.09		0.10	

R2 is a meaningful measure) the one with the best explanatory power is simply slavery regressed on female participation, bridewealth, and the war–slavery interaction term, restricted to societies with extensive farming. We found that, among extensive farmers, the interaction of warfare and polygyny increases the odds of slavery by a factor of 22, when compared with extensive farming communities where there is no farming or polygyny, holding constant bride price and female participation. It is interesting that once we control for the interaction of polygyny and warfare the interaction between warfare and female participation becomes insignificant. Polygyny, then, emerges as the critical variable.

DISCUSSION

How do we make sense of all these relationships? My explanation is summarized in the causal model graphically depicted in Figure 2.9.

Consistent with previous work, I argue that female participation is not just strongly *associated* with polygyny in societies with extended farming but is an important *causal* factor. Where women are in great demand as producers, polygyny enhances the wealth and power of men who can afford additional wives, usually older men. Since bridewealth is, literally, an index of women's socio-economic value, high female participation also partly generates both the likelihood and, we suspect, the property and services exchanged for brides. We have seen also, that both polygyny and bridewealth strongly increases the likelihood of slavery and we are arguing that both of these associations reflect direct causal links to slavery. This causal relation is greatly enhanced by warfare; the interaction of polygyny and warfare, as we have seen, enormously increasing the odds of slavery. Similarly, bridewealth is causally linked to slavery but, contrary to the

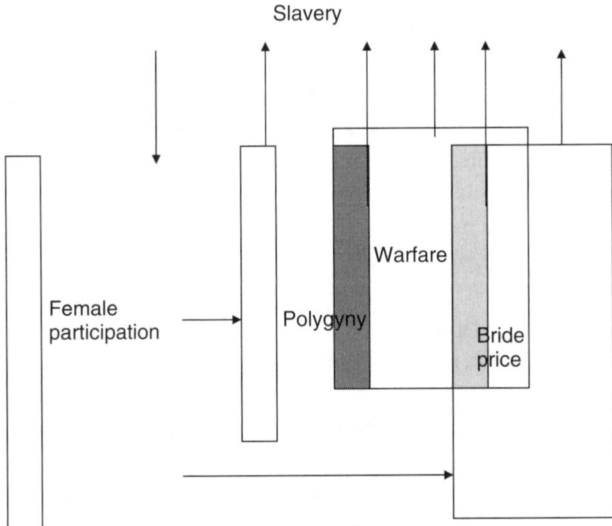

Figure 2.9. General model of slavery

conventional anthropological wisdom, only in societies with intensive farming where it also has a strong interactive effect with warfare (increasing the odds of slavery by a factor of over 4).

Women do sometimes play important economic roles in intensive farming communities (though never participating more than men) and in such cases their value is reflected in the existence of bridewealth. However, the high valuation of women that accounts for the limited number of cases of bridewealth among intensive farmers is due mainly to their roles as reproducers, wives, and concubines. This is consistent with the fact that polygyny is very strongly associated with the existence of bridewealth among intensive farmers under all controls but the association becomes non-significant once we control for female participation among extensive farmers. Warfare also interacts with bridewealth in generating slavery among intensive farmers, though not to the same degree, as the interaction of polygyny and warfare in extensive farming economies. In short, the causal link between bridewealth and slavery in intensive farming societies is due mainly to the value of women as spouses, concubines, and reproducers, whereas both their productive and reproductive as well as other sexual roles lead to slavery among extensive farmers.

But now we face a paradox. The principle of causal transitivity would suggest that increased female participation should lead both indirectly and directly to slavery. However, what we have found is that not only is there no direct association between female participation and slavery, but that when we control for the other variables in our models, a strong negative relationship emerges. How can this be?

The failure of causal transitivity is, actually, not uncommon in statistical analyses and it sometimes goes by the name of Simpson's paradox, where the problem is primarily the result of the quirks of aggregation. In our case, however, there is a substantive rather than purely technical explanation for our seemingly paradoxical claim that slavery is the cause rather than the effect of female participation and, what's more, that the relation is negative; meaning that more slavery causes more men to be in the dominant mode of production. Our explanation requires a dynamic, rather than purely static or cross sectional, perspective.

Let us consider, first, situations where men outnumber women in the dominant mode of subsistence. Where there is warfare, both male prisoners of war and captured women are reduced to slavery. Male slaves reinforce the male predominance in the workforce but captured women would have the opposite effect. And in the absence of warfare we know that most slaves bought in the pre-modern world would be women. So why doesn't slavery tilt the participation rate in favour of more women? The answer is the role of polygyny and the differential assimilation of male and female slaves. Goody has observed that 'there was a constant drift of the offspring of slave women into non-slave status', and that male slaves had less opportunity to reproduce themselves.[57] This is true, but his point is that this resulted in the constant natural decline of slave populations, which must, therefore, be replenished through external trade and/or warfare. While this is consistent with what we have found, my point here is that there was also a gender bias in this drift, with female slaves and the female children of slaves moving into free status to a far greater degree than male slaves and male children.

Most men who were enslaved in the less advanced slaveholding societies of the pre-modern world tended to remain slaves for life. (This is less true of advanced systems, especially those with large urban centres and skilled slaves.) Women, on the other hand, even when used for productive purposes are invariably also used as additional wives or concubines. As secondary wives most were eventually manumitted. Among the Marghi of northern Nigeria, for example, women were the main captives in their frequent inter-village wars; but most were soon absorbed as wives and their status was similar to that of 'a wife acquired without benefit of bride-wealth'.[58] Male slaves, on the other hand, who were usually purchased, tended to remain slaves for life. They were bought to be workers and to 'found a line of mafa (slaves)'.[59] In Islamic slaveholding societies there is a religious requirement to manumit a female slave who bears her master a child, regardless of whether he has married her or not. The Koran also explicitly encourages younger men to solve the problem of a shortage of marriageable women in polygynous societies – most women being monopolized by older and more powerful men – as well as the temptations of adultery, by taking slaves as wives.[60] Indeed, the 'primacy' of the female slave's role 'as sexual object and as a potential mother of free children in the Mamluk empire', writes Shaun E. Marmon, 'is made quite clear by the fact that the statement "your sexual organ is free," *farjuki hurrun*, serves as a formula of manumission for female slaves'.[61] Yet another factor that accounted for the retention of male slaves among less advanced pre-modern societies is what I have called the 'honorific trap' that captured males faced.[62] Having experienced the devastating loss of honour in their enslavement, there was no place for them among the free men, especially

57 Goody 1980: 41. 58 Vaughn 1977: 89. 59 Vaughn 1977: 91.
60 Patterson 1982: 228–32. See also Gordon 1990. 61 Marmon 1999: 4. 62 Patterson 1991: 51.

where honour was prized, as was usually the case in small-scale societies. Women did not face this trap; enslavement did not preclude them from entering the roles of wife or concubine. In the long run, then, slavery in polygynous societies resulted in a selective bias in favour of the retention of males as slaves. To be sure, not all female slaves were absorbed and manumitted, especially those that were unattractive, but, at best, what we find is a shift toward more equalization of the genders in the dominant subsistence mode.

Now consider societies where women were the primary producers. As in all societies, the fact that women dominate an occupation usually means that it has lower status among men. Where women are the primary producers, in fact, men are often engaged in warfare or struggling for status. To do women's work would be dishonouring. But, as we have shown, slaves are quintessentially people without honour. Hence, male slaves in such societies would be incorporated as workers alongside women, in this way tilting the workforce toward a greater number and proportion of men.[63]

This male bias would also be reinforced by the reproductive process. With the exception of some of the more advanced Islamic societies, the male children of both male and female slaves tended to remain in slavery to a far greater degree than the female children of both. In polygynous societies such second-generation slave girls and young women would become prime targets for sex- and wife-deprived younger and poorer men, especially in societies with high bride prices.

Another role of the female slave, not open to men, which facilitated her assimilation into free status was that of wetnurse and nanny. Indeed, in Songhay-Zarma, a special bond emerged between free men nursed by the same slave wetnurse – 'kin through the women' – and this invariably resulted in the 'integration of slave women as "mothers"'.[64]

Another factor that shifts the sex ratio in favour of men, even though women are normally recruited at greater rates, is the re-sale of slaves. In the Sahel, like most other parts of Africa, female slaves were worth more than male slaves and in many cases it was more profitable for the owner of captive females to re-sell them and keep the males for his own uses. Thus, according to Manning, slave captors in the Savanna sell 'two-thirds of the

[63] For examples, see Sardan 1983: 135; and MacCormack 1983: 287. According to Klein, in one case of slavery in the western Sudan, the humiliation of mixing roles was so great that it led to a slave revolt; this, however, was clearly the exception that proved the rule. See Klein 1983: 85.

[64] Sardan 1983: 142.

female captives and one-third of the males' across the Sahara. However, they further remove a significant number of the women from slavery to become wives and concubines in polygynous unions. At the same time, slave men suffer a severe shortage of spouses and many end up in 'nearly all male barracks'.[65]

In the long run, then, increased slavery would eventually lead to growing numbers of men in the labour force, even if the initial effect was to increase the number of women; hence, the negative association we observe between slavery and female participation. Note, once more, that my argument holds only where full polygyny is the norm, that is, where over 20 per cent of marriages are polygynous, especially where there is warfare, and to a lesser extent, where there is bridewealth. In the absence of these factors or controls, there is simply no bivariate association between slavery and female participation; slavery in such cases simply reinforces established patterns and hence is as likely to be found in male dominated as in female dominated subsistence systems.

IMPLICATIONS FOR WESTERN HISTORY

Let me conclude with a few comments about some possible implications of this study, and approach, for the understanding of slavery in the ancient Mediterranean West, and especially Greece. The types of societies I have examined are mainly tribal and small-scale communities and, as such, our analysis would seem to be of relevance mainly to the societies described in the Homeric poems and Hesiod – in other words, Dark Age Greece, the world of Odysseus and the period of the *basileis*, or chieftains, somewhere between 900 BC and 700 BC. This is precisely the period of Greek history most in need of illumination.[66]

We know that the subsistence pattern was a mixed one in these societies, with pastoralism very likely predominating, until about the middle of the eighth century, when there was a gradual shift toward predominantly agrarian societies.[67] Warfare was frequent, possibly chronic.[68] And its

[65] Manning 1990: 45–6. John Thornton, however, is critical of Manning's assumption that the societies victimized by slave raiding and war lost equal numbers of men and women. His alternative model assumes that chronic warfare would be biased toward more men being taken and cites the case of nineteenth-century Angola where census data indicate this to have been the case. See Thornton 1983: 39–48.

[66] Osborne 1985. [67] See Murray 1993: 45–7; Finley 1979: 69; and Hanson 1995.

[68] Finley 1979: 53–4, 62, 85–6; Murray 1993: 39. See also Garlan 1988: 32–3.

main purpose, as Hanson points out, 'was *not*, to storm cities, *not* to gain advantage over foreign troops, *not* to protect the Greek polis from outside challenges – but rather to fight each other',[69] which is similar to how we would describe warfare among the small-scale agro- pastoral communities of the Sahel and other societies in our sample. It was a primary means of acquiring wealth and slaves, especially females. It appears, also, that in the societies Homer wrote about, women, especially the women of the better-off *basileus* families, had relatively high status, both socially and economically, and could move about on their own to a degree unthinkable during the classical period.[70]

These facts alone would lead us to expect well institutionalized patterns of slavery in these societies. In fact, we know that slavery was widespread, that male and female slaves worked at all the main subsistence tasks – as swine- and goatherds, in the farming of grain and other agricultural products and in the household of the more prosperous as nurses, housemaids, and retainers. Many female slaves were also taken as concubines and secondary wives. A good many of the skilled workers (weavers, smiths, butchers, and potters) would have been slaves or ex-slaves and we know that there were women among the skilled. Among the gifts offered Achilles by Agamemnon in the event of his victory were 'seven captive women from Lesbos skilled in crafts'.[71] Significantly, a leading student of ancient Greek slavery concludes that, outside of the household, males and females were about equal in numbers.[72] A striking feature of these societies is that there seem to have been few taboos relating to the kind of work people were expected to do: apparently even *baseleis* sometimes participated in hard manual labour, when they were not away fighting, as Odysseus' famous boast about his ability to handle the scythe and plough, work with leather and build his house suggests.

The parallels between the societies described here and those we have examined, especially in regard to the agro-pastoral slave systems, are remarkable. It is precisely in such agro-pastoral systems that slavery elsewhere has the highest levels of development in the small-scale, pre-modern world, most notably in the Sahel, where one finds among some groups of Tuareg slave populations that were well over a half of the total.[73] Slaves are not only incorporated in great numbers as a result of warfare in such

[69] Hanson 1995. [70] Murray 1993: 44. [71] Finley 1979: 70. [72] Garlan 1988: 33.
[73] See Lovejoy 2000b; and Bernus and Bernus 1975: 27–47.

systems but are often the primary agricultural producers, in addition to their roles in the less desirable areas of animal husbandry. As we have seen, there is a tendency in such societies for second generation slaves to be semi-manumitted or 'hutted' in farm villages where they exist in a semi-servile status. Additionally, manumission tends to be high among household slaves, especially the children of concubines. Homer's depiction of Eumaeus, Odysseus' slave swineherd, well describes the fate of the typical male slave in all small-scale pre-modern societies, especially agro-pastoral systems with their marked emphasis on honour and warfare. A former prince, who had suffered the ultimate dishonour, he knew only too well that 'Zeus of the wide brows takes away one half of the virtue from a man, once the day of slavery closes upon him.'[74] Although well treated, it is significant that there was no social space or niche for him as a freedman in the *oikos*-centred community of his enslavement, unlike the numerous female attendants. The best he could hope for was his master's kindness as a result of serving him faithfully. But however well treated, he knew he would forever be a stranger in a strange land. Hence, to the disguised Odysseus, who has just thanked him for his hospitality he replied: 'stranger, I have no right to deny a stranger . . . that is the way of us who are servants and forever filled with fear when they come under power of masters who are new'.[75]

Two other generally accepted features of Dark Age Greece are of considerable comparative significance. One is the fact that slave status was inherited through the male line.[76] This is an unusual pattern, its best modern counterparts being found among the Migiurtini Somalis, another warring agro-pastoral group, and the Margi of northern Nigeria.[77] The other feature is the large group of landless, low-status persons known as the *thetes*. Most commentators claim that this group was worse off than the slaves.[78] Yvon Garlan argues that there was considerable ambiguity in their status and that the difference between them and slaves was blurred.[79] John Fine's guesses about their origins and condition are interesting: they were 'descendants of earlier inhabitants who had been dispossessed by immigrants, runaway slaves, people expelled from some kinship organization, refugees from a blood feud'.[80] He also adds that 'in a world where one's welfare depended on belonging to a kinship organization or possessing a

[74] Homer, *Od.* 17: 322–3. [75] Homer, *Od.* 14: 55–60. [76] Finley 1979: 67.
[77] Patterson 1982: 137–8. [78] Finley 1979: 65–6. See also Fine 1983: 42.
[79] Garlan 1988: 36–7. [80] Fine 1983: 42.

profession or craft . . . the *thetes* were people without land, a trade, or family connections'. Now, what I find remarkable about this passage is that this description perfectly matches the basic definition of the slave as I understand the term. In most kin-based societies elsewhere the slave was, quintessentially, a kinless person, one with no claims on the community. *Thetes* were the perfect exemplification of the condition I have called 'natal alienation', a fundamental element of slavery.[81] Did this mean that they were slaves? Very likely; or else they were descended from slaves. There are numerous modern parallels, the most striking being perhaps the *irewelen* people of servile ancestry among the more sedentary Tuaregs of states such as Damagaram, Kano, and Katsina.[82]

Why have historians of ancient Greece been reluctant to recognize what seems obvious to any student of comparative slavery? The answer, I believe, is found in the definitional trap that most modern historians are ensnared by in their usage of the term, 'slavery'. The Roman legal definition of a slave as one who is essentially owned, the property of another, has dominated western thinking about the nature of slavery. However, as I have shown in *Slavery and Social Death*, both the Romans' view of property and their conception of slaves as the quintessential kind of property were very peculiar in comparative terms.[83] All over the world, people who were not slaves were frequently bought and sold; this being true of Euro-American indentured servants until well into the nineteenth century, and of serfs in Russia and Eastern Germany until as late as the mid-nineteenth century. It is also a fact that, in bridewealth systems, wives were bought without any notion of them being slaves; indeed, their purchase price was an honourable index of their social value. Conversely, the fact that a group of people were no longer bought and sold does not mean that they were not slaves or very close to that status.

Once we rid ourselves of the view that slaves have to be persons who could be bought and sold, we can more easily grasp the fact that the *thetes* were largely semi-manumitted slaves, no longer always under the direct control of a master but very much at the mercy of most genuinely free persons in the society; akin to groups such as the Irewelen of Hausaland and even the Afro-Americans during the post-emancipation Jim Crow era. And, like all such semi-slave groups, they were usually worse off than slaves who were directly tied to a master. One other piece of evidence lends

81 Patterson 1982.

82 Baier and Lovejoy 1977; 391–411 For other examples, see Hill 1976 and Hogendorn 1977.

83 Patterson 1982.

weight to our argument. It is the fact that one of the major elements of Solon's reform was his plan to buy back Athenians who had been sold abroad into slavery. To a student of comparative slavery the necessity for such a reform, and the pre-existing practice it implies, are quite extraordinary. It is rare indeed for people to sell the members of their own community abroad. Rare, unless those sold were regarded as slaves or hardly better in status by the sellers. There could be no better proof of the slave-like status of the mass of *thetes*, a status against which they were on the verge of revolting. The *seisachtheia* of Solon is usually interpreted as a discharge of the burdens of debt bondage, but this leaves unresolved the question of how the mass of the Athenian population could, in the first place, have been reduced to such a condition with the ultimate sanction of outright slavery in the event of defaulting on their debts. We need go no further back in history than the share-cropping and debt-servitude of the post-emancipation black population of the United States to understand how this was a fate that easily befell all recently enslaved groups.

Dark Age Greece then, was a collection of genuine slave societies, in which a sizeable proportion of the population were either slaves or semi-slaves directly descended from slaves. The ancestors of this servile population would have been mainly women captured in warfare. Most of their male ancestors would have been killed or sacrificed, but some of them were also enslaved especially if taken as boys. Like in most agro-pastoral societies, the sexual division of labour was, in the long run, heavily influenced by the strong female bias in assimilation to free or semi-free status, resulting in the roughly equal distribution of men and women in most occupations both in farming and animal husbandry, even though more women would have been initially captured. The strong presence of women in all areas of these rudimentary agro-pastoral communities and the tendency for such equalization in work to lead to a highly developed sense of their own equality with men suggests the existence of women with attitudes that would have been anathema to men with patriarchal views. Strong, independent and assertive women are a hallmark of post-slavery societies, as anyone familiar with the black Americas will attest. Men, such as Hesiod, were clearly of the view that the women of their time were out of control. We can now better understand the source of his gratuitously vicious, and otherwise perplexing, misogyny.[84]

[84] See, for example, Hesiod, *Works and Days*, 65–9; 373–5; 700–1, and Hesiod, *Theogony*, 570–93; see also, Arthur 1984: 23–5; and Rogers 1966.

APPENDIX: THE SOCIETIES OF THE STANDARD CROSS-CULTURAL SAMPLE.

No.	Societal name	Date[1]
1	Nama Hottentot	1860
2	Kung Bushmen	1950
3	Thonga	1865
4	Lozi	1900
5	Mbundu	1890
6	Suku	1920
7	Bemba	1897
8	Nyakyusa	1934
9	Hadza	1930
10	Luguru	1925
11	Kikuyu	1920
12	Ganda	1875
13	Mbuti	1950
14	Nkundo Mongo	1930
15	Banen	1935
16	Tiv	1920
17	Ibo	1935
18	Fon	1890
19	Ashanti	1895
20	Mende	1945
21	Wolof	1950
22	Bambara	1902
23	Tallensi	1934
24	Songhai	1940
25	Pastoral Fulani	1951
26	Hausa	1900
27	Massa (Masa)	1910
28	Azande	1905
29	Fur (Darfur)	1880
30	Otoro Nuba	1930
31	Shilluk	1910
32	Mao	1939
33	Kaffa (Kafa)	1905
34	Masai	1900
35	Konso	1935
36	Somali	1900
37	Amhara	1953
38	Bogo	1855
39	Kenuzi Nubians	1900
40	Teda	1950
41	Tuareg	1900
42	Riffians	1926
43	Egyptians	1950

44	Hebrews	621
45	Babylonians	1750
46	Rwala Bedouin	1913
47	Turks	1950
48	Gheg Albanians	1910
49	Romans	110
50	Basques	1934
51	Irish	1932
52	Lapps	1950
53	Yurak Samoyed	1894
54	Russians	1955
55	Abkhaz	1880
56	Armenians	1843
57	Kurd	1951
58	Basseri	1958
59	Punjabi (West)	1950
60	Gond	1938
61	Toda	1900
62	Santal	1940
63	Uttar Pradesh	1945
64	Burusho	1934
65	Kazak	1885
66	Khalka Mongols	1920
67	Lolo	1910
68	Lepcha	1937
69	Garo	1955
70	Lakher	1930
71	Burmese	1965
72	Lamet	1940
73	Vietnamese	1930
74	Rhade	1962
75	Khmer	1292
76	Siamese	1955
77	Semang	1925
78	Nicobarese	1870
79	Andamanese	1860
80	Vedda	1860
81	Tanala	1925
82	Negri Sembilan	1958
83	Javanese	1954
84	Balinese	1958
85	Iban	1950
86	Badjau	1963
87	Toradja	1910
88	Tobelorese	1900
89	Alorese	1938
90	Tiwi	1929
91	Aranda	1896
92	Orokaiva	1925
93	Kimam	1960

94	Kapauku	1955
95	Kwoma	1960
96	Manus	1937
97	New Ireland	1930
98	Trobrianders	1914
99	Siuai	1939
100	Tikopia	1930
101	Pentecost	1953
102	Mbau Fijians	1840
103	Ajie	1845
104	Maori	1820
105	Marquesans	1800
106	Western Samoans	1829
107	Gilbertese	1890
108	Marshallese	1900
109	Trukese	1947
110	Yapese	1910
111	Palauans	1947
112	Ifugao	1910
113	Atayal	1930
114	Chinese	1936
115	Manchu	1915
116	Koreans	1947
117	Japanese	1950
118	Ainu	1880
119	Gilyak	1890
120	Yukaghir	1850
121	Chukchee	1900
122	Ingalik	1885
123	Aleut	1800
124	Copper Eskimo	1915
125	Montagnais	1910
126	Micmac	1650
127	Saulteaux	1930
128	Slave	1940
129	Kaska	1900
130	Eyak	1890
131	Haida	1875
132	Bellacoola	1880
133	Twana	1860
134	Yurok	1850
135	Pomo (Eastern)	1850
136	Yokuts (Lake)	1850
137	Paiute (North)	1870
138	Klamath	1860
139	Kutenai	1890
140	Gros Ventre	1880
141	Hidatsa	1836
142	Pawnee	1867
143	Omaha	1860

144	Huron	1634
145	Creek	1800
146	Natchez	1718
147	Comanche	1870
148	Chiricahua	1870
149	Zuni	1880
150	Havasupai	1918
151	Papago	1910
152	Huichol	1890
153	Aztec	1520
154	Popoluca	1940
155	Quiche	1930
156	Miskito	1921
157	Bribri	1917
158	Cuna (Tule)	1927
159	Goajiro	1947
160	Haitians	1935
161	Callinago	1650
162	Warrau	1935
163	Yanomamo	1965
164	Carib (Barama)	1932
165	Saramacca	1928
166	Mundurucu	1850
167	Cubeo (Tucano)	1939
168	Cayapa	1908
169	Jivaro	1920
170	Amahuaca	1960
171	Inca	1530
172	Aymara	1940
173	Siriono	1942
174	Nambicuara	1940
175	Trumai	1938
176	Timbira	1915
177	Tupinamba	1550
178	Botocudo	1884
179	Shavante	1958
180	Aweikoma	1932
181	Cayua	1890
182	Lengua	1889
183	Abipon	1750
184	Mapuche	1950
185	Tehuelche	1870
186	Yahgan	1865

[1] Dates are the focal points of the earliest reliable ethnographies

CHAPTER 3

Slaving as historical process: examples from the ancient Mediterranean and the modern Atlantic

Joseph C. Miller

This chapter explores dynamic aspects of the book editors' challenge to consider the rise and demise of 'slave systems' in the ancient Mediterranean and in the emergently modern Atlantic – but it offers a *historical* approach to recurrent *slaving* as incremental processes of change in place of the structural premise of abstract and implicitly static 'slave systems' that underlies the method of comparison implicitly proposed, and also nearly all the current literature on slavery.[1] Slavers marginal to particular historical contexts in which they lived, earlier and later, found both means and motivation to advance themselves, at the expense of rivals in control of, but limited to, local resources by acquiring outsiders whom they exclusively controlled. This recurrent historical dialectic, uniquely contextualized in both ancient times and the modern Atlantic, as well as elsewhere in the world, identifies similarities and differences in the historical dynamics that explain the resulting parallels and contrasts that conventional comparisons in structural terms describe.

Slaving is fundamentally a historical process, as slaving strategies achieved prominence primarily in times and places where rapid military or economic expansion facilitated access to outsiders. It was also, thus, generally a by-product, a secondary strategy, arising from specifiable tensions within larger and more complex historical processes. Significant slaving and integration of the slaves in turn contributed to still others. Slaves were, by definition, novel components of the historical contexts into which they were brought, and they were, in effect, deployed at the cutting edges of major innovations throughout the history of the world. A historical analysis of slaving thus adds understanding by contextualizing unique

[1] I will thus attempt to problematize the inherently static logic of Moses Finley's widely popular (but highly structural, and hence historically inert) contrast between 'slave societies' and 'societies with slaves'. See Finley 1968: 307–13.

processes of change rather than by comparing *a priori* defined static institutions abstracted from their historical contexts.

The following sections set familiar outcomes of slaving in the ancient Mediterranean region and in the Atlantic in broader contexts of the long-term historical changes that produced them. It positions the slavers, often merchants, in worlds dominated by military, land-owning, and priestly rivals rather than focusing on the masters' domination of their slaves. It contextualizes the slaves also in worlds more complex than the singular 'domination' of masters presumed in the conventional, essentially socio-logical, literature, and differently so in the Old World than in the New World. The singularity of the masters' control was relative to their rivals, whom it excluded from access to the enslaved. The exclusive access of masters to significant numbers of slaves in turn empowered the slavers to effect innovations in complex, tense working partnerships with their more established rivals. Depending on the specific times and places, military innovators used slaves to challenge landed interests, or merchants used slaving to challenge either of these two. Slaves were thus aggregated in the largest numbers and became objects of the greatest preoccupations of their masters as products of major changes under way and also as means of consolidating the differences they made.[2]

My emphasis here is on the dynamic aspects of *slaving* that I regard as inherent. That is: how and why certain people recurrently resorted to this strategy from time to time and in place after place throughout human history. The historical 'problem' of slaving, thus, consists in seeing who, under what circumstances, by what means, with what ends in mind, and with what failures as well as what successes, managed to get their hands on individuals – 'outsiders' in origin – so culturally and socially isolated upon arrival that they could be induced, if not compelled, to give personal advantage, even at their own expense,[3] to those in socially conceded exclusive control of their presence. As for those enslaved, in contrast to

[2] Consider this phrasing as a less teleological, less evaluative, phrasing of the important idea that David Brion Davis presents in modern and Europe-centred contexts as 'progress' – that is, as moments of clarification, or at least ideological definition, that subsequent generations appropriated and modified for historical purposes of their own; see Davis 1984. Finley – in Finley 1959: 145–64 – first proposed the ironic association of slavery with the moments in the past, particularly ancient Greece, identified as paradigmatic for what nineteenth-century Progressives celebrated as 'progress'.

[3] Here is the defining element of exploitation *in extremis* emphasized as defining by Meillassoux 1991. For Meillassoux, slavery is distinguished from other 'modes of [exploitive] production' by extraction of a population's labour effort beyond the point of allowing it to bear and nourish children to the age of further reproduction. Reproduction of an enslaved labour force then falls to the masters' violent captures (the 'iron' of the title alluding to the sword or other weaponry) and/or by purchase (the 'gold').

Patterson's sociological accent on the intimate relationship between masters and slaves in his famous definition of slavery as '*the permanent, violent* [personal] *domination of natally alienated and generally* [that is, socially] *dishonored persons*',[4] the historical approach to their active presence (rather than their social absence) emphasizes the contexts in which this definitionally isolated dyad in fact, even primarily, lived. It emphasizes the slavers' relations with their social, or economic, or political, or military rivals rather than masters' relations only with their slaves. It accents motivating and enabling strategies of change rather than Patterson's ironic emphasis on the failure of total domination to achieve ultimate dependence. It also emphasizes alternative identities and communities that the enslaved forged among themselves, inevitably independently of their masters' attempts to obtain their exclusive loyalty.[5] If slaves are defined primarily as being 'dominated', as Patterson's and virtually all other abstract efforts to conceptualize 'slavery' define them, they may play off the contradictions within the (presumed, axiomatic, accepted, given) confinement of 'slavery' to preserve some sense of personal dignity and even create opportunity within their captivity, or eventually to assert themselves beyond it in society as well, but they are unpromising agents of *historical* change.[6] 'Socially dead' thus translates into historically inert. Within this logic, they make a historical difference only in rebellion, preferably violent, mass revolt, that is, no longer as 'slaves' but rather in asserting themselves outside their would-be masters' assumed control.[7] Historians instead might better identify and appropriate for their analytical purposes the vitality that slaves, ineluctably human beings, possessed.

[4] Patterson 1982: 12 [Patterson's italics, but my parenthetical glosses for implied emphasis relevant to the arguments of this chapter]. A more historical definition of 'slavery' includes the experiences of enslavement and thus the perspective of the enslaved, emphasizing meaning, capability, and hence motivated action. The contextual aspect of enslavement then centres on ephemeral isolation, and the resulting but temporary disability and vulnerability, followed by strategies of constituting new social relationships. Patterson assumes the singularity and persistance of the slave's relationship with the master alone. A more fully contextualized setting of the experience focuses on slaves' agency directed initially, and under some circumstances primarily, at 'belonging', or at constituting relational identities. On the premise that sociability defines humanity, slavery thus literally 'dehumanizes' to the extent that it isolates, and slaves seek to recover the recognition that constitutes identity, the self, humanity itself. See Miller 2004b.

[5] See Miller 2003b: 81–121.

[6] The general literature is at extreme pains to detect and celebrate slave agency, but it does so against the historical red herring of assumed total domination of the masters, which – unsurprisingly enough – no historian who has looked has ever found.

[7] And, elsewhere, I posit an alternative vision of the strategies of the enslaved that complements my accent here on uprooting and transfer as the definitive moment in the *process* of being enslaved; see Miller 2003a. For parallel concerns in the United States context, see Johnson 2001: 148–67; and Johnson 2003: 113–24.

ANCIENT NOVELTIES OF SLAVING, BROADLY SKETCHED

Having, thus, suggested how viewing 'slavery' as an 'institution', peculiar or not, has neglected key historical aspects of what was in fact always a process, and thereby also missing the vital presence of the enslaved, I now devote the remaining space in this chapter to a historicized sketch of (inevitably highly) selected but suggestive elements of what could become a global history of slaving.

Slaving was a strategy focused specifically on mobilizing directly controlled *human* resources. On the scale of world history, established interests eventually fought back by intensifying their utilization of the local resources that they controlled and that had no external counterparts. Land in confined river valleys became scarce relative to agrarian populations, and lands improved to increase their productivity became the focus of significant investments of labour. Military technologies, trained coordination of large bodies of fighters, and logistics to support concentrated armies replaced massed individual human agility, personal valour, and clever deceit as the keys to winning violent confrontations. Eventually, loaned commercial assets became means of rendering others dependent through personal indebtedness.[8] As these *internal* resources increased in efficacy and hence value, predation on outsiders – including slaving – remained the peculiar resort of those marginalized by others' control of them. Thus, those who slaved are understood historically not by 'correlation' of consistent descriptive 'variables' isolated from their contexts – as comparisons of 'cases' in the social sciences would do – but rather as whoever managed to step beyond the changing specific, complex, multi-faceted, and contradictory contexts of specific controls on the internal assets otherwise key to individual success.

The 'empires' of ancient southwestern Asia – and also Greece, Rome, and throughout the Islamic world, no more than human society itself – were not a 'natural' unfolding of some ancient potential; they too had to be created. No one planned them; many resisted them. In all these cases, they were imposed militarily on, rather than induced among, integral domestic communities that they converted to peasants who remained capable of supporting themselves but were able also to contribute, under duress, to the

[8] Some readers may be tracking the partial parallel of these differing historical strategies with Marxian 'modes of production'; shorn of his structural framing, Marx acutely sensed some of the key strategies of individuals' exploitive control, from a perspective that valued balance and reciprocity parallel to (but in a very limited material sense) what I am here calling a 'communal ethos'.

maintenance of overlords and the wealth of merchants.[9] The autonomous power of a single nominal authority – figureheads we might term 'rulers' only by not quibbling over relevant historical distinctions – to exploit ruthlessly rested on their ability to set themselves above – that is, outside, and independent of – the communal politics of reciprocity otherwise prevailing. Such political authority was not inherently militarized, since religio-political ideology easily sufficed in the 'animate', rather than technological, worlds of those times. 'Rulers' usually consolidated this splendid isolation primarily by surrounding themselves with others similarly free of competing obligations to anyone else in the local communities they sought to transcend, that is, with slaves captured from wars undertaken abroad.

In ancient Mesopotamia – where long-distance trade put military elites in contact with distant populations susceptible to capture, removal, and integration as isolated newcomers, and also provided wealth to purchase people captured on the battlefields – warrior elites surrounded themselves with slaves to support enormous personal households and also those of the priests of cults deifying them, so to frame ideologically the separateness they sought from the communities of peasants whom they ruled. Egypt, earlier in time than Mesopotamia, less commercialized in underlying strategies, and only belatedly in contact with significant enslaveable populations, relied on captives to correspondingly lesser degrees. In all cases, the slaves – mostly female – were thus assembled in skilled, ongoing, often intimate capacities close to their masters. 'Domestic' roles like theirs subsequently characterized slavery everywhere in the Old World, and also in more of the New World than the plantation paradigm of male slavery in the Americas acknowledges.[10]

Slaving represented the strategy by which military elites, in contexts where they were marginal to a predominantly rural and communal ethos – indeed, quite unable to depend on the people they attempted to claim as 'subjects' beyond understood limits, consolidated the ideological, and then the key infrastructural, strength to assume the physically dominating positions their successors claimed. Such positions historians who see these historical processes of initiating radically new forms of authority only as static, enduring 'civilizations', usually attribute anachronistically

[9] The key dimension of the famous 'river-bottom' or 'hydraulic' states of that era and area was not state interference in production but rather state facilitation/coordination of the hydraulic infrastructure, both water to irrigate, and thus increase, production and river transport to remove (and control) production that remained in the hands of viable local communities, on whom the 'state' was fundamentally dependent. Hence, the resort to slaving by such regimes, as follows.

[10] See Campbell, Miers and Miller 2005: 163–82.

to the founders without problematizing how they accumulated the power they left to their heirs.[11]

But they concentrated their slaving on the central innovation, the creation of autonomous power. Broadly, ancient military elites drew on the loyalties they claimed from local populations to celebrate themselves through intermittent monumental construction, or military plundering, of the occasional, and often seasonal, rhythms that peasants could provide without compromising the economy's underlying reliance on their routine agricultural labours. The issue of slaving was not 'labour' in some abstract sense, nor 'product', but rather the politics of isolation of themselves, and of their palace and personal slaves. Slaves employed in ongoing military capacities were devoted to the limited, special purposes of protecting the palace, or its occupant, as militarized extensions of the much earlier use of women and girls (and eunuchs) there in domestic capacities. To the extent that ancient rulers thus succeeded in implementing a religious cover of god-given separateness and loyal subjects, they structured these outsiders ideologically by reducing them ethnologically to caricatured 'enslaveable barbarians'. Greeks eventually characterized those whom they excluded in these classic terms,[12] as they included themselves in a pan-peninsular identity built around civic honour, although philosophers still acknowledged the – at least theoretically – random quality of earlier slaving of the opportunistic sort as a way of reminding the mighty, surrounded by their slaves, of the ephemerality of the human condition. Collective identity was once again, as commonly throughout human history until the dawn of nationalism,[13] defined by slaving.

Early commercial slaving transferred captives taken in remote military campaigns to domestic households at home, backed crucially by state authority.[14] Merchants marginal to the process of military expansion by their warrior rivals thus thrived, serving well the military and priestly elites building their autonomy on the services of outsiders delivered to them. However, by the mid-first millennium BC their successors began to invest the liquid assets they derived from disposing of plunder from abroad to

[11] An axis along which to problematize historically the long run of events on the lower Nile; according to this hypothesis, internal infrastructure would have yielded coordination capable of sustaining external military adventures only after several centuries and 'dynasties'.

[12] Elsewhere 'cannibals', 'witches', 'polluted', 'animality/bestiality', 'heathen', and 'stupid' served as demonizing inversions of the varying ideological claims of other communities to their own superiority.

[13] Miller 2004a.

[14] Hence the legal codes that are principal sources of the scattered available evidence. I am aware of the other epigraphic and papyrological evidence of individual circumstances and transactions.

intrude on the access of domestic elites to populations at home.[15] They indebted local farmers otherwise beholden exclusively to rulers, or priests. By shifting their investments from external trade to local populations, they claimed access to the basic labour of the agrarian economy or – in the likely event of default – seized their persons. They extended the proprietarial and contractual provisions of emerging commercial law[16] to seize local peasant debtors as slaves, either by selling themselves to relieve their relatives of their secondary liability, by the rules of collective responsibility, or – more often – giving up female dependants through 'sales' to their merchant creditors.

'Proprietarial' interests in both outsiders and local debtors, commercialized for purposes of negotiability, thus appeared several millennia ago in Mesopotamia. However, to construe these atypical transactions, or transactional moments in lives otherwise spent within domestic households, as comprehensive, or as defining of 'slavery', would then indulge the selective fallacy of origins – in relation to modern thoroughly proprietarial slavery – to an extreme degree. Contextualized historically, such personal rights of transfer of interests in persons, as distinct from the collective responsibility of the communal ethos for and over members of its communities, applied only to fleeting moments of definitive transfers between contracting strangers. The full historical context included many other kinds of less individuating transfers of personal responsibility and allegiance – as wives and wards, orphans and widows, or slave girls among friends or to confirm mutual obligations – among resident communities in ongoing relationships of mutual responsibility to one another. 'Property' in persons, in the modern commercial sense, was present, but it was far from pervasive, and commercial strategies of slaving were significant primarily as mercantile means to subvert the still prevalent, if also tenuous, claims of military rulers to legitimacy in fundamentally communal societies. Proprietarial rights in the sense of an individual 'owner's' exclusive personal possession were not a prominent aspect of what defined an individual as a slave; rather, contextualized origin as an outsider, recency of arrival, conditionality (or

[15] The brevity of the schematization possible within the confines of this essay forces me to focus on the transformative elements in much more complex historical situations. In the Peloponnesus, for example, naval power (and piracy) also produced captives who were enslaved.

[16] Which gave legal – that is: collective – sanction to the rights of individuals as opposed to the prevailing ethos of communal responsibility; the later distinction between 'personal' (moveable) property and the 'real' wealth held in communal/societal trust presumably derives from this transition from collective to private interest.

contingency) of standing, and – above all – initial isolation and vulnerability were.

In Europe and Africa, and also in Asia, most – perhaps the great majority – of the people enslaved had been female,[17] often sent or carried off at very young ages. Women and girls there had been taken into large households and thus distributed in small numbers among a great many people native to wherever they were placed. Where slavers occasionally had, for whatever reasons, aggregated large numbers of adult males, these experiments with setting enslaved men to productive gang labour had soon ended in revolt.[18] The resulting Old World practices of slavery were essentially female, private, and broadly incorporative and assimilative within the strongly hierarchical, patriarchal, households within which the great majority of the enslaved lived. However, they remained correspondingly obscure in the written records of the time, when writing was confined largely to the public sphere. The historian must contextualize the limited written records of transactions involving slaves in the much larger, only minimally commercialized, hence unrecorded circumstances of those times. Public law, intended to regulate affairs among strangers or among contracting partners otherwise unrelated, thus took little notice of 'slavery' of this female sort. Commercial law regulated public transactions, including those transferring rights over people, but markets probably accounted for only a small portion of transfers that otherwise distributed enslaved girls and women through networks of kinship and alliance – by analogy with other forms of personal, hence negotiable, property – as distinct from the estate of the household or other collectivity. Most transactions, including those involving people, and particularly females, left no record.

Public involvement with the presence of the enslaved remained in the realm of personal ethics and the responsibilities of honourable men, in two senses. Positive morality emphasized the personal responsibility of the master, or household head, for all the lesser, weaker members of the 'family' he assembled, including women and children as well as outsiders

[17] Miller 2007c. See also the probably more-than-coincidental argument of Orlando Patterson that the slaves who invented the idea of 'freedom' in ancient Greece were women; see Patterson 1991. Rather than, as he implies, that women as dominated had a particular insight into slavery, the case may have been that most slaves were women. This hypothesis would then raise the additional question of why enslaved males feature so prominently in Greek (and Roman) theatre. One component of an answer would then be the dramatic potential that arises from the ironies and contradictions of men confined in a condition so abnormal against the background of slavery naturalized as female.

[18] One thinks, of course, of the slave wars in the late centuries BC in southern Italy and Sicily as well as the famous 'Zanj' revolt at the end of the ninth century AD in what is now southern Iraq. On the Zanj, see Popovic 1998.

present through enslavement. Particular injunctions against mistreatment of the vulnerable enslaved may have derived from their utter lack of personal networks of support, unlike wives and their 'legitimate' children with in-laws devoted to their interests.

Negative collective awareness of the slaves was similarly personal and consisted of stereotyped constructions of the limited ability of the enslaved within the household to defend themselves, hardly treating them as the depersonalized 'things' referenced by analogy, rather than as substantive description, in commercial law.[19] The core images caricaturing the enslaved exaggerated the limitations of the recently arrived, varying over time and space with the backgrounds of the individuals stereotyped. This exclusionary caricaturization of difference remained essentially ethnic into the first century of slaving in the Atlantic.[20] It also arose less from public legal categorization than from complex competitive dynamics within the large compound households in which slaves were congregated. Individuals tried to convert their slaves to advance their own standing within them, and legitimate wives struggled to claim heritages of respected lineage and current wealth for their own children at the expense of infants that the men of the household might father with the slave girls within it. The ancient struggle over outsiders brought into a strongly communal ethos, between individuals and the claims of their communities, thus recurred in the wealthy and aristocratic households of the ancient Mediterranean. It was an inherent tension where slaving focused on women to reproduce – in one way or another – domestic institutions.[21] The civic exclusions of modern slavery were muted, secondary at most as historically motivating considerations.

Large households or other sorts of corporate activities (municipal, artisan, commercial, etc.) engaged in non-seasonal enterprises sometimes held moderate numbers of enslaved men, in some instances as the skilled members at the group's core and in other cases deployed in dangerous or demeaning capacities. Yet, the seasonal bulk of agricultural production throughout the Old World fell to resident peasant communities, able to support themselves during the non-productive months of the year and to yield up a portion of their harvests and other produce, as well as military and other occasional service, to the military or ecclesiastical elites. Male

[19] Here, again, Patterson 1982 is implicitly right: the inverse of the non-existence of the slave outside of the master–slave dyad translates to vibrant vitality within it.

[20] Thus the ethnically etymological 'Slavs' at the root of the word for 'slave' in all western European languages other than Celtic and Scandinavian; for further detail, see Miller 2004c.

[21] More contextualization of this theme in Miller 2007c.

slaves were generally too costly and too much in demand in the cities to serve as supplements to resident rural labour, except where triumphant military aristocrats brought significant numbers of captives from the fields of battle to intensify occupation and exploitation of under-utilized, otherwise claimed, or unavailable, local labour forces.

The prominence of slaves in parts of late-Republican and early imperial Roman rural Italy would thus have marked a significant shift toward a more commercially integrated countryside in response to burgeoning urban needs at Rome. Generals in Rome's sweeping military campaigns on the frontiers of its expanding conquests thus used their captives to displace previous and less market-oriented landowners – a characteristic example of figures marginal to an older Republican order using resources, human in this case, originating outside its boundaries so as to challenge, and in this case to overcome, an *ancien régime* of land-owning aristocrats.[22] The historicized version of the conventional, but misphrased, question of what analogies the Roman *latifundia* bore to 'plantations' on the modern model would examine the differences between established peasant and landlord labour arrangements and the novelties new landowners introduced, with slaves, in the late centuries BC, together with the specific (skilled?) categories in which men or women might have served the retired military command as slaves.

Other warlords used captives seized abroad to assert themselves against domestic challenges of growing commercial wealth at home throughout the following millennium and a half in Afro-Eur-Asia.[23] Territorial conquests enriched the traders, who relieved victors on the battlefield of the spoils of their triumphs to increasing degrees, and thus merchants surrounded themselves with slaves in such numbers that, if allowed to continue to grow unchecked, could constitute political commercial threats to military power. Rulers responded by employing slaves themselves in specific sensitive capacities, which varied according to the contexts in which they found themselves but which almost never included basic agricultural labour.[24] The famous military slavery of Islamic regimes and other polities in Africa and Asia – what Patterson calls 'palatine slavery' – resulted from

[22] I am well aware of the debates surrounding the extent and functions of enslaved labour on the Roman *latifundia*.

[23] But not in the pre-Columbian Americas, where lack of the military power that the horse allowed forced continued reliance on spectacular displays of immolated enemies or – more terrifying still – subjects presented as less than utterly loyal to the regime.

[24] The famous Spartan *helot* communities of rural cultivators had been clearly tightly controlled and carefully allocated among an evidently very competitive local military elite, one deprived of opportunities for supporting itself by military expansion. *Helots* thus represent the outcome of a

the great seventh- to fifteenth-century commercial prosperity in the Muslim *oecumene*. Regimes in western Europe – too poor to compete for captives with Muslim commercial markets, too Christian to enslave locally, and increasingly too politically inclusive in a monarchical style to need slaves to support royal power or, more important, to tolerate the use of slaves by potential opponents within the realms being constituted – turned to slaves to guard their regimes only very marginally.[25] There, the struggle for the hearts and minds of local cultivators became a three-way contest between the Catholic Church with its vast landed interests, monarchs who subtly appropriated the overarching legitimacy that the Church had built over the preceding millennium as defenders of the faith, and the local ('feudal') warlords gradually reduced to the splendorous and impoverished impotence that culminated in eighteenth-century France.

Throughout the expansive Islamic world, on the other hand, infidel populations accessible to plunder steadily dwindled, and commercial consolidation of the far-flung frontiers of the *dar-al-Islam* intensified from the tenth to the twelfth centuries (AD). Warlords accordingly became increasingly marginal to the realities of daily life, and thus more and more reliant on military palace slaves to protect them. These captives they self-defeatingly purchased from, and thereby enriched, the very mercantile interests who were challenging them, rather than capturing them directly. In part since they found it less risky to turn to foreign merchants for the slaves they needed, the door of slaving in the Muslim eastern and southern

rare instance of military involution, a military elite that did not collapse when deprived of plunder from abroad but instead intensified its claims on its own local population in a collaborative (republican) style, rather than the usual dictatorial outcome of militarized competition intensified by turning inward. The Spartan cultivators were not composed of vulnerable and isolated newcomers but rather lived in functional resident communities. The Spartan rulers seem to have retained control by excluding the commercial impulses of their era. For background, see Hodkinson 2003: 248–85, and numerous other publications. Elsewhere, e.g. Asia, when military elites exhausted their expansive capabilities in commercially dynamic circumstances, landlords and merchant creditors became the strong influences over peasants' lives, with great rural debt, and many children and women were released into enslavement to sustain it; see Miller 2003b and sources cited. The medieval European counterpart, but in a less commercialized environment, became the manor dominated by a local warlord living in his palace; 'serfdom' there developed only belatedly as landowners, who retained only a faded aura of former military autonomy, appropriated the legal frameworks then being asserted by monarchs-on-the-make to redefine their claims on, and often making concessions to, the rural populations of their lands in order to retain them against the brightening lure of employments in adjacent growing commercial sectors (e.g. the valleys of the great central European river arteries in the thirteenth century, or the eighteenth-century commercialization of eastern European agriculture), or against the assertions of strong military monarchs (e.g. so-called 'serfdom' in the great days of the tsars in Russia). For central European serfdom, see Bush 1996a. For Russia, though in a different vein, the basic work is Hellie 1982; see also Kolchin 1999: 87–115, and earlier publications cited therein.

25 For a slightly more developed exposition of this argument, see Miller 2004c, and Miller 2002b: 1–57.

Mediterranean opened to northern Italian traders selling captives from the Slavic-speaking regions of the Black Sea. They profited sufficiently – among their many other mercantile strategies, primarily by distributing the Indian Ocean spices they received in return – that in the fourteenth and fifteenth centuries they extended this strategy of commercial slaving to selling these (etymological) Slavs to the prosperous merchant households in the cities of the Christian Mediterranean. In the fifteenth century the northwestern Italian Genoese, marginal to Venetian successes derived from mercantile strategies oriented to the south and east, carried this slaving strategy on westward into the Atlantic, in partnership with the Portuguese, where they drew on new sources of captives in Africa to acquire the labour needed to produce sugar on the islands of the eastern Atlantic. Thus they set the stage for two very different subsequent Atlantic elaborations – in Africa and in the Americas – of this newly commercialized trans-oceanic process of slaving.

NOVELTIES OF SLAVING IN THE NEW WORLD, BROADLY SKETCHED

Slaving in the Atlantic basin thrived in entirely novel contexts that severely limit the relevance of direct comparisons with, or continuities from, the Old World predecessors just sketched. The background to Atlantic slaving consisted not of precedents but rather earlier and very different strategies of other players marginal to radically distinct historical contexts who had used the exclusive control they gained by importing vulnerable outsiders to their own advantage. To review the contrasts introduced thus far: implicit in the preceding sketch of slaving strategies over the course of the world's history before *c.* 1500 were largely domestic circumstances that – while they recurred in a few places in the New World – did not motivate the strategies developed in the highly commercialized contexts developed there. In addition, the economic resources of two vast continents and the commercial opportunities of linking American specie and then plantation-grown agricultural commodities to growing consumer markets in Europe and to artisan production in Asia generated unprecedentedly rapid growth for the European merchants who thus integrated the four continents surrounding the Atlantic.

The slavers there were other merchants marginal to the specie, commodity processing, and early industrial sectors that generated the investment capital that fuelled this vast and fast-expanding commercial engine. In the Americas they created communities of slaves, mostly men, far more numerous, dynamic, and differentiated over time – and incidentally also spatially from the earlier colonies to later ones – than the (once again) paradigmatic but uniquely homogeneous and North American racial stereotypes of 'blacks' held in perpetual bondage – or, even more reductively, just as 'slaves', the least dynamic and most tautological characterization of all. In Africa, marginal figures appropriated the capital that they extended to build new commercial networks, through slaving, within the framework of the inherited ethos of communal and relational identities.

Historians routinely take elaborate account of wrenching change throughout the Atlantic basin between the sixteenth and nineteenth centuries in nearly every respect other than 'slavery', which they have transferred as an 'institutional' constant from the Old World to the New.[26] However, in fact strategies of slaving in the Atlantic moved through incremental processes no less dialectical and dynamic than the historical patterns evident in the Old World, and eventuated in new institutionalized forms of 'slavery' characteristic of modern civic formulations of community. A first approximation of understanding early Atlantic slaving as a historical process would begin by emphasizing the openness of the commercial context within which Italians developed sugar production on Spanish and Portuguese islands off Africa's Atlantic coast. It would, then, historicize the process of the then only incipient monarchical centralization behind Spain's initial colonizing strategies in the New World, where *conquistadores* enslaved native Americans in large numbers that threatened the interests of monarchs in Madrid.[27]

Spanish uses of Africans in the Americas in the late sixteenth and early seventeenth centuries were more limited and more politically benign than the more commercial practices that Portuguese and Dutch-based collaborators elaborated on larger scales in the initial stages of using Africans for plantation production in Brazil. They produced sugar there in late-medieval arrangements less integrated than the classic industrial 'plantations' on the sugar islands of the Caribbean. These – and key elements of the ideology that became the paradigm for all modern studies of slavery – developed as the British and French adapted to the much more thoroughly integrated commercialization of the eighteenth century. Atlantic slaving thus developed slowly, contradictorily, and incrementally.

[26] And the associated stereotypes of 'race', 'plantation', 'African cultures' as 'retentions', and so on. The fixity of the concept, which evidently extends to the full complex of phenomena associated with it, must stem from its utter centrality to modern (often national, but also racial, biologized) identities – taken as inherent, stable – throughout the Americas; see Miller 1997, and Schwartz 2004a.

[27] Excepting, of course, sugar and coffee later in Cuba, which represented entirely different adaptations to much more commercialized contexts in the nineteenth century.

In North America, as in the early Spanish colonies, strategies of slaving began in Old World tones that historians thinking in terms of subsequent standards of institutionalized ante-bellum slavery in the United States hesitate even to designate as 'the institution'.[28] Enslavement there acquired its formal, legal institutionalization only in the 1670s. It established its distinguishing demographic base of women giving birth to future generations of enslaved children in both the Chesapeake and the Carolina Lowcountry only in the eighteenth century, creating communities of the enslaved that resembled self-reproducing peasant communities. Owners broke up these 'plantation communities' between the 1770s and 1807 – both in the Chesapeake, as the old Tidewater families took their slaves westward into the Piedmont and tried to retain them against British offers of liberty during the American War of Independence, and as the formative cotton frontier in the southern states drained the coastal rice plantations of generations-deep enslaved families. Slavery in the United States became focused on the expanding cotton regions in the succeeding two decades as new arrivals from Africa disappeared and coastal owners of slaves sent more than a million American-born, English-speaking, increasingly Christian individuals to carve plantations out of the southern forests. At the same time, federal judges attempted to frame a national categorical law, including (or rather excluding) slaves, thus introducing slavery in a starkly institutionalized, highly public form.

The paradigm(s) of 'slavery' that emerged during those brief, late decades of highly emotional conflict between northern abolitionists and southern defenders of an institution increasingly condemned as 'peculiar' incorporated the politicized mutual caricaturizations of all the parties to the conflict more than they reflected the actual practices of slavery on the side of the masters or the experiences of the enslaved.[29] These incompatible views emerged within a political culture (always a primary aspect of slaving contextualized historically) that assumed more modern features in the Americas – in no small part through the discourses of abolition itself – of national communities thought of as homogeneously inclusive, and earlier in the United States than elsewhere, but – contradictorily – filled with slaves excluded from the emerging political community.[30]

28 See Breen and Innes 1980.

29 See Salman 2001 and most of the recent studies combining political, cultural, and social history to show competitive constructions of selves and others.

30 Miller 2004c.

To historicize Atlantic slaving fully, one must also take account of circumstances changing over the same centuries in Africa, and in ways more parallel than is usually recognized to the historical processes of commercialization on the western shores of the Atlantic. To summarize: slaving in Africa, as in other parts of the world, for a long time had been a significant means by which marginal figures – younger males, recent arrivals, contingent guests – had eroded the control of older elites. In the seventeenth century, commercial contacts with European merchants had strengthened these legacy authorities. In the eighteenth century the younger men, as well as collateral members of political aristocracies, and communities subordinated in other ways reacted by seizing on the mercantile credit that European slavers offered as their own means of aggregating the people who constituted new centres of power. These trade goods, distributed in the right ways, obligated and otherwise acquired followers, mostly women retained in support of their ambitions at home, but, in the process, also selling as many (or as few) as necessary to keep themselves supplied with the distinctive and empowering imported goods they obtained from the Europeans.

As Africa's terms of foreign exchange moved strongly in their favor, in the eighteenth century these textiles, copper, cowries, and other striking adornments became principal means by which ambitious individuals drew more and more of the continent's domestic communities into the commercial world of the Atlantic. Or rather, they created new (pseudo) communities around commercial slaving while (ironically, perhaps, but only to us[31]) preserving the earlier communal ethos as an ideology that obscured their fundamental violation of its reciprocities through slaving strategies by embedding the women they kept as 'wives' and 'wards'.

More and more of the largest and most prominent communities of the continent – some ethnic, others 'political', and more and more of them fundamentally entrepreneurial – consisted of people they assembled through slaving. The still further intensification of slaving in the nineteenth century to keep up with the growing internal competition extended to the use of slaves to produce commodities for export. By the time colonizing Europeans attempted to estimate these proportions in the early 1900s, people of slave origin were large majorities, approaching 80 or 90 per cent in the most commercialized areas. Even before abolition in the Americas, the largest aggregation of slaves in the world living under one

[31] For thoughts on the distinctions between modern historical epistemology and the historical and political thought of Africans, see Miller 2005.

political authority was in the Sokoto Caliphate, centred in what is now northern Nigeria.[32]

The context from which these incremental steps in constructing the novel, highly commercial strategies of slaving around the Atlantic did not 'begin' – as it is conventional to emphasize – is the late medieval eastern Mediterranean, though incremental processes of change have roots there – as well as in many other parts of the world. One must approach 'slavery' in thirteenth-century Crete historically by emphasizing not its anticipations of eighteenth-century Jamaica, which were in fact all but non-existent, but rather the contrasting context there of the thriving urban markets for female slaves, Islamic and later Christian. From the point of view of the Italian merchants selling these women, the utility of selling slaves to building rural productive capacity was minimal in comparison.

They also took into account the ecclesiastical and aristocratic control of Christian lands and their resident peasant populations – none too numerous in the lingering demographic wake of the Black Plague. Commercially oriented entrepreneurs, still marginal to the historical contexts in which they operated, were confined to investments in further distant trading opportunities rather than in local agricultural production. Blocked by religious hostilities from the lands of Islam, merchants therefore channelled their wealth into urban property, artisanal production, and loans to the landed military nobility and its increasingly costly military adventures.[33] Thus, they created the magnificence of Florence, Siena, Venice, and other monuments to late medieval and Renaissance commercial wealth and urbanity. These growing cities they staffed in spite of the restricted local sources of labour by buying mostly Slavic-speaking women and incorporating them in their magnificent households as domestics. Muslims and other captured men they employed in other artisan production and as staff for municipal services in the growing cities. Slaving thus both resulted from the marginality of Christian merchants in Europe and accelerated the rate at which they began to move from the margins of a political economy dominated by military and ecclesiastical owners of the land, and its resident populations of peasants, toward the commercial and industrial dominance of their successors four centuries later.[34]

[32] With apologies for the overly rapid sketch of slaving as history in Africa, which I have developed more fully in Miller 2007a. For some of the details cited, see Klein 1998; Lovejoy 2000b and 2005.

[33] They also faced other competition, in the form of emerging civic monarchical protections that excluded slaves from much of the proto-industrial sectors in central and northern Europe.

[34] The longstanding sensitivity of military aristocrats and other land-holding interests to the threat posed by excessive aggregations of slaves beyond their control underlay both the reservations of the

The ensuing long, incremental historical track of their expanding commerce led out into the Atlantic, beyond these inhibiting contexts of continental Europe, and specifically through their mobilization of more than ten million Africans as slaves engaged in agricultural production in the Americas. The more marginal mercantile interests in Genoa, central Europe, and Sephardic Jews took the initial lead in the fifteenth and sixteenth centuries under the sponsorship of the marginal military monarchs of the Iberian peninsula. They found investment for their lagging financial capabilities in production itself – initially sugar – in the much less politically constrained contexts of uninhabited islands off Africa's western shores. Critically for this historically contextualized focus on incremental changes, the Canaries (in fact depopulated), Madeira, and eventually equatorial São Tomé and Príncipe in the Gulf of Guinea were beyond the development capabilities of their aristocratic and ecclesiastical sponsors, and rivals, in Europe.

Cultivation of cane for sugar offered viable commercial prospects on these eastern-Atlantic islands, but in such remote, and hence risky, environments merchants would venture the capital required for land improvements and the equipment necessary to produce *mascavado* on large scales only with some sort of financial collateral to guarantee their investments, as well as military protection.[35] The high cash values that Africans were bringing as slaves in the cities of Renaissance Iberia and in the Mediterranean, together with their potential utility as producers of sugar, made commercialized rights of ownership of captives from the adjacent mainland create the necessary assets out of human productive potential controlled as negotiable property.[36]

This commercialization of human relations in the Atlantic – in Africa as well as in the Americas – over the next two centuries raced ahead of the accumulation of liquid capital in Europe to use as wages to entice workers there away from relations of production established within other relationships of dependency. Phrasing the point in terms of alternative strategies of capital accumulation, or creation, highlights the subsequent process of converting the once intimate relation of (domestic service and artisanry, largely female) slavery in Europe, Asia, and Africa to personal 'property' in

Catholic Church in allowing enslavement of local (Christian) populations and the outright prohibition of owning slaves to the principal marginal merchants of the time, the Jews. For a different emphasis on European Christianity as background for Atlantic slaving, see Eltis 2000.

35 In economic terms, historical contextualization must consider 'opportunity costs', in this case alternative investment opportunities in the Mediterranean or elsewhere in Christian Europe.

36 An important accent on labour as collateral is in Solow *et al.* 1987: 711–37; Solow and Engerman 1987; Solow 1991: 43–61.

male labour producing commodities in the Americas. That is, slaves in the Americas became negotiable for cash and therefore also protected prominently by public commercial laws of property.[37] However, contextualizing slaving in terms of the commercializing context of the Atlantic also suggests a broader *process* of 'commercializing human relations' that in Europe took the form of expanding the use of wages from covering temporary engagements for specialized purposes to a generalized strategy of ongoing employments.

As historical process, these alternative means to the converging end of commercial integration arose from the differing incremental steps through which investors moved the process, often in complementarily differing regional components of commercial networks expanding toward global proportions.[38] Early Iberian slavery in the New World drew on non-proprietarial bonds derived from Old World premises of domestic intimacy and integration in extending sacralized domestic ties for the enslaved through Catholic baptism, god-parentage, marriage, and lay brotherhoods. These alleged continuities are usually attributed to an unproblematized 'originary' vein running back through cultures of southern Europe essentialized as Catholic. As history, however, it is important, instead, to accent the early sixteenth-century timing of their extension from a religiously distinguished population in *reconquista* Iberia to Slavic women domestics, then African men in Iberia, and on to aggregating African men and women on unprecedented scales for hard labour in mines and cane fields in the Americas.

By the historical macro-logic of slaving as the strategy of marginal challengers, slavers are inherently a problem for the establishments challenged. In the initial phases of Atlantic integration, the landed and clerical establishments of Spain and Portugal were protecting themselves at home

[37] Thus, a key moment in the legal definition of modern slavery was the elimination of residual public interest in slaves in the 1670s through redefinition of their property status as 'personal' rather than 'real'; see Morris 1996.

[38] The first proprietarial claims to slaves as commercial, and individualized, assets elaborated earlier (in the late medieval, family based or otherwise corporate) entailments of lands, workers, skills for similar purposes of commercial investment, by landed families and 'master' artisans through orders, guilds, apprenticeships, and serfdom. The accent on these collective qualities in Europe is meant to emphasize parallels with what I have termed the communal ethos in contemporaneous Africa. In the sixteenth century, Spanish law extended the legal strategy underlying these 'entailments' to include slaves within a legal sphere of indissolubility of the complex of commercial assets – crushing mills, land and improvements (particularly irrigation), and human beings – assembled in the Spanish Americas on first-generation 'plantations'. A parallel sequence of strategies (not a time-transcending sociological typology of abstractions) ran through negotiable short-term personal entailments as contracts of 'indenture' toward the eventual ideological separation of individual 'wages' as 'free' and slaves as 'bonded'.

by displacing the dangerously dynamic potential of capitalist development, initially via slaves and sugar, to safely remote domains in the Americas. In this political sense, as well as the more familiar economic one, the unprecedented wealth in precious metals in the Americas enabled them to do precisely this, often spectacularly in the short run but ultimately to their own disadvantage in Europe, as they succeeded in limiting expansive mercantile investment on the home front through the restrictions and monopolies and licences familiar in the conventional narrative of early imperial administration in the Atlantic.[39]

The aspirant monarchs of sixteenth-century Castille and Aragon, and their successors as rulers of Spain, faced the challenge of controlling American colonies with the clear economic potential to escape their nominal masters in Europe, as they all eventually did. For the Spanish monarchs, the first step (as is widely recognized[40]) was to limit the private and autonomous access of the first generation of *conquistadores* to the native Americans they conquered as slaves. The 1520s and 1530s saw massive military slaving in Central America and elsewhere around the Caribbean to replace declining populations in the islands of the Indies. The huge mainland estates that Cortéz and other *conquistadores* claimed in the next generation threatened to support independent break-away military lords, if they gained exclusive control over the native Americans, rather than create the loyal, and dependent, servants that Spanish kings intended. Enslaving the conquered populations would have placed them in vast private domains, beyond the control of the monarchy. The resulting 'New Laws' that Charles V proclaimed in 1542 – whatever the theological and legal discourse of saving Indian hearts and minds for Christ and Crown in which they were debated – effectively asserted the direct authority of the Crown, through its appointed representatives in the Americas and its allies among the Catholic missionaries, over these people, their bodies as well as their souls. The New Laws were a critical moment in consolidating both monarchy in Europe and European monarchical authority in the Americas.

The Spanish Crown then limited mercantile investment in its New World colonies to foreign interests and restricted the supplies of Africans they delivered to them as slaves under the famous series of *asiento* contracts, similarly playing each off against its rivals. As for the merchant slavers, the

[39] And the parallel in Africa took the form of its ethical exclusion from the commercial ethos as 'witchcraft', with alleged witches physically expelled as slaves, some sold to Europeans.

[40] But primarily as an a-historical/teleological/originary anticipation of abolition, or humanism, and then always acknowledging the paradox thus created out of its apparently 'racist' toleration of, even encouragement of, slaving for Africans; see, e.g., Blackburn 1997: 150–6.

initial commercial investors thus protected were all foreigners marginal to the accelerating commerce of continental Europe, Genoese and Germans and – later – Dutch linked to Sephardic Jews.[41] As foreigners in the New World, from the perspective of the only formative Iberian monarchies of the time, they were also safely marginal to remote and problematically controllable colonial domains.[42] By controlling access to Indian labour, the Crown controlled the key to agricultural, and then mining, production; it also limited uses of Africans as proprietarial slaves, whom it did not control directly, to much less politically sensitive functions in the domestic retinues of its appointees and allies in the cities, or in familiar and controllable artisan and other urban employments. Sixteenth-century Spanish slaving in the Americas thus extended the Renaissance Mediterranean reliance on foreign slavers and retained direct ecclesiastical and monarchical authority over the agricultural populations of the colonies.

In thus preserving the Old World politics of slaving, Spanish authorities also avoided – or rather again displaced – the incremental novelty of New World slaving, the massive numbers of males assembled by the seventeenth century on cane-growing plantations in Brazil and then the Caribbean region. Their *asiento* contracts indirectly enabled Portuguese, and then others similarly marginalized by the unprecedented flows of silver to Seville, to build the capacity to deliver significant numbers of African men to Brazil. The initial phases of Portuguese slaving in Africa had sent small numbers of captives along relatively short sea routes to the Gold Coast, to sugar islands in the eastern Atlantic, and to Iberia. Maritime slaving, even on these limited scales, challenged the logistics of carrying large numbers of people over long distances on the open ocean, as devastating shortages of food and water demonstrated all too often on the lengthy *carreira da Índia* to Portuguese trading posts in the Indian Ocean. The first Africans taken to the Spanish Americas were few in number, often skilled and arriving after first passing through Iberian ports; they were thus high enough in value to repay the costs of

[41] The relevant comparisons lie not in the immediate, very different contexts in Europe but rather at similar points in parallel historical processes; in this case, the process involved the recurrent contest between incipient military regimes and the merchants on whom they depended, but who simultaneously threatened political consolidation on monarchical terms. Earlier instances had occurred in and around the eastern Mediterranean basin, late in the second half of the first millennium BC, and much of the history of slaving in the Muslim world revolved around the same struggle; for the context of this argument, see Miller 2007b.

[42] Compare the parallel exclusion of resident merchants from the domestic sphere in Africa under terms usually translated into English as 'landlord/stranger' relationships. For one useful discussion (though not in these terms), see Brooks 1994; see also Curtin 1975.

transporting them across the Atlantic. Trans-Atlantic carriage of much larger numbers of less valuable captive Africans in the sixteenth and early seventeenth centuries would – and did – incur catastrophic and commercially ruinous mortality, until the Dutch, and then the English, worked out viable commercial techniques to bring people across alive (if only barely) in the seventeenth century.

Only the silver paid for enslaved Africans delivered to Spanish domains could cover the considerable mortality costs of learning to carry large numbers of people long distances on the high seas. Fortuitously, the Angola region in southwestern Africa came under Spanish control under the union of the two Iberian crowns in the 1580s, at the same time that severe drought in the region provoked conflict and created captives and refugees whom *asientista* merchants purchased in unprecedented numbers. We do not know how many deaths among the enslaved crowded below the decks of *asiento* ships en route from the southern Atlantic would have been prevented by calling at Recife in the northerly Brazilian captaincy of Pernambuco, where sugar production first developed. The almost entirely extant official documentation, carefully construed to obscure what the king had prohibited, would not feature captives sold to pay for food and water for the remainder of the human cargoes in their overcrowded ships, except perhaps as entirely plausible 'deaths'. New World slaving thus began to shift from domestic artisans to field hands accidentally, opportunistically, as well as incrementally, as marginal interests in slavery appropriated secondary strategies of the primary investors in silver as strategies of their own.

The Portuguese Crown's territorial claims in Brazil, which lacked silver, rested on greater dependence on merchant investment in production, and specifically foreigner, from the beginning. Dutch-based commercial capital seized on the drought-induced distress in Angola, as well as growing Portuguese experience with trans-Atlantic transport of large numbers of captives to finance the costs of Africans delivered to the Americas in multiples of previous numbers.[43] Africans – mostly men – arriving in the northeastern captaincies as isolated individuals in turn found themselves

[43] The epistemology of history depends on reasoning from the fullest possible – here global – contexts ('thick description' in Geertz's ethnographic phrasing). Brazilian sugar was a substantially new creation built from elements originating in Spanish law, drought in Africa, the dispersal of the Sephardic community from Spanish Inquisitorial persecution in Portugal, and silver mining in Peru and Mexico, as well as often-cited developments in Muslim nautical sciences, Ottoman closure of the eastern Mediterranean to Christian merchants, and Chinese invention of the three-roller mill for grinding sugar.

assembled in large aggregations that made it possible for them to convert Old World strategies of 'belonging' from seeking places within their master's households to developing associations within what can very loosely be termed 'communities' among the enslaved.[44] This prospect of community – or at least association – within slavery was radically new, and it enabled later Africans elsewhere in the Americas to act from it publicly, as slaves within their enslavement, in ways that their predecessors had found themselves able to do only very rarely. In Brazil the Catholic lay brotherhoods provided recognizable – and seemingly controllable – vehicles for doing so. Elsewhere, slaves built quasi-ethnic New World 'nations' from the commercial identities given them according to the ports in Africa where they had been 'reborn' in the commercial context of the Atlantic as property rather than the home communities of reproduction into which they had been born.[45]

In the Caribbean and in Brazil, the increasingly diverse backgrounds of successive waves of captives introduced to American slavery – and, of course, mortality – from a wider and wider array of regions in Africa turned their agency toward working out neo-'ethnic' identities reflecting the succession of cohorts, distinguished as much by the order of their arrival as by the differing regions of Africa from which they had come. The *nações* (*cabildos*, nations, etc.) that they created thus represented their reactions to the ongoing dynamics of slaving in the Atlantic. They served – in ways that differed from context to context – multiple purposes, for their masters as well as for themselves. Among the enslaved, they served to negotiate places for individuals arriving or being moved from owner to owner or plantation to plantation and also to provide a decent burial, thus commemorating those who departed through death. Among the quasi-ethnic guilds thus created, they also served to protect claims to distinctive treatment or privileges, particularly against newcomers, whom they thus forced to respond by organizing in similar fashion. Finally, with regard to their masters, they served to assert a positive character, allegedly inherited from somewhere and someone, thus denying the consummate isolation of enslavement. Moreover these 'nations' were public identities useful in New

44 As distinct from the notion of the 'slave community' as a stable, or at least consolidated, entity, as developed, and criticized, in the US historiography; for the original notion, see Blassingame 1979. Initial criticism is in Gilmore 1978. For the peculiar instability of community under slavery in the Americas (as distinct from the relative, or at least presumed, continuity of the Old World domestic household) see Miller 2003b.

45 For a recent survey of the vexed issue of African 'ethnicity' in the Americas, see Hall 2006, though with much greater emphasis than I would allow on the directness of the 'links' emphasized in the title.

World settings increasingly categorized publicly, however unreflective they may have been of the socially irrelevant personal biographies in Africa of the people claiming them. These 'African ethnicities' in the Americas were New World ideological identities, parallel to those of the slavers then being formed out of the presence of Africans enslaved in socially and culturally viable aggregations. Thus, historicizing Neo-African 'ethnic' identities in the New World reveals them as more modern and manipulated than inherited and inert.[46]

Following the historical lines developed here, the slaves created these incipient 'communities' also as processes, and in terms of their potential to motivate and enable individual, as well as collective, strategic action. Associations available to slaves had to sustain involuntary movements of people through them, unlike – say – any stable peasant community based on shared descent, and hence on biological reproduction. Slaves in the commercial context of the Atlantic were negotiable property, and so they were *essentially* mobile, unwillingly and damagingly so, from the violent uprooting of their capture in Africa, through the trans-Atlantic transfers that landed them wherever they happened to end up, and also in eventually being moved on again through sale in the Americas, or departing through early deaths at any point in the inherently processual experience of enslavement.[47]

Hence, we should expect – and the first hints of research along these lines are starting to appear – that the strategies of the enslaved centred on

[46] The literature on 'ethnicity' in Africa has turned strongly toward a parallel emphasis on historicity, flexibility, and contextualization; with regard to Atlantic identities constructed out of the slaving process, the most thoroughly explored, so far, is 'Yoruba'. See Law 1997: 205–19; Matory 1999: 72–103. See also Northrup 2000: 1–20; and Gomez 1998. The abstracted 'cultural traits' that form the focus of studies of 'Africanisms' in the New World take little account of these initiatives of the enslaved; one must approach the identities they asserted instead as symbols adapted and applied to the circumstances in which they found themselves, and not necessarily Africans but perhaps even more urgently American-born slaves seeking signifiers distinguishingly their own. Since public meaning in slave societies was largely in the hands of the masters, 'looking African', in terms of masters' stereotypes of 'Africa', would have been at least as important as derivation of behaviour from antecedents in Africa. See Chambers 1997: 72–97 and Chambers 2002: 101–20. Hall 2006 has a modulated version of the continuity thesis. John Thornton has argued repeatedly for such continuities but in fact documents them only in contexts in which self-presentation to masters had broken down in revolt or escape, when small groups among the enslaved fell back on military training from Africa designed there to transcend the divisions of descent in moments of emergency mobilization. The African 'precedents' were thus in the multiplicity, flexibility, and situationality of identities there rather than in stable, singular continuities of 'culture'. See Thornton 1991a: 1101–13, 1991b: 58–80, 1993: 181–214, 1998: 161–78, and 2000: 181–200. For a much broader assertion of continuities, see Heywood 2002.

[47] Escape and manumission were more voluntaristic ways of leaving; no one entered voluntarily.

avoiding repeated uprooting and on their vulnerability to mortality.[48] Those whom enslavement had otherwise isolated focused on creating techniques of social reconstitution and on staying in contact with the lost and departed in their spiritual imaginations, if not in person. Leaving slavery voluntarily through escape succeeded only when seeking refuge in 'maroon' communities established in the wilderness but those tended to stay in close touch with the slaves they had left behind, and sometimes also with the masters. Leaving slavery through manumission was no less ambivalent in the limited degree of separation sought, or attained, since those 'freed' normally remained in continuing, if more elaborately negotiated, dependence.

The 'communal' character of slaves' lives in most times and places in the Americas was therefore barely incipient, since it was anything but static in terms of personnel. Membership in these associations – however large they may have been in numbers – was constantly renewed by mortality, manumission, maroonage, and sale, with new Africans replacing those who moved or were sent onwards. This inherent and ongoing process of social recomposition at given moments in specific colonial contexts, and its varying rhythms of entering and leaving, are the proper focus of *historical* analysis of the slaves' experiences of their slavery. Over time, the slaves' inability to generate the kinds of integral community that transcended the generations helps to explain – to take an example from among the clichés of 'slavery as an institution' – why collective attempts at revolt were so infrequent, so partial when they did occur, and so often betrayed from within, as well as why they succeeded in only a single instance, Haiti, and then only momentarily in any unified sense. American slaves' agency lay in their struggle to create a contingent sort of 'community' among themselves, prior to any presumed solidary 'institution' available to use against their masters. The fundamental isolation of enslavement nurtured the fierce individualism that sustained its survivors in slavery, and later also in freedom.

For masters in the Americas, aggregations of male slaves in such massive numbers and the opportunities that the enslaved made of them posed entirely novel and largely unanticipated problems of a public order. They first of all tended to become disorderly in public. Further, the public aspects of the commercial debt used to assemble them brought government

[48] Notably Troutman 2000; see also the panel (chaired by Walter Johnson) on 'Political histories of death in the black diaspora' (Organization of American Historians annual meeting, Washington DC, 13 April 2002). A published paper from that occasion is Brown 2003: 24–53. The theme of 'death' given a social significance by Patterson is thus being extended in more physical senses; also see Miller 1988.

attention to what had previously been essentially domestic affairs within private households. Merchants who sold the slaves – often on credit – summoned the backing of public authorities to collect what they were owed, and planters were left to force their slaves to work off the burden of debt that they had contracted to have them brought to America. Analysts in Europe – political economists more sensitive to the New World commercial realities than theologians keyed on Old World personal ethics – acutely, and immediately, recognized their presence as a public concern. Recognizing the disquieting scales of commercialized slaving in the Americas helps to resolve David Brion Davis' classic 'problem' of why Europeans began to doubt the political and economic viability, as well as (and distinct from) the private morality, of newly institutionalized – in the senses of public and ideologically obfuscated – *slavery* in the eighteenth century. Since Spain had headed off the political 'problem' of massive slavery in the sixteenth century, nothing like it had existed before. Governments in Europe – other than Lisbon's monarchy, weak and distracted as it became – tried to respond in the seventeenth century with legal codifications that blended the ethical standards of the domestic slavery in the Old World that they knew with the New World novelty of large gangs of enslaved men.[49] Governments stepped in, social philosophers redefined these issues in the language of liberal economics, and populist politicians eventually took them up as vehicles integral to creating the emerging nations of the nineteenth century.

A different dynamic prevailed in North America, of course. There, as early as the middle of the eighteenth century in the Chesapeake, the ability of the women enslaved to reproduce shifted their strategies from neo-ethnic (or ethnicized) competition among cohorts of new arrivals from Africa to family formation among themselves. Their principal concerns became surviving dispersal of their formative families among many small, often isolated residential units and a near-total definition of their enslavement in proprietarial terms that facilitated unpredictable break-ups of formative families through sales of their individual members. The slaves, thus, turned from pursuit of public recognition of their exotic presence to exploiting the possibilities of private patronage from 'owners' radically empowered by the democratic politics of the new nation.[50]

[49] In the Iberian *Siete Partidas* (1275), the Manoeline ordinances of Portugal (1516), the French *Code Noir* (1685), and eventually the Spanish *Codigo Negro* (1789).

[50] And from this dynamic, the entire historiography of the enslaved in North America, from Blassingame's (undated but implicitly) ante-bellum 'slave community', Genovese's elaboration of its (Christian) spirited and spiritual ideological content, and Walter Johnson's elaboration of the

In the United States, all of the significant dynamics of Atlantic slaving were unique – 'peculiar' indeed.[51] By the time the realities of making one out of many in the new Republic forced former rebellious colonials to face themselves and their slaves, most of those enslaved in the ideologically formative Chesapeake were Americans, not Africans. They were also increasingly English speaking, their children eventually also Christian, and more often than not unacknowledged children of the same extended '*American* famil[ies] black and white' that owned them.[52] To indulge in a 'Charlottesville moment', Mr Jefferson and Ms Hemings remain powerful symbols of this transgression of all of the subsequently dichotomized ideological premises of modern slavery because she was a woman enslaved (not a man), racially ambiguous, included intimately in a paradigmatically American household, clearly not culturally disabled, perhaps not even vulnerable – but also prominently including her implied, and therefore also powerfully denied, status as consort of one of the nation's 'founding fathers'. If acknowledged, Ms Hemings would take her rightful place as a 'founding mother' of the nation.

The people enslaved by the nineteenth century in the United States thus met none of the premises on which viable slaving elsewhere had rested for tens of thousands of years. They knew well the culture of their masters, better than the masters knew themselves. Most of them were anything but isolated. Simultaneously, and contradictorily, the proprietarial characterization of these 'Americans' (if not also kin) became exaggerated, both because of the profound commercialization of slavery in North America and because of their value as collateralized property to 'farmers' who were seeking dignity and autonomy by mastering slaves but whom creditors in Britain, later northern banks – and eventually a federal government and its armies – were increasingly 'mastering' in a commercial sense. Mr Jefferson was once again prototypical for the United States; when he died, his slaves were sold from his estate – except for a few, perhaps his children, whom he freed – to pay off debts left from his otherwise rich and creative (whether or not also procreative) life.

These contradictions of slavery in colonial North America were exaggerated in the early nineteenth century in the nascent United States. Ideals of civic inclusiveness and the challenges of forming a coherent national identity out of residents of probably unprecedentedly – even increasingly – diverse

moral anguish that commercialization and the constant threat of sale provoked in Johnson 1999, regardless of the physical welfare that enabled the creation and survival of family (see Fogel and Engerman 1974), or the ambiguities of resistance and escape (see Berlin 2003).

[51] To recall Stampp 1956. [52] Playing on the titles of Wiencek 1999 and Ball 1998.

origins, their recency of arrival relative to the ancestors of most of the enslaved, and operatively participatory politics brought these contradictions into public affairs to an unprecedented degree. These ambiguities generated distinctively intense pressures on both slavery and perceptibly African ancestry, creating one of those fleeting moments of uniting around exploiting the vulnerability of the enslaved alien within – if not also against 'enemies' defined without – that go back to the very origins of humanity.

The accepted political ethic of civic inclusiveness declared the exclusion of residents (and native-born!) from the political community as slaves not only anomalous and immoral but also potentially corrosive of the integrity of a body politic thought of in corporate terms. In fact, the human bodies acquired through slaving had long supported personal ambition and sustained the marginalized within communities of all sorts. In a formative not-yet-nation like the new United States, the process of consolidating a truly national – in the senses of popular, participatory, and trans-regional – politics generated the political alarm that large numbers of slaves, as 'private property' entirely beyond the reach of civic regulation, had previously generated, much more than concern for the personal welfare of those enslaved.[53] By the mid-nineteenth century, the compromises possible in Constitutional times, among parties thinking of themselves as independent negotiating partners, had become impossible among participants competing over who would define the necessarily single paradigm of an integrated nation.

The emergent premise of a single nation recast the conservative federalists of former times as radical separatists. Abolitionist counter-tropes, of course, played off the proslavery defences as they developed in the 1840s and 1850s as violations of, or regressions from, the integrative, commercial, and unified identity of a progressive 'nation', with mostly incidental acknowledgment of the more complex realities of living in, or with, slavery.

'Black' Americans of African descent, however partial, thus, entered a highly ideological and institutionalized *slavery*, rendered more and more perpetual by the proprietarial concerns of debtors attempting to finance a major new agricultural sector in the cotton South and by the growing political sensitivity of their presence. Everywhere else in the world,[54] these locally born children of their masters would have been acknowledged as the

[53] Again underscoring the vital importance of separating 'race' from 'slavery'.

[54] With the possible exceptions of the similarly commercial French and English plantations in the Caribbean, but even there 'amelioration' publicly acknowledged maternity, and status as 'coloured' and 'freedman' recognized their children as native born.

natives they had become, and the survivors of enslavement would have moved through some form of release into other kinds of dependency within private, domestic households. But no form of such corporative dependency was possible in a 'democratic' nation of recognized – even participating – individual voting citizens, starkly contrasted with, even defined by, the ultimately non-participatory status of the enslaved. Hence, 'sale' to other owners, not self-purchase as a form of manumission, became the principal, highly commercialized, strategy of recognizing personal skills and ability, by realizing it in a financial sense, for the owner and at the crushing personal expense of separation of the owned from kith and kin.

The slave families and plantation communities in the Chesapeake and Carolina Lowcountry became the principal sources of mobile people who replaced Atlantic imports in the nineteenth century. Sales 'down the river' to Mississippi or New Orleans removed recalcitrant individuals who strained at restraint and severely challenged the communal strength built up by then by the enslaved through family strategies, in some areas for generations. The people whom such removals isolated again upon arrival on the highly commercial plantations in the fleeting, ephemeral ante-bellum moment of the cotton South in the 1840s and 1850s had to find other ways to create communities of their own, significantly through Christian religious communion. The question, thus, considering the ante-bellum years as a brief moment in a process influenced profoundly by attempting to hold native-born Americans in slavery, is what 'problems' their children would have united to create for their owners in the 1860s and 1870s, had the national 'problem' of slavery not provoked war and emancipation of the principal (human) assets of the enemy.

The accidents of war released them to reconstitute their recently dispersed families and then, betrayed by the failure (for them) of Reconstruction, left them to live in commercial tenancies not unlike the personal dependency that had followed individual manumissions elsewhere in the world. Commercialization had, by then, proceeded far enough – though, in the impoverished post-war South, not sufficiently to fund wages – that modern strategies of direct, individuated debt smoothly succeeded the vulnerabilities of slaving.

CONCLUSIONS – THE LIMITS OF COMPARISON

Historicizing slaving along lines suggested by the preceding illustrative elements of an integrated history of the strategy thus allows us to describe processes of commercialization unique to the Atlantic in language developed from analysis of earlier processes, and similarly to move from the very modern characteristics of commercial slavery in the United States South back to parallel processes known in very different specific forms in the Old World, from the ancient Mediterranean to medieval Europe to modern Africa.[55] The comparative method conventional in sociological studies of 'slavery as an institution', on the other hand, compares specific manifestations of these recurrent processes by extracting them from the historical contexts that in fact generated and thus explain them. Comparison of similarly denominated phenomena, even claimed direct continuities – as in the instance of 'Roman law' in the Americas, fails as history because 'tradition' is always 'reinvented', giving new uses and applications, in novel historical circumstances, to legacies from the past thus revered. Reasoning by analogy, a form of implicit comparison, assuming parallels or even identities rather than making processual sense of contrasts, must rest on establishing similar historical contexts of the instances compared. For the ancient Mediterranean, for example, more relevant analogies may come from Africa than from the modern Americas.

As history, recurrently through the millennia sketched here, people 'marginal' to given contexts used slaving to challenge established insiders. Slaving, thus, figured prominently in the commercially oriented growth at Athens that left Greece the paradigmatically 'classical' age of both Renaissance Italian merchants and of the enlightened commercialism of the eighteenth-century North Atlantic. The marginal challengers were not 'outsiders' or even dominated insiders: rather, they tended to have positions of sufficient strength, close enough to the very power that they sought slaves to overcome, to be able to build on their superiors' initiatives, but mobile enough to manoeuvre – most effectively on remote frontiers – with independent initiative sufficient to appropriate the assets of those in control for purposes of their own. On the frontiers, they had ready access to people of backgrounds very different from their own. Put in this way, it is almost truistic to observe that a slave's vulnerability, and therefore utility, derived from the structural quality that Patterson and Moses Finley[56] and many other students of slavery have stressed: her, or his, *origin* 'outside' the social context into which she, or he, ended up confined, and constrained.

[55] See the theorized statement of this principle of the 'reversibility of comparisons' in Salman 2004: 30–47.

[56] Patterson 1982; and most famously, Finley 1968.

Contextualized in terms of the internal politics at stake from the point of view of the marginalized slavers, the outsider origins of the enslaved meant that they constituted new resources, adding to the strength of challengers otherwise too weak to compete effectively for resources available at home. Slavers introduced slaves to evade the zero-sum and self-defeating calculus of attempting to mount a challenge from within, to confront empty handed those who held all the cards.[57] Slaving, thus, recurred again and again at the innovatory edges of change. The heirs and successors to those who had used slaving as the means to initiate change no longer needed slaving to build on success, and so they shifted to less risky, more respectable means of maintaining the control their ancestors had won.[58] Paradoxically, slaving continued only in unresolved, persisting confrontations, as throughout the full course of the history of the Muslim stand-off between military rulers, clerical popular and legal authorities, and marginalized merchants.

The dynamics of such slaving had complex and contradictory, and therefore historically interesting, outcomes. Depending on how many slaves the challengers managed to acquire – and these numbers were fundamentally contingent historical results of the shifting circumstances of their times and places – they produced changes of many sorts by resorting to slaving. Most of the people brought in as slaves in the Old World had been females, girls and women. These women had enabled *nouveaux riches* masters to join the old guard rather than to replace it. Or the *ancien régime* might, in effect, buy out the slavers by making them suppliers of labour for their own households, or enterprises, leaving them with politically less sensitive assets of merely material or financial sorts.

On the other hand, the merchant slavers turned loose without restraint in the Atlantic acquired more captives, particularly men, than their aristocratic rivals could relieve them of. The men accumulated in the Americas in the hands of the challengers empowered them commercially. In the Old World, slaving led to no structural transformation, in spite of the expansion of the human basis of the society, or polity, or economy. In the Atlantic, before the modern era, when direct control of human loyalties and skills counted for more than arms or other technology or currencies, the slavers were likely to move from their positions of marginality to mount

[57] As Engels had it, correctly, for the relief that imperial expansion gave to tensions between the industrial magnates who directed it and the home-based working classes who created their wealth; the same point may be stated in terms of 'nationalism' as a sentiment blurring distinctions of wealth, as money replaced ancestry as a means to power, with abolition covering the less seemly aspects of the process in the populist cause of saving the poor and powerless.

[58] Thus Davis 1966.

direct challenges – and even achieve dominance – within, thus accomplishing what, in structural terms, we recognize as a transformative change. In either case, consistent with what David Brion Davis and others have observed, slaves huddled, or toiled, or fought, or contributed at the very cores of the expansive eras that conventional history, devoted to money and monumentality, recognizes as 'progress', not least because the slaves' enslavement made them serve effectively and thus enabled the thinkers and actors of those eras driven to innovate by their marginality.[59]

APPENDIX

Table 3.1 *Epochs of the past and strategies of slaving*

Epoch (approximate dates)	Historical challenge(s)	Strategies of slaving (responses)
'Prehistory' (~20,000–3,000 BC)	Formation of community ethos	Ritual immolation
Age of empires (~3,000–1,000 BC) [and later, elsewhere]	Formation of military/ political institutions	(Ritual immolation) Military seizure, temple, 'state' slaving
Classical (a) (~1,000 BC–varying dates in first millennium AD)	Mercantile challenge (inclusive polities) (universal religions)	(Military seizure, temple, state slaving) Household administrative staffing
Classical (b) (~1,000 BC–varying dates in second millennium AD)	Preservation of ethos of community (era of ethnicity, kinship)	Differential incorporation within ethos of homogeneity; hostages, 'pawns', wives, slaves
Commercialization (~1000–1800)	Mercantile challenge (and triumph)	Urban services, households – extension to production (American plantations)
Modernization (~1800–1920)	Civic polities/nations (early colonial rule)	Survival/defensive [abolitionism]
Contemporary (1920–present)	International human rights Wage economies eroding dependencies Weak governments	Totalitarian states [hidden – prostitution, other sexual labour, 'migrant labour', undocumented aliens, child labour, other commercialized forms of exploitation]
The Future?	[Local warlords??]	Child soldiers, hostages . . .

[59] 'Innovative' and transformative are more contingent, hence historical, analogues of what, in a teleological mode, is classed as 'progress'.

Table 3.2 *Novelties in the Atlantic (1)*

Background (approximate dates)	Historical challenge(s)	Strategies of slaving (responses)
European 'domestic' Slavery (14th C.)	Merchants constrained to trade; superior Muslim markets for captives	Sales to Islamic markets secondarily to Christian cities (merchants)
(1450s–90s)	Portuguese seeking African gold	Incidental slaving, significantly within Africa
Atlantic islands (1490s–1530s)	Merchants (foreign) licenced to move into production (sugar) – Madeira, São Tomé Managing slaves assembled	Shift to Africans, collateralize-ation of labour, elaboration of proprietarial principle Manueline Code (Portugal – 1516)
Spanish colonies (1520s–1530s)	Containing *conquistadores*	Native American slaving 'New Laws' (1542), *asiento* to contain slaving to foreign merchants and domestic contexts
	Legal protection of assets	Sugar lands, equipment, and labour 'entailed' (1529?)
(1580s–1590s)	Silver mining	Supports early technical challenges (and costs) of trans-Atlantic transport of Africans
(1590s)	Containing merchants	*Asiento* (to foreign merchants)
Brazil (1610s–1620s)	Technical advance in mech-anical processing of cane; financing from Dutch	Massive imports of Africans, for agricultural production; male majorities (1610s–1620s)

Table 3.3 *Novelties in the Atlantic (2)*

Barbados, Martinique (1650s)	Shift to large-scale, inte-grated 'plantations'	Europe: chartered companies (focused on American silver, African gold), debt financing of start-up costs (plantations, Jamaica acquired by English sugar) (1670s)
	Male majorities of (almost entirely new) slaves	*Code Noir*, Barbados (and Virginia) slave codes (1670s–1680s)

Table 3.3 (*cont.*)

Caribbean (18th C.)	Sustaining large-scale sugar plantations Philosophical/economic/ ethical/disciplinary challenges *Period of formulation of (European) ideologies of plantation model* (England) Haitian revolution	Companies fail, 'private' investors pick up the pieces Political economy in Europe. Police regulations in Americas (Male) slaves forming pseudo- 'communities' in Brazil, Caribbean; families in North America Confirms stereotypes of both 'savage' Africans and liberal-inspired leaders
North America (1770s–1790s)	Elaboration of civic politics Native-born slaves come of age, slave families consolidated Forming a new 'nation'	Exclusion of native-born 'blacks' First rebellions (Gabriel, etc.) Cotton gin (1793) Imports end (1808) Assimilating immigrants
(1820s–1830s)	Development of cotton Internal slave trade Popular political culture	Breaking up slave families Slave communities forming along racialized and religious lines

Table 3.4 *Novelties in the Atlantic (3)*

Background (approximate dates)	Historical challenge(s)	Strategies of slaving (responses)
	(Emancipation in British Caribbean colonies – 1834/1838)	
(1840s–1850s)	'Old South'	Establishing new plantation systems Establishing new forms of slave 'community'
(1860s)	Civil War	'National' crisis Emancipation

PART II

Economics and technology of ancient and modern slave systems

CHAPTER 4

The comparative economics of slavery in the Greco-Roman world

Walter Scheidel

INTRODUCTION

Genuine 'slave economies' – in which slave labour permeated all sectors of the economy and played a central role in economic output outside the sphere of family labour – were rare in history.[1] Classical Greece and the Italian heartland of the Roman empire are among the most notable cases. This raises important questions: how did the Greeks and Romans come to join this exclusive club, and how did the circumstances that determined the development and structure of their regimes of slave labour compare to those that shaped other slave-rich systems? This chapter has two goals. The first one is to improve our understanding of the critical determinants of the large-scale use of slave labour in different sectors of historical economies. This calls for a comparative approach that extends beyond classical antiquity. I hope to show that by adjusting and fusing several existing explanatory models, and by considering a previously unappreciated factor, it is possible to make some significant progress toward the creation of a cross-culturally valid matrix of conditions that situates the experience of ancient slave economies within a broader context. In brief, I argue that the success of chattel slavery is a function of the specific configuration of several critical variables: the character of specific economic activities, the incentive system, the normative value system of a society, and the nature of commitments

I am grateful to Paul Cartledge, Stanley Engerman, Joseph Miller, Ian Morris and Peter Temin for comments on earlier versions of this chapter. Proper consideration of their input would have required a book-length study.

[1] I use 'slave economies' as the specifically economic correlate of the familiar term 'slave societies' (as opposed to the much more common 'slaveowning societies' or 'societies with slaves' which permitted slaveownership but did not depend on it); for definitions and discussion, see Turley 2000: 4–5, 62–100. The conventional canon includes Greece and Rome in antiquity, and the United States, Brazil, and the Caribbean from the fifteenth to the nineteenth centuries: e.g. Hopkins 1978: 100–1; Finley 1998: 298. Dutch South Africa and the Sokoto caliphate (in nineteenth-century Nigeria) surely belong in the same category, with late medieval Korea as another candidate. For the somewhat more inclusive concept of 'large-scale slave systems', cf. Patterson 1982: 353–64.

required of the free population. My second objective is to explain differences in the relative prevalence of chattel slavery in different periods and parts of the ancient Mediterranean world with the help of data on prices and wages, a body of evidence that has never been fully exploited in this context and which again allows some genuine progress. I argue that high real wages and low slave prices precipitated the expansion of slavery in classical Greece and Republican Rome, while later periods of Roman history may have witnessed either a high equilibrium level of slavery or its gradual erosion in the context of lower wages and higher prices.

Whereas slavery as an institution used to be truly ubiquitous in world history, the use of large numbers of (often male) slaves for productive purposes was not.[2] In most settings, at least insofar as the demographic and occupational structures of slaveholding are at all perceptible, slaves were often female and/or employed in the service sector. American slavery provides an obvious counterpoint, with its emphasis on slave labour in agricultural production, and a comparatively minor role in manufacturing and services. Where does Greek and Roman slavery fit in on this spectrum?

Unfortunately, even the most basic properties of the classical slave economies remain obscure. The number or proportion of slaves in a particular ancient state or in particular sectors of its economy is invariably unknown. The widespread notion that slaves accounted for approximately one-third of the population of classical Athens and Roman Italy is devoid of any evidentiary foundation and owes much to the corresponding share of slaves in the population of the Old South in the 1860 census.[3] The only usable quantitative evidence, gleaned from the census returns of Roman Egypt in the first three centuries AD, yields different percentages for different parts of the country, from 7 per cent in one city in Upper Egypt to 14.7 per cent in the cities of Middle Egypt.[4] None of this can be taken to be representative of conditions in Greece or Italy.

In the absence of quantitative data, modern observers deal in impressions. Our sources leave little doubt that in Athens slaves were essential in mining, worked on the rural estates and in the workshops and businesses of the wealthy, and served them in their homes. There is no sector of the elite economy in which slaves were not commonly employed, and the same is true for Rome.[5] In this regard, the convergence of the qualitative evidence

[2] For general surveys, see Patterson 1982; Finkelman and Miller 1998; Turley 2000.

[3] Scheidel 2005a: 64–79, *contra* Finley 1998: 148; Brunt 1987: 124–5; Bradley 1994: 12.

[4] Bagnall, Frier, and Rutherford 1997: 98.

[5] Westermann 1955 is still the most detailed survey of the evidence. See also Garlan 1988; Fisher 1993; Bradley 1994.

is overwhelming, thereby reducing the need for (otherwise desirable yet impossible) quantification. The opposite is true of the much more controversial issue of the extent to which slaves were employed by commoners, above all in farming. This problem cannot be addressed without statistics; such evidence does not exist; therefore, no amount of scholarly debate will ever yield compelling answers.[6] However, although the true scale of sub-elite slaveownership may well be critical for our understanding of the psychological and cultural significance of slavery in Athenian or Roman society,[7] it does not necessarily have to be known in order to analyse economic behaviour in elite circles. For that reason, I shall confine myself to an analysis of the use of slave labour by the upper classes, in an environment where we may take its significance in all sectors of employment as a given.

INCENTIVES AND CONSTRAINTS

Why would individuals who relied primarily or exclusively on the labour of others choose to employ slaves for a particular type of activity? Fenoaltea's model, familiar to students of modern slavery but far less known among ancient historians, envisions a fundamental divide between two categories of slave labour.[8] Effort-intensive activities are amenable to close supervision and 'pain incentives': these include mining and quarrying, lumbering, basic construction work such as digging, and certain forms of farming, primarily work that can be performed by gangs and does not require high levels of care (such as sugar and cotton production). Conversely, care-intensive activities require rewards to motivate slaves and reduce ill-will that fosters carelessness, shirking, and theft. This category includes artisanal and commercial activities, domestic service, and even some forms of farming, such as viticulture, as well as animal husbandry – in brief, any activities that either depend on a certain accumulation of human capital or are not readily susceptible to close supervision. While the pain-incentive regime allows owners to minimize investment in subsistence and rewards,

[6] The debate has centred on conditions in classical Athens. Many slaves among family farmers: e.g. Jameson 1977: 122–45, 1992: 135–46, 2001: 167–74. Few slaves: e.g. Wood 1983: 1–47; Ameling 1988: 281–315. In principle, a similar (and similarly aporistic) controversy could be launched regarding Roman Italy. Current population estimates for classical Athens make it seem rather unlikely that many smallholders owned enough land to make proper use of slaves, regardless of slave prices: see my addendum in Garnsey 1998: 195–200; see also Foxhall 2001: 209–20. In the United States, farmers who did not own slaves did not employ other people either, at least not in the long term. The real divide is between farms that (can) use additional (long-term) labour and those that cannot, not between those which do or do not use slaves. See Rosivach 1993: 551–67.

[7] Finley 1981: 97–115; Cartledge 1998: 156–66, 2001: 247–62.

[8] Fenoaltea 1984: 635–68.

it raises supervision costs. Care-intensive activities demand better provisioning and general rewards, and more often than not some realistic prospect of manumission. In Fenoaltea's words, '[t]he proposed model thus predicts that the continuum of activities from land- and effort-intensive to capital- and care-intensive will be matched by a continuum in the treatment of unfree labour from harsh and closely supervised to benign and unsupervised (. . .) and that over this continuum the likelihood of manumission will grow from negligible to substantial'.[9] He observes that, for activities that are conducive to pain-incentives, a low subsistence/high supervision regime of slave labour will always yield higher returns than any form of free labour.[10] By contrast, reward-rich activities are intrinsically more suitable for free labour, and the use of slaves in these sectors is therefore inherently unstable. Manumission in particular will tend to erode slavery in this context.[11] This model chimes with the view, advocated among others by Fogel and Engerman, that slavery works best in the context of gang-labour, especially for sugar and cotton, which required 'a steady and intense rhythm of work'.[12] It also fleshes out Canarella and Tomaske's earlier optimal utilization model that shows that 'force intensive slave management techniques [i.e. the equivalent of Fenoaltea's 'pain incentives'] are optimal if as the intensity of labour extracted from slaves increases, the marginal product of force per additional dollar of expense declines less rapidly than the marginal product of bribes [i.e. 'reward incentives'] per additional dollar of expense in bribes'.[13]

However, notwithstanding the overall plausibility of this model,[14] serious problems remain. From an Americanist perspective, critics have cited the case of tobacco farming, which relied on plantation slavery although the crop requires care, and where gang labour was uncommon, while in those cases where gangs were employed, this appears to have happened in

[9] Fenoaltea 1984: 640. This represents a significant improvement over Hicks 1969: 127–8, in which the author considers the value of slaves the main criterion for good or poor treatment (but see 131).

[10] Fenoaltea 1984: 641 (and see 644), for the fact that in America, post-slavery contracts did not generate comparable productivity.

[11] On the role of manumission as an incentive, see also Findlay 1975: 923–34.

[12] Fogel and Engerman 1974: 204; also Fogel 1989: 26, 34, 78, 162. Cf. Metzler 1975: 123–5, for rational management and economies of scale on US plantations.

[13] Canarella and Tomaske 1975: 626.

[14] I note in passing that the use of slaves in unhealthy locales must have been closely linked to a pain-incentive system; see Sallares 2002: 247–55, in which the author suggests that agricultural slaves were common in central Italy because of the spread of malaria in the Roman Republican period. Cf. Dusinberre 1996, for slave labour in the rice swamps of South Carolina and Georgia. Work in fever-ridden areas was surely an 'unpleasant' activity that was conducive to the use of some form of coerced labour. Cf. already Engerman 1975: 504–5.

order to ensure careful treatment of the plants.[15] Moreover, under the right circumstances, slave labour could become common and highly profitable in grain cultivation as well; as a notable example I would like to mention the Virginia Piedmont.[16] In general, the focus on gang labour and brute force also makes it hard to explain why so many farmers benefited from keeping just one or a few slaves.[17] Consideration of ancient slave labour compounds these problems. Fenoaltea seeks to accommodate Greek and Roman evidence within his model, but only with mixed results. It is true that the widespread use of slaves in effort-intensive activities such as mining and the prevalence of reward-incentives in care-intensive sectors, such as crafts and management, support his argument. Then again, large-scale grain farming by slaves was also known in Roman Italy.[18] More importantly, large-scale viticulture in the same region was consistently associated with chattel slavery (even including *servi vincti*, chained slaves of ill repute), although vines are clearly highly care-intensive.[19] To evade this contradiction, Fenoaltea maintains that slavery in viticulture was in fact unsustainable in the long run, a mere 'short-term phenomenon' that appeared to ensure the transfer of expertise among workers.[20] Thus, slave labour would have worked best to set up new wine and oil plantations, a process that involved a lot of digging. He even goes so far as to conclude that 'the contrast between the land- and effort-intensity of the modern Southern and Caribbean staples and the capital- and care-intensity of the ancient Mediterranean staples appears to provide much the most significant single explanation of the viability of plantation slavery in the New World and its non-viability in antiquity'.[21] This claim would seem to hinge on a very peculiar definition of 'viability': after all, slave-driven viticulture flourished in Roman Italy for a period several times as long as the period of large-scale cotton production on American slave plantations. In fact, in what amounts to a complete reversal of Fenoaltea's position, the prominence of slaves in Roman wine and olive cultivation prompted de Neeve to consider these

[15] Hanes 1996: 309, and n. 13.

[16] Irwin 1988: 295–322; Wright 2003: 527–52. This speaks against the exclusive association of slavery with 'crops such as tobacco or cotton, which demanded sustained attention during a long growing season' proposed by Earle 1978: 51–65 (quote at 51).

[17] Kolchin 1987: 54 (71.9 per cent of US slaveowners in 1860 owned 1–9 slaves).

[18] Spurr 1986: 133–43; Scheidel 1994: 159–66.

[19] Kolendo 1971: 33–40; Etienne 1978/9: 206–13; Carandini 1988. Chained slaves in viticulture: Cato *Agr.* 56; Colum. *De Re Rustica* 1.9.4–5; see generally Backhaus 1989: 321–9.

[20] Fenoaltea 1984: 647–8. [21] Fenoaltea 1984: 653.

activities typical of plantation-style slave labour.[22] It is also telling that, contrary to Fenoaltea's assumptions, the most detailed account of Roman arboriculture envisages not merely the use of slaves in skill-intensive long-term activities, but even the employment of *external* workers for the purpose of digging up vineyards.[23]

Further difficulties arise from Fenoaltea's contention that slavery was a more competitive labour regime for intrinsically 'unpleasant' occupations.[24] While the use of slaves in mining is perfectly consistent with this observation,[25] the apparent dominance of slave labour in Roman domestic service and animal husbandry compel him to argue that both sectors belong in this category. In his view, domestic service was 'unpleasant' because it placed servants in close proximity to the owner and subjected them to close control and abuse: thus, domestic slavery in antiquity 'seems second only to mining in its suitability to slave labour'.[26] While comparative evidence certainly suggests that slaves considered domestic service a mixed blessing,[27] it is not at all clear that this kind of employment would necessarily have appeared undesirable to the wives and children of displaced Roman farmers who were looking for sustenance.[28] Somewhat paradoxically, the herding of livestock is likewise thought to have been 'unpleasant', partly because of the solitary nature of this activity.[29] In other words, we are asked to assume that workers didn't want to be close to their employers, but they didn't want to be far away from them either. Yet it is not at all obvious that a pastoral lifestyle, free from close supervision and abuse, should have been an inherently unpopular field of employment. Moreover, even Fenoaltea prudently refrains from labelling artisanal and commercial activities 'unpleasant', despite the fact that Greek and Roman slaves appear to have flourished in these spheres for hundreds of years.

[22] de Neeve 1984a: 75–82. He was, however, mistaken in doubting the suitability of slavery in grain farming: see above, nn. 16 and 18. Wright 2003: 532–5 observes that in the United States, slaves were concentrated on the most valuable land. The situation in Roman Italy may have been similar: compare de Neeve 1984b. This relationship could at times be reversed, in the sense that some land became valuable only because it was worked by slaves, primarily in the case of unhealthy land that would not otherwise have been intensively cultivated: see above, n. 14.

[23] For the latter, see Scheidel 1989: 143, on Colum. *De Re Rustica* 5.1.8, 5.2.2. Compare also Colum. *De Re Rustica* 2.2.12; Labeo *apud* Ulp. *Dig.* 43.24.15.1, for the use of external labour for comparably unskilled tasks.

[24] Fenoaltea 1984: 655. See also Barzel 1977: 93–4.

[25] The persistence of 'collier serfdom' in Scottish mines up to 1799 is a good example for the utility of unfree labour in mining.

[26] Fenoaltea 1984: 655. [27] E.g. Genovese 1974: 331–8; J. Jones 1985: 25–8, N. T. Jones 1990: 113–17.

[28] Evans 1981: 101–65. [29] Fenoaltea 1984: 656.

Fenoaltea's model helps to account for the success of slavery in domestic service, animal husbandry, manufacturing, and commerce in the classical world: reward incentives are well documented in all these areas.[30] At the same time, there is no sign of erosion through manumission: slave herdsmen are still attested in late antiquity,[31] and domestic service seems to have been a quintessentially unfree activity from classical Greece to the end of antiquity, for over a millennium. To complicate matters further, slave employment in these sectors coincided with the presence of free rowers in Greece and Italy and free miners in Roman Spain, Dacia, and Egypt, although it is hard to imagine more 'unpleasant' and dangerous activities.[32] In sum, Fenoaltea's model explains the use of slaves in certain areas and makes a valid point about the correlation between the character of work and the incidence of manumission, but fails to account for the apparent success of slavery in many care-intensive activities, mostly in ancient Greece and Rome, and to a lesser extent in the Americas as well. I want to suggest that this is because the model is incomplete, and needs to incorporate additional variables to provide a more cogent explanatory framework.

In this connection, Hanes' focus on turnover costs and the benefits of guaranteed long-term labour obligations assumes special importance.[33] The need to replace workers creates transaction costs, including the costs of searching for a replacement, the loss of labour in the meantime, providing the replacement worker with job-specific skills, and supervising an unfamiliar worker. More specifically, in an agrarian context, turnover may cause particular damage if it interferes with time-sensitive activities, when labour input cannot be substituted across time and the loss of a labourer may cause irremediable harm, as in the case of a harvest or other critical seasonal activities.[34] Turnover costs are more likely to become a serious issue in 'thin' labour markets where labour cannot be quickly replaced. In such cases, slavery is attractive not only because it ensures the availability of labour and full control over the labour force but also because gender norms are less likely to interfere with labour needs. Hanes argues that, in consequence, US slavery worked well in 'thin' labour markets such as rural plantations, mines, rural foundries, and rural

[30] Bradley 1987 is the most detailed study. See also Klees 1998 and Weiler 2003.

[31] Russi 1986: 855–72.

[32] Mrozek 1989: 98–9 (wage labour in Roman mines). Galley slaves became common only in the early modern period; see Scheidel 1998: 355–6.

[33] Hanes 1996: 307–29.

[34] This aspect received particular attention from contemporary observers in the USA; see ibid. 321–4.

construction projects, as well as in domestic service – partly because of the rural setting of many 'Big Houses', and partly because of the information costs inherent in selecting suitable domestic staff. This model works similarly well for antiquity, and much improves on Fenoaltea's model in accounting for the popularity of slave labour in viticulture. By the same token, it is consistent with the comparatively small importance of slave labour in ancient Egypt, a country where unusually high population densities and low normative living standards supported a 'thick' labour market that facilitated the substitution of free labour.[35] Further analogies can be drawn regarding close alternatives to formal slavery. As Hanes points out, indentured servitude and slavery represent similar solutions to the problem of turnover: the former preceded the latter in the same sectors of the American economy because it generated similar benefits. The same may be assumed for debt-bondage in archaic Athens and in early Roman society, until it was in both cases eclipsed by the use of chattel slaves.[36]

One notable deficiency of Hanes' model concerns the apparent indifference of southern factory owners to high turnover rates:[37] the logic of the argument suggests that the significance of human capital in this sector ought to have encouraged the use of slaves even in otherwise 'thick' urban labour markets. This is all the more true as a combination of concerns about turnover costs and the desirability of accumulating human capital goes a long way to explaining the widespread use of slaves in Greek and Roman craft production. In my view, Watson's well-known distinction between 'open' and 'closed' slave systems helps to account for this otherwise unexplained discrepancy. In 'open' systems, slaves could be freed and fully assimilated into society, whereas in 'closed' systems, slaves remained a separate group even after manumission and were barred from intermarriage with the free population.[38] This distinction allows us to locate historical slave systems on a spectrum that puts sub-Saharan African slavery (where slaves often came to be incorporated into the owners' families) at the 'open' end, and US slavery (where manumission did not ameliorate the racially constructed inferior status of (ex-)slaves) at the opposite extreme. By implication, one would expect not merely the *quality* but also the

[35] See Frier 2000: 787–816, at 814 for population densities, and below, in the following section, for low rural real incomes.

[36] See below, in the following section. Further corroboration is provided by the recrudescence of dependent contract labour after the abolition of slavery in several parts of the world: e.g. Engerman 1986: 263–94.

[37] Hanes 1996: 319. [38] Watson 1980.

Table 4.1 *The Temin matrix*

	Frequent manumission	Only exceptional manumission
Open systems	Early Roman empire	
Closed systems	Classical Greece, Nineteenth-century Brazil	Southern United States, the Caribbean

overall *frequency* of manumission in a particular slave system to be correlated with its 'openness'. The main question is whether the relative degree of 'openness' should be regarded as a function of economic structure (such as the relative prevalence of certain types of economic activity that did or did not rely on slave labour) or rather as an independent and antecedent factor. In the latter case, 'openness' or 'closure' may have mediated the actual extent to which slaves were employed in effort- or care-intensive activities. For instance, slave labour might not flourish in care-intensive activities that thrive on the prospect of tangible rewards, manumission, and proper integration into free society, if it is employed within the constraints of a 'closed' system that militates against the conferral of such rewards or lessens their appeal. This handicap may account for the under-representation of slave labour in the most care- and reward-intensive sectors of the US economy. By contrast a high degree of 'openness' would make it easier to align economic interests with overall socio-cultural conventions and expectations.

Temin classified five leading slave systems as either 'open' or 'closed' and grouped them according to the frequency of manumission (Table 4.1).[39] However, the dual dichotomies of 'open' vs 'closed' and 'frequent' vs 'exceptional' seem unduly blunt even as ideal types. For instance, it is not at all clear that Brazil was as 'closed' as the USA, or that ancient Greeks 'frequently' freed their slaves. A sliding scale is more suitable for the purpose of capturing the relative standing of each system (see below). More importantly, though, Fenoaltea's model ought to discourage attempts to assign quasi-typical manumission frequencies to entire slave systems. While 'openness' or 'closure' may well have been overarching and culturally pervasive qualities, the actual probability of manumission was primarily a function of the specific properties of different types of work (Table 4.2).

[39] Temin 2004: 525 table 1.

Table 4.2 *The Fenoaltea matrix*

	Frequent manumission	Exceptional manumission
Effort-intensive/Pain incentives	No	Yes
Care-intensive/Reward incentives	Yes	No

Table 4.3 *Composite sliding scale*

	Frequent manumission		Exceptional manumission
Open system	⟶		
	Rome (c[are]/r[eward])		Rome (e[ffort]/p[ain])
↓		19C Brazil (c/r)?	19C Brazil (e/p)
		Athens/Greece (c/r)?	Athens/Greece (e/p)
			USA, Caribbean (c/r, e/p)
Closed system			

I believe that a composite model is required to take account of both sets of criteria (Table 4.3). In my composite model, manumission frequencies are specific to particular types of labour (effort/care-intensive) and incentive patterns (pain/rewards), while the overall degree of 'openness'/'closure' logically predicts the actual significance of slave labour in either one of these categories. Thus, in a 'closed' system with very low manumission rates (such as the United States), slave labour is much better suited to effort-intensive activities than to care-intensive work. At the other end of the scale, Romans were free to select whichever incentive scheme was appropriate to any given type of labour in the knowledge that societal conventions would not interfere with that scheme's successful implementation: while secure property rights facilitated ruthless exploitation in sectors where it worked best, a high level of 'openness' permitted the application of reward-rich incentive strategies in human capital-intensive occupations. As far as we can tell, classical Athens and Brazil occupied an intermediate position.

This expanded model also addresses some of the problems raised by existing mono-causal explanations. For example, it suggests that it made sense to employ slaves in vineyards, animal husbandry, and crafts not because any of these activities were somehow inherently 'unpleasant' but because turnover costs and the benefits of human capital accumulation favoured the utilization of slave labour in those sectors. At the same time, if task-appropriate rewards cannot readily be bestowed because they are incompatible with societal norms, slavery will not thrive in those sectors. Finally, the fact that 'closure' can easily clash with economic interests indicates that it does indeed constitute a (largely) independent factor.

But even an eclectic approach can answer only part of my original question – why did Greek and Roman and American elites rely on slave labour for certain activities to the extent that they did? While we may have gained a better understanding of the set of circumstances that made the use of slaves a more or less promising strategy, we are still unable to account for its actual prevalence. Once again, Fenoaltea and Hanes' models show the way. As Fenoaltea points out, free labour may (at least to some degree) be substituted for slave labour if the free labour force is abundant and impoverished, and can therefore be subjected to more slavery-like working conditions. As a logical corollary, high real wages among the free denoting scarcity of labour are more conducive to slave labour *per se*, and forestalls this kind of substitution. This, in turn, chimes with Hanes' argument about turnover costs: turnover was not just a static problem (as in the case of 'thin' rural labour markets created by low population densities and the dominance of family labour) but also a dynamic phenomenon: if labour becomes scarce, the cost of turnover rises, rendering slavery a more attractive option.

In the Americas, slavery was at a disadvantage in care-intensive activities not merely because of 'thin' settler-society labour markets, but more generally because the 'closed' nature of the slave system impeded the application of the appropriate reward incentives. Owing to colonial 'virgin soil' land/labour ratios, rural labour markets were necessarily 'thin', and effort-intensive slave labour was common and profitable. Greeks and Romans managed to employ slaves in both care- *and* effort-intensive occupations. Therefore, labour markets must have been 'thin' in terms of real wages and turnover costs. At the same time, the densely populated classical city-states deviated profoundly from the New World scenario of readily available land and manpower shortage. If classical Athenian or Roman Republican labour markets were indeed 'thin', and hence conducive to the use of slave workers, they must have been 'thin' for very different reasons. I explore this issue in the following section.

COMMITMENTS

In the most general terms, the emergence of large-scale slavery across economic sectors depends on two fundamental preconditions: (1) a relative shortage of labour (i.e. of labour relative to exploitable resources), and (2) access to slaves. We may also identify several contingent secondary variables: for (1), they include demand for goods and services that could be produced by slaves (1a), and high real wages among the free labour force (1b); for (2), the accumulation of capital (i.e. financial access to slaves) (2a), and physical access to enslavable persons (2b). Accumulation of capital (2a) also feeds back into (1).[40]

This scenario applies to New World slave systems that benefited from growing demand in Europe (1a) and an exceptionally favourable land/labour ratio (1b) that induced endemic labour scarcity, as well as from the accumulation of capital (2a) driven by (1a) and access to an unusually abundant supply of slaves in sub-Saharan Africa (2b) (and, later in the United States, rapid natural reproduction).[41] In ancient Greece from the archaic period onwards, the opening up of the Mediterranean through mass emigration created new commercial opportunities and markets (1a), while a beneficial configuration of economic and political conditions and developments appears to have raised real incomes (1b),[42] thus promoting the accumulation of capital (2a) and access to foreign slaves (2b). However, since slavery appears to have thrived as much in the core regions of Aegean Greece as in peripheral Greek overseas settlements we face the question of whether any of these factors necessarily generated a sufficiently significant shortage of labour in that core. The same is true for Roman society in the late Republican period: capital accumulation (2a) and access to slaves (2b) increased dramatically during the last two centuries BC (in both cases ultimately because of successful warfare) but slave labour came to be concentrated in central western Italy (as well as Sicily). Again, it is unclear why these changes should have precipitated labour scarcity.

Finley looked for an answer in political and ideological conditions: for him, the abolition of debt bondage (in early sixth-century BC Athens and late fourth-century BC Rome) created a new dichotomy of (fully) free and

[40] This schema differs in points of detail and perspective from previously identified sets of criteria. Compare Finley's three conditions for the emergence of a proper 'slave society', of (1) inequality in assets, (2) developed commodity production and markets, and (3) 'unavailability of an internal labour supply' (Finley 1998: 154). It seems to me that all three can be collapsed into a single factor, i.e. labour scarcity, whereas access to slaves is a missing and altogether independent variable. Cf. Rihll 1996: 95, rightly stressing the importance of supply. Cartledge 2001: 162 treats (1) inequality, (2) access to slaves, and (3) labour shortage as the main variables.

[41] This summary is limited to the most fundamental economic features. For an extremely rich explanatory analysis of the emergence of New World slavery, see now Eltis 2000.

[42] Expansion and growth of slave trade: see Rihll 1993: 77–107. Rising living standards in mainland Greece: see Morris 2004: 709–42, Morris 2007.

(fully) slave, leaving slavery as the only viable form of readily exploitable labour for those whose assets required them consistently to employ others for work. In Finley's perspective, class relations take centre stage: 'The peasantry had won their personal freedom and their tenure on the land through struggle, in which they also won citizenship, membership in the community, the *polis*. This in itself was something radically new in the world, and it led in turn to the second remarkable innovation, slave society.'[43] Rihll drew attention to another crucial variable, namely the growing availability of slaves.[44] Recently, Morris sought to fine-tune this model by stressing the interplay of a variety of factors such as 'demography, technology, the attitudes and responses of the wealthy, Solon's role as negotiator, Athens' international situation, the relative price of different forms of labour, the specification of property rights in people and things, the creation of institutions for measuring and enforcing them, and the legitimacy of Athenian culture'.[45] Ultimately, however, his reconstruction maintains Finley's emphasis on the consequences of the withdrawal of dependent labour that used to be provided by members of the local in-group of free citizens.

Labour may become scarce for two reasons: a rapid increase in resources such as land relative to the labour force, and by rising commitments among the free population that conflict with economic activities. Small and socially cohesive polities may be particularly likely to experience the latter phenomenon. The recent comparative survey of thirty-six city-state cultures throughout world history undertaken by the Copenhagen Polis Centre has highlighted certain features that tend to be common to polities in that category. Hansen defines a city-state as 'a highly institutionalized and highly centralized micro-state . . . with a stratified population' whose 'political identity is focused on the city-state itself and based on differentiation from other city-states'.[46] Furthermore, city-states disproportionately often featured 'debating and voting councils and assemblies', institutions that most readily develop in the context of micro-states.[47] I hypothesize that the more city-states conformed to the ideal-typical 'polis' model of high political and military participation rates and a clearly

[43] Finley 1998: 157–8, also quoted in Morris 2001: 28. Finley did not fully develop this argument with regard to Rome but suggested an analogous process (see Finley 1981: 165–6). Harris 2002: 415–30 argues that Solon abolished enslavement for debt rather than debt bondage, and that the latter continued to be attested (420–5). However, there is no sign that the latter arrangement represented a common alternative to slavery in the late archaic or classical periods.

[44] Rihll 1993, 1996. [45] Morris 2001: 29–41 (quote at 41).

[46] Hansen 2000a: 19. [47] Hansen 2000b: 612.

defined citizen-insider/foreigner-outsider dichotomy, the more likely they were to resort to chattel slavery when the standard requirements ((1) and (2) as defined above) were met.[48] In addition, non-city-state polities that nevertheless experienced comparable inducements were likely to adopt similar solutions. A comprehensive survey and any systematic testing of this hypothesis are well beyond the scope of this chapter. For a start, I limit myself to nine very brief sketches of historical cases from five millennia and four continents.

Classical Athens provides a suitable starting point. From the end of the tyrannical regime onwards (and increasingly so in the wake of imperial expansion and political democratization after the Persian invasions) adult male citizens accepted growing commitments to the political and judiciary process and especially to the military sector.[49] The growing involvement in these activities of the wage-earning elements of the citizenry would have interfered with long-term or time-sensitive labour arrangements.[50] At the same time, the influx of imperial rents and commercial revenue facilitated the accumulation of capital, growth in demand, and rising wages. Some poleis averted labour shortages by subjugating and collectively enserfing or enslaving neighbouring populations: Sparta is only the best-known example of a seemingly widespread phenomenon.[51] By contrast, islands or central Greek poleis that were surrounded by more formidable neighbours were severely constrained in their ability to adopt this strategy. It is therefore perhaps not by coincidence that Greek sources convey the impression that large-scale slavery was particularly common in a central-Aegean zone of shared economic development that stretched from Corinth and Megara to Athens, Aegina, and Chios.[52] In this area, the combination of high time-commitments of fairly closed citizen-populations, commercial and/or expansionist opportunities, maritime access to slave markets in Asia Minor, the northern Aegean (Thrace) and the Black Sea region, and the

[48] Cf. Rihll 1993: 109–11 for the nexus between the Greek militia system, politics, and the emergence of a slave society.

[49] See Hansen 1985, 1988: 14–28, for the demographic background.

[50] The nexus between the expansion of naval service and the public involvement of Athenians of modest means is well established and was already noted by contemporary observers: e.g. Strauss 1996: 313–26. Note that Athens may have been a latecomer on the scene: slave-rich poleis such as Corinth or Chios appear to have developed sizeable navies well before Athens did (Thuc. 1.13; Hdt. 6.8).

[51] See most recently Luraghi, and Alcock 2003 on Sparta, and Van Wees 2003: 33–80, on other captor societies.

[52] Salmon 1984; Legon 1981; Cohen 1992; Jew 1999; Figueira 1981; Roebuck 1986: 81–8; Sarikakis 1984: 121–31. Slaves: Athen. 6.265b–267b, 272b–d.

lack of readily exploitable neighbours may well have been instrumental in precipitating the intrusion of chattel slavery into all sectors of the economy.

Republican Rome followed a comparable trajectory. Starting out as a city-state at the intersection of two different city-state cultures (Latin and Etruscan) and retaining its principal military and governmental institutions in increasingly fossilized form for hundreds of years, Rome placed heavy commitments on the adult male population of its expanding citizen core. Exceptionally high levels of military mobilization and large-scale migration militated against stable long-term employment.[53] These processes coincided with unprecedented growth in the accumulation of capital among the elite and equally abundant opportunities for the enslavement of defeated enemies and the purchase of foreign slaves.[54] Rome dominated its Italian neighbours by incorporating them into a military alliance system instead of turning them into a dependent (non-military) labour force. Combined with a fundamental societal 'openness' and inclusiveness that co-existed with a strong concept of citizenship and thereby facilitated the adoption of reward-intensive slave labour regimes, all these factors converged in producing an environment that was strongly conducive to the spread of chattel slavery throughout the economy.[55]

Other city-state cultures experienced similar inducements on a more moderate scale. In the fifteenth and sixteenth centuries, the *negeri* – a cluster of Malay-speaking city-states in Sumatra and Java – relied on a captive labour force of slaves that had been acquired largely through purchase or conquest.[56] The 'open' character of the slave system encouraged manumission and the use of slaves in care-intensive tasks. The price of labour was unusually high, supposedly ten times subsistence in rice according to astonished European observers. With regard to disruptive commitments, the 'Malayan' insider core of these *negeri* resembled the 'Roman' citizenry in its porosity and inclusiveness, and in its military commitment to its polity.

The Yoruba *ilu*, city-states in what is now south-western Nigeria from the sixteenth to the eighteenth centuries, provide a somewhat different

[53] Brunt 1987; Scheidel 2004: 1–26; Scheidel 2006.

[54] E.g. Hopkins 1978: 37–96. To some extent, relative labour scarcity at the core may even have been complemented by a more 'colonial' situation in those parts of Italy where mass killings and displacements had altered land/labour ratios in ways that were conducive to the introduction of slave labour. However, the extent of any such developments is controversial, and bound up with the question of how badly some regions of Italy had been affected by warfare and confiscations.

[55] Cf. Jongman 2003: 100–22, for the argument that Italian urbanization was closely associated with the growth of the slave population.

[56] Reid 2000: 424–6.

example.[57] Just as in Greece, citizens were typically farmers who resided in the city; the distinction between citizens and strangers was crucial, and citizen status underpinned the exploitation of slaves, who were outsiders bought or captured in war.[58] Power depended on control over people rather than land, the latter being plentiful and the former scarce. In this case, the combination of citizen commitments and a quasi-colonial land/labour ratio favoured the employment of slaves.

However, city-state status is not *a priori* conducive to large-scale slavery, and needs to coincide with other crucial factors (most notably (1) and (2) as defined above) to produce this particular outcome. The Hausa city-states in northern Nigeria (*c.* 1450–1804) illustrate this basic point.[59] The period preceding the takeover of the Sokoto Caliphate in the early nineteenth century was characterized by ongoing conflict between the various city-states: the sources frequently refer to slave-raiding expeditions, tribute paid in slaves, and gifts of slaves between polities. The Hausawa – the free citizenry – dominated cities and countryside. Apart from herders and merchants, almost all foreigners who were absorbed into these city-states were slaves or members of certain 'unfree' occupational castes. 'Slaves were unquestionably of central importance to the growth and development of Hausa city-state culture.'[60] Even so, slavery never came to define Hausa society or became essential to its economy. Pre-imperial Hausa society differed from Greece and Rome in important respects. As slaves were used in military capacities (including the guarding of cities), and elite cavalry was at the centre of military operations,[61] the overall incidence of extra-economic commitments that were specific to the working citizenry appears to have been low. Moreover, access to new slaves was limited compared to conditions under the jihadist Sokoto regime of the Fulani in the nineteenth century when warring and enslaving greatly expanded.[62] These constraints are consistent with the limited development of slavery prior to that period.

As already noted above, other city-states fell back on collective slavery (Sparta and other poleis) or serfdom, such as the city-states of Etruria[63] and the Mixtec city-states in Mexico (*c.* 900–1521), where elites owned large numbers of *tay situndayu* ('serfs', mainly of foreign origin) who worked their estates.[64] In the absence of critical incentives, slaves remained comparatively unimportant in several other city-state cultures. Slaves did not

[57] Peel 2000: 507–17. Just like 'polis', '*ilu*' refers to both the city-state and its urban core (ibid. 508).

[58] Peel 2000: 515. [59] Griffeth 2000: 482–506.

[60] Griffeth 2000: 491–2, 494 (quote). [61] Griffeth 2000: 500.

[62] Lovejoy 1981: 201–43, 2000b: 201–8. See also Jumare 1996: 31–8.

[63] Frankfort 1959: 3–22; Harris 1971: 114. [64] Lind 2000: 572.

play a major economic role in the independent Sumerian city-states (from *c.* 3000–2300 BC) and were primarily used as domestics.[65] The limited scope for expansion in this period and the lack of labour shortages were the main structural constraints, analogous to conditions in Old Kingdom Egypt. This situation only changed in the post-Akkadian Ur III empire (*c.* 2100–2000 BC) when slaves assumed greater importance,[66] comparable perhaps to the expansion of slavery following the transition from the independent Hausa city-states to the imperial Sokoto caliphate. Likewise, slaves were of minor significance in the core coalition of Aztec city-states of the imperial period (1428–1520), arguably due to the fact that military commitments tended to be modest,[67] and landless workers were both numerous and readily available for long-term employment (that is, real wages and turnover risks appear to have been low).[68]

Conversely, it is possible to identify systems that were not city-states but nevertheless experienced the specific configuration of demand, opportunity, and 'insider' commitments that is conducive to the spread of slave labour. Medieval Scandinavian societies are a case in point. There, we witness a combination of a strong commitment to military activities within the in-group; an egalitarian ideological superstructure that reinforced the free/slave divide (esp. in the 'New World' environment of Iceland) and propped up the myth of popular political participation; disproportionate capital accumulation among elites; and access to an abundance of enslavable persons (both Norse and non-Norse) and to a variety of slave markets.[69] In the Viking Age, significant levels of slaveowning were perhaps confined to the West Norse of Norway, Ireland, and Iceland. Later on, slaves may have been employed on large estates in Denmark, Norway, and Iceland but were mostly found on family farms where one or two slaves provided domestic service and support in farming.[70] It was only when military commitments subsided and overall population increased that slavery was eroded by a shift to tenancy arrangements.

Portugal in the age of exploration, though likewise not a city-state, offers another and much better documented example. Slavery greatly expanded

65 Westenholz 2002: 31. 66 Siegel 1947.

67 See Hassig 1988: 59–60, for estimates of the relationship between army strength and population size.

68 Smith 2000: 581–95, 588. Even the concept of citizenship was lacking (589). For the modest economic importance of slavery, see Smith 2005: 138, and cf. also Clendinnen 1991: 38. An ample supply of *mayeque* (dependent tenants, ? serfs) reduced demand for chattel slaves: for the former, see, e.g., Clendinnen 1991: 20; Zantwijk 1985: 270–1.

69 City-states were not completely absent from this environment: see Holm 2000: 256–7, for estimates of military commitments in the Norse city-state of Dublin; and Holm 1986: 317–45, on slavery.

70 Karras 1988: 69–95, who stresses the shortcomings of the evidence.

in the second half of the fifteenth century and peaked in the sixteenth, when it had come to assume a critical role in the overall labour supply.[71] In this case, the crucial determinants were the extension of Portugal's reach into sub-Saharan Africa from the 1440s onwards, opening up abundant slave markets that replaced earlier sources of supply which had depended on successful conflict with Muslim polities; and an endemic and intensifying labour shortage caused by the ambition of a tiny population of some 1.5 million Portuguese to establish some measure of control over vast parts of the planet, and consequent (and often permanent) losses to the domestic labour supply. Slave labour became so profitable that the purchase price could be amortized within two years, and even faster for skilled slaves. Whilst concentrated in the cities, especially the capital of Lisbon,[72] slavery spread into both care-intensive and effort-intensive sectors of the economy (viz. artisanal and commercial activities, and work in foundries, on river barges, etc., respectively). Slavery subsequently declined in the seventeenth and eighteenth centuries in response to a demographic recovery, a decline in wages, and the increasing pull of the Brazilian labour market that drove up slave prices.

These observations support the assumption that rising commitments within clearly defined groups of stakeholders that coincide with rapid capital accumulation and improved access to slaves create favourable conditions for the spread of slave labour in the economic sphere.[73] This process differs from the standard 'New World' scenario that pits scarce labour among settler population against abundant natural resources, and offers a more suitable explanatory model for the creation of large-scale slave systems at the core rather than the (colonial) periphery of powerful polities.[74] In the most general terms, we may expect any large-scale slave system to conform to one of two ideal types: 'peripheral' systems with favourable land/labour ratios, and 'core' systems in which a combination of high commitment levels, capital inflows and overseas expansion raises demand

[71] Saunders 1982.

[72] For a counterexample, compare the situation in the Netherlands that subsequently faced similar commitments (in terms of the out-migration/population ratio) but mitigated manpower shortages through large-scale immigration of German and Scandinavian men who married Dutch women, esp. in the large cities (see de Vries 1986: 107–10), rather than by the importation of slaves. Portugal's comparatively isolated position may have curbed free immigration.

[73] In the context of city-state cultures, the spread of slave labour may, in turn, free citizens to devote (even) more time to war and politics, a reciprocal process that forces neighbouring polities to follow suit or risk defeat, and favours the emergence of a cluster of closely interconnected slave societies.

[74] Both models (for core and periphery) are consistent with Miller's argument (in this volume) that slavery is a strategy to secure the labour services of vulnerable 'outsiders' for tasks that cannot easily be imposed on 'insiders'.

for labour. However, as I indicated earlier, this rapid survey can be no more that a pointer for future research.[75] A systematic comparison between different categories of states would be required to identify significant correlations between specific features and levels of slave ownership.[76]

COSTS AND TASTES

Is it possible to measure the significance of the two key variables (1) and (2) in the ancient Mediterranean world? As I have shown elsewhere, we may gain at least a vague impression of the economic impact of (1) labour shortages and (2) access to slaves by comparing price and wage data from different regions and periods.[77] The principal contrast is between the expanding slave economy of classical Greece and the more mature slave system of the Roman empire during the first few centuries AD (Table 4.4).

Within ancient Mediterranean history, the 'mature Roman slave system' of the first three centuries AD stands in marked contrast to conditions in classical Athens in the fifth and fourth centuries BC. Athenian valuations are significantly lower than comparable rates for the Roman empire. This interpretation is strengthened by the ratio of slave prices to daily wages. Jones and Duncan-Jones, in their earlier more limited attempts to assess the value of slaves in different times and places, were right to maintain that Athenian slaves were significantly cheaper than Roman imperial slaves.[78]

These findings shed new light on the dynamics of chattel slavery in the ancient Mediterranean. Roman Egypt was endowed with an unusually 'thick' rural labour market: population densities were much higher than in most pre-industrial countries, and population pressure may well have been an issue.[79] At the same time, slave prices were relatively high – that is, broadly in line with Mediterranean averages (see Table 4.4) – thanks to the pull of the Italian market rather than local demand. In this environment, slaves were luxury items: most households did not own any slaves, and most that did had only one or two.[80] As far as we can tell, slave labour did not play a great role in production. Hired labour and tenancy were the dominant labour arrangements. Classical Athens provides a counterpoint

[75] Pertinent conditions in late medieval Italian city-states in particular varied considerably and merit more detailed analysis. See, e.g., Haverkamp 1974: 160–215, for the significance of slavery in medieval Genoa.

[76] Cf. Chapter 2 in this volume for methodological issues.

[77] Scheidel 2005b: 1–17.

[78] Jones 1956: 194; Duncan-Jones 1978: 162–4.

[79] See above, n. 35, and Frier 2001: 139–59.

[80] See above, in the opening section, and also Bagnall, Frier, and Rutherford 1997: 98, for low levels of slaveownership in the census register *P.Oxy.* 984 (from Ptolemais or Lykopolis): 5 out of 36 households owned a total of 13 slaves.

Table 4.4 *Regional variation in real slave prices in the Greco-Roman Mediterranean (male and female; in wheat equivalent)* *

	Slave prices expressed in:		
	(1) Wheat equivalent (in tons)		
Context	(1a) Range	(1b) Rough mean	(2) Annual wages of unskilled rural labour
Classical Athens			
(5th/4th C. BC)		~ 1.2–1.6	0.3–0.5
(Delphi)			
(2nd C. BC	?<3.5–4.7	?<4)	
(1st C. BC	?<3.8–7.2	?<5.5)	
Roman Italy			
(1st/2nd C. AD)	2–9	5.5	
Roman legal			
(2nd/3rd C. AD)	3–7	5	
Roman Egypt			
(2nd/3rd C. AD)	[3.5 or] 4.–4.5	4	3
(Levant, 2nd C. AD			similar?)
(Dacia, 2nd C. AD			similar??)
(Dura, 3rd C. AD			similar?)
Roman price edict			
(AD 301)	(2.5–3?)	(2.5–3?)	(2–2.5?)
Roman empire (overall)			
(1st–3rd C. AD)			~ 4 (+/– 50%)

*For detailed discussion of the evidence, see Scheidel 2005b.

to this 'low-equilibrium' scenario: given high real wages and low slave prices, it must have paid to buy slaves instead of relying on hired labour. This is true *a fortiori* if we consider the impact of the comparatively 'thin' free labour market of the classical Athenian polis (see above). High real wages indicate labour scarcity. Imported slaves were both cheaper and more dependable than free wage-labourers. In this environment, it may even have been profitable to keep slaves simply to hire them out.

In this comparative evaluation, the Roman Republican period assumes the role of the missing link. In the absence of quantifiable evidence, we can only hypothesize that conditions in Italy and Sicily during the last two or three centuries BC bore a greater resemblance to classical Athens than to Egypt or even Italy itself in the first few centuries AD. As I have argued in the previous section, high demands on the free population, rapid accumulation of capital within the elite, easy access to slave markets, and the growth of markets for goods and services both within and outside Italy can be expected to have generated a similar environment of relatively high real wages and low slave prices.[81]

When commitments fell dramatically following the Augustan transition, population grew, and export markets shrank, the comparative advantage of slavery relative to free wage labour and tenancy must have declined.[82] It is frequently assumed that this process gradually eroded large-scale slavery at least in certain sectors of the Italian economy.[83] This is certainly plausible but perhaps not an inevitable outcome. We also need to take account of the limited flexibility of established institutions.[84] Path dependence militates against gradual fine-tuning of institutions until worsening sub-optimality triggers sudden adjustments.[85] The feedback loop between institutions and belief systems also merits attention. Once a slave-owning ideology is firmly established, it may prove hard to dislodge it not only in the owner class but also among free workers.[86] There is no sign that the Roman empire experienced anything remotely comparable to the severe shocks that destroyed large-scale slavery in the Americas and in other colonial settings: the emergence of an abolitionist ideology at the core of the dominant world system that came to affect elite behaviour; the unilateral and coercive curtailing of the international slave trade by the world's leading naval power; a massive civil war in North America; and later colonialist interventions in Africa. In the Roman empire, by contrast, rule over slaves continued to be a defining element of elite identity; ideological or economic challenges were absent; and the socio-economic standing of the ruling class did not depend on the intrinsic competitiveness of the preferred system of labour. At the very least, we have to allow for the possibility that economic incentives and established tastes diverged over time, and that continuity in tastes helped prop up an increasingly inefficient system. Moreover, we must allow for the probable growth of natural reproduction: once a large slave population had been put into place and sex ratios evened out over time, a steady supply of replacements was guaranteed.[87] Moreover, qualitative evidence points to continuing imports from

[81] For discussion, see Scheidel 2005b.
[82] See Scheidel 1996: 93–7, for rough quantification of changing labour commitments.
[83] For (sceptical) discussions, see Garnsey and Saller 1987: 72–3; Morley 1996: 55–82.
[84] E.g. Aoki 2001; Greif and Laitin 1984: 633–52.
[85] For path dependence, see David 2001: 15–40. Note that susceptibility to 'market failure' (as intimated here) is merely a special sub-category of the more general property of path dependence.
[86] Cf. Scheidel 2001: 175–84, for the impact of slavery on attitudes toward labour among the free.
[87] Scheidel 1997: 156–69; Scheidel 2005a: 64–79.

outside the empire.[88] While dumping prices may well be a vital element in the rapid expansion of a slave system, steady supply at stable price levels suffices to service an existing if bloated system. In consequence, the core of the Roman empire may have entered a prolonged 'high-equilibrium' state of slaveholding.[89]

There can be no simple solution to this problem. Our answers are inevitably conditioned by our perspective. In the idealized universe of neo-classical economics, efficient markets and rational actors who enjoyed costless access to perfect information would not have hesitated to use their resources as efficiently as possible by adjusting the relationship between free and unfree sources of labour as factor endowments changed over time. In the fuzzier but more realistic world of sociology and the humanities, concerns about status and the meaning of freedom and slavery would have constrained economic forces and helped perpetuate a well-established regime of labour and domination with all its social and cultural implications even as its efficiency declined over time.[90] Efficiency and utility are not the same thing. This is not to say that neo-classical market forces were unimportant or did not gradually assert themselves over time: it simply means that we are unable to tell whether changes in the economic incentive structure from the beginning of the monarchical period onwards triggered immediate or much delayed adjustments to labour markets, or none at all. In the absence of reliable statistics, our answer will always be coloured by preconceived notions – perhaps not of what mattered at all, but surely of what mattered *more*: market or mentality, economics or culture.

88 See now Bradley 2004: 298–318.

89 The available evidence – in so far as it can be taken to reflect the actual diffusion of slave labour in different periods, a notion that well may be largely illusionary – does not indicate a dramatic drop in slave employment even in late antiquity: see MacMullen 1987: 359–82. Cf. also Whittaker 1987: 88–122.

90 See Patterson 1982, for the importance of domination in slavery. Cf. also Kyrtatas 2001: 140–55, for the Greeks' general emphasis on domination rather than exploitation.

CHAPTER 5

Slavery and technology in pre-industrial contexts

Tracey Rihll

INTRODUCTION

In this chapter I will endeavour to develop a general model of the relationship between slavery and technology in ancient Greece and Rome. This model is informed by comparative evidence from other periods and places and, consequently, may also be applicable to other pre-industrial societies.

In the ancient world, slaves who were skilled artisans or service providers were usually paid for their skills and products. Most people in this sector were paid piece rate, per unit that they made or performed. For example, stonemasons working on the Erechtheion frieze were paid per figure, those fluting the columns, per foot.[1] As a rule of thumb, the more products or services the person sold, the more money she or he made. Slaves could raise the money needed to buy their freedom through saving the residual income from their earnings. Purely on an abstract, theoretical level, we can appreciate that the ancient, independently living slave had good reason to be industrious and to want to increase his or her output in terms of quantity or quality, since every obol earned was an obol closer to freedom. Indeed, the prospect of freedom may have been a more powerful motivator than any felt by a free worker. The prospect of freedom at a price would have provided a powerful motivator for those in the manufacturing sector to improve their productivity and/or the quality of their product. Consequently, we may speculate that slaves were responsible for at least some of the many inventions and technical developments of classical antiquity.

I believe that the key parameters that shaped the relationship between slaves and technologies were:

(1) the skill or care level of the work being performed
(2) the motivation provided to the workers

[1] *IG* I^2 374. Translation in Austin and Vidal-Naquet 1977: 276–9.

(3) the technical education of the workers
(4) the material or cash capital investment required by an innovation
(5) the physical and socio-economic benefits of an innovation
(6) the physical and socio-economic risks of an innovation
(7) the physical mobility of skilled workers and transaction costs.
We will examine each of these in turn.

(1) THE SKILL OR CARE LEVEL OF THE WORK BEING PERFORMED

People are diverse in tastes, habits, and abilities and, therefore, make different choices and show different preferences, especially with regard to their jobs and their methods of earning the basic means of survival. Self-appointed rationalists may claim that some people take control of and turn distasteful situations into palatable ones by finding some virtue in them; and this may be true in certain cases. The phrase 'an honest day's work' smacks of such efforts at redemption, as does the claim to be 'only obeying orders'. All manner of outrage have been perpetrated on selves and others by such mind-bending exercises.

However, coerced labour cannot be expected to perform effectively work that requires a lot of care and attention or delicacy or sensitivity.[2] It has been suggested that coerced labour will perform work, but it will be the minimum required, and that does not normally coincide with high-skill or high-care jobs.[3] Consequently, coerced labour is suitable mainly for work that requires little if any skill or training and little care in its execution. In addition, it is risky to use coerced labour in an environment where the value of deliberate breakage or damage done by the worker (sabotage) could outweigh the benefit of their labour. Indeed, the more expensive the environment, the more likely is the cost of sabotage to outweigh the value of the work, or of the worker. It is not surprising, therefore, that coerced labour is typically found in jobs where a worker's ill-will can find little if any means of expression that can harm the coercer. Management of coerced workers is more challenging than management of willing workers, as it depends almost entirely upon the exercise of condign power.[4]

Coercion may be physical, psychological, or financial. Ordinarily, we might think of slaves as people who are physically coerced, the intimidated

[2] See Fenoaltea 1984: 635–68.
[3] For an alternative theory on the rewards of slaves see Scheidel, this volume.
[4] I use the term condign power in Galbraith's sense; see Galbraith 1984.

as those who are psychologically coerced, and the impecunious as those who are financially coerced. Impecunious here needs to be understood as meaning not having sufficient money for his/her perceived needs, rather than with reference to any particular sum (conversely, the term does not refer to those who are persuaded by the promise of extra money, rather than coerced by the lack of it, to perform unpleasant work). All these people may have been coerced for different reasons into doing jobs that most rational human beings would not do if they did not have to. For this reason, there is a possibility that people of very different backgrounds and statuses may be found working in the same low-skill or low-care job, side by side.

In the modern world, wherever possible, machines have been invented to 'do the donkey-work'; that is to replace physically coerced (and low-skill) animal workers. Animals, in turn, replaced physically coerced slave workers, and according to some ancient writers, slaves replaced subordinate family members, who probably were coerced sometimes.[5] But in antiquity, too, the 'donkeys' were replaced by machines in some contexts. Man-powered versions of mills, to grind small hard bodies into dust, whether organic (grain to flour) or inorganic (mineral grains to powder), were supplemented first by animal-power versions and then water-powered versions. Most of the current evidence for the mechanization of milling is Roman in date, but it is in the nature of archaeological evidence that all such chronological statements are provisional; a Greek mechanical mill could be unearthed tomorrow.

High-skill jobs, by contrast, or those requiring great care in their execution demand the worker to be committed to the work. For example, no one wants an incompetent or resentful surgeon to operate upon them, or a nurse with a grievance to be responsible for their personal care when incapacitated. For these sorts of jobs, modern managers usually exercise compensatory or conditioned power over the workers, rather than condign, and so it was in antiquity. Slaves performed high-skill and high-care jobs, as well as the unpleasant ones, for example as teachers, assayers, doctors, and secretaries.[6] They too were motivated by compensatory and conditioned power, exercised by the market, the state, and their masters. They too were committed to the work, even though they were slaves. Some masters rewarded their slaves not only with freedom or an inscribed

[5] See, e.g., Herodotus 6.137; Pherecrates fr. 10.1.147 Kock; Timaeus *FGH* 566 F 11; Aristotle *Politics* 6.8.23.

[6] There is a great deal of primary evidence for slaves in high-skill or high-care work in ancient Greece and Rome. For a selection, see Wiedemann 1981.

tombstone but with real assets reflecting reciprocal concern, if not affection, precisely because the slaves in question had shown high levels of care and consideration for their masters. Pliny, for example, not only gave his old nurse a farm valued at 100,000 sesterces, but even sent in a manager, when its income fell off, to look after it, and her.[7]

Innovators care about their work almost by definition; they would not innovate, if they were not motivated by the problems as well as the opportunities presented by their work. Let us then turn to consider motivation.

(2) THE MOTIVATION PROVIDED TO THE WORKERS

In ancient manufacturing, free staff were almost impossible to recruit, never mind to retain. This may have happened because citizens were 'committed', in Walter Scheidel's terms,[8] or because they were prejudiced against crafts, or prejudiced against working for others, or a combination of such factors. An Athenian whose father had irresponsibly failed to teach him any skill, thus preventing him from making a living, was released from the legal duty to look after his father in his dotage.[9] Consequently, fathers competent in specific craft skills would have taught these to their children, and there would have been much continuity of occupation in families through time. Children did not have to use the skills taught, if they could make ends meet through other methods; Socrates is not known for his stonework, nor Theophrastus for his whites. People already in crafts could and did change trades, for example, from cobbler to doctor (about which Aesop tells a nice cautionary tale). Lucian gives a number of reasons for his pursuit of a career in letters rather than in various family members' occupations, notably that of sculptor (*The Dream*). He was blessed with a particularly fine intelligence; most freeborn children, whether of citizen or freedmen parents, would have had no option but to continue in the occupation(s) they could learn from family members. Crafts were thus passed on from father or mother to son or daughter. What is odd (not exceptional, but unusual) about ancient Athens, in comparison to most societies, anywhere, anytime, is that the free appear always to be

[7] Pliny the Younger, *Letters* 6.3.

[8] By this, Scheidel means otherwise occupied, especially with politico-military matters, hence labour recruitment and retention could become problematic and unpredictable; see Scheidel this volume. For Scheidel, the high turnover cost is one of two key factors leading to the development of a genuine slave society in ancient Greece (the other being high real wages). See further Scheidel 2005: 1–17.

[9] Plato *Protagoras* 327a; Vitruvius *De Architectura* 6 praef. 3.

self-employed. This fact points in the direction of attitudes rather than economics as the driving force behind self-employment.

The ancient Greeks themselves express free men's refusal to take on permanent posts as employees largely in terms of a perception that this is tantamount to voluntary slavery. For example, Eutheros, an old friend of Socrates, had lost his farm and his father during the war and had nothing left. He told Socrates, 'I was obliged to gain subsistence by my labour wherever I could, thinking that this is better than begging.' Socrates wondered how long he could carry on like that and suggested that he went 'to some wealthy citizen, who may want someone to help him gather in his fruits, inspect his affairs, and oversee his slaves'. Eutheros equated this with enslavement: 'But slavery, my dear Socrates, is a thing I can ill submit to.'[10]

Although Socrates obviously entertained the idea of the free employee, I know of no example of a free man working as an employee in a craft shop in ancient Athens. This is, I think, evidence of absence rather than absence of evidence. For there is quite a lot of evidence to show that free poor would hire themselves out on an *ad hoc* basis as labourers or runners or something similar (see e.g. last quote). There is a rationale for this behaviour. What we might perceive as job security, the ancient Greeks might have seen as bondage. By taking only piecework, the ancient workers preserved their right, and thus their freedom, not to take orders from an employer on a daily basis.[11] They did not want to work every day, or have a regular job, and they did not want to take orders from a superior. Instead, they preferred to control their work, to decide themselves what to do and when to do it. Thus, attitudes created a situation where exactly the same actions could be viewed as positive or negative, depending upon the circumstances of the act. 'Anything done to satisfy a personal need, or to help a friend, or to attain goodness, will not be illiberal; but the very same act, when done repeatedly at the instance of other persons, may be counted menial and servile.'[12] The Saraguro of Ecuador, who like the ancient Greeks had a strong sense of personal autonomy, also preferred piece-rate work because it allowed them to work unsupervised, without a 'boss'.[13]

10 Xenophon *Memorabilia* 2.8.

11 The concept of freedom and its origin in the experience of slavery in ancient Greece is the subject of Patterson 1991.

12 Aristotle *Politics* 8.2.6.

13 The ancient evidence supports the Belotes' suggestion that 'preference for piecework rather than time-based wages is probably common among people who place a high emphasis on personal autonomy'; see Belote and Belote 1984: 40.

Some of the slaves manumitted in Baltimore also preferred, for the same reasons, to take jobs with large measure of independence in terms of freedom to control one's own time and space, jobs such as chimneysweeps and washerwomen.[14] These attitudes to working for others have nothing intrinsically to do with status, for example *qua* 'elite' attitudes not shared by the 'hoi polloi'. We do not know whether the free poor who behaved like this in ancient Athens were citizens or freed slaves. Metaphorical uses of slave terms in the ancient sources, prejudicial attitudes to metics (resident aliens), and stigmas attached to ex-slaves combine to make it extremely difficult to unpeel the possible layers of meaning and processes of reasoning that ultimately led people to behave in certain ways. Nor do we know which of the two attitudes came first: did free people think and act this way because slaves habitually or historically performed these jobs, or were slaves recruited to perform these jobs because free people considered these tasks appropriate only for slaves and thus refused to do them? There is a self-sustaining aspect to all this, like the proverbial chicken and egg. Still, the pattern is consistent and clear: ideally, one works for one's own, not others. This created a fundamental structural constraint on businesses (whether farm, workshop, or other): staff recruitment, when extra hands were needed, was an *ad hoc* process that had to take place on a daily basis, *if* the extra hands were free.

Staff recruitment and retention was not a structural problem, however, if the staff were slaves. Forensic speeches and other evidence from classical Athens suggest that a free artisan often trained one or more slaves in that craft either to help or to replace him/her.[15] Once trained, the slave either worked side by side with the master, or was sent to work in the master's place. Slave artisans and service providers, whose work involved artistic skill, professional knowledge, or sound judgment were exploited for their special skills rather than wasting their talents as general assistants. The Greeks understood well that slaves were motivated by rewards as well as by punishments and that those incentives are better motivators for skilled slaves and those performing jobs requiring care.[16] This phenomenon is widely confirmed historically. It is explained by the fact that threats and violence tend to cause counter-productive attitudes in jobs requiring high skill or care, such as high anxiety levels and ill will towards the master.[17] Normally, slaveowners had to spend time managing their slave(s),

[14] See Whitman 1997.

[15] The classic example is Lysias 24, on behalf of a disabled citizen to retain his state pension.

[16] For example, Xenophon *Oeconomicus* 5.15–16. [17] Fenoaltea 1984: 637–8, 654–8.

although some Athenians got along with minimal supervision, by enticing their slaves to work well on their own.

This is because the slave could earn a living from his or her skill, much as a free worker did. Both artisans and service providers were normally paid on a piecework basis: so much per pot, per foot of plaster, or per evening. Phrynichus refers to a potter making a hundred wine cups a day.[18] The principal capital asset that the slave used in order to perform the work, namely his/her body, was not his/her own. Therefore he/she had to hand over to the owner part of his/her earnings as rent on his/her body. This rent was sometimes called *apophora*,[19] sometimes *ergasia*.[20] An obol per day seems to be a common *apophora/ergasia* rate for a slave in Athens. For the sake of comparison, at the same time, a citizen was paid three obols per day for service in the courts or the assembly and a state pension was one obol per day. The rest of the slave's income was his/her own. This residue (*kermation*, small change) would have provided an incentive payment for the slave to work without supervision.[21]

Some skilled slaves were allowed to live alone, separately from the master.[22] Archaeologically, slaves' homes are indistinguishable from those of free people. Somewhat ironically, in economic terms, of all the different types of people living in classical Athens (or ancient Rome[23]), the independent slaves lived the life most familiar to adults living in modern western societies. Five similarities should be mentioned: (1) These slaves typically worked in manufacturing or the service sector rather than in agriculture. (2) They were paid in money rather than in kind. (3) They bought rather than grew their food. (4) They had to pay for their accommodation. (5) On a daily basis, they chose how to spend or save what cash they had left after necessary expenditure. The opportunity to live like this, separate from the master, making decisions about how to live one's life – and who to share it with – was surely an incentive in itself. Some, though, saved money to buy their freedom.[24] Manumission documents from Athens usually record the slave's skill. While most slaves mentioned worked in the craft and service sectors, some of them were specialist

[18] Phrynichus, *Revellers* 15. [19] For example, Menander *Epitrepontes* 380.

[20] For example, Hypereides 3 [*Athenogenes*] 22. [21] Fenoaltea 1984: esp. 639.

[22] Garlan 1988: 70–3 for the Athenian evidence. Slaves living independently would tend to live near regular markets where they procured their daily bread, as would anyone who did not grow their own food. In Attica, the regular markets were in the agora and the Peiraeus.

[23] For the Roman evidence see Temin 2004: 513–38.

[24] Skilled slaves appear to have had to pay considerably more for their freedom than they probably cost the master. This has an economic logic, since the master probably invested time, energy, and materials in training the slave; see Forbes 1955: 321–60.

agricultural workers such as vine dressers.[25] These manumitted slaves then joined the ranks of the free, and at least in the case of some Greek slaves, they continued to perform their craft or trade, now as metics, free resident aliens.[26]

We have documentary evidence for thousands of individual cases of slaves manumitted, but relative to the number of people enslaved at the time, it is a fraction. It is a reasonable assumption that many more people were enslaved than were freed. Nevertheless, based on a range of evidence and coherent argument, the position widely held by scholars is that manumission was normal for slaves performing skilled or sensitive work and abnormal for those involved in hard physical labour such as mining. For the Roman world, the satirist Lucian observed that even a natural slave (φυσείδουλος) would expect to be freed by the time he got to the approximate age at which some (free) Greek scholars sought the 'voluntary slavery' of salaried posts in great Roman houses.[27] Lucian may have been satirizing his compatriots, distinguished old Greeks, but in the process gives us more information about manumission in the Roman world than any number of inscriptions could do. Most scholars believe that manumission was even more common in Rome than in Greece.[28]

(3) THE TECHNICAL EDUCATION OF THE WORKERS

Most machines and techniques were developed and built anonymously in antiquity; in this respect, the ancient world strongly resembles the medieval and early modern worlds.[29] Obviously, the people who made these machines and used these techniques had the requisite skills to do so, although they almost certainly had no qualification as such. Experience, in fact, was the key in the productive sectors. They also had the appropriate

[25] See Tod 1901: 197–230.

[26] For example, those who formed a loan group stayed on at least until the last member of the group was released; see Westermann 1968: 17–32.

[27] In his work of that name; see Lucian, *On Salaried Posts in Great Roman Houses*, section 24.

[28] See Scheidel, this volume. See also Patterson 1982: 271–8; and Temin 2004: esp. 523–35.

[29] Zilsel points out that in the early modern period 'the artisans, the mariners, shipbuilders, carpenters, foundrymen, and miners worked in silence on the advance of technology and modern society. They had invented the mariner's compass and guns . . . [more examples] . . . they were no doubt the real pioneers of empirical observations, experimentation, and causal research . . . today we do not even know their names.' See Zilsel 2000 (1942): 940. See also Epstein 1998: 699–705, for a more recent statement of the case with examples of innovations in many crafts. However, note that 'the possible solutions' to the problem of why people deliberately invent something new (703) cannot be confined to the three Epstein proposes, because none of them worked for antiquity, when there was much inventiveness.

education, if they followed an established design, and the imagination, if they were inventing or innovating. Technology involves techniques as well as machines, materials, and power. This is most apparent with the largely immaterial technologies such as counting methods, musical notation (a Greek invention), and shorthand (an invention of a Roman slave called Tiro).[30] Experience and technique involves knowledge and skills, and they reside mainly in people's heads and hands.

In antiquity, the people in question were both slaves and free. For there were no tasks in antiquity carried out exclusively by slaves – though there are some noticeable variations in the sectors occupied by slaves between Greece and Rome. For example, some of the most successful bankers in the Greek world were slaves (becoming rich and famous in the process), while in the Roman world free citizens dominated the financial sector. These distinctions are not readily apparent in manufacturing, however, which is the main focus of this chapter. In both societies manufacturing was undertaken by both slave and free (freeborn and emancipated).

The apprentices of the Middle Ages were quite different from the ancient craftsman's or service provider's slave, who was bought and trained up to assist or replace him. This is evident in certain sectors. In the medieval world, where *free* staff had to be recruited and retained, high-risk industries like mining and metalworking did not attract many apprentices from families not already involved in them.[31] In addition to medieval metalworks, we can consider the modern period. The ironworks staffed by free labour in the early American Republic suffered very high turnover rates. On average, only half the furnace hands at one works were there a year later, and only 20–30 per cent of the workforce were retained over a five-year period at each of three different free labour ironworks.[32] But the ancients could 'recruit' as many slaves into these areas as they could afford and manage, and as a result, for as long as there were slaves to work the mines, Greek and Roman metalworking produced vast riches for individuals and the state. That in turn fuelled the Mediterranean economy, and polluted the planet on a scale not matched until well into the Industrial Revolution.[33] In ancient Greece and Rome, the number of people trained

[30] Teitler 1985 covers the subject from the early principate to the mid fifth century AD. See 172–3 for Tiro.

[31] Epstein 1998: 684–713. [32] Bezis-Selfa 1999: 694, and n. 59.

[33] Wilson 2002: 26–8 gives figures for Roman mining. Whilst generally sympathetic to his argument, I think that to lose sight of the slaves in ancient manufacturing, as he does, is to paint a picture as partial as that which sees not the technology. The Roman mines were not fully mechanized. For numbers of slaves and quantities of material processed in the Athenian silver mines, see Rihll 1999: 115–42.

and educated in any and every craft did not depend on and was not restricted to the number of people who wanted or chose to follow those occupations, as it did in non-slaveholding societies; it was significantly higher, because the workers were not there by choice.

As an alternative to training a slave, an ancient artisan might have bought a slave who was already skilled in his or her craft. This was an expensive option, but one that might bring new skills and knowledge into this artisan's production processes. In surviving slave sales documents, slaves skilled in crafts and services were commonly valued at twice or three times the value of an unskilled slave. This raises the issue of capital investment, the subject of the next section.

(4) THE MATERIAL OR CASH CAPITAL INVESTMENT REQUIRED BY AN INNOVATION

Ancient crafts and services varied with regard to the level of investment required to start a business; mining, for example, required significant time and expenditure before a grain of silver was produced, while it risked no financial return at all. Slaves and technologies were not normally rivals for funds, but were coterminous.

The development of innovative technologies that require very heavy capital investment can only be undertaken by the very wealthy. In the ancient world this generally means the state and/or a few extremely rich individuals (even though in some cases politics constrained the actions of private individuals irrespective of their wealth). For example, some Hellenistic and Roman ships were of a type best understood as a luxury liner or floating palace. These lead-lined behemoths came complete with separate accommodation and decks for different classes of passengers and crew and were fitted out with, amongst other things, gymnasia, promenade decks, container plants, and statues; we even hear of a hemispherical planetarium for a ceiling in one very posh room onboard one very posh ship (the *Syrakosia*).[34] The *raison d'être* for ships of this sort was conspicuous consumption and display of the owner's good taste. The Nemi ships were built to sail on a lake while the *Syrakosia* was too big to enter any harbour in the Mediterranean basin other than the one in which it was built, which rendered it useless as a genuine merchant vessel.[35] Monarchs – kings,

[34] Moschion *apud* Athenaeus *Deipnosophistae* 5.206d–209e.

[35] For an idea of the size, tonnage, and cargo of regular merchant ships, see Gibbons 2001: 273–312, with a useful catalogue of significant wrecks at 297–304.

tyrants, and emperors – built such ships to display their power, both economic and organizational; republics, of democratic or oligarchic persuasion, did not build them. Any private individual even thinking of building one would almost certainly have been seen as a threat, either to the state or to the monarch. Advanced military technologies and mining operations were also in a class apart from other ancient technologies, since they required big budgets and offered big rewards. We are told explicitly that the great leap forward in catapult technology – the discovery of the formulae that related machine component sizes to the missile to be discharged – was the result of extensive experimentation by engineers working directly on the problem because of the generous patronage of the Ptolemaic kings.[36]

However, most ancient innovations were apparently developed in the more humble confines of the ordinary workshop, and did not require much expenditure of materials or cash either in their development or in their adoption, as we shall see in section (5). The process of invention was celebrated and considered part of human life.

(5) THE PHYSICAL AND SOCIO-ECONOMIC BENEFITS OF AN INNOVATION

The Greeks and Romans associated inventions with individuals: although these associations may have been accurate or inaccurate, real or imaginary, the habit reveals clearly that inventors could be celebrated in their lifetimes and even immortalized in literature. Daedalus and flight is perhaps the most famous association; while the most surprising is perhaps the mathematician Archytas' invention of the baby's rattle.[37] Pliny's *Natural History* contains hundreds of putative inventors' and discoverers' names, most of them otherwise unknown. Some famous Greeks wrote books about inventions, e.g. Theophrastus and Strato (consecutive leaders of the Lyceum after Aristotle); no such book has survived the past 2,000 + years unfortunately. Intellectuals were not the only ones who wrote books on inventions; artisans, such as Melanthius the Painter (who wrote a work *On Painting*)[38] were also responsible for similar works. Likewise, Hermippus of Berytus (Beirut), who was born into slavery in the time of Hadrian, wrote a multiple-volume book entitled *Slaves who were Famous in the Cultural*

[36] Philo, *Belopoiika* 50.24–6. [37] Aristotle *Politics* 8.6.2.
[38] Diogenes Laertius *Lives of the Famous Philosophers* 4.18.

Domain.[39] The loss of these works is a real handicap to modern study of this topic. However, the very existence of these stories shows that the Greeks and Romans perceived ideas, tools, and techniques as inventions not givens, and they knowingly changed, improved, and supplemented the technical base over time. At the same time, they expected innovations to bring concrete benefits.[40]

Mechanization is not motivated solely by a concern to save labour, even in slave environments such as Jamaican plantations, as Satchell showed clearly in relation to the development of sugar mills.[41] Strikingly, more than 60 per cent of the patents recorded in England in the period 1660 to 1799 were for innovations that aimed to save capital or improve quality; less than 20 per cent of them aimed to save labour.[42] Epstein argues that patterns elsewhere in Europe were probably similar, and according to the model of Guild activity that he develops, this preference for skill-enhancing, capital- (rather than labour-) saving innovations is to be expected. Guilds were largely concerned with the reduction of transaction costs,[43] and the challenges were rather different in slave economies such as those of ancient Greece and Rome. Nevertheless, generally speaking, the ancients also developed machines to perform the sort of work that (1) could be done better by machine, or that (2) could not be done at all by people, rather than that (3) aimed to save labour.

For example, a Roman shield press is a fine example of type (1), having been designed to hold curved strips of wood in place while they set. Indeed, although it is possible to make a legionary's plywood shield by hand, ideally with the aid of a substantial tree trunk (to act as a former) and a lot of string, it is extremely fiddly and time-consuming. To make a plywood shield, each individual strip of wood needs to be bent to shape and held firmly in place until it sets, and, when the wood is dry, the pieces have to be assembled and glued and again held firmly in place until the glue sets. The shield press holds all the wooden strips needed to make a shield in place for however long they require. It is also a valuable tool of mass production, of course, and helped meet the legionaries' demands for thousand upon thousands of shields. The catapult is a fine example of

39 *Suda* (*c*. 10 AD) s.v. *Istros*: 'Hermippos in book 2 of *Slaves who were famous in the cultural domain* says that Istros came from Paphos.'

40 On the issue of progress in general, see Edelstein 1967.

41 Satchell 2002: 93–111.

42 Epstein 1998: 693–6.

43 The transactions costs Epstein has in mind are: 'the unattributed costs and benefits of training . . . to teach skills . . . to allocate costs to provide teachers and pupils with adequate incentives . . . to monitor the labour market to avoid major imbalances between supply and demand for skilled labour'; see Epstein 1998: 688.

type (2) invention, being able to throw missiles much faster, and therefore further, than is possible by hand or with a staff sling.

Nevertheless, ancient interest in type (3), labour-saving devices, may have been underestimated. For example, at Barbegal near Arles in France,[44] sixteen wheels were powered by one purpose-built aqueduct that was divided into two races. A similar multi-wheel facility was recently found on a steep slope of the Ianiculum in Rome.[45] The Romans mechanized a chore that was normally done by those people who occupied the lowest registers on the social scale: women, slaves, and criminals.[46] What was then perceived as the lowest sort of human labour was relieved, by machine, of the burden of grinding grain to make flour. For an explanation of these innovations, I think, we have to look neither to the technology nor to the slaves but to the *city* of Rome.

My argument, in brief, is this. By the middle of the first century BC, there were perhaps 600,000 people resident in the city of Rome.[47] At some point in that century, the state appears to have contracted miller-bakers to grind and bake some grain (perhaps that for the emperor himself, the Praetorian Guard and/or other state functionaries) and employed magistrates to ensure quality control and honest dealing. Those officers are included in the surviving part of the portrayal of daily life and grind at Eurysaces' bakery, images of which are displayed with pride on his enormous tomb.[48] Henceforth, one can easily imagine a step-change towards mass production in the development of the sector. For now, about three generations after the appearance of professional bakers in Rome,[49] officers responsible for the maintenance of trading standards guaranteed a certain amount of work for some commercial bakeries and promised customers frequent oversight. For the miller-bakers, this meant that the risk associated with making significant capital investment in men and machines suddenly dropped sharply.

[44] Leveau 1996: 137–53. Note that this is now dated to the second century, not the fourth.

[45] See Bell 1994 : 73–89. See also Wilson 2002: 13, and further references there. This is not the main sets of mills mentioned in the literary sources, but a different group.

[46] The first two categories were closer than one might think. Aristotle observed that very poor men were forced to use their women and children as slaves; see Aristotle *Politics* 1323a5–6. On criminals, see Pliny *NH* 18. 83–112.

[47] I adopt this from Garnsey's estimate for the late 70s BC; see Garnsey 1988: 212. The population of Rome is a much disputed topic but it is generally agreed that the numbers are rising dramatically through the last two centuries BC. Brunt suggests *c.* 180, 000 around 270 BC, rising to *c.* 750, 000 by Augustus' reign and the turn of the millennium; see Brunt 1971: 376–88. Stambaugh supposes there were as many as a million residents of Rome by that time; see Stambaugh 1988: 89. Storey argues that the number was half a million; see Storey 1997: 966–78.

[48] Curtis 2001: 358–70.

[49] Professional bakers first appeared in 171 BC according to Pliny, *NH* 18.107.

For some residents of Rome, ready-made bread might have appeared as a wonderful new convenience, much as white sliced bread appeared to our forefathers' generation[50] and ready-made meals appeal to many now. Around the turn of the era, Antipatros of Thessalonike celebrated the new technology and opportunity:

Hold back the hand that works the mill; sleep long
  You grinding-women, though cocks announce the day
Demeter has put your work out to the nymphs
  Who jump onto the very top of the wheel
And spin the axle which with twisting cogs
  Revolves the Nisyrus millstones' hollow weights.
A golden age has come again, we learn
  To feast on Demeter's produce without work.[51]

In exchange for a relatively small fee paid in cash or in kind (for those who could afford it) there was an opportunity for many more people to buy themselves or their slaves out of the hard and time-consuming daily chore of milling grain, kneading dough, and baking bread. The arrangement for the machines to be powered by water (as, for example, in the Baths of Caracalla, where the mills were built into the extensive substructure of this grandiose facility soon after AD 212) demanded considerably higher investment and advance planning – they could not be installed as an afterthought.

Some people had bought their bread since at least the fifth century BC, when professional bakers sold their wares, one tray-full at a time, in the agora and streets of Athens. Aristophanes portrays a baker-woman whose fourteen loaves were spoiled and she seeks restitution to the tune of fourteen obols.[52] If the figure of an obol per loaf is reliable, this was a very expensive convenience, since by this time an obol represented one third of a juror's pay for a day's work in the courts. So, a loaf cost a third of a day's 'satisficing' wages and Aristophanes' baker expected to earn at least 2⅓ drachmas at a time when ½ drachma was considered 'satisficing'. The baker had expenses that the juror did not have, of course, so the 2⅓ drachmas was not all profit.[53]

[50] The impact of white sliced bread was such that it spawned an idiom still applied to welcomed new technologies: 'the best thing since sliced bread'. The bread thus lauded, nevertheless, gave many of that generation health problems in later life, e.g. diverticulitis.

[51] *Palatine Anthology* 9.418, in Jay 1973: 196. Within a hundred years of this date we have a further four surviving references to water mills. See Vitruvius *De Arch.* 10.5.2; Strabo *Geog.* 12.3.30; Lucretius *De Rerum Nat.* 5.514–16; and Pliny, *NH* 18.97.

[52] Aristophanes, *Wasps* 1388–91.

[53] The play was produced in 422 BC. This was a time of stable wages in Athens, according to Loomis 1998: 257.

Xenophon also suggested that bread was an expensive luxury. One Cyribes apparently supported his household comfortably through ownership of a slave-staffed bakery. However, the same source clearly points out that everyone, including members of the best families, knew how to make flour and bread, just as they knew how to spin wool and make cloth.[54] Nevertheless, by the fourth century BC, if not before, magistrates were in place in Athens to protect whoever was buying bread by ensuring that its price was proportional to the price of grain.[55] Unfortunately, we do not know what that proportion was.

By the first century BC, when Eurysaces died, bakers could produce basketfuls of bread more or less continuously and many more people could take advantage of this production. Thousands of people were by now beneficiaries of the *plebs frumentaria*, the grain dole, which Gaius Gracchus had introduced in Rome in 123 BC.[56] By Caesar's time there were perhaps 320,000 beneficiaries in Rome, while grain doles existed in other cities of the empire too.[57] These people represent the first significant group in history – hundreds of thousands of people in one place at one time – who acquired grain freely without growing it themselves. First generation city-dwellers, who had grown up on the farm, would have known all about grain growing and processing. But as they became increasingly urbanized, a rising number of second-, third-, or fourth-generation urbanites might have lost the skills, the tools, or the space, to turn it into edible food. Thus, in the case of mechanical flourmills and dough machines, I believe that mass urban supplies of grain encouraged mechanization of its processing, and the mass production of bread.[58] The terms are relative of course, and Jasny estimated that the inefficiency of the Pompeian 'hour-glass' shaped mill was such that all the many mills in Pompeii would have had to work round the clock to keep the population of that city supplied with flour.[59] The presence of slaves in a given urban area was, I think, essentially

54 Xenophon, *Memorabilia* 2.7.6.

55 Aristotle, *Athenian Constitution* 51.3. They also ensured that the retail grain price was proportional to the wholesale, the milled grain price was proportional to the unground grain price, and the meal price likewise. For details of Athenian grain regulations, see Garnsey 1988: 134–49.

56 Garnsey 1988: 195–6. In time, this became the 'bread' part of the famous 'bread and circuses' (Juvenal *Satires* 10.81) policy that stopped this large urban populace from rioting or starving. The grain dole was distributed to different numbers and types of people over time; see Garnsey 1988: 211–14, and 236–7 for details of the changes.

57 Demonstrated by Caesar's 44 BC *Law on Municipalities* 5 (otherwise known as the *Tabula Heracleensis*) that says 'whenever and wherever grain is distributed to the people'.

58 I have come to this view independently of the arguments of Galbraith and others for supply side economics.

59 Jasny 1950: 240, 252.

irrelevant to the issue here, which is really about the numbers of consumers and the availability of grain more or less guaranteeing a large market for bread makers. Slaves (and metics) were consumers too, but they were not in receipt of the grain dole, and anyway were unlikely to want to spend disposable income on luxuries such as convenience food.

Many ancient machines fall into the category of being not-labour-saving machines; all those designed to entertain, for example. This includes most automata or devices, such as the one that shot a jet of water as high into the air as the top of the arena.[60] Being able to shock and awe the people was, I submit, one of the emperor's means to impress the public and, this way, remain on the throne. Such machines were as necessary to preserve the domestic status quo as monster catapults were to preserve the international status quo. 'To live in peace, prepare for war' is not a modern motto; Hero (or Ctesibius) opens his *War Machines* with precisely that advice, pointing out that, if peace is the aim, an arsenal full of catapults works better than a school of philosophy.[61] In that sense, these were productive technologies. They produced deference and respect, rather than material objects, and they produced it precisely because they achieved what could not be done by human labour alone.[62]

(6) THE PHYSICAL AND SOCIO-ECONOMIC RISKS OF AN INNOVATION

Some ancient inventions failed: 'like mutations, most technological innovations are duds and deserve to be eliminated'.[63] Innovations may be risky in a number of ways, of which economic loss and opportunity costs are relatively benign. One story from antiquity is often quoted. It runs that the emperor Tiberius ordered the execution of the artisan who reputedly invented 'flexible glass', and the destruction of his workshop, 'in case vessels made of such glass should devalue precious metal plate'.[64] Pliny himself observes that this story is not consistent with fact, since certain glass drinking cups fetched HS 6,000 in Nero's time, which was much more than precious metal cups. It is impossible to discover 'what really

60 Seneca, *Natural Questions* 2.9.2. 61 See Cuomo 2002: 165–77.

62 The Roman emperors' desire for novelty, for innovation, and experiment, specifically in the architectural arena, is stressed and discussed sensitively by L. F. Ball; see Ball 2003, especially his final interpretative essay.

63 Mokyr 1992: 328.

64 Told by Pliny *NH* 36.195, who doubted its veracity, and repeated with elaboration by Petronius *Satyricon* 51 and Dio Cassius 57.21.7.

happened' from this story. Did someone invent plastic? Or did someone simply observe a glassworker at work? All glass is flexible when hot, though how many people in antiquity would have known that is a moot point. Most would have no acquaintance whatsoever with the production of glass.[65] There is also a logical problem: how would a flexible plate improve the eating experience and, thus, displace and devalue precious metal (rigid) plate? We have flexible plates and they are generally despised; they are 'party plates' made of paper or thin plastic. It is precisely their flexibility that is the problem; flexibility is not an asset in an object intended to hold food or drink. The story is problematic on a number of levels and cannot be taken at face value as evidence of hostility to innovation, as it sometimes is.

Let us consider how it might have arisen. An inventor, whose invention required capital investment but who was turned down by a potential patron, was hardly likely to have explained this failure as the result of his invention being judged intrinsically bad; consequently, some other reason would have been promulgated. Alternatively, the potential patron might have given some spurious reason for his rejection in order to preserve the artisan's sense of self-esteem. We must always keep in mind that inventions may not have been taken up because the claims made of them were false – they did not deliver what was promised by their inventor – or they were unusable, or the risks or costs of adopting them outweighed the foreseeable potential benefits they could bring.[66] Sometimes such failure was not foreseen, and a technologically challenging project was pursued anyway – perhaps for non-economic reasons; perhaps in optimistic economic error. For example, the cost of draining the Fucine Lake (a truly spectacular feat of engineering not matched in some regards until the twentieth century) to reclaim the 20,000 iugera of land under it was nearly twice as much as the land's worth: it cost HS 36,000,000 to drain, but was worth less than HS 20,000,000 when drained. As Saller observed, the rarity of 'economic investment' on this scale may attest to Roman economic rationality better than this ambitious project itself does, given the costs and benefits of it.[67]

[65] Foy and Nenna 2003.

[66] The story of Vespasian and the transport haulier is often cited as another (*the* other?) example of a technological innovation being deliberately blocked: the emperor allegedly turned down a device to move columns for what we would call political reasons, according to Suetonius *Life of Vespasian* 18. The interpretation of this story is discussed in Finley 1981: 192; Greene 2000: 49–50; and Wilson 2002: 4. Compare the story of a new type of machine to haul loads to the city of Florence a thousand years later (which was awarded the first patent in that city). It 'was a technical fiasco that failed to carry a single load'; see Long 1991: 879.

[67] Saller 2002: 264.

On a more everyday level, innovations might involve a raising of standards that could not be maintained in lean times. For example, Galen remarks that, in poor years, farmers and bakers did *not* use a type of sieve specifically designed to remove darnel (a field weed) from the grain crop, because it would reduce the total yield at a time when everything harvested was needed. As a result, he says, consumers suffered headaches in the short term, and skin problems in the long term as the toxins accumulated.[68] From the overall concerns of the text, one should assume that the motivation (at least in Galen's estimation) was simply to have bread in times of dearth, even if the bread was contaminated. What we might call 'fair weather inventions' like this sieve, which was invented sometime before Aristophanes wrote fr. 480 Kock,[69] were probably the first ones to get lost when ancient society came under pressure in late antiquity. Innovations can bring mixed blessings, depending on conditions: what may be a benefit in one set of circumstances may be a detriment in another – most starving people would rather have contaminated food than no food, or bread made of grass rather than no bread at all.[70]

Early mechanization offered, at best, only small improvements of one sort or another over the entirely manual processes that had preceded it, and it sometimes involved a trade-off of one desideratum against another.[71] Roman mechanical flour mills may represent an improvement upon human (slave) performance in terms of quantity of grain processed through the bakery in a given period.[72] Nevertheless, this does not mean that the product was better or even more efficiently ground. The quality of the flour was probably little or no better, at least in the machine's early versions. There might have been quite a lot of versions, driven by the desire to improve the quality or quantity of product or to reduce costs or by fortuitous accidents or for a host of other reasons that we can now only guess. For example, from invention in the first century BC through to the second century AD, the shape of mechanical millstones changed from

[68] *Properties of Foodstuffs* 1. fin. Other dearth-time foods were worse; acorn bread, or the leather straps from beds for example.

[69] See Amigues 2003: 17–22.

[70] See e.g. Polyaenus *Stratagems* 8.23.24, reporting an episode in the civil war, when Caesar's troops were reduced to eating grass bread, and Pompey, on being brought a loaf of it, hid it, 'as he did not want to reveal to his own troops the enemy's self-control'.

[71] For comparative evidence, see Rosenberg 1976.

[72] For example, it has been estimated that the Barbegal mill could produce *c.* four and a half tonnes of flour per 24 hours, assuming 50 per cent down time; enough for 12,500 people to eat 350 gr. of bread per day. See Sellin 1983: 100–1. Wilson points out that comparable figures are obtained by a traditional water mill in Bosnia in the twenty-first century AD; see Wilson 2002: 12, and n. 70.

conical to flat and striations on the grinding faces were introduced in the second century.[73] Nevertheless Galen, who moved in the highest circles of imperial Rome at a time generally regarded as Rome's zenith mentions a type of bread that floated on water like a cork.[74] One deduces from this that most breads of the time, besides being grey in colour, sank, either totally or nearly so. Neither image is particularly appealing to the modern consumer, for whom there was still some way to go in the development of milling and baking technology. It is a common error[75] to assume that the initial development of a new tool or technique is what matters, instead of subsequent improvements and refinements to that technology. Historical studies suggest that quite the opposite is the case.[76]

Aufhauser first drew attention in the mid 1970s to the fact that machinery is often associated with deskilling (loss of skills), pointing out correctly that technological change could make production less complicated, and require less skilled labour per unit produced.[77] Although deskilling can lead to a decline in the quality of the product, not a rise in it, mass production can also raise the quality of base-line products, so that, for example, oil from a press was normally better than oil from treading.[78] Mass produced terra sigillata or red-gloss ceramics (what used to be called Samian ware) was probably better quality than the average local potter could produce and, interestingly, there is no obvious difference in quality between slave-made mass-produced ware and freeman-made mass-produced

[73] Wikander 2000: 392. [74] *Properties of Foodstuffs* 1.5.

[75] And one that Finley consistently makes. See Finley 1998(1980): 138; and Finley 1999(1973): 109, 114, and 146–7, and his 'Technical Innovation' chapter – despite his apparent awareness of the problem as stated in his second paragraph there. It is because of his misunderstanding of this and related technological issues that his interpretation *was* 'repeatedly challenged' (see Finley 1998(1980): 108). Keith Hopkins did not make this error; see Hopkins 2002: 190–230, at 219.

[76] For examples, see Rosenberg 1976 *passim*; De Long 1992: 321; and Malanima 1988, on the early fulling mill that damaged high quality cloth and was thus rejected by the makers of such fabrics until the machine was redesigned to eliminate the problem, whereupon they adopted it. Other examples come from the plantations in the New World, where a switch from horizontal to vertical axes in sugar mills and the addition of a third roller made a huge difference to output (and worker safety); see Fuente 2004b: 135–6, and n. 74, and Schwartz 2004a: 163. Thanks to Alejandro de la Fuente for drawing my attention to this book. There is an overview of the debate on the geographical origins of the vertical mill in Vieira 2004: 42–84 at 52–3. The vacuum pan distillation process is another example from the sugar plantations; see Aufhauser 1974: 41–2.

[77] Aufhauser 1974: 43.

[78] Note D. J. Mattingly's observation that 'the purchase or construction of olive mills and presses is commonly an indication of surplus oil production. Subsistence production of olive oil for a peasant family can be carried out using more rudimentary equipment [i.e. treading]. The existence of presses of whatever size in the archaeological record may be an important indicator of more market orientated rural economies.' See Mattingly 1993: 485. See also Foxhall 1993: 183–99.

ware. This is apparent if one compares, for example, Arretine products, produced largely by slaves, with Gaulish products produced (with one exception) by free men.[79] However, neither of these mass-produced wares is as good as the best artisans could produce, and the best red-slip ware was no Portland Vase.

(7) THE PHYSICAL MOBILITY OF SKILLED WORKERS AND TRANSACTIONS COSTS

Transaction costs were highlighted in section (3): having slave workers did not necessarily evade transaction costs for the master, because high-skill or -care workers were motivated by pay and manumission and therefore periodically needed replacing, while the replacements needed training and supervision until trained. However, free workers were more or less unobtainable in some ancient states (probably more in those where craftsmen were not admitted to the citizenship), so transaction costs associated with slave workers had to be borne.

Slavery forced skills and techniques across linguistic and cultural boundaries in a way that war and persecution did in later ages, as, for example, some pagan philosophers left Rome for Persia when Justinian forbade them to teach, some Catholics left Elizabethian England, some Huguenots left seventeenth-century France, and some Jews left 1930s Germany.[80] For most of human history, most people's circumstances have not been sufficiently bad to drive them to cross linguistic barriers and to brave new worlds. But when it has happened, they inevitably took their knowledge and technologies with them, as, most famously, did France's Huguenots and Germany's Jews. Although it is impossible to demonstrate, I believe that slavery must have been responsible for much technology transfer and innovation diffusion in the ancient world. I also believe that much hybrid vigour resulted from it – but that is another story altogether, which I must reserve for a different occasion.

[79] See Peacock 1982. I owe this excellent example to Nigel Pollard. For a comparative case, with fascinating insights into the potential advantages and disadvantages of slave versus free labour in manufacturing, see Bezis-Selfa 1999: 677–700. For slave and free working side by side in the same works, see Dew 1966. I am grateful to Susan O'Donovan for these references.

[80] For a less famous example of technology transfer by free technicians fleeing persecution, but one which happened in environments that also involved both slavery and technology, see Portuondo 2003: 231–57, at 256.

CONCLUSION

Slaves in the manufacturing and service sectors typically performed high-skill or care-intensive work. Such slaves were normally motivated by compensatory and conditioned power, the prospect of reward ('carrot in front') or sense of duty, rather than by condign power ('stick behind'). They were educated in the skills and techniques needed to perform their work, either before or during enslavement. They had good reason to want to improve their productivity – the prospect of freedom. Slavery is not antithetical to technical progress when the slaves are motivated by reward, rather than punishment.

There was a great deal of technical progress in classical antiquity. Most innovations required little capital investment. Those innovations that did generate an advance in the quality or quantity of production usually generated only marginal benefit. Step-changes in production were possible only when favourable technical and social circumstances coincided, as they did in catapult development in third-century BC Alexandria, and bread production in first-century BC Rome, for example.

Slavery forced people with diverse technical skills and education across linguistic and cultural boundaries, and tended to concentrate them in large cities and in monarchs' capitals and palaces. Slavery was perhaps the main agent of technology transfer and innovation in any society in which physical mobility amongst the free was unusual.

CHAPTER 6

Comparing or interlinking? Economic comparisons of early nineteenth-century slave systems in the Americas in historical perspective

Michael Zeuske

INTRODUCTION

As a historiographer of the Americas, I have sought to illuminate the facts through the employment of comparisons and statistical surveys and, thus, provide proof to my ideas.[1]

With these words, Alexander von Humboldt began the chapter on slavery in his *Political Essay* (*Essai politique*) on the island of Cuba, published in 1826. The chapter represented the most important argument made by a liberal thinker against slavery in the Atlantic world in the first half of the nineteenth century. Understandably, when John Thrasher omitted it from his 1856 translation of the *Essai politique* into English, Humboldt protested openly and forcefully against the omission.[2]

The origins of systematic comparison between slave systems, however, can be traced back to earlier than the publication of Humboldt's *Essai politique* and can be linked directly to the Haitian revolution. Already by 21 August 1791, immediately after the outbreak of the rebellion in the Acul region's plantations, in the north of Saint Domingue, terror struck throughout the world of slaveholders in the Americas. A powerful fear travelled through the Atlantic world in a pattern of concentric rings; one could appropriately describe this phenomenon by saying that 'a spectre wandered through the Americas'. It was, thus, the 'suspicion of an analogy between the contemporaneous shocks experienced by all the American slave systems' that was to trigger scientific comparison. It started when, in an attempt to find an explanation, masters and spin-doctors in the different slave societies concocted a true comparative question in systemic terms: is the situation in Cuba, Venezuela, New Granada, Louisiana, Virginia or Bahia exactly the

[1] Humboldt 1826a: 154.
[2] See Humboldt 1826b; and Thrasher 2001: 253–65. See also Zeuske 2001a: 30–83, and 2003.

same, or at least similar, to the one in Haiti and, if it is, what is to be concluded from this for the future of 'our own' slave system? Likewise, intellectuals also took this fundamental question as their starting point for their enquiry. Some even made trips with a comparative intent, for a variety of purposes. For example, Moreau de Saint-Méry, acting as a spy, travelled the areas of uprising of the Saint Domingue slaves and the outskirts of the United States in order to make comparisons. Also slaves and many former slaves found that the question of comparison between slave systems suddenly made sense, but, obviously, they asked it in reverse.[3]

Yet, another question could arise from the comparison between slave systems and it was one that, instead, focused on the differences and, specifically, on how the experience of the slaves' rebellion could be utilised for the correct development, or for the destruction, of a specific slave system. Ultimately, this latter question – that of the discovery and exploitation of differences – provided a line of enquiry for the first political and anthropological operation of comparison between slave systems – an operation that had much to do with the degree of mobility and transfer of information in the intra-Caribbean setting. In short, the shockwaves propagated concentrically from Saint Domingue and, as they did, they were communicated in oversimplified talks. The closer these talks occurred to the source, the more they were characterized by questions about 'pre-scientific' comparisons and transfers.

The questions asked the most were those about possible direct contacts and exchange of information between Saint Domingue and other slave systems, as well as about the spread of the revolution. Predictably, gentlemen discussed, above all, matters of safety and safety measures, whereas their counterparts mostly discussed the requirements for a successful uprising. Reaction by the participants to the discussions was immediate. In 1808, Francisco de Arango y Parreño, a friend of Alexander von Humboldt, still remembered how 'on 20th November, 1791, the news of the rebellion in Guarico [an old Spanish name for Le Cap] arrived in Madrid'. The same day, Arango wrote to the king, outlining comparisons of a bold nature, about sugar production in Saint Domingue and Cuba, about how it should be changed and how control of the slaves could be achieved in both regions.[4]

Later on, in his renowned *Discurso sobre la agricultura de la Habana y medios de fomentarla* (1792),[5] Arango not only wrote: 'the insurrection of

[3] See Zeuske 2004b: 157–90; Naranjo Orovio 2005: 101–78; and Saint-Méry 1913.
[4] Arango y Parreño 1952 (1792), I: 55 ; Arango y Parreño 1952 (1791), I: 111–12.
[5] Arango y Parreño 1952 (1792), I: 115–62.

the Negroes of Guarico enlarged the horizon of my ideas',[6] but also employed the comparative method to construct the myth that slavery was better in the Spanish than in the French colonies:

> the fate of our freedmen and slaves has been better and they have been happier than the slaves and freedmen in the French colony [of Saint Domingue]. Their numbers are smaller than those of the white population and, aside from that, they could never take over the important garrison of Havana. My great endeavours [to ensure safety against a slave rebellion] foresee a future, in which the prosperity of the island [of Cuba] will increase and she will have 500,000 or 600,000 Africans at her borders. What I talk about is that time in the future and I want our precautions to start from today.[7]

So, the pragmatist Arango was sharper (and earlier) than the scientist Humboldt in his analysis, while he was also quicker at utilizing the comparative method. We know very little about reaction from the other side – about the way slaves engaged in comparison and about their renewed efforts to escape slavery now boosted by the Saint Domingue Revolution, or about the way coloured seamen, smugglers, fishermen and militia, who were in direct contact with Saint Domingue, reacted in east Cuba and in the world of the Lesser Antilles.[8]

Humboldt arrived in the Americas only in 1799, but he had already heard about Saint Domingue. In general, it took more than ten years, from the beginning of the slave revolution in Saint Domingue in August 1791, for public opinion to acknowledge that a problem existed. It was precisely in connection with his studies on the slaves' revolution in Saint Domingue that Humboldt first labelled himself a 'historian of the Americas'; in modern terms, this can be seen as a way of politicizing history, of making it a history of the present.

At the beginning of 1804, Humboldt spent his last days in Mexico City. From there, he journeyed east, to Vera Cruz. Finally, he arrived at Havana, in Cuba, on 19 March 1804. While Humboldt was on his trip, something truly inconceivable for the majority of his contemporaries occurred. Former slaves, who had, by then, become soldiers and officials in an army of black citizens, proclaimed the existence of a new state. They did so in Saint Domingue, the French part of the Caribbean island of La Hispaniola, after winning the war against an expedition of French soldiers sent by Napoleon – the first decisive defeat ever suffered by a Napoleonic army.[9]

[6] Arango y Parreno 1952 (1792), I: 149. [7] Arango y Parreno 1952 (1792), I: 148–9.
[8] See Scott 1996: 128–43; Ferrer 2003b: 333–56, 2003a: 675–93; and Gonzalez Ripoll *et al.* 2005.
[9] See Leitner 2002; Fick 2000: 961–82; Geggus 2001; and Dubois 2004a and b.

Yet, in the diaries that have been published until today, Humboldt does not make a single mention of this momentous historical event. He does not mention it in the diary of his trip to Mexico City, nor does he mention either the revolution in Saint Domingue (1791–8) or the French intervention in the former colony (1802–3) during his stay in Vera Cruz. And yet, the significance of the Saint Domingue Revolution for Humboldt and, in general, for the studies in comparative history of slavery became evident in the course of the intensive transatlantic debates that were held as part of the celebrations for the 200 years anniversary of the event in Haiti. The year 2000, then, saw the resurfacing of a previously unknown section of Humboldt's diaries from the Jagiellońska Library in the Polish city of Kraków.[10]

THE BEGINNING OF SCIENTIFIC COMPARISON: HUMBOLDT'S CUBA DIARY OF 1804 AND THE '*ESSAI POLITIQUE*' ON CUBA

Humboldt's Cuba diary, recently found in Kraków shows that, in 1804, he effectively began comparative scientific research on slavery. In particular, Humboldt's short essays, with titles such as 'Slavery' (*Esclavage*) and 'Slaves' (*Esclaves*) contain his ideas, analyses, and evaluations of the slave systems in the Americas. Topics treated range from the slaves' setting light to the fields in Cuba and elsewhere – a sort of narrative of events related to the repercussions of the slaves' revolution in Saint Domingue; slave rebellions and slave rights; and legislation on slavery in comparative historical perspective. Humboldt examined also the sugar production of Saint Domingue until 1788 and the impact that the slaves' revolution in Saint Domingue had on the prices of sugar and coffee, as well as the slave trade and the origins of slaves in the Antilles in 1788. He, then, attempted to assess the long-term repercussions of the Saint Domingue Revolution on Cuba and on other slave societies by grouping such repercussions under particular headings, such as 'Landscapes of Slavery (and Soil Types)', 'Statistics and the Origins of the Slaves', 'Revolution and Terrorism in the Caribbean' and 'Revolution, Rebellions, and the Slave Trade'.[11]

[10] See Faak 1982, 1986/90, 2000; and Humboldt 1804.

[11] Humboldt 1826b: 1–5; 10. With 'terrorism', Humboldt refers to physical violence in politics, but not to the Haitian experience as it was constructed after 1804 by intellectuals and writers mostly belonging to the planter elite. See also Geggus 2003: 38–59 and Leitner 2005.

Taking as his starting point the concrete situation of Havana, where he resided, and the surrounding regions of Güines and Bejucal on the south-east, Humboldt analysed, again under different headings, 'revolution, rebellion, resistance and slave-dogs', 'revolution, rebellion and the rights of the Negroes in 1804', the 'character of the Negroes in Africa', and the 'situation of the Caribbean around 1804'. As Humboldt did so, he engaged thoroughly with colonial demography, examining issues such as the total number of the slaves, the caste structure of Cuban society, and the so-called 'masculinity rates', meaning the ratios of men to women among the slaves. Humboldt ended his analysis in the diary with a vision of slavery ending in some twenty years in the Caribbean and in the rest of the Americas. He could have not known anything about the action that the Cuban slaves took against slavery to solve the problems he outlined, an action that took place as he was working on his manuscript of the *Essai politique*, which was finally published around 1825.[12]

Despite Humboldt's hopes and predictions, twenty years after the composition of his 1804 diary, slavery had not yet been abolished. In fact, 'second' slavery itself prospered, while slave smuggling reached a new climax. Humboldt's *Essai politique* is clearly a more explicit political essay about Haiti and the black Caribbean. It is also an essay focusing on explicit comparisons, as well as implicit transfers. In the *Essai*, Humboldt analysed all aspects of slavery, several of which he also recorded in the diary; he did so, though, in a systematic form.

Humboldt's employment of a comparative method in investigating slave systems shows clearly in three particular chapters of the *Essai*. In the chapter about 'Population', he took into account all aspects of modern demography, but he focused particularly on the differences between rural and urban slaves, as well as on the increase of the slave populations. In the chapter on 'Trade', he analysed the sugar and coffee exports, the slave trade and the wood, cattle, and flour imports. Finally, in the chapter on 'Land-Economy' [agriculture], he took a look at the sugar landscapes, at the reasons for Cuba's prosperity, at the creators, and at the economics of sugar production, at its structure and costs. Interestingly, Humboldt omitted from his treatment his knowledge of incidents in which slaves claimed to be granted rights. Instead, he depicted Haiti as an entirely different story altogether. He called the newly born state the 'Kingdom of the Ethiopians' and he saw it as the possible core of

[12] Humboldt's diary 'Cuba 1804' is not yet published. See Paz 2000.

an 'African Confederation of the Free States of the Antilles'. Today, we would think Humboldt's characterizations as akin to the concept of 'Africa in America', that is the idea of a Caribbean Afro-America, or a 'black' Caribbean.[13]

Together with the coloured population of Cuba, enslaved and free, the Caribbean islands included more than 2 million people, as Humboldt correctly calculated. In the *Essai politique*, in fact, Humboldt talked of 2,360,000 coloured people, or 83 per cent of the Caribbean population, including Cuban slaves and free people of colour. In Brazil, instead, the estimates for the year 1819 gave a population of 1.1 million slaves and a population of 2.5 million free for a total of 3.6 million people.[14]

All in all, we can see the *Essai politique* on Cuba (and also on Haiti) as characterized by a type of politico-scientific and historical argument that sought to appeal to the slave owners. Humboldt mostly ignored the fact that Cuba was still a colony and the role that the Church, and religion in general, played in it. Humboldt interpreted the behaviour of the Cubans according to his own reasoning: according to him, if the Cuban elite did not change its practice of mass slavery with radical reforms, it was to suffer 'the revenge of the population of slaves', or what he called 'the bloody catastrophe(s)', referring to the fate of Saint Domingue. Humboldt counted on Francisco de Arango y Parreño, a congenial partner, to achieve this goal. Though for different reasons, Arango had, in fact, arrived to similar conclusions to the one that Humboldt had attained after twenty years of study. This was the main motive behind the friendly correspondence between the two, which went on even though Humboldt's essay on Cuba was banned from the island almost immediately after its publication.[15]

Humboldt's *Essai politique* deals with statistical comparisons – focusing on people, 'natural reproduction' and production of goods – in the same way as they are still dealt with in the twenty-first century, that is, in the context of the sociological and historical literature. Humboldt compared the overall numbers of the population of different areas and also the particular ratios of individual groups – slaves, free blacks, and whites – in Cuba, Jamaica, the British Antilles (today the British Caribbean[16]), in

[13] Humboldt 1826a: 64, 80–1; and Thrasher 2001: 124. [14] Marcílio 1987: 37–63.

[15] Humboldt 1826a: 64, 159; Thrasher 2001: 148; and Francisco Arango y Parreño to Humboldt, La Habana, 30 July 1827, Staatsbibliothek zu Berlin – Preuβischer Kulturbesitz, Handschriftenabteilung, Nachl. Alexander von. Humboldt, K 7b, Mp. 68.

[16] Engerman and Higman 1997: 47–57.

total, the 'Antilles-Archipelago', the USA, and Brazil. According to him, the highest ratio of slaves to the overall population was in Jamaica, where the population was divided between 85 per cent slaves, 10 per cent free blacks and 6 per cent whites. Then followed the British Antilles (with 81 per cent slaves, 10 per cent free blacks and 9 per cent white), Brazil (with 51 per cent slaves, 26 per cent free blacks and 23 per cent whites), Cuba (36 per cent slaves, 18 per cent free blacks, 46 per cent whites) and the USA (16 per cent slaves, 3 per cent free blacks, 81 per cent whites).

The explanation offered by Humboldt for the population ratios in the entire 'Antilles-Archipelago' (40 per cent slaves, 43 per cent free blacks, 17 per cent whites) was the following: 'one should not forget that, since the liberation of Haiti, there are more free Negroes and mulattoes than slaves in the entire Archipelago and the Antilles'.[17] He, then, particularly emphasized this point in connection with his argument on the need for reforms:

in the entire Archipelago of the Antilles, the coloured people (Negroes and mulattoes, free and slaves) make up a mass of 2,360,000 [individuals], or 83% of the total population. Soon, the legislation in Antilles and the legal status of coloured people ought to undergo positive developments. When one continues to draw attention to advice instead of acting, the political power falls into the hands of those who have the strength to work, the will to be free and the courage to endure continuous deprivations.[18]

In addressing the issues of the 'natural increase' of slave populations and of the slave trade, Humboldt came close to an explicit comparison between Cuba and Jamaica. The results of this comparison led Humboldt to believe in 'the advantage of the Spanish legislation and the customs of the residents of Cuba. The comparisons show [that there are] favourable circumstances vis-à-vis the physical treatment and the liberation of the Negroes on this island.' In short, Humboldt's conclusions agreed with those of modern historical studies by Frank Tannenbaum and Stanley Elkins.[19]

Then, Humboldt wrote a passage that Robert Fogel and Stanley Engerman, authors of *Time on the Cross*,[20] would have been glad to read:

it is impossible for me not to praise the treatment of Negroes in the southern part of the United States. At the same time, there is a certain generational

[17] Humboldt 1826a: 63–4. See also Thrasher 2001: 124.
[18] Humboldt 1826a: 64; and Thrasher 2001: 124.
[19] See Humboldt 1826a: 90–1; Thrasher 2001: 142–3; Tannenbaum 1946; and Elkins 1959. For a systematization of the historiography, see Kolchin 2003a; unfortunately, Kolchin does not refer to Humboldt.
[20] Fogel and Engerman 1974.

dimension to their tribulations. The [American] slave, who has a shack and a family, is not as unlucky as the one who is huddled within a [confined] space with others as if he belonged to a flock [here Humboldt implicitly refers to Cuba's *Barracones*]. The larger the number of those who live with their families in shacks which they consider theirs, the more settled the Negroes and the quicker their reproduction.[21]

In analysing the rate of reproduction of the slave population in the USA from 1780 to 1820, Humboldt noticed that it rose by '26 ‰'.[22]

Humboldt also made a specific comparison – the most extensive in the *Essai* – between sugar production and sugar 'export' in Cuba, Jamaica, Barbados, Granada (Grenada), Saint Vincent and Trinidad, the 'British Antilles', the 'French Antilles' and the 'Antilles-Archipelago', the British, Dutch and French Guyana, and Brazil. Not surprisingly, Louisiana only deserved a passing mention. Then, Humboldt compared the total figures with the figures for Saint Domingue in the years 1788, 1799, 1825. Around the year 1825, Haiti's sugar exports were 'close to zero'; at the same time, Brazil, Cuba, and Guyana, with their 2,526,000 slaves, exported three times as much sugar as Saint Domingue had done at the time of the latter's greatest productivity, in 1788.[23]

Humboldt engaged in further comparisons, some in relation to sugar prices and their fluctuations and some on the statistics arising from the different censuses taken in Cuba in the period 1784–1829. Humboldt also treated, albeit implicitly, the issue of transfers, especially when he talked about the internal organization of the plantations, the techniques utilized to process sugar, and in general the yields of the soil and the sugarcane; he did so also when he talked about the effects of the Saint Domingue Revolution on the different sugar-producing colonies of Europe, including Java. Of special interest are Humboldt's ideas on how to widen and secure the gentlemen's political cultures as these acted as transfers in the slave societies of the Americas. Equally interesting is Humboldt's comparison between the abolition of slavery in the 'new republics' – which had emerged in Latin America from the Creole wars for independence from Spain – and the situation in the south of the USA, where there were increasing numbers as a result of 'careless and perishable laws [the reference here is to the 1820 Missouri Compromise]'.[24]

[21] See Pérez de la Riva 1975; and Zeuske 2007. On traditional and written ownership rights in slavery, see Scott and Zeuske 2002: 669–99. See also Humboldt 1826a: 90–1; and Thrasher 2001: 142–3.

[22] Humboldt 1826a: 90–1. [23] Humboldt 1826a: 104; 100–6. [24] Humboldt 1826a: 154–9; 160–1.

THE HISTORICAL ORIGINS OF COMPARISON AND THE REPERCUSSIONS OF THE SAINT DOMINGUE REVOLUTION ON THE 'SECOND SLAVERY'

Until the nineteenth century, the Saint Domingue Revolution was mostly referred to as the cause of a 'great fear' (*grande peur*) for slave resistance and rebellion. Humboldt's writings were an exception, especially when, in his 1804 diary, he described the events in Saint Domingue as the 'liberation' of the slaves. He also wrote that 'terrorism ruled over the colonies in 1803' (*le terrorisme regnait en 1803 aux colonies*). By this, he meant the Jacobin 'terror' unleashed by the 'white' French Leclerc and Rochambeau as opposed to the fear induced by rebellious slaves. For his part, Francisco de Arango y Parreño, still considered the creator of the Cuban system of mass slavery, wrote that 'as the divine Providence brought the whip over France and [still] brings it on her nowadays [Arango here refers to the Saint Domingue Revolution]... the confusion and the disorder, which prevailed in her colonies, reduced their production and enhanced the value of ours'.[25]

As cold and calculating as he was, Arango thought that, to take advantage of the situation, certain measures needed to be taken: liberalization of the slave trade, revoking of the *Código Negro Español* (the 1789 slave laws, which were valid throughout the Spanish empire), accumulation of capital, free export and technological improvements of the sugar production in Cuba, and exploitation of scientific discoveries, particularly in the fields of botany and chemistry. Arango and Nicolás Calvo, together with the rest of the group of Humboldt's acquaintances, started to work on the concept of complete liberalization of the slave trade – and we might notice that they did this virtually next door to the place where the most important slave revolution in world history had occurred! As a consequence, the Spanish authorities promoted 'free trade' in slaves – while they also made plans for a 'white' immigration – but they restricted it to *muzzles* (*bozales*; black slaves from Africa) and excluded from it 'French' *ladinos* (slaves born in Saint Domingue).[26]

[25] Arango y Parreño 1952 (1792), I: 169. See also Humboldt 1826b; Callahan 1967: 177–205; Ferrer 2003b: 333–56, and 2003a: 675–93.

[26] 'Expediente relativo a las precauciones y seguridad a los negros en general y en particular a los introducidos de las colonias extranjeras' (1795–1801), Archivo Nacional de Cuba, La Habana (ANC), Real Consulado (RC), leg. 203, no. 8993; 'Expediente sobre prorroga de termino concedido por S.M. en Real Orden de 22 de Abril de 1804 para traer negros de la costa de Africa', fol. 1–3, ANC, RC, leg. 74, no. 2836. See also Arango y Parreño 1952 (1791), I: 111–12; Konetzke 1958–62, III: 643–52; González-Ripoll Navarro 1999: 205–22; Naranjo Orovio 1999: 121–38; Kuethe 1998 : 209–20.

At about this time, Cuban planters in Havana developed a strong interest in the exact disciplines, in science (mostly chemistry and botany), in safety measures, and in colonial demography. Despite the influence of the Saint Domingue experience, changes in slave law, with reference to the revolution, were rejected. The planters' power was clearly stronger than the crisis that gripped the empire. In fact, the planter's strategy had much more success than the strategy devised by the imperial elites of the Spanish metropolis to disable France's colonial competitors by conquering her most important colony, exploiting the weakness caused by the slave revolution.[27]

Thus, the Havana elites developed Cuba's sugar plantation economy by exploiting the same markets that had made the fortune of Saint Domingue. In the long run, this move resulted in a shift of the centre of gravity of these markets and in its replacement with North America. Both Nicolás Calvo, one of the largest and most influential plantation owners, and Arango tirelessly argued in favour of a stronger use of scientific methods for the improvement of the Cuban sugar economy and of its infrastructures.[28]

Similar to Cuba was the situation of Jamaica. Yet, barely forty years later, the British sugar island ended up committing what Seymour Drescher has called 'econocide', that is, a kind of 'economic suicide'. Cuba, instead, continued to have one of the most efficient agrarian economies in the world and her domination of the sugar markets remained relatively unchallenged until 1954. At the same time, Cuban culture remained centred upon both sugar production and slavery and developed its characteristics through an ideological spin, that is, through the manipulation of 'Haiti' as the very icon of fear. In 1792, Arango could rejoice in proclaiming that 'the era of our prosperity has arrived' (*la época de nuestra felicidad ha llegado*), a claim that did not conform to the general feeling of fear, silence, and confusion.[29]

The members of the elite who did engage in the exercise of comparison also acted as agents for cultural transfers. In general, gentlemen knew very well how to utilize comparative colonial demography – a type of precise sociologic and politico-scientific study, which inevitably resulted in an analysis of the causes of the Saint Domingue Revolution – to exercise their rule over those who served them, and sometimes also against their own motherland. In this connection, Manuel Moreno

[27] See Zeuske 2007; Yacou 1996: 277–93, and 1973: 73–80. [28] Puig-Samper 2000: 19–68.

[29] Arango y Parreño 1952 (1792), I: 134. See also Craton 1997: 161–84; Drescher 1977, 2002; Holt 1992; and Zeuske 2004a.

Fraginals, rather than speaking of cultural transfers, has talked about travels made by relatives of members of the Cuban sugar-growing elite to other countries and to other sugar- growing islands, primarily Saint Domingue – and, later, Haiti, in order to see if there was still competition to fear – but also Jamaica, Barbados, and even Portugal, because of the slave trade.[30]

As a result of his own residence in England, Arango became persuaded that the path to the future lay in technological progress based on mechanics and in the transformation of slavery in massive business through the slave trade. Arango's admiration for England seems to echo a later conclusion drawn by Marx, according to whom, when compared to the more industrialized countries, the less advanced countries looked inferior, because the latter only had a glimpse of their own future. From the purely historical point of view, this was and is truly incorrect; yet, the sugar-growing Creole patricians would have gladly made Cuba the Albion of Spanish America. In any event, the Cuban planters did bring with them, from their trips to Saint Domingue, French experts in the production of sugar, so that they could install their modern sugar industries.[31]

The year 1796 was one that aroused high feelings of insecurity, due to the prolonged revolution in Saint Domingue. In that year, a debate was held in the *Real Consulado* between advocates of a 'white immigration' (followers of General Captain Las Casas), advocates of the rise in the number of slave imports (followers of Arango), and advocates of the use of Mexican and Yucatan Indians (followers of the Marquis de Casa Peñalver), all categories who were to work under conditions of forced labour. In the end, Arango's ideas prevailed. Nicolás Calvo clearly saw the best side of the situation, even though war and revolution continued in Saint Domingue, when he wrote that:

> it will not be easy for the French to produce so quickly that volume of sugar, [simply] because their Negroes are in revolt and at war and for [a] long [time] work, obedience and order will be absent. The English no longer have even a fraction of good soil on their stony island that has not been cultivated already, and

[30] See González-Ripoll Navarro 2002: 85–101, and 2001: 291–305.

[31] See Arango y Parreño's travelogues in ANC: 'Expediente sobre las noticias comunicadas por el Sindico Don Francisco de Arango y Parreño, adquiridas en el viaje por encargo de S.M. ha hecho a Inglaterra, Portugal, Barbada y Jamayca', 30 September 1795, ANC, RC, leg. 92, no. 3923; and 'Expediente relativo a las noticias adquiridas por el Sindico de este cuerpo en Inglaterra y Jamayca, sobre refinerias de azucar', 28 October 1795, ANC, RC, leg. 93, no. 3924. See also Marx 1999 (1867–95).

so they will not be able to increase their production much more [than what they already have].[32]

The shock of the revolution in Saint Domingue is, however, not to be underestimated. It was as a consequence of the terror – which all the cultivated gentlemen had to endure in the greater Caribbean – that Simón Bolívar, a revolutionary aristocrat, had to relinquish his home and leave for Haiti in 1816. An English captain expressed correctly the opinion of his contemporaries, who knew of the explosive effects of the reality, symbol, and icon that Haiti represented, when he wrote that 'this alliance [the one between Pétion and Bolívar] opened the eyes of the nation about the true intentions of the leaders of the insurgents, and changed essentially the nature of things. It holds command upon the same people, but it is not the same party any longer'.[33]

This statement outlines, in general terms, the effects of the single successful revolution of slaves in world history in the Americas. The cultural transfers and the influences of the revolution upon people in other territories and of different classes and groups among the slave societies of the Caribbean were, of course, much more extensive, and also they expressed themselves through considerable politicization. Possibly, there was a revolutionary situation in the Caribbean between 1794 and 1798. Perhaps Humboldt had really sensed that a general revolution of slaves and free blacks was in the air shortly before his arrival in America. We have in fact only clues, and too little hard evidence, which tell us about the vision of the slaves – the other protagonists, besides the slaveholding elites, of the comparison between slave systems – since, naturally, all the slaves compared their situation with what they knew about Saint Domingue/Haiti. Yet, this spread of information did not generate either one or more successful large rebellions of coloured people. The slaveholding elites opted for a detailed and comparative analysis of the 'Haiti experience' and, through this, they constructed new mechanisms of domination. During the process, they made frequent use of the example of Haiti as the 'icon of fear', while they utilized the results of comparative political and scientific studies of slavery.[34]

32 'Informe de Nicolás Calvo' ; See also Naranjo Orovio 2000: 188. Humboldt mentioned the debates on reform and abolitionism; see Humboldt 1826a: 163–4.

33 Captain Stirling to Admiral Harvey, February 1817, quoted in Parra-Pérez 1954–7, II: 307. See also Geggus 2001.

34 See Geggus 1987: 274–99, 1997: 1–50, and 2003: 38–59.

SLAVERY'S DETERIORATION AND POWERFUL IDEAS: THE LONG SHADOWS OF THE REVOLUTION

To recapitulate, one could agree with David Geggus that 'the black Jacobin Toussaint Louverture and the revolution of Saint Domingue' – as C. L. R. James' famous title calls them – affected slavery's further development, both in the sense that it stimulated it and in the sense that it contributed to its decline. The question is only: which local, or regional, slave systems moved toward the deterioration and which ones moved toward further development within this 'big picture'? In this connection, one should notice that the shock of the slave revolution also led towards new forms of science, and specifically that of historical comparison within the framework of the contemporary political debates and of the contemporary politicization of history.

Arguably, deterioration hit, in any case, the French 'Pearl of the Antilles', as Saint Domingue was known – a change symbolized by its different name of Haiti – while also the export sector of Jamaica, the British 'Pearl of the Caribbean', was destroyed forever. After ten difficult years and a relatively short 'golden year' of Jamaican sugar production in the period 1805–20, the Saint Domingue Revolution affected favourably, in the long-term, the development of Cuban sugar production. The Spanish 'Pearls of the Antilles' carried for almost one hundred years the burden of agricultural, scientific, and financing centre of Spain's Atlantic empire. The example of the three islands of the Caribbean where slavery was employed on a large scale during the *Ancien régime* – Saint Domingue, Jamaica, and Cuba – shows the unfolding of three completely opposite decisions and paths taken in regard to future developments and also in regard to ways of bringing about emancipation or abolition.[35]

In Jamaica and in other islands of the British Caribbean, due to political and geo-strategic reasons, a process of restructuring through abolition, first of the slave trade, and somewhat later of slavery took place in the period 1808–1834/38. The causes of the abolition of both slave trade and slavery in the Atlantic part of the British empire were structural and political and were related to the wider context of the historical process. Thus, they had to do with the strategic retreat of the British empire from the Atlantic hemisphere; with soil depletion on the relatively small islands of the British West Indies (a phenomenon only partly balanced by the economic rise of British Guyana); and with the rise in the cost of man-power after the abolition of the British slave trade. As regard to the historic processes, but

[35] See Sivers 1861; and Gallenga 1873.

also in terms of performance, as Seymour Drescher has written, 'England contrived directly as a new global freedom-power from the spirit of conservatism and the radically heretic/unorthodox Protestantism. After the abolition of slave trade and slavery, arrived a ridge of high pressure for sugar production and finally – after a bloody slave rebellion 1831–1832 – an "*Econocide*".'[36]

The first act of slave emancipation in world history occurred between 1791 and 1803 in Saint Domingue. In Saint Domingue, the revolutionary outbreak took place because of both political and structural reasons, among which a shortage of land in the north of the island and a slow rate of development, mostly in the south. In this case, emancipation and abolition were enforced by the slaves themselves and by the (Jacobin) state by force. In the war, the military leaders of the free black population (Rigaud, Pétion, Boyer and others) ended up joining the black 'slave-generals'. Thus, in Haiti, a new nation arose, which was formed by the different populations of ex-slaves, free blacks, and free mulattoes and by those who, from the start, had arrived with the steady influx of immigrants from other slave societies. Also in other societies, such as Venezuela, where there were fewer black slaves and more free coloured, the experience of the equivalent of the *gens de coleur* resembled that of Saint Domingue during the revolution. As a consequence, Haiti developed as a state (or, rather, a series of states) in its own right. At the same time, Haiti became an Atlantic icon of fear for slaveholders – an image whose construction related to the image of the Haitian situation of 1804. This image led to the resurgence of racist feelings, while, as a consequence, slavery itself became politicized.[37]

However, for the former Haitian slaves, the main achievement of the revolution was not the creation of either a new state or a constitution. The main achievements were freedom and ownership of land; thus, former male and female slaves, mostly those who lived in the republic of Haiti headed by Pétion and Boyer, benefited from the destruction of great plantations and of landowners' power. The revolution of the slaves led to one of the greatest rearrangements of land property that history ever witnessed. This rearrangement was really started by Pétion, and continued by Boyer, but, later, it was only partly controlled by the elites of the new state. Together with the land, the now free Haitians could preserve their life and that of their families and could leave behind their experience of life in

[36] See Viotti da Costa 1994; Drescher 1977; Craton 1997; and Davis 1975.

[37] Trouillot 1995: 70–107.

bondage; unconsciously, but very effectively, they relied on the island's underdevelopment to maintain their familiar culture of subsistence.[38]

Even before the developments in Saint Domingue/Haiti, other parts of the old island of Hispaniola had been strongly affected by the deterioration of the slave system and by a general change in the shape of the state. Haitian armies conquered the Spanish part of Hispaniola, proclaimed the abolition of slavery, and unified the two parts of the island in 1822. Then, in 1844, Santo Domingo, the old Spanish part of the island, was decolonized in a conservative way and from this act ensued an enduring crisis between the 'white' elites and the mulatto majority of the population.[39]

In Cuba, under the influence of the Napoleonic wars, the extreme liberalization of economic policies by the Spanish crown went to the advantage of Havana's Creole elite and led to the virtual collapse of the imperial states' operation of order. The colonial elite took its chances with the production of sugar, one of the booming industries of the second episode of globalization. Immediately, it became clear to the elites that the demographic patterns of Jamaica and Saint Domingue were not going to be repeated; for this reason, they planned with the crown the establishments of 'small', 'white', Cubas. Fundamentally, the Creole elite remained voluntarily on the island in a colonial status. A similar pattern arose in Puerto Rico, between 1820 and 1850, with, on one hand, a sugar economy even more booming and, on the other hand, a strong coffee sector. The Caribbean elites in Puerto Rico were even stronger than the 'imported elites' in Cuba. To them, Spain had little power left to bargain on the interests of the colonial elites. Sugar economy and mass slavery became, thus, ubiquitous in the Spanish Caribbean economic structure from 1820 until 1886, even though in Puerto Rico, the crisis in sugar production started as early as 1850; the exception was, since 1822, Saint Domingue.[40]

Broadly speaking, the delay of the revolution of Saint Domingue affected the development of slavery in Nueva Granada (later Colombia) and Venezuela, both already in crisis beforehand. The elites there became, so to speak, pre-emptive about the movement of autonomy against Spain, so to eventually anticipate the uprising of the Pardos, following the example of Haiti.[41]

In the long term, the revolution in Saint Domingue stimulated and affected the development of slavery in the new Southern Interior of the

[38] Fick 1998: 1–15. [39] See San Miguel 1997.

[40] See Díaz Soler 1965; Scarano 1984; and Picó 1993; and Martínez-Fernández 2002: 91–115.

[41] See Zeuske 2004b: 154–90

USA. Here, the Jamaican (centre) and Louisiana (periphery) types of slavery, although similar in regard to the politico-legal conditions at least until 1820, led to completely separate ways under the influence of Saint Domingue. This can be seen in the integration of different political systems, the demographic patterns, the economic areas, and the forms of resistance and legal orders that characterized them.[42]

Finally, Saint Domingue also stimulated sugar production in Bahia and Pernambuco until around 1840, while, later, it also affected coffee production in southern Brazil. Brazil became part of a cultural area in which Haiti played and still plays a very important role as an icon of fear and as a real standard against which to measure slave rebellions and slave conspiracies.[43]

In the background of these three distinctive paths to modernization through mass slavery in Cuba, Louisiana, and Brazil, upswings occurred also in Puerto Rico and Vieques, Martinique and Guadeloupe, British Guyana, Danish Saint-Thomas (in relation to the slave trade), Swedish Saint-Barthélémy, and Dutch Surinam. As part of the reflux occurring after the 'era of democratic revolutions' (1789–1848) and also as a result of the breakdown of Jamaica, a highly state regulated slavery in the Dutch region was maintained for a particularly long time. By 1850, it had become clear – mostly as a result of the success of a great 'modern' land economy based on mass slavery in the USA – that 'nation', modern republicanism, and slavery were imaginable and attainable together. This is the reason Cuba also experienced a movement in favour of the so-called 'annexation', essentially an attempt carried out by parts of the planter elites to join the southern states.[44]

These episodes were not always cultural transfers, but rather symptoms of a real failure in the relationship between producer and competitor, since they denoted the not completely voluntary transfer of 'market shares', and people and capital, together with that of objects of study for matters of security questions and icons of fear that could be easily manipulated. In terms of these transfers, thus, Saint Domingue became an agent of acceleration in the development of the three paths of development to modernization including mass slavery in the Atlantic American space. As a result, the road was clear for the development of the nineteenth-century black Caribbean. Its centres were no longer the coastal plains of relatively small

[42] See Berlin 2003: 163–209; see also map at 160. See also Tadman 2000: 1534–75; and Berlin 2003.

[43] See Reis 2003; Vidal Luna and Klein 2003; Reis and Gomes 1996; Gomes 1999: 225–318, 2003b: 253–87, 2003a; and Del Priore and Gomes 2003.

[44] See Scarano 1984; Dorsey 2003; Tomich 1990, 2004: 120–36; Oostindie 1995; and Kellenbenz 1966: 152–74.

islands, but, rather, large valleys and savannas, larger islands, coastal plains in the Mexican gulf, and vast continental areas in the Mississippi valley. To the slavery landscape belonged also large rivers, such as the Mississippi, and sophisticated cities, such as Havana, Matanzas, and New Orleans. All of them acquired an even closer connection with the larger 'seascape' of the Atlantic.

In terms of both historical structure and culture, the case becomes relatively clear, when one compares with one another the works of Ira Berlin, Dale W. Tomich, and Peter Kolchin. According to all of them, in the second half of the eighteenth century, as in the entire American continent with the exception of Saint Domingue, Jamaica, and Cuba, in North America also, there was a crisis of the traditional types of slavery present on islands and coasts. Three slave systems had been developed in British America, later USA, under the favourable terms of the massive request for unskilled manual labour in the peripheries of the second globalization. In the North, the northern non-plantation system of the New England type stood in sharp contrast to the Virginian type 'old slavery' system centred around Chesapeake Bay. In the South, the plantation system of the Carolina/Georgia/Florida type was formed by a 'rice belt' (also partially cultivated with indigo) that stretched from the Carolina Lowcountry to Georgia and as far as Florida, or from Cape Fear in North Carolina to St Johns River in western Florida. It is what Ira Berlin has conceptualized with the term 'seaboard South'.[45]

In the lower Mississippi valley arose a new booming zone in the slave economy: the 'southern interior'. This new area was roughly divided into a very small sugar zone in the southern parishes around New Orleans and a very large cotton district that spread over the states of Louisiana, Arkansas, Mississippi, Alabama and Georgia, and later other states. Louisiana's newly acquired slave system, in particular, was started in the first instance by Louisiana Creoles and Acadians, but was soon taken over by the Americans. As a result of these changes, the old centres of slavery in North America became double peripheries, both in relation to the world market and in relation to the new core area in the South, while New Orleans turned into a metropolis built with the profits of a new, internal, slave trade within the USA.[46]

45 See Tomich 1988: 103–17, 2003: 4–28, Tomich 2004; Morgan 1998; and Landers 2000b.

46 See Berlin 1980: 44–78, 2003: 160 (see especially the map); Tomich 1988: 103–17, 1991: 297–319; Kolchin 1993; and Tomich 1997: 67–80; 140–63. See also Scarano 1984 and Kolchin 2003a (for a definition of 'South'); for a case-study, see Dunaway 2003; and Johnson 2004.

Within the territories that later included the heart of the slave states in the South of the USA, the model of slavery that developed at the beginning – the Louisiana type – was strongly influenced by Saint Domingue. Its centre was Louisiana, where French who had been removed from Cuba in 1809 joined a fairly large number of migrants from Jamaica. Planters in Louisiana turned fairly quickly to sugar as their main product and this remained an important product even later next to 'King Cotton'. All these immigrants engaged, in one way or another, in some sort of historical comparison, while, through their experiences, *entanglings* and *transfers*, through their life stories and relationships with people, they were themselves the embodiment of *histoire croisée*. We know a great deal about these 'comparisons' they engaged in, but, aside from them, male and female slaves also must have done the same. About this, we know almost nothing.[47]

It was the increasing demand of cotton and stimulants, such as sugar and coffee, that had made large-scale slavery efficient and profitable. However, the institution of slavery, which the 'Founding Fathers' of the American Republic protected in the Constitution of the United States with a rhetoric derived from the Enlightenment, was soon to become unfashionable as a foundation for modernization. In this context, the transfers appear especially clear, despite, or perhaps because of, the comparative perspectives embedded in the respective national historiographies. Slavery and slave trade were trans-national and even cosmopolitan in their structure and in their relation to the cultural world to which they belonged, both of them shaped by the masters, as Humboldt's work attests; slavery, in particular, was both trans-local, often concealed, and local in the specific slave cultures that it originated.

In these cases, slavery functioned as an agent of transfer of an economic culture that moved from Saint Domingue to Cuba, to Louisiana, and later also from the English-speaking North American areas to Louisiana, together with a prosperous internal slave trade, which moved along the Mississippi and from the East to the Southwest. In total, slaves were sold and bought two million times in the entire pre-Civil War period. The new type of slavery that arose in the South of the USA probably originated from these transfers. In this sense, the USA, or at least the coastal and estuary

[47] See Zeuske 2006b; Debien and Wright 1975: 3–216; Cauna 1994: 333–59; and Meadows 2000: 67–102. On the reasons for emigration from Saint Domingue, see Nash 1998: 44–73; and White 2003: 103–21.

regions in the South and the trade and port cities on the East Coast, were also part of the black Caribbean.[48]

However, as a result of the revolution of Saint Domingue and the manifold transfers that it generated, from this very region came also an idea of 'a Caribbean', and indeed 'an Atlantic of freedom', which simply overcame the traditional localism of initiatives of resistance against slavery. The ideas of equality that arose from the Saint Domingue Revolution were very radical and militant and their influence continued at least until the Cuban War of Independence of 1895–8 and later.

SLAVERY AND COMPARISON TODAY: ENTANGLING HISTORY, *HISTOIRE CROISÉE*, TRANSFERS AND COMPARISONS

What does 'historical comparison' mean today? This issue has clearly changed in shape with the current trend of abandoning the study of slavery in terms of structures and types to focus on the slaves themselves as individuals and participants. Yet, if we take into account the historical dimension of the participants, historical comparisons in these terms today seem to have a lot in common with the ideas and writings of Arango and Humboldt, who, in some sense, had initiated them.[49] In other words, historical comparison was there from the beginning. The biggest difference in terms of content between the works written in 1800 and those written in 2007 is probably that in 1800 somebody like Humboldt did not treat the USA as a fundamental part of his study, while today the USA are essential to every historical study of slavery.

Secondly, today's historical method has to solve the difficult problem of comparing different spaces, or landscapes, of slavery – an operation which, under certain circumstances, could act as a deductively configured framework – including, at the same time, the slave participants' mobility and agency, as well as the information flow that occurred between them. Eventually, such an operation should also include the slaves' respective world-views.

Thirdly, today, it hardly seems meaningful to reflect upon trans-cultural operations without the benefit of comparison. The foundation of every comparison is still always a deductive approach through which to arrive at a development of types and typologies – or 'forms', 'formations', 'structures' – so to be able to discover similarities. In the German tradition,

[48] See Johnson 2000: 1–18, 2004; May 1973, and 1995.
[49] Middell 2000: 7–40; Werner and Zimmermann 2003: 36–77; and Zeuske 2006b: 297–360.

'comparisons' (*Vergleichen*) have to do with the 'same' (*gleich*) – a term which really means either 'same' or 'similar,' according to the context. This notion of construction of types derives implicitly from the idea that, under similar conditions, in different places, something similar arises; this is even harder to carry out in the case of comparison between similar types at different times ('structural comparison'). In order to even begin a comparison, anything that, through a deductive operation, can be classified as similar must be always considered, or perhaps even feared. This is regardless of whether the method adopted is historico-political/scientific, as in the case of Arango, or whether it is particularly elaborate from the scientific point of view, or including both a politico-scientific and a historic dimensions, as in the case of Humboldt.

Without the fundamental 'similarities' that can be inferred through these methods, there is no comparison. No one commences such an operation expecting only to find differences. Yet, it is possible to discover differences by analysing specific phenomena or their contexts that, at the outset, are classified as 'same' or 'similar'. In so far as the comparison does seem to be distinctive and a sub-area of the transfer analysis, then Jürgen Osterhammel's sentence describes it well: 'no transfer [occurs] without a perception of difference'.[50]

Construction of types is a recognized sociological method; when, however, both construction of types and typology depreciate the empirical-anthropological point of view privileging, instead, a completely philosophic or rather abstract method, only a bad, or a very limited, explicit type of comparison is possible. The theme of the comparison should have the same effect of a weapon, or of an instrument that can be found in different cultures, and thus it could be something like 'the effects of different slave systems on male slaves or female slaves, and how they relate together in cross-cultural fashion'. This understanding of historical comparison, in fact, is very close to the idea of cultural transfer and to the study of cultural perceptions, although the elements of comparisons here play also an implicit role. Today, comparison no longer includes just construction of types. Instead, it focuses as well on the historical succession of events, on the passing of time, and on both development and structure, together with the very world-views in which the 'types' are developed and in which they interact. These are equally components of a comparative historical study as the participants, and the constructors, and their experiences in different respects.[51]

[50] See Osterhammel 2003: 439–66; 443. [51] See Tomich 2004: 120–36.

More importantly, the perspectives have changed in several respects since 1800: the post-colonial view now perceives as the main participants in historical events the slaves, no longer the local elites, or the structures, or the classes, as Humboldt thought. To be sure, the slaves were more or less bound to the different places where they were, in particular houses, or in the plantations of their masters. Yet, from there they succeeded in affecting in different ways the process of cultural formation in the emerging nations of the Americas. This was, in essence, the foundation of the Afro-American culture. At the same time, the slaves preserved hidden information, memory, and culture of one or more traditions and world-views – such as Islam and some form of animism – which became, then, trans-local ahead of time as a result of the Atlantic slave trade. The process of 'creolization' started in Africa and was at the basis of a diaspora, which was all centred on that continent. With this observation, we can introduce another perspective within the historical analysis: that of the micro-history, or the dimension of the particular experiences that different participants had at different levels within the Atlantic macro-space.[52]

As a fourth point, we might add that we now reflect critically upon the past through post-colonialism. In practice, the reflexive attitude derives, to a large extent, from methodological features related to the concept of '*transculturación*' – a concept influenced by both the ideas of *transferts culturels* and of *histoire croisée*. Material of this type can be found also in older studies that focused on 'stories of relationships', keeping a philosophical basis of evaluation, and in equally old travel literature as well. In the field of study that researches on diaspora, things are in reverse; here, the starting point is, rather commonly, a more ethnic, more linguistic, and more cultural type of essentialism, sometimes as an answer to the American based slave studies which tend to give a non-historical view of West Africa. Then comes the investigation of the process of '*transculturación*' (or hybridization) and, only afterwards (if at all), historical comparisons, which are treated mostly in terms of transfers of culture, or as comparisons of situations before and after, as well as of interactions between them from both temporal and special points of view.[53]

[52] See Scott 2001: 181–216, 2002: 191–209; Zeuske 2002a: 235–66; Rubin and Tuden 1977; Moulier-Boutang 1998; Mintz and Price 1992; and Lovejoy 2000a: 1–29.

[53] See Coronil 1995: IX–LVI; Werner and Zimmermann 2004; Kilson and Rotberg 1986; Terborg-Penn *et al.* 1987; Lewis 1995: 765–87; Lovejoy and Law 1997: 181–200; Desch-Obi 2000; Mann 2001: 3–21; Heywood 2002; Lovejoy and Trotman 2002; Edwards 2003; Falola and Childs 2004; Law 1997: 205–19; Lovejoy 2004b: 1–29. See also Lovejoy and Law 1997; Lovejoy 2004c: 40–55; and Price 2006: 115–47.

As a fifth and final point, we should notice that, within the slave cultures and the histories of the slaves' lives, we look both at the middle level in terms of structures and landscapes – thus, for example plantations and their development – and at the macro level – thus, at seas and seascapes, continents, and ideologies ('big picture'). In this perspective, nations and states become rather secondary. Yet, a comparison understood as such comes without the enrichment that the idea of cultural transfer can offer, thus without the benefit of looking at the trans-local and trans-national, since everything needs to be 'before the nation', and thus without a proper look at networks, let alone a reflexive discourse. In this sense, the history of historical constructions through comparative perspectives, such as those, is relatively undisputed. These are mostly colonial perspectives, which often present the slaves only as victims, or perspectives that concentrate on structures and on the masters' cultures, or perspectives that often explain slavery through the logic of economic systems, but neither of them seeks to understand the point of view of the slaves as participants.

The starting point for comparative analysis and its adjustments is the revolution of Saint Domingue. A rather discursive and scientific type of comparison focusing on this event preceded implicit historic comparison in the work of prominent members of the planter elites, such as Francisco de Arango y Parreño in regard to Jamaica and Portugal, and also in the communications between male and female slaves and free blacks and coloured. Historical comparisons that focus on the lives of protagonists and prominent travellers or artists, who engaged with the problems of their time as contemporaries, commonly taking the side of the slaveholding elites as to theoretical culture and historical perception, and incorporate relations between different peoples and groups, involve an implicit type of comparison.[54]

This implicit type of comparison, or 'entangled history', or *histoire croisée*, is ubiquitous – mostly in the format of 'reports' and 'travels' – at this particular time and in the traditional historical depictions of it. The problem of race, for example, is one of the most important features of slave societies, most of all in post-emancipation societies; it was from the latter's perspective that comparative histories of slavery were often written. Most of the male, and female, travellers, or even historians, who engaged in comparison in the late eighteenth and early nineteenth centuries, kept as

[54] To be sure, explanatory history and comparison are close, being both highly theoretical and very static. See González-Ripoll Navarro 2002: 85–101; Ferrer 2003b: 333–56, 2003a: 675–93; and Gonzalez-Ripoll Navarro *et al.* 2005.

starting point the idea of European and 'white' hegemony together with the mystified myth of the 'races'. All these writers constructed their comparisons according to such criteria. Thus, the true meaning of post-colonialism needs to be sought therein, as an answer to these works. The new basis for comparison in the history of both slave societies and post-emancipation societies has, in fact, focused on a critique of those race constructions that has generated an even larger body of works.[55]

As for Humboldt, he compared Cuba with all the most important slave societies of his time, aside from the US South which was not yet fully formed, in the period 1825–30. In terms of method, he used mostly a mathematical approach, with demography and statistics. However, his systemic-scientific comparison remained rather an exception in his own time, since historical comparison done through travel continued to be the most popular. To be sure, a reason could have been also that the earlier scientific operations of 'comparison' around 1825–30 dissented completely from the two pre-eminent evolving methods of historical writing: Leopold von Ranke's historicism and Hegel's dialectic and history of philosophical ideas.[56]

Contemporaries and travellers compared, most of all, Saint Domingue with Cuba, then Cuba with Jamaica and, after 1850, Cuba with the US South, or vice versa – this latter type of comparison was also common as a result of the different options for a travel route, as Humboldt had already maintained, in his letter to Willdenow. Or else, travellers compared Brazil with other continental Spanish colonies, though this was rather rare, since Brazil was also mostly considered an exception, due to its sheer size. Interestingly, Ulrike Schmieder, who carried out research on travelling women and their views on slavery, race, and gender, visited most of the slave societies that we have discussed here: the US South, Cuba, and the Northeast and Southeast of Brazil, with the cities of Bahia, Recife, Rio, and São Paulo.[57]

In historical terms, it is Cubans such as José Antonio Saco, who condemned the slave trade and defended slavery, who have mostly opened up comparative perspectives that are still valid despite their relativity. Saco used as his argument to explain the existence of slavery its presence within the same types of historical dimensions – the Roman and Greek worlds – that

[55] See Hannaford 1996; Berlin 1998: 1–14; Hodes 2003: 84–118; Degler 1971; and Marx 1998.

[56] See Zeuske 2001a: 30–83, 2001b, and 2002b.

[57] Moheit 1993: 124. See Pérez Jr 1992, 1999: 24–38; and Schmieder 2003. On three slave systems – Brazil, Mexico, and South Carolina – in relation to the question of 'Why African Slavery?', see Menard and Schwartz 1993: 89–114.

were still popular in gentlemanly culture in the era of Enlightenment and at the time of the abolitionist movements. Saco examined particularly Brazil. He referred to similarities in structure and politics, as well as in the behaviour of the elite. Saco considered the presence of that giant empire as a form of 'protection' for the system that kept slavery intact in his own world. Even more meaningful was the idiosyncratic search of other writers for imperial slipstreams, naturally with a particular regard to the USA, which were often set against Great Britain. In time, a critical perspective of slavery emerged in reaction to the position of representatives of British interests, such as Richard Madden.[58]

The Brazilian Executives followed, in a way, the Spanish-Cuban political and legislative guidelines with the interdiction of the slave trade in 1845 in Cuba and in 1850 in Brazil. Then, with the *Ley Moret* and the *Lei Rio Branco* – the so-called laws of the 'free womb' – the children of slaves were to be free from a certain age in 1870 in Cuba and in 1871 in Brazil. Finally, slavery was abolished in Cuba in 1886 and in Brazil in 1888 respectively. In systemic terms, exchange, transfers, and comparisons often underwent disturbances caused by Great Britain.[59]

Scientific types of historical comparison in the USA have been mostly linked to the work of Frank Tannenbaum and Stanley Elkins. Both, along with other scholars, based their research on the writings of Alexander von Humboldt, Fernando Ortiz, and Gilberto Freyre and argued mostly in reaction either to the thought of Ulrich B. Phillips, within the USA, or of Fernando Ortiz and Gilberto Freyre, outside the USA. To be sure, the earliest works of this kind were the product of black intellectuals such as W. E. B. DuBois and anthropologists such as Melville Herskovits, Sidney Mintz, and Eric R. Wolf. Great sociological and historically informed syntheses of slavery through the ages, with strong comparative elements, then followed, notably with the work of David Brion Davis and Orlando Patterson.[60]

A type of socio-historical mid-level comparison was further developed by Herbert S. Klein in his work on Virginia and Cuba and in his great panorama of slavery in Latin America and the Caribbean. An altogether

[58] Saco 1961 (1832), II: 71–2. Saco also wrote a history of slavery; see Saco 1982 (1862–74). See also Paquette 1997: 204–25. Richard Madden criticized the argument about the relative mildness of Cuban slavery; see Madden 1849: 142.

[59] See Eltis and Walvin 1981; Engerman 1995: 223–41; and Chalhoub 1989: 64–84. See also Bethell 1970; and Drescher 1988: 429–60.

[60] See Tannenbaum 1946; and Elkins 1959. On the debates, see Fuente 2004a: 229–69 and Fuente 2004c. See also Phillips 1908, 1963; Ortiz 1906, 1916, 1940a, 1940b: 273–8; Freyre 1946 (1933); Davis 1975; Patterson 1982, 1991; Davis 2000: 452–84, and 2006.

different type of comparison is found in the work of Peter Kolchin who has argued in favour of the study of self-contained cases in a somewhat narrow way. His particular comparison was surely based on his earlier experiences of contemporaneous, but genetically unconnected, systems of work enforcement. In Stanley L. Engerman's work it is also possible to find examples of self-contained, 'external', macro-comparisons.[61]

More to the point, methodical historical comparison of slave systems has been practised by Alain Yacou in regard to the Spanish and French Antilles, Dale Tomich in regard to Martinique and Cuba, and Barry Higman in regard to North America and the Caribbean. These macro-comparisons have also been tied together in a global view through the use of Marx-Williams' thesis on 'primary accumulation', no longer employed by European scholars, but still popular in the United States, where it actually originated. Also part of the historians' research culture is the rhetorical image of 'free' labour as characteristic of the centres of capitalist development, where work legislation, though, still continued to have features of legal quasi-enslavement, while production of resources took place through a system of actual slavery, only contractual.[62]

Even more rare are comparative studies whose focus originates from the experiences of the slaves as participants, studies which include examples of *histoire croisée* and show a micro-level perspective of life lived by participants on the macro-structures, but also on concrete 'landscapes of slavery'. Also very rare, but somewhat wider, are panoramas of slavery in the Americas focused on different parts of the system: division of labour, methods of control, structures, plantations and architectures – such as studies of wooden huts of slaves in west Africa, Brazil, and Cuba – and processes – such as abolition and emancipation with the respective laws.[63]

Cuba plays only a marginal role in the present day research on the Diaspora. Yet, complete silence on transition societies such as today's Columbia and Venezuela, or even Guyana does not appear a viable option. A truly critical post-colonial history should not just analyse the interweaving of trans-cultural and trans-local and the interlinking of slave regions or slave landscapes in the Americas. First and foremost, it should analyse the hidden interweaving of slave cultures and the 'reflux' of former slaves in the

[61] See Klein 1967, 1986; Engerman 1996: 18–41; Kolchin 1987, 1990: 351–67, and 1996: 42–67. For Kolchin's ideas on comparisons, transfers, and reflexive entanglings, see Kolchin 2003a: 2–6, 74–115.

[62] See Yacou 1987: 287–305; Tomich 2004: 120–36; Higman 2002: 9–23; Mörner 1992, I: 347–63; Mörner 1993: 57–87; Mann 2003: 7–22; Klein 1994: 197–220; Blackburn 1997; and Van der Linden 2003.

[63] See Scott and Zeuske 2002: 669–99, 2004: 521–45; Zeuske 2004b; and Marquese 2004.

transatlantic space in connection with the participants to those cultures: slaves, former slaves, slave traders, sea people, sailors, outlaws, ostracized rebels, ship doctors, travellers, soldiers, Atlantic-Creoles, and even plants, animals, and pathogens. At the same time, such a history should also analyse the social dynamics of the multi-fold master–slave relationships. Some specific features of the behaviour of slaves from areas influenced by Islam – areas in which arose specific traditions of manumission, military service, patron–client relationship, or attempts to use writing – are potentially explained through examples and transfers, issues which in American studies are not commonly taken into account.[64]

The complex connection among all these relationships formed the historical basis of the so-called 'globalization', today so successful and usually presented as if it were only a western, technological, 'post'-modernity. In reality, 'globalization' revolves around a post-colonial, and in some cases even still colonial, type of trans-locality, which must include even the last of the Pacific islands, and certainly Africa, within its concept of 'modern'. This interweaving was characterized by a thick grid of exchange relationships and back and forth movements to and from the basis, not always possible to be described as the usual arrows going from Africa to America on the maps of the traditional depictions of slavery and the slave trade.[65]

Translocation and transculturation to some degree are undermining the tendency to typify. Then, the interweaving has also to be analysed in the sense of a trans-cultural space characterized by the slaves' concealed African-American culture, by the presence of slave traders and Atlantic creoles, by the 'material culture', and, as well, by the impact of the 'creolization' of specific groups of people. Such a space should not be analysed just as an Anglo-American 'Black Atlantic', although the original idea is correct and shows how far scholars can reach keeping in mind trans-cultural transfers, or as an 'English plantation America', with numbers and economic cultures as the ultimate criteria for comparison. Historiographic imperialisms of this type are, unfortunately, widespread. Even the best researchers of slavery are not completely free from them.[66]

[64] Among the exceptions, see especially Mann 2001: 3–21. See also Verger 1968; Sarracino 1988; Berlin 1998: 17–28; Crosby 1994; Ortmayr 2004: 73–99; and Lovejoy 2004a: 233–62.

[65] See Freitag 2005.

[66] See Linebaugh and Rediker 2000; Brooks 1994; Bartens 1994; Lienhard 2001; Van der Linden 2003; Curto and Lovejoy 2004; Berlin 1998: 251–88; Zeuske 2006a: 9–44; Eltis 2000: 193–223, Drescher 2004: 31–69; and Gilroy 1993. A well-done critique of 'historiographic imperialism' is in Craton 1997: 161–84.

CUBA AND THE UNITED STATES

Frank Tannenbaum was not correct in his comparison between the USA and Cuba, at least not in regard to the sources he used and the ideas he held as given, most of all because he simply did not include within his study the slave culture itself, and thus the male and female slaves as participants. Still, Tannenbaum had referred to a set of elements, which are, nonetheless, the subject of contemporary comparative research: the role of the law and of particular institutions and the duration of transition from the status of slave to that of citizen, among others. For his part, then, in his comparison of Virginia and Cuba, Herbert Klein had compared the proverbial equivalent of apples and oranges, mostly because of the great differences between tobacco and sugar and because Virginia was at its peak in the seventeenth and eighteenth centuries, while Cuba reached it only in the nineteenth century. A similar case is that of Gwendolyn Midlo Hall's acclaimed comparison between Saint Domingue and Cuba.[67]

In general, Cuba in the period between 1800 and 1840, and also later, should not be compared to the USA. Before 1840, Cuba – as part of the Spanish colonial empire – was far more important than the slave regions of the USA, which were at the periphery of global history. Afterwards, however, Cuba's significance was simply too small. The differences in size and power became clear from around 1850: the USA and Brazil were the giant slave societies, while Cuba was little more than a small part of a colonial empire. Cotton, coffee, or tobacco, and sugar were worlds apart. Thus, the two cultures of slavery that they produced could not, and cannot, be analysed as clearly separate entities in self-contained comparisons. Nevertheless, many contemporary travellers, such as Ulrike Schmieder, have compared the US South with Cuba. On one hand, this was a result of the pragmatic 'model-search' engaged in at that time by comparers, individuals who often originated from the elite cultures and wished to show their particular political liabilities, that is how much more politically aware one elite was compared to another. This is the idea behind John S. Trasher's 1856 publication of Humboldt's essays on Cuba in the USA. On the other hand, comparisons served the purpose of stressing the differences between different slave systems.[68]

[67] On the debate over Tannenbaum, see Fuente 2004a: 339–69. See also Klein 1967; Sio 1965: 289–308; and Hall 1972.

[68] See Schmieder 2003; and Thrasher 2001.

If one wishes to engage in a practice of research that takes into account all the levels of analysis – space, structures, social history, and quantities – self-contained types of comparisons between the USA, Brazil, and Cuba after 1850 are virtually impossible. It is better to utilize implicit comparisons placing transfers and networks in the foreground. Explicit comparisons are possible only if one chooses selected, partial themes, such as *Cuba grande* ('greater' Cuba) and sugar-cultivated Louisiana, as the work of Rebecca J. Scott shows, going from 'external' comparison to the micro-historic life histories – 'play of levels', partly in relation to different 'landscapes of slavery'. The results of this implicit type of comparison usually show some similarities, but, most of all, fundamental differences, such as the well-known ones in regard to racial issues.[69]

Rebecca Scott is also known for having been the first to dare an implicit comparison of slavery in the sugar producing regions of Cuba, Brazil, and Louisiana in the immediate aftermath of emancipation, incorporating actual connections into her narrative. Through her empirical work, one becomes aware that it is only possible to carry out meaningful comparisons between Louisiana and Cuba, by all means and purposes two relatively small and compact sugar-growing worlds (*mundos donde crece la caña*), mostly because of the similarity in scale and material and, thus, of their effects on the lives of individual participants. Of these similar and inter-connected worlds, also the trans-cultural and interwoven life histories of many participants of slavery – participants of the strife against slavery and colonialism, as well as of the post-emancipation struggles – were an integral part.[70]

The continental US South, planted mostly with cotton, and its variations had, instead, a completely different culture. Most of all, the problems one faces in studying it are related to the size and origin of the slave population, to the scale of the continental space – which was continuously enlarged by the employment of railway and steamboats, products of the industrial revolution – to the difference in sizes and types of location, as in the case of the Mississippi fields, and also to the number of structures essential for the presence of slavery, thus planters and plantations. All these problems make a coherent type of comparison certainly not impossible, but very expensive to carry out. To this, one should add the fact that the elites in power in Cuba – first the slave traders and later the rich merchants and the imperial elites – as a result of the transatlantic slave trade and of imperial

[69] See Scott 1987: 565–83, and 1994: 70–102. [70] See Drescher 1988: 429–60.

corruption – were much wealthier and much more powerful than the elites of the US South.[71]

The sugar-growing elites of Cuba also had an advantage in the technology which was thirty to fifty years ahead of the one employed by the Brazilian coffee and sugar elites. They turned a substantially rural sugar culture, and with it a series of dynamic state-based economies centred on Havana, Matanzas, Cárdenas and Cienfuegos, and, until around 1850, also Trinidad and Santiago de Cuba, into an unparalleled slave region in the western world: *Cuba grande*. It was unparalleled, most of all, in its combination of cultural, social, religious, political and technological dynamics in a relatively narrow geographical space – dynamics typical of a large island. *Cuba grande* came to be seen, thus, as the most efficient slave system in modern history, after 1820; but, in reality, this was so only in relative terms. In absolute numbers, *Cuba grande* did not come even close to the size and level of production of slavery in the United States or southeast Brazil after 1850. Between 1830 and 1840 a *Cuba grande* myth of supremacy of the island, placed in a strategic position, became widespread because of the power and influence of its elite, and this myth had a lasting effect until the present day.

More to the point in regard to *Cuba grande*, the slave culture of the island of Cuba – which actually includes within itself five or six different slave cultures, and sugar regions as well (Havana-Matanzas, Trinidad, Cienfuegos, Sagua, etc.) together with the dynamic cultures of the free coloured and the free blacks – is simply not comparable to that of the USA, especially if one focuses on the study of slaves individually recognized as participants. Early racism in Cuba has been formulated theoretically in sharper and clearer tones than in the USA; this was, however, the result of a politicization of social categories and historical constructions and could not prevail as such. Racism in twentieth-century Cuba has been always inclusive; it has never given way to white supremacy.[72]

Slave cultures alone – which in the USA are mostly Creole, while in Cuba include a large number of different Bozal cultures, as well as Afro-Cuban slave cultures – are not comparable, with the exception of the one in the Mississippi Delta sugar-producing district and in its dynamic centre, New Orleans. Still, between the Caribbean, Spain, the colonial imperial power and the USA, there were probably transfers and connections, which affected both slaves and masters. Louisiana's 1804 and Florida's 1819 sales to the USA,

[71] See Kolchin 2003a: 39–73. See also the map in Marquese 2004: 336.
[72] Arango y Parreño 1952 (1811), II: 145–89.

as well as the emergence of a slave system based on sugar, together with a number of other influences that the slave system in the 'new' US South incorporated, resulted in direct transfers from Saint Domingue, whether to Cuba in the period 1792–1809, or to Jamaica or Florida respectively.[73]

Yet, important to post-colonial endeavours are not only the *histoire croisée* of slavery, but also the type of comparison stemming from a micro-historical perspective and the idea that slaves were not isolated and that their hidden living worlds have existed to this day. These viewpoints have been linked to one another, most of all through the study of the slave trade and of trans-Caribbean, transatlantic, and trans-American migrations and diasporas *per se*, though Jane G. Landers' concept of 'Cimarrón' ethnicity, or counter-creole Spanish ethnicity, stands out in this respect. These viewpoints are also the object of research on cultural transfer, or on *histoire croisée*, or on diasporas and *entangled histories*.[74]

However, such viewpoints also built on the influence of pre-existing cultures, whether they were colonial, imperial, or masters' cultures, most of all those related to particular territorial formations, religions, discourses, economic systems, rights and punishments. They also built on the influence of slave traditions, the different slave societies, from where the immigrants predominantly categorized as 'white' arrived, and the relatively self-contained and self-sustained Afro-American cultures in the landscapes of slavery. The comparative analysis can be carried out in this respect at the micro-level of life experiences and at the discoursive and representational level through the analysis of *mémoires*, biographical descriptions, and slave voices, or at the macro-level of big pictures. A suitable key concept in a horizontal perspective, in this sense, can be found in Fernando Ortiz's idea of *transculturación*; while, in a vertical sense, 'Creolization', a concept already used in regard to Africa for the 'Atlantic-Creoles', must be conceptualized more strongly.[75]

Altogether, especially in relation to our historic understanding of the slaves' worlds, both slavery and the slave societies it generated are studied much better through the two-side comparison typical of the *histoire croisée*, or 'entangled history'. And yet, the possibilities of a self-contained type of comparison based on similarities or of a structural type of comparison are in no way exhausted. On the contrary, the very objects of one or more such

[73] See Rehder 1999; Walker 2004; Paquette 1997: 204–25; Debien and Wright 1975: 3–216; Cauna 1994: 333–59; Landers 1999, and 2000b.

[74] See Landers 2000a: 30–54.

[75] See Woodward 1985: 48–59; Zeuske 1997: 265–79; and Lovejoy 1997: 119–40; Price 2006: 115–47; and Zeuske 2006b.

comparisons lie in front of us, in the study of Havana (or Matanzas) and New Orleans, Trinidad, San Juan de los Remedios and Baracoa, as well as San Agustín and Pensacola. Moreover, these comparisons would still have the advantage of incorporating trans-cultural elements and transfers, because of the frequent changing of these places from one colonial power to the other. It would have been equally significant to make one or more comparisons focused on slavery in the sugar-producing areas of Louisiana, Cuba, and Puerto Rico, and, as already mentioned, Bahia, or Recife.[76]

Next in importance to comparisons between the 'great' slave societies, there were comparisons made by travellers between the different types of slavery in the Caribbean. This practice occurred with particular intensity in the milieu that witnessed the abolition of slavery in the British Caribbean colonies (1834–8) and it was carried out, significantly, by travellers who belonged to European colonial powers that continued slavery in the Caribbean. By way of example, I mention here the names of Granier de Cassagnac, Rosemond de Beauvallon, and Victor Schoelcher, and also writers such as Gómez de Avellaneda and Merlin, who were particularly inspired by the experiment in abolition. Incidentally, Victor Schoelcher, a French abolitionist and connoisseur of Cuba, was challenged by the countess of Merlin, a Cuban citizen and a defender of slavery; she was certainly able to see the damage done to the so-called 'masculinity rates' – or ratios of men to women – amongst slaves.[77]

Altogether, historical comparison between the regions of the apparently 'small' area of the Hispano-Caribbean slave cultures in Cuba, Puerto Rico and, in the twentieth century, Santo Domingo (the Dominican Republic) seems to have been considered rather unsuitable from the point of view of 'large' slave systems such as Brazil and the USA. This was because many specialists who have spent years researching and analysing the sources of their particular field in slavery studies have simply developed a natural hostility toward every form of historical deduction.[78]

CUBA AND BRAZIL

There were between Cuba and Brazil, at any moment in time, similar wide transfers or known connections as there were between Cuba and the USA.

76 See Werner and Zimmermann 2003: 36–77; and Tadman 2000: 1534–75.

77 See Cassagnac 1842–4; Schoelcher 1843; Campuzano 2004: 475–86; Schoelcher 1843, 1: 348; Yacou 1986: 457–75; and Rosemond de Beauvallon 2002.

78 See Fraginals 1983: 56–117; Marte 1989; Schmidt-Nowara 1999, and 2000: 188–207.

Within the milieu of the slave trade and through the slave smuggling, the captains and those who funded the smuggling operations, there existed, doubtlessly, wide networking and transfers; yet, these are to a large extent unknown. So, for example, Ramón Ferrer, the murdered captain of the ship *Amistad*, had been previously appointed a Portuguese (or Brazilian) captain on a ship named *Bella Antonia*, which he purchased around 1835, aiming at profiting from direct slave smuggling between Africa and Cuba. Researching those links opens up interfaces and gateways to the hidden African Atlantic of slave trade, transculturation and Atlantic Creoles, which empirically means, that the slave smugglers of Brazil and Cuba, their crews, and cooks met on African shores – an extremely big field of further research.[79]

In the history of the debates about slave trade and slavery in Cuba, there is in the work of Arango, as in the work of José Antonio Saco – the most important historian of slavery of the second half of the nineteenth century – clear evidence of elite transfers between Brazil and Cuba. Arango suggested, already in his famous 1792 *Discurso sobre la agricultura*, to establish Spanish-Caribbean branches of the slave trade in Brazil instead of at Rio Gabon and Fernando Poo. Instead, José Antonio Saco, in his dual capacities as intellectual representative of *Cuba grande* and critic of the slave trade and of the immigration of Africans to Cuba, was a comparer *par excellence*, and one who focused exactly on Brazil and Cuba.[80]

Mostly due to the scale and the problems related to the bulk of statistical data, though, macro-comparisons between Cuba and Brazil are, without doubt, unlikely to yield particularly meaningful insights. Brazil had, in temporal sense, given its older tradition of mass slavery than Cuba's in the plantation sector, in both spatial and quantitative senses, completely different dimensions from Cuba; this can be seen particularly well through a sort of David vs Goliath analogy to describe the slave mining industries of El Cobre in Cuba and Minas Gerais in Brazil. The same goes for the gigantic external and internal slave trades of Brazil, and of the USA, as well as for the diffusion of slavery in other regions of Brazil – for example in Maranhão or in Guayana – all the way to what were, effectively, also gigantic borders and transit zones. The similarities and transfers to Venezuelan regions of South

[79] 'Ferrer, Ramón. Intestado de D. Ramon Ferrer', interrogatorio cerrado de D.a Juana Gonzalez, en la morada de D. Juana Gonzalez, f. 93r-95v, La Habana, Regla, 4 June 1840, ANC, Escribanía de Marina, leg. 39, no. 385 (1839). See also Röhrig-Assunção and Zeuske 1998: 375–443; Lamounier 1995: 185–200; and Jones 1981: 89–106. Some sources in the ANC on the purchases of ships from the USA or Portugal point to this connection.

[80] Arango y Parreño 1952 (1792), I: 135.

and East (oriente) are striking, meanwhile the coastal slaveries of Caracas or Cumaná are very close to Caribbean patterns.[81]

Yet, this does not mean that comparisons conducted at the macro-level would not yield any result, simply because there are no explicit south to south historical comparisons. Also, the problem of dimensions should not simply be read from today's experience into the past. Until the middle of the nineteenth century, Brazil consisted mainly of a chain of coastal societies with little access to the interior, with the exception of Minas Gerais and São Paulo. Similarly to the way Cuba and other coastal colonies of Spain were connected to the Tierra Firma, Brazil's local slave societies were mostly connected through coastal navigation – and actually, from today's perspective, they were rather unconnected. Bahia, Rio, and Santiago de Cuba, Matanzas, Trinidad, or Havana in the period 1750–1800 are, thus, theoretically comparable. For this reason, Laird W. Bergad emphasized the 'striking similarities in American slave systems' in regard to their internal economic aspects. Similar is the case for the systemic aspects of slave control.[82]

On the other hand, Brazil's southern area, in the nineteenth and twentieth centuries was too far away from Cuba for the possibility of meaningful connections and transfers. At the same time, sugar differs from coffee, in that it demands more techniques and technology. The labour requirements for coffee were no 'lighter' than for sugar. However, demography was a different case. Slaves from the sugar regions of Cuba were never used in Brazil and vice versa. Also cotton cultivation in Natal and Recife is different from sugar cultivation in Matanzas or Cienfuegos. Given this structural difference between Brazil and Cuba, a search for slaves of the same ethnic African origin should be, so to speak, closer here to the participants, as Martin Lienhard had shown in regard to 'voices', discourses, and words.[83]

From 1800 to 1844, from the Cuban perspective, there was a sort of internal and external competition between sugar and coffee. In 1844/45, after Cuba's coffee plantations were heavily damaged by two hurricanes, Cuban coffee production was surpassed by sugar production in the interior, also thanks to the coming of the railway. In addition, competition on the world market boosted coffee production in Brazil, Venezuela, and New

[81] See Díaz 2001; Bergad 1996: 67–97, 1999; Graham 2004: 291–324; Slenes 2004: 325–70; Röhrig 1993; Gomes 1999, 2003b: 253–87, 2003a; Del Priore and Gomes 2003; and Pollak-Eltz 2000.

[82] See Bergad 2004: 219–35; and Marquese 2004.

[83] Michael Tadman has argued that sugar was likely best grown by men; see Tadman 2000: 1534–75. See also Lienhard 2001.

Granada, among other places. First Rio de Janeiro, and then, also São Paulo, turned into the centres of the largest coffee economy in the world and into Afro-American societies *par excellence*.[84]

Within this frame, *Cuba grande* continued to be unique, along with the sugar regions of Bahia, Recife, and west of São Paulo – in the perspective of a possible comparison of similarities – until around 1840/50. With similar caution, one can envisage also self-contained comparisons between 'small' Cuba and 'small' Brazil around 1850, focusing on free farmers, slave resistance, individual uprisings and also attempts – as in the case of the Malé uprising and comparable attempts in Cuba in 1833 – or even slave families. Alternatively, one can envisage comparisons between slave societies and micro-regions, as has been done already in regard to Vassoura, Rio Claro, Bahia, and Matanzas.[85]

By employing spatial separation, self-contained comparison becomes theoretically possible, without too much focus on connections or on examples of *histoire croisée*. It is, though, hard to carry out, from the empirical point of view, due to the unsteady situations of the sources in the nineteenth century. At the same time, both *Cuba grande* and Bahia/ Pernambuco, the Brazilian Northeast, were located within an ideological, religious, cultural and symbolic historical network, as well as in a systemic network, through the traditions of Catholicism, political culture, the influence of the Church, the administration of slavery, and even through the ideologies that dominated the city and the slave areas, through the fears for slave revolutions related to the 'icon Haiti', but also through the elites' perception of modernization, whether these included slavery or its abolition.

Such was the substance of the most elegant, self-contained, historical comparisons between Havana and Rio de Janeiro, Santiago de Cuba and Bahia, comparisons which are also possible from a trans-cultural Atlantic macro-perspective. In particular, the imperial metropolis of the Atlantic, Rio and Havana, show clear similarities in the period between 1820 and 1850, and so do Santiago de Cuba or Trinidad with Bahia or Recife. Around 1820, Rio and Havana resembled one another, like two Atlantic sisters, also in terms of slave numbers. In 1830–40, Havana was the world's capital of slavery. However, this situation did not last long. Among the

[84] See Pérez Jr 2001; Zanetti Lecuona and Garcia Álvarez 1987; and Vidal Luna and Klein 2003: 53–78.

[85] ANC, Comisión Militar, leg. 540, no. B (1833). See also Carvalho 1998; Schwartz 1992: 65–160; Mattos de Castro 1988: 461–89, 1995: 83–100; La Rosa Corzo 2003 ; Reis 2003; Slenes 1999; Zequeira 2003; Stein 1985; Dean 1976; Queirós Mattoso 1988, 1992; and Bergad 1990.

reasons were the independence of Brazil and the failed independence of Cuba. In Rio de Janeiro alone, in 1850, there were around 80,000 (78,855) slaves, out of a total population of 205,906 people. At around the same time, in 1846, Havana had a total population of 84,930 free individuals (56,558 white and 28,422 free coloured) and 21,988 slaves.[86]

Still, from the point of view of a comparison not just focusing on similarities, already by 1850, Havana was connected, through the first railway network and through coastal steamboat services, to the most important Cuban regions, as well as to the areas of *Cuba grande* and to the harbours of Cárdenas, Matanzas, and Batabanó. At around the same time, the coffee from Vale do Paraíba was still brought to Rio or Parati on mule caravans. Thus, in the nineteenth century, *Cuba grande* and the area between Havana, Matanza, and Cienfuegos was a landscape characterized by high technology, mass slavery, urban and rural elements, and by highly modern intersection points, or harbours, of the global world economy. In its compactness and technological modernity, Cuba was temporarily unattainable and incomparable – a true *Silicon Valley* of sugar.[87]

CONCLUSION

What is going to be important in future comparisons will be the search for new theoretical models and new empirical research on the basis of a different perspective, one that will move away from structures and masters and will focus, instead, on actual experiences and traditions, going beyond the simple analysis of impacts of globalization processes on male and female slaves. From the new possibilities offered by technologies and specializations, in fact, arose new social dynamics and new connective processes between slaves, attendants, and masters, but also between the slaves living in the cities and free coloured, as has been researched by scholars such as Matthias Röhrig Assunção, Martin Lienhard, and Priscilla Naro.[88]

For her part, Jane G. Landers, has stressed the trans-imperial dimension of the circum-Caribbean slaves and their premature *Cimarrón*-ethnicity. Once this is granted, then the question becomes: how did the *Cimarrón*-mentality affect the evolving nations? At least in the case of Cuba's former slaves such as Esteban Montejo, the *Cimarrón* held a trans-racial and rather

[86] Comisión de Estadísticas 1846: 53; and Humboldt 1826a: 107. See also Karasch 1987, and 2000.
[87] See Schmieder 2003: 139; and Zanetti Lecuona and García Álvarez 1987.
[88] See Röhrig-Assunção 2003: 159–76; Lienhard 2001; and Naro 2003.

inclusive *Mambi*-mentality, while in Brazil the same can be said for the *Quilombola*-mentality; both arose within new nations. A further question is that of the place of the descendants of slaves in today's nations, conditioned by globalization. The next step in comparison could, then, be a self-contained contrast of those slavery landscapes, of their slave economies, as well as of their complementary and contrasting economies, of the material culture, of resistance and/or other Afro-American forms of organization, and also of statistics of the slave trade, of slaves' reproduction, of slave dwellings, of practices of release and politics of freedom, of geographical-physical relations and infrastructures, and of African sources of particular features of slavery.[89]

Against the background of these similarities, differences soon become apparent. Despite the massive population of slaves in Brazil, Cuba maintained its unique leading position in the sugar economy and its system of mass slavery throughout the period 1820–1950. In reality, Bahia and Cuba, or Pernambuco and Cuba, were thought as the *Cuba grande* of sugar. Comparisons between these regions are also about similar landscapes – though with different locations within Atlantic slavery – as well as about similar quantitative dimensions, given the difference of 350,000–400,000 female and male slaves; within the core of scientific structures, the sugar mills (*engenho/ingenio*) contributed in various phases to technological modernity. Despite its many turbulences in the nineteenth century, Brazil was, anyhow, a relaxed empire, which engaged in primary accumulation through contact with the sub-colonies in Africa, as well as through the slave trade and slavery.[90]

Cuba, Brazil, and the US South belong to the American type of plantation societies. This makes them eminently comparative. The main differences between their types of slavery in relation to the cultures of female and male slaves seem to have existed against the cosmological and religious backdrop of social formation in Brazil and Cuba on one side and the USA on the other side. Was Tannenbaum in some way right, after all?

[89] See Landers 2000a: 30–54; Berlin and Morgan 1993; Reis and Gomes 1996; McDonald 1993; Barickman 1998; Howard 1998; Sartorius 2003: 108–27; Klein 2002: 37–49; Fraginals 1978, II: 68–75; Brito 1986: 74–103; Fraginals 1986: 3–12; Chalhoub 1989: 64–84; Zeuske 2004b; and Röhrig-Assunção 2003: 159–76.

[90] See Tomich 2004: 129–32; Schwartz 2004a: 158–200; Law 2001: 22–41; and Soumonni 2001: 61–71.

PART III

Ideologies and practices of management in ancient and modern slavery

CHAPTER 7

Ideal models of slave management in the Roman world and in the ante-bellum American South

Enrico Dal Lago and Constantina Katsari

INTRODUCTION

In recent years, scholarly debate has focused increasingly on the usefulness of comparative history and on the appropriate methods to practise it. Key works written by comparative historians have shown the possibility and advantage of using the comparative approach as a means to shed light on a variety of different issues. For the most part, such works deal with a particular case-study placing it in a broader context of historical comparison. As Peter Kolchin has recently argued in *A Sphinx on the American Land* (2003), this can be characterized as the 'soft' approach to comparative history, since it enables scholars to 'combine attention to two important historical components: specificity and context'.[1] Instead, what Kolchin calls 'rigorous' approach to comparative history, one adopted by works that 'compare and contrast' two cases giving equal weight to both, is still rare. Arguably, the most active advocates of this approach have been experts of the ante-bellum American South. Works such as George Fredrickson's *White Supremacy* (1981), Peter Kolchin's *Unfree Labour* (1987), and Shearer Davis Bowman's *Masters and Lords* (1993) have been hailed as models of specific and rigorous comparison.[2] The method that all the above studies employ in their 'rigorous' approach to comparison can be described as 'contrast of contexts', according to the definition given by sociologists Theda Skocpol and Margaret Somers in an important article published in the 1980 issue of *Comparative Studies in Society and History*. According to Skocpol and Somers, this method seeks to 'bring out the unique features of each particular case ... and to show how these unique features affect the working out of putatively general social processes'.[3]

[1] Kolchin 2003a: 4. [2] Fredrickson 1981; Kolchin 1987; Bowman 1993.
[3] Skocpol and Somers 1980: 185.

In our chapter, we intend to apply Kolchin's 'rigorous' approach to a specific case-study of 'contrast of contexts' that focuses on comparison between the Roman world and the ante-bellum American South. Our comparison, though, differs strikingly from the types of comparative studies previously mentioned in one crucial respect: the fact that it is 'diachronic'. In fact, diachronic comparison between specific features of the ancient and modern world is still in its infancy; only very few examples of it are currently available and all of them in the ever-growing field of slavery studies. Chief among such studies is the exceptionally broad survey of the institution of slavery in its different forms throughout history conducted by Orlando Patterson in *Slavery and Social Death* (1982).[4] More specific studies of classical slavery which hint at possible comparisons with the modern world, and specifically with the Atlantic slave systems, characterize the work of other scholars such as Moses Finley, Keith Hopkins, Keith Bradley, Stephen Hodkinson, Walter Scheidel, Brent Shaw and a few others. Yet, so far, little has been written in terms of providing a 'rigorous' comparison of the type described by Kolchin focused on ancient and modern slavery, though, perhaps, an interesting case of possible comparison through a parallel treatment of ancient and modern cases is in the work of Alan Watson.[5]

In our diachronic comparison, we focus specifically on the analysis of ideal models of slave management in the Roman world and in the ante-bellum American South as one of many possible comparative topics between ancient and modern slavery. While slave management is in itself a particularly promising topic for comparison, we believe that the specific focus on its ideal models can shed light on important and overlooked features of the ideology of the master class and of the master–slave relationship in the two societies. In fact, as in every slave society, also in the Roman world and in the ante-bellum American South debate on the ideal model of the management of the enslaved workforce must have characterized the intellectual activity of educated members of the slaveholding elite. Our argument is that, in both cases, notwithstanding the striking differences, the master–slave relationship can be characterized as involving different degrees of paternalism. To be sure, paternalism has long been the guiding concept used by scholars in describing the master–slave relationship in the ante-bellum American South; yet, the same cannot be said for the Roman world, since references to paternalism in the scholarly interpretation of the

[4] Patterson 1982.

[5] Finley 1998; Hopkins 1978; Bradley 1987, 1994; Hodkinson 2003: 248–85; Scheidel in this volume; Shaw 1998a; Watson 1987, 1989. See also Davis 2006.

different types of relationships, among which is also the one between master and slave, are scanty at best. Despite such differences in scholarly approaches, we still think that it is possible to use paternalism as a useful analytical tool, especially in a specific kind of study, like ours, which focuses on particular descriptions of the types of dependency that tied the slaves to their masters – descriptions that characterized the agronomic literature produced by slaveholders in both worlds.

Comparisons between ancient and modern slavery encounters notorious difficulties, simply because of the sheer difference in terms of evidence and availability of sources. However, in the case of slave management, we are fortunate in having been left with important treatises written by ancient authors, and specifically by famous Roman agriculturalists Cato, Varro, and Columella, all writing between the first century BC and the first century AD. Such works include not only the authors' particular views, but also their advice to slaveholders on the ideal management of slaves. Therefore, we will make constant reference to these sources when explaining slave management in the Roman world in our chapter. As one might expect, in the case of the American South we have, instead, a plethora of available sources with regard to slave management. Yet, there is a particular type of source that reflects the thoughts and views of the master class in relation to ideal ways of managing the slaves. This is especially the case of essays and articles written by articulate southern planters who published regularly on the foremost ante-bellum economic and agricultural journals – such as *De Bow's Review*, *The Southern Agriculturalist*, and *The Farmers' Register* – and of a number of pamphlets – such as *Governor James Henry Hammond's Instructions to his Overseer* – that circulated widely among American slaveholders in the period between 1820 and 1860 and were held as true paradigms of slave management for future generations. Though it is possible that, given their classical education, nineteenth-century American slaveholders might have been influenced by Roman agriculturalists, we will not attempt to discover any possible direct relation between the two in terms of inherited tradition. Rather, our essay aims to compare and contrast evidence from the two sets of sources in order to arrive at a possible definition of paternalism in the two slave societies.

THE SLAVES' WELL-BEING: THE KEY TO IDEAL PRODUCTIVITY

In both the Roman world and the ante-bellum American South, masters considered themselves responsible for the well-being of their slaves. The model for a well-ordered and functioning plantation ought to have provisions regarding all aspects of slave life, given the connection between the slaves' health and their productivity. As a consequence, both ancient and modern ideal models of slave management stressed the importance of housing, food, and clothing. Both Roman agronomists and Southern agricultural writers provided detailed instructions on the construction of the slave quarters, stressing their need to be characterized by particular features, on the particular material that should be used for slave clothes, and on the type and quantity of food that should be distributed to the slaves.

With regard to housing, Roman agronomist Columella recommended the construction of a large kitchen with a high ceiling as a convenient resting place for the slave household and of cubicles that allowed the light of the midday sun at the equinox.[6] Such arrangements aimed at providing a solution to the practical problem of a large household whose members all took their meals in the same area of the building, while they also showed concern for the existence of an adequate amount of light in the particular rooms where the slaves lived. For his part, a southern planter from Virginia stated in 1856 that 'the ends aimed at in building Negro cabins should be: first, the health and comfort of the occupants; secondly, the convenience of nursing, surveillance, discipline, and the supply of food and water; and thirdly, economy of construction . . . Their houses should be provided with large glass windows . . . light and air are necessary to the proper making of blood.'[7] Understandably, health played a major part in the construction of the slave quarters in both the Roman and the southern cases. Yet, a certain concern about the effects of the logistics of arrangements in the construction of slave quarters on the slaves' daily lives seems to have been a common feature as well. Interestingly, a Virginian planter recommended in 1840 that the slave quarters should be built in such a way that the dormitories would be placed around a large common room with stoves for daily usage.[8]

Of equal importance to housing in the mind of the masters was the type of clothing that they distributed to the slaves. Columella repeated his advice on clothing twice in order to stress its importance with regard to the health of the slave household. In the first instance, he mentioned that the *vilicus* – who was the one responsible for choosing the clothes – should

[6] Columella, *De Re Rustica* 1.6.3. [7] R. W. N. N. 1856: 129, 131.

[8] Harrison 1840: 212–13. A South Carolina planter also mentioned in 1857 that 'a negro loves the sun, it is his element and he basks in its raise *con amore*. His quarters should be on the south side of a hill, and never in the shade'; see Gage 1857: 132.

bear in mind their practical purpose, rather than aim at improving the appearance of the slaves.[9] Thus, he should examine and choose the clothes similarly to the way he examined and chose iron tools.[10] More specifically, the vestments should be 'long-sleeved leather tunics, garments of patchwork, or hooded cloaks', capable of protecting the bodies of the slaves from all changes in weather, while they worked in the open.[11] As it happened, such detailed provisions masked the fact that the slaves' change in clothes seems to have been kept to a minimum. According to Roman agricultural writer Cato, tunics, blankets, and wooden shoes were allocated to farmhands only every other year, while in some cases they were meant to be recycled.[12]

Despite this, in Rome's ideal model of slave management as it was expressed in Columella's instructions, the importance of practicality in slave clothing seems to have been paramount. In the ante-bellum American South, celebrated South Carolina planter James Henry Hammond seems to have had similar concerns in his instructions to his overseer, given the fact that he insisted that slaves were given clothes made with the appropriate material for the different seasons: wool for the fall and cotton for the spring. Yet, even though it is true that, not unlike what Cato reported, on Hammond's plantation also, 'each worker would get a pair of shoes every fall and a heavy blanket every third year', it is particularly significant that Hammond recommended that 'jackets or pants maybe substituted for each other whenever the wish is expressed before making them'.[13] Therefore, regardless of whether they actually applied rules and provisions, at the very least both Roman and American masters ideally set out to take care of the health of the slaves at work by attempting to prevent possible sickness caused by the weather through the use of proper material in clothing; at the same time, a limited attention to cleanliness – given the rare change in clothes allowed in both cases – seems to have been common in both cases.

In this respect, a much bigger role in the slaves' health, together with properly arranged housing and weather-proof clothing, was played by their diet. In the American South, suggestions on the proper slave diet abounded both in essays on agricultural journals and in instructions to overseers written during the ante-bellum period. In general, the most important point seems to have been always about fairness in distributing food rations to the slaves. According to Peter Kolchin, food provisions amounted to a standard of '8 quarts of corn meal and 2½ to 4 pounds of pork or bacon per

9 Columella, *De Re Rustica* 1.8.17. 10 Columella, *De Re Rustica* 9.1.21.
11 Columella, *De Re Rustica* 1.8.9. 12 Cato, *De Agricoltura* 59. 13 Hammond 1840–50: 357.

week', though these were 'supplemented by numerous items that varied according to season and region, many of which – including chickens, vegetables, fruit, opossum, fish, and shellfish – slaves grew on their garden plots or hunted and gathered from the forests and waterways'.[14]

Still, whether slaves could supplement their diet with such items or not, the masters' food provisions played the largest role and masters were well aware of this. It is, therefore, not surprising that, in the widely acclaimed management rules for his rice estate in South Carolina, Plowden C. Weston wrote that 'great care should be taken that the negroes should never have less than the regular allowance; in all cases of doubt, it should be given in favour of the largest quantity'.[15] Likewise, an award winning essay written by a Georgia planter in 1852 recommended that 'the allowance now given per week to each hand – men, women, boys and girls that are large enough to go in the fields to work – is five pounds of good clean bacon and one quart of molasses, with as much good bread as they require; and in the fall . . . the addition of one pint of strong coffee, sweetened with sugar, every morning before going to work'. The same planter also recommended that the meat and bread should be cooked by a woman hired specifically for the purpose and that 'each house or family should have a garden attached for raising their own vegetables'.[16] Doubtless, the reason for having a plantation cook was that masters did not want their slaves to have control over the cooking of their food, so that they would not quarrel over it or eat too much.[17]

Unlike the detailed advice given about slave diet in ante-bellum southern articles and pamphlets, the information in our Roman sources does not quite elaborate on the subject of slave diet with an equal degree of precision. Clearly, Columella used the issue of food mainly to make moral comments about the superior character of his predecessors, who would be feeding their slaves with milk, meat, and corn. At the same time, he also attempted to chastise his contemporaries, who abstained from distributing costly foods and probably limited their slaves' diet to the consumption of vegetables.[18] On the other hand, Cato was far more specific on the details of slave diet and mentioned hens, eggs, dried pears, sorbs, quinces, apples, figs and raisins as part of the foodstuff cooked by the wife of the *vilicus*.[19] He also talked about monthly allocations of wine, olive oil, and salt, which seemed to be essential.[20] According to both Cato and Varro, though, the main part of the slave diet seems to have

[14] Kolchin 2003b: 113. [15] Weston 1857: 38. [16] Collins 1854: 20. [17] Kolchin 2003b: 119.
[18] Columella, *De Re Rustica* 10.1.1. [19] Cato, *De Agricoltura* 143. [20] Cato, *De Agricoltura* 56–8.

consisted of bread or grain (*cibaria*) that was distributed to the slaves on a daily basis.[21] Similarly to what happened in the American South, in the Roman world also, some slaves were allowed to add to their diet the meat of the livestock they kept and the vegetables from the kitchen gardens.[22] It is fairly obvious that Roman agronomists were especially concerned about the cost of food, although they realized that adequate feeding was essential to keep the slaves productive.

Both in Rome and the ante-bellum American South it was an intermediate figure of slave manager – the *vilicus* in one case and the overseer in the other – that was directly responsible for the allocation of food allowances to the slaves. This was a task that involved a certain degree of administrative and decision-making abilities. Its importance lay in the fact that adequate – although mostly far from generous – food allowances were crucial in keeping the slaves strong and content, so that their work could continue uninhibited. Both Roman and southern masters strove to achieve the aim of maintaining a healthy workforce, at the same time keeping a tight control over all aspects related to the slaves' food consumption. For this reason, in both cases, aside from the role of the estate manager, an equally essential role was the one of the cook and/or wife of the *vilicus*, who was in charge of preparing the meals according to the exact instructions laid out by the master. By employing such a system of control, masters made the slaves intrinsically dependent for their survival upon their benevolence and also showed a concern for their well-being.

In all fairness, there is little reason to doubt that in both the Roman world and the ante-bellum American South masters felt responsible, to a certain degree, for the welfare and health of their slaves; for a start, such an attitude was, in both cases, a 'logical outcome' of their economic reasoning, since slaves were valuable property. As early as in the Roman period, attention to slave health was an indispensable factor in a well administered estate. Usually, either the *vilicus* or his wife would assume the task of taking care of the sick members of the slave household. In the ideal Roman estate described by Columella, both the fatigued and the sick workers would remain in an infirmary under the care of the wife of the *vilicus*.[23] One obvious reason for such a measure was the masters' concern with protecting their human property from deterioration. However, Columella

[21] Cato, *De Agricoltura* 56–8; Varro, *Res Rusticae* 1.63.

[22] Varro, *Res Rusticae* 1.19.3; Columella, *De Re Rustica* 10.1.1; Pliny, *NH* 19.52.

[23] Columella, *De Re Rustica* 9.1.18 (on the *vilicus* taking care of wounded slaves); and Columella, *De Re Rustica* 12.1.3 and 12.3.7 (on the *vilica* taking care of the slaves).

also gives us another reason by explaining that 'those who recovered their health . . . are eager to give more faithful service than before'.[24] Those slaves who had been taken care of when they were sick were more ready to acknowledge the magnanimity of their master and put themselves under his protection.

For largely similar reasons to the ones of Roman masters, also in the ante-bellum American South planters laid out specific instructions – though in greater detail – with the aim of not leaving anything to chance with regard to slave health. In an ideal southern plantation, a hospital would be a mandatory requirement and would be attended by either one or more nurses with the occasional help of doctors. In his rules, Plowden C. Weston wrote that 'all sick persons are to stay in the hospital night and day, from the time they first complain to the time they are able to go to work again. The nurses are to be responsible for the sick not leaving the house, and for the cleanliness of the bedding, utensils, etc.'[25] Arguably, the most famous example of a plantation hospital was in the Hopeton estate, in South Carolina, significantly held as a model in agricultural and slave management. In Hopeton, planter James Hamilton Cooper built what John D. Legare enthusiastically described in the 1833 issue of *The Southern Agriculturalist* as 'an airy and warm building 80 feet by 24, with four wards, an entry which answers as an examining room, a medicine closet, a kitchen, and a bathing room', all of which was kept by a nurse.[26]

The principles that informed James Hamilton Cooper's building of his model plantation hospital recall comparable ideas that – Columella seems to imply – were behind the construction of the infirmary on an ideal Roman estate. The comparability of this particular feature allows us to make parallels in regard to the idea of care in the master–slave relationship in the two societies. It seems that in their ideal models of slave management both Roman and southern masters sought to convey an image of themselves as protectors and benefactors of the slave population under their control. It was, thus, in both cases, by combining in their minds economic concerns with the objectives of obtaining the slaves' respect and support that masters set to take care of the slaves' health, and their well-being in general. As a consequence, when laying out their management rules neither Roman nor southern masters could afford to spare any effort in attempting to convince the slaves of their goodwill.

[24] Columella, *De Re Rustica* 12.1.3. [25] Weston 1857: 41. [26] Legare 1833: 574.

THE IDEAL TREATMENT OF SLAVES: PUNISHMENTS AND REWARDS

Despite the Roman and the southern masters' show of concern for their slaves' health and well-being, it was hardly the case that the actual work routine on plantations and estates focused only on the benevolent aspects of the master–slave relationship, as both the Roman and the southern ideal of slave management included as an essential feature the image of a well-ordered and disciplined workforce. The proper functioning of the estates' workforces, which was essential to the estates' productivity, could only be ensured by specific measures of control ideally aimed at maximizing the results of a well-ordered and repetitive work pace. Within this ideal model of control, respect for hierarchy played a major role, since it was up to the principal slave managers and to other lesser figures of authority, all of whom were usually directly responsible to the masters, to ensure that the slaves did not violate the rules and regulations that clearly delimited their possibility of action in regard to both work and housing. In this context, discipline assumed a paramount importance especially during the daily work routine and it is clear that both Roman and southern masters thought it could be enforced effectively only by dividing the enslaved workforce into relatively small groups that were easier to supervise.

Accordingly, in Columella's ideal Roman estate, slave gangs employed in the field should not exceed the number of ten men each. In fact, 'that limited number was most conveniently guarded while at work'. As for the reason for having gangs, it also had to do with the fact that, if the slaves were scattered rather than being grouped, it would have been more difficult to watch them.[27] In the American South also, on large plantations, slaves were usually divided into gangs; however, there were customarily twenty-five to thirty individuals working in a gang and their close supervision was ensured by a black driver under the direction of the overseer. Such numbers can be extrapolated from the plantation journals that either the masters or the overseers used to keep. For example, in James Hamilton Couper's journal for his model plantation at Hopeton, the number of workers for each gang in the cotton fields averages between twenty and forty individuals, supposedly the most manageable size in terms of work discipline.[28]

In both the Roman world and the ante-bellum American South, the masters' instructions were very specific on the importance of enforcing orderly conduct upon the slaves, not only during daytime, but also at night.

[27] Columella, *De Re Rustica* 1.9.7–8. [28] Legare 1833: 575.

Instructions to slaveholders on this particular topic abound in the Roman agricultural treatises. In his work, Columella advised the slave manager to walk at the rear of the slaves when they left the fields to go back to their quarters, so that none of them was left behind.[29] Cato also had similar advice in mind, when he wrote that an ideal manager had to 'be the first up and the last to bed, having first seen that the buildings are shut up, that everyone is in bed in his proper place'.[30] Clearly, both writers thought best to stress that the precautions taken to control the movement of the slaves and ensure that they did not break any of the rules laid out by their masters, especially at night when it was easier, were never enough.

A similar concern shows clearly also in works on agriculture and slave management written in the ante-bellum American South. Here, the overseers were specifically charged with the task of ensuring that slaves were confined in their quarters once work was finished in the fields. To this end, overseers were to inspect and periodically check the slave quarters at night. For example, in 1857, Plowden C. Weston recommended that 'the overseer is every now and then to go round at night and call at the houses, so as to ascertain whether their inmates are at home'.[31] What these examples suggest is that, in both the Roman world and the ante-bellum American South, strict discipline at work during daytime and extra security measures at night were used by masters as deterrents, so that the slaves would be prevented from perpetrating any mischief.

When prevention failed to achieve its aim, masters found themselves compelled to resort to punishment in order to keep slaves in their place; significantly, when describing their ideal model of slave management, both Roman and southern agricultural writers always made clear that this was a result of ill attitude on the part of the slaves, who simply had failed to listen to their master's advice. We know that, in the Roman world, the use of the whip was a widespread practice. Yet, among the Roman sources, only Varro mentioned it in his treatise. Specifically, Varro asserted that the *vilicus* should, by all means, use his whip, but only if words failed to achieve the desired result of disciplining the workforce.[32]

In contrast to the evidence from the Roman sources, whipping comes across in the articles and pamphlets written in the ante-bellum American South as the most common form of punishment. For example, a planter from South Carolina made a comparable point to the one made by Varro, when he stated that 'negroes who will not do their work, like boys who will

[29] Columella, *De Re Rustica* 11.1.18. [30] Cato, *De Agricoltura* 5. [31] Weston 1857.
[32] Varro, *Res Rusticae* 1.17.5.

not get their lessons, must sometime be flogged'.[33] As for the object of punishment, planter Joseph Acklen from Louisiana described it particularly clearly when he said that it should be 'first for correction, to deter the offender from a repetition of an offence; and second for example to all others, showing them if they offend they will likewise receive certain punishment'.[34] The idea that punishment was just and should be applied only when necessary is particularly evident in the rules set out in 1847 by a Virginian planter, according to whom 'the hands must be made to obey and work, which may be done by strict attention to business, with very little coercive means'.[35]

Therefore, in their ideal models of management, both southern and Roman masters strove to resort to as little violence as possible and to discipline violently slaves at work only if absolutely necessary. A significant number of planters, in fact, thought that 'much whipping indicates a bad tempered or inattentive manager' and would have agreed with James Henry Hammond that 'a great deal of whipping is not necessary, some is'.[36] For his part, Columella advised slaveholders that the slaves 'may rather fear his [the *vilicus'*] sternness, than detest his cruelty'.[37] Though expressed in different ways, in both cases, the emphasis was on the certainty and fairness of punishment rather than its severity as instrument of prevention of, and response to, slave resistance to the masters' discipline.

Together with beating, a common way of punishment in both the Roman world and the American South was slave confinement; in both cases, slaves were placed inside prison buildings whose construction was characterized by particular security features. In the Roman case, an underground prison (*ergastulum*) whose walls received light only through narrow windows placed high above the ground hosted the unruly slaves, who slept there in chains.[38] It was one of the main responsibilities of the *vilicus* to inspect that such slaves were all properly chained and guarded, following the direct orders of the master.[39] The employment of similar security measures was advised also in the American South, where, in particular, a farmer recommended that thieves, runaways, and unmanageable slaves should all be kept in 'a loghouse, with a good substantial door, lock and key, storey twelve feet high, logs across above, so as to make a regular built jail'.[40]

33 Franklin 1844: 25. 34 Acklen 1856: 617. 35 Blunt 1847: 82.
36 Anon. 1849: 82; Hammond 1840–50: 347. 37 Columella, *De Re Rustica* 1.8.10.
38 Columella, *De Re Rustica* 1.6.3. 39 Columella, *De Re Rustica* 1.8.16.
40 Anon. Small Farmer 1851: 369.

Therefore, confinement was, in both cases, an extreme measure that aimed at separating rebel slaves from their fellow bondsmen; yet, there were important differences. Roman agronomists considered it quite common for a master to have his slaves chained when they were confined in a jail, or else when they were engaged in particular types of agricultural labour, such as the tending of vineyards.[41] On the other hand, masters in the American South only resorted to constraining their slaves with chains and other methods, or confined them in jail, only after every attempt at disciplining them had failed. Instead, besides relying on a more frequent use of the whip, they preferred to send their slaves to particular correction houses where they would be 'broken'.

In both the Roman world and the ante-bellum American South, punishment – however certain and severe – was customarily accompanied by different types of incentives for the slaves. In fact, in the ideal models of management of both slave societies, the existence of a complex system of punishments and rewards was a crucial aspect of the master–slave relationship. Through such a system, masters aimed at showing the slaves that correction was only the other side of the master's care for their well-being.

In the Roman estates, rewards for the enthusiastic work of a slave included additional food and clothing, exemption from work, permission to graze a beast of his own, and other similar privileges. An additional dimension to the motivation for rewards can be grasped from the writings of Varro, according to whom 'any who have been given too hard a task, or so severe a punishment, may thus be consoled and their goodwill and kindly feeling towards the master be restored'.[42] According to Columella, apart from the customary material rewards, acknowledgment for the services of a diligent slave took the form of a dinner invitation by the overseer.[43] Columella also wrote that particular rewards, in the form of exemption from work or even freedom, went to female slaves who managed to provide their master with three or more children.[44]

Similar attitudes toward slave rewards can be observed in the master class of the ante-bellum American South. Typically, rewards to particularly diligent slaves would include time off from work, extra food and clothing, and even cash payments, or the permission to cultivate a plot of land. A planter from Mississippi clearly stated that rewards should be allocated 'to each one upon his good behaviour, his activity, obedience and efficiency during the year'.[45] Curiously, inviting loyal slaves and their family to

[41] Columella, *De Re Rustica* 1.9.4. [42] Varro, *Res Rusticae* 1.17.6. [43] Columella, *De Re Rustica* 1.8.5.
[44] Columella, *De Re Rustica* 1.8.19. [45] Townes 1851: 258.

dinner was a customary practice among many planters, but usually only on particularly meaningful occasions, such as Christmas or the Fourth of July, during which large celebrations were held on plantations across the South.[46]

Also, like Roman masters, southern masters gave rewards to female slaves who were particularly prolific. This comes hardly as a surprise, though. The presence of slave children was an indication of the general good health and stability of slave families – both factors that loomed large in the planters' ideal model of slave management. Short of promising freedom, the best reward to a prolific female slave was also in the ante-bellum South time off from work. Thus, a Georgia planter who wished to reward a particularly prolific mother significantly stated that 'when the family increases to ten children, I will require no other labour from the mother than to attend for her children'.[47]

Arguably, very specific reasons led both Roman and southern masters to treat rewards as a particularly important aspect of their relationship with the slaves. In both cases, the masters thought that, in the ideal world that they sought to construct on their estates, slaves could be kept content only if the masters gave proper attention to their good behaviour and acknowledged their goodwill in tangible ways. Yet, in both cases, the system of punishment and rewards also made clear in an equally tangible way that the slaves' improvement of their own condition could occur only within the set boundaries of the master–slave relationship. In other words, such an improvement could occur only through the slaves' acknowledgment of their masters' authority and their acceptance of their absolute dependence on his goodwill for their well-being. As a consequence, in both the Roman world and the ante-bellum American South, the ideal model of slave management came to be based on a system of punishment and reward that was not only strongly ideologically charged, but that was specifically meant to reinforce the hierarchy and structure of power that had originated from the formation of the slave society.

DEPENDENCY, PATERNALISM AND RECIPROCITY IN THE ROMAN WORLD AND THE ANTE-BELLUM AMERICAN SOUTH

All the examples we have provided point to the existence of a constant feature in the master–slave relationship in both the Roman world and in the ante-bellum American South. This feature can best be described as an

[46] Blassingame 1979. [47] Hazard 1831: 350.

extreme form of dependency. There is little doubt that, in both societies, slaves found themselves completely dependent on their masters for their survival. Such dependency defined in both cases the legal aspects of the master–slave relationship through the existence of codified measures. At the same time, dependency as a concept was a particularly important element of the specific ideological dimension of the master–slave relationship. It was in connection to such an ideological dimension that the dependency that bound the slaves to their masters was highly idealized in the models of management that both Roman and southern agronomists and intellectuals put forward for the benefit of the master classes.

Significantly, in the first century AD, the Roman philosopher Seneca compared the dependency of a slave on his master to the relationships that bound a subject to his king and a soldier to his commander.[48] A century later, Tertullian thought that, within the household, the ties that bound a slave to his master resembled the ties that bound a wife to her husband or a son to his father.[49] Clearly, in the Roman world, sets of dependent relationships defined the social and family structures and legitimized the power of some members of society over others. Modern scholars have defined such social and legal institutions as *patria potestas*, *amicitia*, patronage, and, slavery. Since all of these were forms of dependency, they naturally shared common characteristics.

For example, Claude Eilers has noticed that in the sources slaves were styled as humble friends (*humiles amici*).[50] In other cases, several terms are used to describe the relationship between masters and slaves as similar to the one between patrons and clients. The same idea appears in the work of Richard Saller, who has implicitly connected the idea of slavery with some form of patronage, when he referred to the bestowal of the *beneficium-gratia* by a master on his slave and/or by a patron on his freedmen.[51] In view of the evidence at our disposal, we cannot disregard the fact that notions of reciprocal exchange, such as the *beneficium*, probably characterized part of the master–slave relationship. Yet, despite the few similarities between slavery and *amicitia* and slavery and patronage, we should always bear in mind that, as Orlando Patterson has remarked, 'slavery is a permanent, violent domination of natally alienated and generally dishonoured persons'.[52] Therefore, slaves were, in any case, perceived as less than human and, thus, their relationships with free men or with freedmen were constructed according to different rules. Significantly, the objectification of

[48] Seneca, *De Beneficiis* 3.18.3. [49] Tertullian, *Apologeticus* 3.4.
[50] Eilers 2002: 15; Cicero, *Fam.* 16.16.1. [51] Saller 1982: 24. [52] Patterson 1982: 13.

the slaves was described vividly in the writings of Roman agronomists. Specifically, Varro placed slaves in the same category as tools, when he wrote that agricultural instruments

are divided by some into two parts, namely (1) men who work, and (2) men's tools without which they cannot work. Others divide them in three classes, namely (1) the class gifted with speech, (2) that which has inarticulate voice and (3) that which is voiceless. To the first belong slaves, to the second oxen and to the third wagons.[53]

Comparably to what happened in the Roman world, in the ante-bellum American South also, forms of dependency abounded in free society and tied in different ways the less powerful to the more powerful; and yet, none of these came close to the extreme form of dependency that characterized slavery. Perhaps the most striking difference between the two case-studies is the fact that, in the South, the predominance of the factor of race led to a situation in which the extreme form of dependency related to slavery affected exclusively the African-American part of the population. Therefore, relations between white masters and black slaves had a particular connotation, one that implied the existence of a perceived inferiority of the black race in comparison with the white race. Numerous scholars have described the relation of dependency that tied black slaves to their white masters with the term 'paternalism'. This term relates specifically to a rhetorical device used by southern masters in their ideological defence of slavery. At its most basic level, the term refers to the notion that slaves were like children who could not take care of themselves and benefited from the slaveholders' use of them. During the period between 1830 and 1860, when slavery came under considerable attack as a consequence of the formation of an abolitionist movement in the North, this idea was at the heart of a 'pro-slavery argument' advanced by such leading spokesmen as James Henry Hammond, George Fitzhugh, Thomas Roderick Dew, and Henry Thornton Stringfellow, who justified the necessity of the existence of slavery based on these grounds.[54]

Yet, modern scholars have differed widely in their interpretation of the reality of paternalism. Notably, Marxist historian Eugene Genovese, has argued that paternalism was the defining 'non-capitalist' feature of antebellum southern slavery. For Genovese, paternalism was based on an individual relationship between master and slave that led the slaves to accept the ideological premises of the slave system, and yet it also allowed them to carve room for bargaining the day-to-day details of their

[53] Varro, *Res Rusticae* 1.17.1. [54] Hammond 1842; Fitzhugh 1988 (1857); Dew 1832; Stringfellow 1860.

condition.[55] On the other hand, neoclassical economists Robert Fogel and Stanley Engerman believe that paternalism worked on southern plantations similarly to the way it works in modern firms. Thus, just as a 'capitalist' boss does with his workers, the master motivated his slaves giving them rewards and allowing them to assert, at least partly, their rights.[56]

In our chapter, in describing our interpretation of the ideal model of slave management, we will take the view that, ideally, southern masters tended to emulate their supposed role of heads of extended households by dealing with slaves as if they were helpless children. Yet, it is clear to us that the difference between the ideal and the reality was related, on one hand, to the contractual nature of the daily activities on the plantation and to that slave resistance to the masters' design for total control that is central in Genovese's interpretation and, on the other hand, to the different measures that the masters took to maximize their profit through accommodation, as Fogel and Engerman's studies have shown. In other words, the ideal model of slave management rested on a reality that included features and dynamics in the master–slave relationship that have been described by both schools of thought – the 'non-capitalist' and the 'capitalist'. Such an idea, which is central in our view, forms an essential part of a new interpretative departure that characterizes a small group of recent studies on the ante-bellum South.[57]

Most scholars would agree that an essential feature of paternalistic ideology resided in its metaphor of the family as an ideal model of social relations. In general, it is possible to say that a reason for this was that, in the ante-bellum South, family relations were supposed to provide the standard for social relations at large. Yet, in the case of slavery, this metaphor was also related to the late eighteenth-century rise and spread of a particular paternalistic ideal through a historical process that Willie Lee Rose has described as the 'domestication of domestic slavery'. According to Rose, through this process, masters intended to convey 'the qualities so much admired in the Victorian family; cheerful obedience and gratitude on the part of children (read slaves), and paternalistic wisdom, protection, and discipline on the part of the father (read master)'.[58] In the mind of the masters, this ideal was not just mere fiction, since, in the nineteenth-century American South, children and wives were dependent,

[55] See Genovese 1974, 1969; and Fox-Genovese and Genovese 1983.
[56] See Fogel and Engerman 1974. See also Oakes 1982; and Scarborough 2003.
[57] See especially Smith 1998; Young 1999; Follett 2005; and Dal Lago 2005. [58] Rose 1982: 21.

both legally and economically, on the head of the household, and therefore were subordinate to him.

It is, therefore, not surprising to see that masters, in their ideal model of relationship with their bondsmen, came to see the latter as equally dependent and subordinate in an extended household that included family and slaves alike. In fact, just as family dependants had both rights and duties to claim and to respect in the relation of reciprocity that they entertained with the head of the household, slaves under the paternalistic system were supposed to have particular rights and duties in their relationship with their master. By the 1850s, the idea that the enslaved workforce had particular rights was not just codified by the law, but was also present in several pamphlets and articles that defined the ideal model of slave management.[59]

In his work, Eugene Genovese has brought to our attention the fact that 'the expression "our family, white and black" . . . became ubiquitous during the 19th century'.[60] Significantly, time and again, in the pamphlets and articles written by planters, we can see the metaphor of the family in the description of the master–slave relationship and of the rights and duties that were attached to it. In these documents, it is implicit that the authority of the father ruled unchallenged over both family members and slaves. Such an idea even found a particular justification in the scriptural defence of slavery as 'ordained of God'.[61]

In fact, it is clear that, much as slavery was seen as divinely approved, the family, as a consecrated institution and one strictly related to the emergence of bourgeois capitalism, provided the perfect metaphor for a comparably reciprocal relationship – the one between master and slaves – that had to function as efficiently as possible in order to ensure that the planters obtained maximum profit in their agricultural enterprises. As a result, the paternalistic metaphor of the family functioned for the masters as a truly ideal rhetorical construction of the master–slave relationship. Yet, ultimately, the reciprocity implicit in such an ideal, by allowing slaves some room for bargaining over their own rights, influenced and shaped to the masters' advantage the internal mechanics of plantation management and, by contributing to diffusing labour-related conflicts, was partly responsible for the spectacular ante-bellum increase in southern agricultural production.

Similarly to what happened in the American South, in the Roman world the Latin words *familia* and *domus* referred to an extended household that

[59] See, for example, Lee 1857: 486–91. [60] Genovese 1992: 69. [61] Ross 1857: 106.

included both the nuclear family and their slaves.[62] According to Roman law the *pater familias*, the head of the household – the father, the grandfather, or even the great grandfather in some cases – held the *patria potestas*, which included the power of life and death over the members of his *familia*. However, he had also responsibilities towards his subordinates, since he was legally accountable for the actions of his children and his slaves.[63]

The importance of the figure of the *pater familias* in relation to the slaves is evident in the writings of the Roman agronomists. In particular, they described in minute detail the benefits that a slave would receive from the master/*pater familias* with regard to food, clothing, housing, and healthcare. In return, the slaves were obliged to show both *fides* (loyalty) and *obsequium* (obedience) towards their master as an acknowledgment of their gratitude for all such benefits they had received over the years.[64]

Roman agronomists clarified that, if a master wished to be treated by his slaves with both *fides* and *obsequium* he had to follow a specific piece of advice they gave him: he had to help the individual slave to feel that he/she was, by all means, a member of the household, with his/her own rights, as well as with his/her own obligations. For example, being taken care of after returning from the fields and being provided with food and drink 'without their being defrauded' were rights that the slaves who worked the entire day for the benefit of the household had earned. Interestingly, Columella also specified that the slaves should always dine close to the hearth of the household; this assertion strengthens the idea that the members of the enslaved workforce, ideally, were to 'feel', rather than just 'be', members of the *familia*.[65]

Particularly interesting is the fact that Columella seems to have been specifically concerned about possible abuses of the rights of the slaves. In fact, he wrote that 'the investigation of the householder should be the more painstaking in the interest of slaves of this sort, that they may not be treated unjustly (*iniuriose*) in the matter of clothing or other allowances'. He, then, concluded with more advice, suggesting that 'a careful master inquires . . . whether they are receiving what is due to them (*iusta precipiant*) under his instructions'.[66]

To be sure, in the Roman world, the rights of the slave do not find their roots in the supposed justice of a system 'ordained of God', but in the unwritten laws that permeate the 'aristocratic' ideals of the period. The *pater familias* assumed the responsibility of providing his slaves with an

62 Saller 1984: 336–55. 63 Watson 1977: 23–30. 64 Bradley 1987: 33.
65 Columella, *De Re Rustica* 9.1.18–19. 66 Columella, *De Re Rustica* 1.8.17–18.

acceptable standard of living, expecting in return their loyalty and commitment to work for the benefit of his household. In turn, the reciprocal exchange that characterized the master–slave relationship eventually bore its long-sought fruits, since, according to Columella, 'such justice (*iustitia*) and consideration (*cura*) on the part of the master contributes greatly to the increase of his estate'.[67]

Therefore, in both the Roman world and the ante-bellum American South, the ideal model of master–slave relationship revolved around the essential feature of reciprocity. Masters were supposed to provide for the well-being of their slaves in return for their loyalty and the work that they performed. Within the boundaries of this ideal model, the slaves could and did become an integral part of an extended household with their rights and duties. On one hand, this clearly increased their dependency on the masters; on the other hand, in the masters' mind, this also allowed them more chances to survive. More importantly, it is evident that in both cases, though under very different social and economic circumstances, the masters' acknowledgment of certain rights of the slaves was related to their attempts to diffuse conflict, and, thus, have a better working environment. Such an environment, in turn, would produce the ideal conditions for the optimization of the resources of the master's plantation or estate.

THE IDEAL PATERNALISTIC SYSTEM: BENEVOLENCE, INTERFERENCE, AND EXPLOITATION

Clearly, in its daily reality, the paternalistic system must have been characterized by the masters' combination of cruelty and kindness in the treatment of their slaves, though there is no doubt that it always maintained as a central feature its exploitative nature, however filtered through measures of reciprocity and accommodation. Still, we cannot overlook the fact that, in stark contrast with this often grim reality, there existed ideal models of management that Roman and southern masters had constructed – models that, according to ancient and modern agronomists, should have informed and shaped the actions of masters toward the slaves in the two societies. In such models, the masters' benevolence, kindness, and care toward his slaves – all qualities related to the rhetoric of paternalism – played a large role and need to be analysed in their right context.

As a consequence of the importance of these qualities, in the ante-bellum American South the ideal model of management relied on the fabrication

[67] Columella, *De Re Rustica* 1.8.19.

of the myth of a fair relationship between masters and slaves. In numerous articles and published tracts, planters exalted the masters' paternalistic benevolence and clearly related it to the condition of dependency of their workforce, by claiming that enslavement, in fact, was of benefit to the slaves – a central point in the writings of George Fitzhugh and other major ideologues of the 'proslavery argument'.[68] Particularly interesting, in this context, are the published recollections of Amanda Washington, which, similarly to other famous published diaries by southern women, supported a highly idealized paternalistic view of the southern slave system – a view in which benevolence played a large role in the moral justification of slavery.[69] Thus, not surprisingly, Washington stated that 'noblesse oblige was recognized everywhere, and we felt bound to treat kindly the class dependent on us [the slaves]'.[70]

To be sure, benevolence could take many different forms in a master's treatment of his slaves; yet, most of the time, the master manifested it by granting rewards that were related to specific aspects of the slaves' daily lives, as we have seen previously. As a result of the influence of paternalism and the rhetoric subsuming the proslavery argument, masters took for granted that an implicit benevolence stemmed out from their condition as slaveholders. For this reason, they considered as exceptional acts of benevolence concessions such as extra food, extra clothing, moderation in punishment, and the construction of proper slave quarters. The consequence of this ideal model of reciprocal relationship present in the masters' mind was that masters expected gratitude from the slaves. And, as Genovese has pointed out, gratitude implies a relation among equals. Therefore, by refusing in practical terms to show gratitude to their masters, slaves refused to acknowledge the inner quality implicit in the relation of dependency and, ultimately, forced the masters to bend their ideal model of management in such a way that they had to acknowledge the slaves' rights as human beings.[71] This is the reason why a number of planters complained about the general ingratitude shown by their slaves, while they did not understand the real meaning of it.[72]

On an ideal Roman estate, as on an ideal southern plantation, the benevolence of the master would have been exhibited also by granting various rewards, such as food, clothes, and other items, as we have seen. Such rewards would be dispensed, according to Columella, on a regular

68 See Fitzhugh 1854. 69 See Washington 1907; see also Woodward 1981. 70 Washington 1907: 64.

71 Genovese 1974: 146–7.

72 See, for example, Mary Jones to Charles C. Jones Junior, July 7, 1858, in Mayers 1984: 162.

basis to those workers who 'have been found constantly busy and vigorous in their performance'.[73] At the same time, though, Columella gave specific instructions to the master to 'talk rather familiarly with the slaves, providing that they have not conducted themselves unbecomingly', so to lighten their unending toil through such friendliness. Interestingly, Columella also thought that the master should 'jest with the slaves and allow them also to jest freely', or in other cases even consult the workforce on the new work to be done.[74]

The above examples suggest that the masters' expression of kindness and concern for the well-being of the slaves was combined with their acknowledgment that their fair treatment was indispensable for the functioning of the estate. Still, the expected outcome of the master's fair treatment of his slaves was supposed to be gratitude in the form of explicit submission to his authority. The Romans used such moral terms as *beneficium* (benefit, kindness, or favour) and *benevolentia* (goodwill), in order to describe the reciprocity implicit in the master–slave relationship.[75] In most of the cases, though, *beneficium* and *benevolentia* referred specifically to the favours that the slaves made their masters in return for the consideration he had shown toward them. Still, if the slaves did not fulfil their roles in this type of reciprocal relationship and did not respond accordingly to the master's show of benevolence, their behaviour would be taken as an exhibition of disloyalty to be punished.

Therefore, notwithstanding the different results of its practice, in both the Roman world and in the American South benevolence was a distinguishing feature of the reciprocal relationship that was at the heart of the ideal model of slave management. At the same time, benevolence was also a prerequisite for the masters' claim of fair treatment of their workforce. Such claim was crucial for the smooth functioning of the actual mechanics of management and of the daily working activities. And yet, its very existence created a host of situations in which the masters' recognition of the existence of their own and their slaves' rights and duties could have a potentially disruptive influence, if the claim did not match the reality of their actions.

The paternalistic fiction of masters' benevolence and the latter's attempts to exact gratitude from the slaves – so that the perfect working environment could lead to the optimization of resources on the estates – ultimately led to a system according to which masters attempted to control

[73] Columella, *De Re Rustica* 1.8.5. [74] Columella, *De Re Rustica* 1.8.15.

[75] Cato Maior, *Agricola* 5.2.; Valerius Maximus 6.8.3; Seneca, *Ben.* 3.18–27.

every aspect of the slave's life. In the ante-bellum American South, masters interfered constantly in the slaves' activities and tried to control them, so to achieve complete domination of their workforce. By doing this, southern planters took paternalism a step forward from the simple acknowledgment of rights and duties. As Eugene Genovese has explained, through their attempt at control, southern masters sought to achieve a social and cultural 'hegemony' over the slaves' minds, so that the latter, in turn, accepted the ideological premises upon which the slave system was founded.[76]

As a consequence, as numerous studies have proven, interference did not confine itself to work, but it extended to areas such as religion and family. In fact, on a number of plantations, if slaves were not practically indoctrinated by their masters, they were required, at the very least, to attend proslavery sermons in the masters' churches and listen to words that stressed their duty of being obedient. In more than one extreme case, particularly religious masters – chief among them Virginian John Hartwell Cocke of Bremo – enforced moralistic restrictions through which they sought to both ideologically control the activities of the slaves and, at the same time, improve their efficiency in their working performance.[77] On his own South Carolinian plantation at Silver Bluff, James Henry Hammond went as far as forbidding all African religious practices to his slaves, but to no avail.[78]

Similarly, the masters' attempts to control slave families were numerous and are well documented. Although slave marriages were not recognized by the law, masters, nonetheless, encouraged slaves to marry so that they could have a stable and self-reproducing workforce on the plantation and also in order to prevent slaves from running away. In time, this attitude was embellished in moralistic tones and masters claimed that they encouraged slave marriages as part of a general moralization of plantation life.[79] Yet, southern masters also found out that slaves were more than ready to put up a staunch resistance to their plans for total control. Significantly, one Mississippi planter explained that he had tried 'for many years by preaching virtue and decency, encouraging marriages, and by punishing, with some severity, departure from marital obligations, but it was all in vain'.[80]

Methods of interference in the slaves' daily lives, similar to a certain extent to the ones employed by masters in the ante-bellum South, existed also in the Roman world. In all likelihood, Roman masters allowed their slaves to form families, so that they could increase their slave population

[76] Genovese 1974: 4–7. [77] Willis 1991: 37–55. [78] Faust 1982: 69–104.
[79] Kolchin 2003b: 123–4. [80] Anon. Mississippi Planter 1851: 623.

and also control the slaves better psychologically.[81] The slave couple, though, would have been able to marry and have children only if the master or the *vilicus* gave their explicit permission to their union.[82] This was, possibly, not just another type of interference in the slaves' lives, but also a further attempt to integrate the enslaved workforce in the household and make it feel more dependent upon the master and, consequently, more attached to his estate. In fact, slave families brought financial advantages and other types of benefits to the master, even though their existence was not legally recognized.[83] By encouraging slaves to engage in a marriage that was not recognized by the Roman law, the master achieved the double objective of increasing the stability of the estate through the creation of slave families and to attach the latter, as legal non-entities, more firmly to the central *familia*.

With regard to the master's control over the religious beliefs of his slaves, it seems that there are, instead, significant differences with the situation predominant in the ante-bellum American South. In fact, there is no doubt that the Romans were particularly tolerant and accepted the existence of a number of religions, as long as these did not harm the Roman state. Moreover, according to the writings of the Roman agronomists, the restrictions and impositions on religious matters, particularly the performance of rites, seem to have affected specifically the managerial figure of the *vilicus* – who could have been equally a slave or a freedman – rather than the enslaved workforce. In particular, Cato insisted that the *vilicus* should not perform rites at crossroads or near the hearth; the master was responsible for the performance of all rites in the household.[84] Similarly, Columella suggested that the *vilicus* should not carry out any sacrifices without the permission of the master. Significantly, Columella also warned that soothsayers and witches should not be admitted in the master's estate, so that they could not fill the minds of his slaves with superstitious beliefs.[85]

The master's interference in the life of the *vilicus* is also reflected by the prohibition of establishing a friendship (*amicitia*) with persons other than the friends of the master.[86] It is commonly accepted that the term *amicitia* indicated a reciprocal relationship based on fidelity between two persons who did not necessarily share the same social status.[87] It is possible, therefore, that the prohibition of engaging in friendships that were not condoned by the master might have aimed at controlling the private

[81] Bradley 1987: 80. [82] Varro, *Res Rusticae* 1.17.5. [83] Buckland 1908.
[84] Cato, *De Agricoltura* 5, 143. [85] Columella, *De Re Rustica* 1.8.5–6.
[86] Columella, *De Re Rustica* 1.8.7. [87] Saller 1982: 11–15.

associations of the *vilicus* outside the family, and thus at protecting the unity of the household.

It is clear that, in both the Roman world and the ante-bellum American South the particular features of the master–slave relationship led to a constant interference of the masters into aspects of the daily lives of the slaves. As a result, special importance was given, in both cases, to the idea of the masters' continuous presence on his estate. To this end, both Roman agronomists and southern agricultural writers repeatedly advised slaveholders about the importance of their constant residence so to be able to manage both their estates and their workforces as effectively as possible. One of the consequences of the masters' constant residence was, thus, that they could gain more control on the crucial dynamics of slave demography by using their power of interference – as they did – particularly to promote the existence and stability of slave families. Clearly, in both cases, the reason was related as much to the masters' concern for the reproduction of their workforce as to the fact that both the slaves and their families were considered part of the extended households of their masters.

Yet, a crucial difference was in the fact that many American slaveholders were particularly weary of the indoctrination of the slaves through religion and, thus, during their periods of constant residence on their plantations, they interfered in the lives of their slaves paying particular attention to their religious practices. As in the above-mentioned case of James Henry Hammond, many ante-bellum southern masters not only forced slaves to worship in their churches and gave their approval only to religiously celebrated weddings, but also forbade their slaves to engage in African practices altogether. Conversely, Roman masters were not particularly interested in this aspect of control and tended not to attribute much importance to the slaves' religious practices. As far as we know, the only example of a comparable attitude in religious matters is in the case of Cato's and Columella's advice to the master not to allow the *vilicus* to perform rites or sacrifices on his own or, in any case, without his approval.

Yet, the Roman *vilicus* himself was a particular type of managerial figure with little correspondence in the ante-bellum American South. Clearly, his authority, his rank, and his supervising tasks were those of an overseer. However, the fact that, in several cases, he happened to be a slave made his relationship with the master more comparable to that of a head driver with a southern planter. Doubtless, regardless of the fact that the *vilicus* could equally be a freedman or a slave, the master expected from him absolute loyalty and trust. Yet, if the *vilicus* was, indeed, a slave, he was much more likely to be forced into a position in which he was obliged to give his loyalty to the master.

In fact, the master's demand for loyalty from particular slaves on a personal basis, as in this case, was a crucial feature in the paternalistic relationship that bound the slaves to a master; it was what weakened the unity of the workforce and created its dependency through a complex system of obligations based on rights and duties. Similarly to the *vilicus*, in those cases in which he was a slave, also the head driver was expected to show absolute loyalty to his master at all times. As James Henry Hammond wrote, 'the head-driver is the most important Negro on the plantation . . . is a confidential servant, maybe a guard against any excesses or omissions of the overseer".[88] Therefore, the slave *vilicus* and the head driver shared an important feature in their close and preferential relationship with the master. As such, they acted as crucial liaisons between the master and the workforce in the ideal models of paternalistic slave management that Roman and southern masters tried to enforce on their estates.

One of the essential features of the paternalistic ideal of the master–slave relationship was the implication that, within the extended household of the masters, slaves were assimilated to children. As we have already seen, for a host of different reasons, it suited both Roman and southern masters to assimilate the master–slave relationship to the one between the patriarch head of the household and his family dependants. In the case of the American South, both Kenneth Stampp and Stanley Elkins have argued that the specific characteristics of the masters' assimilation of the slaves to children led to a process of infantilization of the slaves.[89] In Kenneth Stampp's words 'the master used the most perfect products of the system to prove that Negroes were a childlike race, needing guidance and protection but inviting paternal love as well'.[90] Therefore, children and slaves were thought by the masters to share characteristics such as irresponsibility, incorrigibility, and also the fact that the needs and worries of both were not taken too seriously.

In reality, as Eugene Genovese and a number of other historians have demonstrated, slaves did not passively accept their infantilization but fought back by faking their submission or otherwise resisting in any possible way to their masters.[91] Yet, in their ideal world, masters did not take into consideration the significance of slave resistance and continued to regard slaves as children who simply needed to be corrected when they

88 James Henry Hammond quoted in Phillips 1968 (1918): 272. 89 Stampp 1956; Elkins 1959.
90 Stampp 1956: 322. 91 Genovese 1974.

made mistakes. Perhaps, the clearest evidence of this was the fact that all masters called adult slaves until their old age with the appellation 'boys' and 'girls'. New York journalist and architect Frederick Law Olmsted was certainly well aware of this when he made his travels in the South during the 1850s. Interestingly, in his traveller's account, though not mentioning directly the naming custom we have referred to, Olmsted reported the case of a planter whose slaves 'came to him like children who have been given some task, and constantly are wanting to be encouraged and guided'.[92] What this excerpt shows is that, in practice, paternalism in the American South rested on the fundamental assumption that masters would always consider slaves as inferior specifically because – in the masters' minds – the slaves' behaviour toward them resembled in many ways, especially when they rebelled against their masters, the behaviour of insubordinate children towards their parents.

Similarly, the free members of the Roman household addressed a male slave as *puer* in Latin and *pais* in Greek – both of them meaning boy – no matter how old he was. Such a way of addressing slaves was commonly used in everyday life; it was not just the comedians' invention. Moreover, a similar idea of diminishment of the personality of the slave can be seen also in the iconography, where it informed the hierarchic scaling of figures in reliefs and sculptures in which slaves were usually depicted much smaller than their masters.[93]

It has already been suggested by Richard Saller that the use of the term 'boy' might have implied that slaves, like children, did not have the right or the responsibility to make independent choices.[94] As a consequence, the master was the one who was responsible for taking the appropriate decisions that pertained to the daily lives of his slaves, similarly to the way he was morally obliged to care for the well-being of his subordinates. Despite the fact that there is no evidence in the writings of the Roman agronomists of the use of the term 'boy' in reference to the slaves, it is almost certain that, nevertheless, they did not consider them capable of fending for themselves or of taking important decisions. And still, it is interesting to notice that Columella advised masters to let their slaves express their views freely. In his opinion, this practice allowed the masters to both assess the intelligence of their slaves and also to flatter them and, thus, make them become more enthusiastic about their work.[95] There is no evidence,

[92] Olmsted 1968 (1861): 45–6. [93] See Finley 1998: 164. [94] Saller 1996: 114.
[95] Columella, *De Re Rustica* 1.8.15.

though, that indicates that a master ever acknowledged the validity of a slave's advice or that he actually followed it.

CONCLUSION

The analysis of the master–slave relationship as it expressed itself through reciprocity, interference, and the fiction of father–child relations highlights what in our view are the main features of the ideal models of slave management in the Roman world and the ante-bellum American South. Several differences have arisen from the comparison that we have outlined. First and foremost, it is very likely that paternalistic attitudes were related to a capitalist concern for the maximization of production in the ante-bellum American South. On the other hand, even though Roman masters were clearly concerned about profit returns, they did not pursue its maximization. Furthermore, in the American South, slavery was related to the racial exploitation of African Americans, while, in the Roman world, race was never a factor that conditioned the ideology and practice of slavery.

Yet, unlike the actual practices of slave management, the ideal models created by the Roman and southern slaveholding elites do not seem to have been particularly affected by these crucial differences. The two models were clearly characterized by comparable paternalistic concerns with regard to crucial areas of the slaves' lives and, specifically, to those areas that affected the well-functioning of the estates. This was far from being the result of a simple coincidence or, as other studies might show in the future, of the direct influence of classical authors. The truth is that the two slaveholding elites were confronted by comparable problems in terms of slave management. Largely for this reason, they sought comparable solutions in ideal terms.

CHAPTER 8

Panis, disciplina, et opus servo: *the Jesuit ideology in Portuguese America and Greco-Roman ideas of slavery*

Rafael de Bivar Marquese and Fábio Duarte Joly

INTRODUCTION

By the end of the fifteenth century, when medieval manuscripts containing works of Greek and Roman writers began to be rediscovered and read, their study led to comparisons between past and present, sometimes with a clear and positive preference for the former. In the European Renaissance, Greco-Roman culture was taken as an example of perfection, an idea that would endure unshaken until at least the eighteenth century. For example, in modern political theory, historians such as Sallust, Tacitus, and Livy, and philosophers such as Aristotle and Plato, were mentioned as sources of precepts for political action and for the analysis of state systems.[1] In the making of modern economic thought, a similar process took place. The Latin agronomists – Cato, Varro, and Columella – were read as if their works formed a single unit, a model of agricultural writing in western Europe and in its colonial universe.[2] The same could be said about the other surviving treatises on household management: the *Oeconomicus* of Xenophon and the *Oeconomica* of Pseudo-Aristotle.

Historians of the colonial world have already pointed out the presence of Greco-Roman ideas of slavery in the ideology of the master classes in the Americas.[3] There are also studies on the influence of Roman legal sources on slave colonial legislation.[4] However, it is not simply a matter of showing that the ancient culture supplied an intellectual framework for the understanding of modern slavery. The subject is more complex than is conventionally presumed.

Firstly, it should be stressed that the recovery of the classical tradition with the intention of legitimating slave labour did not occur with equal

[1] About the idea of history subsuming such a perspective, see Koselleck 1993: 41–66.

[2] Marquese 1999: 56. See also Schumpeter 1994: 157.

[3] See Davis 1966.

[4] See, for example, the most famous slave code of the New World, the French *Code Noir*, in Sala-Molins 1987.

intensity throughout the colonial Americas. Rather, it varied in accordance with the historical dynamics of the European maritime empires. Between the decades of 1660 and 1720, a series of writings on slave management in the American plantations were published. The issue of slavery in the New World had attracted the attention of European theologians, jurists, and intellectuals since the beginning of the sixteenth century; however, their interest lay mainly in the legitimacy of captivity, focusing upon the enslavement of the natives.[5]

The literature that appeared after the second half of the seventeenth century had a different character. It concentrated on the behaviour of masters toward their slaves and not on the legitimacy of captivity. Written by Dominican, Jesuit, and Anglican missionaries, those texts – texts such as Jean Baptiste du Tertre, *Histoire Générale des Antilles Habitées par les Français* (Paris, 1667); Morgan Godwyn, *The Negrós & Indians Advocate* (London, 1680); Jorge Benci, *Economia Cristã dos Senhores no Governo dos Escravos* (Rome, 1705); André João Antonil, *Cultura e Opulência do Brasil* (Lisbon, 1711); and Jean Baptiste Labat, *Nouveau Voyage aux Isles de l'Amérique* (Paris, 1722) – addressed the classical tradition, and specifically the Roman agronomists and the Greek writings on *oikonomia*, combining it with the biblical discourse about reciprocal obligations, and thus fashioning their ideas for dealing with the colonial slave societies. Nevertheless, a systematic appropriation of the classical and Christian traditions is only observable in the works of the Jesuits established in Portuguese America, Jorge Benci and André João Antonil.

The main objective of this chapter is to analyse such peculiarity. Benci's and Antonil's ideas on slave management were related to their perception of the structure of the Portuguese imperial power in a context of struggle for pre-eminence between the Church and the State. The loss of prestige of the Church as the leading institution of colonial sociopolitical order corresponded to attempts by the Society of Jesus to reaffirm its importance through the construction of an ideal patriarchal and Christian master. Not only did such an ideal emphasize the masters' authority over their dependants (women, children, and slaves) in a set of relationships that presupposed rigid hierarchy between commanders and commanded, but it also implied the existence of a series of reciprocal obligations between them.

It was in view of these ideological guidelines that the Jesuits appealed to the writings on household and husbandry of the ancient world. In the texts

[5] See Pagden 1982; Davis 1966: 167–96; and Zeron 1998.

of Xenophon, Pseudo-Aristotle, Cato, Varro, and Columella, slavery is mentioned as an essential part of a system of power relationships between the *despotes* or *pater familias* and his subordinates in the household or in the rural property. It was precisely this aspect that allowed a conjunction between Christian and classical thought on slavery. But such a combination only becomes fully understandable if set in the context of the Portuguese empire and its Atlantic colonies in the seventeenth century.

PORTUGUESE AMERICA, SLAVERY, AND THE JESUITS IN THE SEVENTEENTH CENTURY

Portuguese America was the first area of the New World where the slave-based sugar plantations were firmly established. Between 1580 and 1620, there was an accelerated growth in the industry of sugar on the Brazilian coast, especially in Bahia and Pernambuco. In the 1620s, the Portuguese colony already monopolized the supply of sugar to Europe. However, this situation did not last long. The Dutch occupation of Pernambuco between 1630 and 1650 made possible the emergence of new areas of sugar production in the New World: the French and British Caribbean islands.

The rapid establishment of the sugar plantations in the West Indies from the 1650s had a negative impact on the sugar economy of Portuguese America. The growth of the English and French production in the Caribbean lowered the prices of the product in the European markets. At the same time, the demand for black slaves in the West Indian plantations raised the price of slaves on the African coast. Besides this, Brazilian landowners also had to face another problem. Due to the French and British mercantilist policies in the second half of the seventeenth century, which attempted to stimulate production through monopolistic guarantees, Brazilian sugar was practically excluded from these two European markets. From then on, the Brazilian product had to compete with the English and French in the 'open' markets of the Mediterranean and the Baltic Sea.[6]

The unfavourable position of Luso-Brazilian masters in the sugar world market was largely a result of the weakness of the Portuguese Crown in European economics and geopolitics. The Union of the Iberian Crowns in 1580 certainly contributed to the precarious situation of Portugal, because the Habsburg empire was already in the deep economic crisis that would

[6] See Schwartz 1985: 157–63; Ferlini 1988: 70–80; Castro 1976: 31–3, 50–1.

lead to its collapse in the next century.[7] When Portugal obtained independence from Spain in 1640, its standing in Europe was peripheral. The political and economic costs of the Restoration were very high for the weak Portuguese Crown. Consolidation of the new Bragança dynasty demanded submission to a double dependence. To maintain the kingdom against the threats of a Spanish re-conquest, the Bragança ratified a series of military and commercial treaties with England (1642, 1654, 1661), thus enhancing the subordinate position of Portugal in western Europe. On the other hand, with the collapse of the 'Empire of Pepper' in the East, the possessions of the New World became the main economic support for Portugal: a heavy taxation on Brazilian sugar was enacted to finance military and diplomatic expenses.[8]

Such tribulations did not endanger completely the survival of the sugar economy in Portuguese America. Despite the disorganization brought by the South Atlantic wars in the decades between 1620 and 1650, the post-1650 heavy taxation, the structural problems of the Portuguese mercantile fleet, the West Indian competition, and the restricted access to certain European markets, the Luso-Brazilian master class of Pernambuco, Bahia, and Rio de Janeiro was able to maintain a stable sugar production, which was also guaranteed by the consolidation of the Atlantic slave trade.[9] Thus, there was a growth in the number of black slaves in the sugar plantations. Although it is not reasonable to establish a direct causal link between the increase of the captive population and the increasing number of black revolts, it is certain that, during the course of the seventeenth century, slave resistance reached unparalleled proportions in Portuguese America, as the wars of Palmares clearly show.

Significantly, the first texts printed in Portuguese on the theme of black slavery in Portuguese America appeared in the second half of the seventeenth century. Such literature was written exclusively by Jesuits and included some sermons by Priest Antônio Vieira, the *Christian Economy in the Government of the Slaves* (1705) by Italian Jesuit Jorge Benci, and *Cultura e Opulência do Brasil* (*Culture and Opulence of Brazil*) (1711) by João Antônio Andreoni under the pseudonym of André João Antonil. The major focus of these works was on the government of slaves, as the title of Benci's work reveals.

[7] See Wallerstein 1974: 165–99.

[8] See Wallerstein 1981: 179–87; Hanson 1986; Mauro 1987: 39–66; Mello 1998: 248–9; Schwartz 1985: 164–5; Castro 1976: 51.

[9] See Alencastro 2000: 186–7, 325.

It is significant that the Jesuits were the only authors in colonial Brazil to deal with this theme. They had not only formed the main intellectual nucleus of Portuguese America – until the expulsion of the Society of Jesus in 1750 – but they had become particularly known for promoting the counter-reformation ideas and designing a plan for evangelization of the whole colonial population: white men, black captives, and free natives. Yet, if the Jesuits had been established in the main colonial centres of Portuguese America since the sixteenth century, why only in the beginning of the eighteenth century did they compose treatises, such as those of Jorge Benci and André João Antonil, which dealt with master–slave relationships? Indeed, texts written previously by Jesuits did not confront the problem of slave control, despite the facts that the Society of Jesus owned several rural properties run by slaves and that the issue of slavery was a widespread topic of discussion among its members.[10] The answer to this question should be sought in the changes that took place in the colonial context and in the situation of the Society of Jesus in the Portuguese empire.

The end of the seventeenth century was a period of stark social tensions on the sugar coast of Portuguese America, above all between masters and slaves. Although it was not called into question, the institution of captivity in the northeast coast was shaken by the eruption of several episodes of slave resistance, especially the one at Palmares, in the second half of the seventeenth century. Fear of slave resistance was one of the elements that motivated the appearance of innovations in the Portuguese legislation regarding the *quilombos* (fugitive slaves' settlements) in particular, and black slavery in general. The Portuguese legislative tradition on black slavery was not a codified one like that of the French empire. The Manueline and Philippine Ordinances did not explicitly regulate the ownership and control of slaves, but limited themselves to indicating the foundations that legitimated black captivity. Even the complementary legislation to the Ordinances dealt basically with the slave trade and the resulting incomes. During the reign of D. Pedro II (1667–1706), however, a clear modification in this legal tradition is observable, since, from 1688, laws concerning the harsh treatment of slaves were continuously enacted.[11]

In this period of social conflict involving masters and slaves, the Jesuits in Brazil also faced some challenges. In the whole empire, ownership of vast

[10] On the Jesuits and slavery, see Zeron 1998; and J. Eisenberg 2000. On the Society of Jesus' estates, see Assunção 2004.

[11] See the collection of documents in Lara 2000 (cd-rom) and particularly the author's introduction. On the legislation concerning the Brazilian *quilombos*, see Lara 1996: 81–109.

properties (rural and urban) by the Society of Jesus, as well as its exemption from paying tithes, were under attack. Since the 1650s, the Municipal Councils of Bahia and Rio de Janeiro presented petitions against the privileges allowed to the Jesuits. The settlers of the State of Maranhão criticized the use of an Indian workforce by the Jesuits, since it contradicted the defence of the indigenous freedom proclaimed by the Society of Jesus. In the 1690s, the Crown tried to force the Jesuit Order to pay the tithes. All such attacks to the Company were little more than an expression of the loss of the Jesuit pre-eminence in the metropolitan and colonial societies.[12]

This context helps us to understand the formulation of Jesuit projects to guide colonial Christendom and, particularly, to regulate the government of slaves. In view of the problem of slave revolts and the legislation enacted during the reign of D. Pedro II, between the seventeenth century and the beginning of the eighteenth century, the Jesuit treatises and sermons, especially those of Benci and Antonil, tried to respond to the settlers' attacks by showing the faults committed by Luso-Brazilian masters in the control of their slaves.[13] The basic message of the Jesuit texts was that the masters were unable to govern their slaves correctly, because they had moved away from the precepts of Catholic morality.

THE JESUITS, SLAVERY, AND THE CLASSICS

We will first examine Jorge Benci's book, written in the city of Bahia, in sermon-like form, in 1700, and printed in Rome in 1705. Aimed at slave-holders, as well as non-slaveholders, the book is composed of an introduction and four speeches. In the introduction, Benci exposes the idea that the origin of the institution of human captivity goes back to the original sin. With man's rebellion against God, his Creator, human passions generated wars and endless strife. Captivity emerged as a means of preserving the life of the subdued, who therefore ended up in the 'perpetual domain and lordship' of the victorious. As Benci argued, 'as lordship is born from sin, is it surprising that faults derive from it and offences to God take place because of the unreason, injustice, harshness and tyranny that you practice against the servants?' To prevent these faults and offences committed by the masters against God, Benci elaborated his *Christian Economy of the Masters in the Government of the Slaves*, defined as the 'rule, norm and

[12] See Auden 1996: 439–60, 601–3; and Koshiba 1988: 270.

[13] The relation between the slave revolts and the Jesuit writings was highlighted by Vainfas 1986: 84–91, and 1996: 60–80.

model, which the Christian masters must observe to achieve their duties as true masters'.[14]

The foundation of the *Christian Economy* rested upon reciprocal duties between masters and slaves, because 'as the servant is obliged to the master, likewise the master is obliged to the servant'. What were the obligations that the masters owed to the slaves? Benci writes that, in agreement with the Holy Spirit, as expressed in Ecclesiasticus (33.26), 'bread, and discipline, and work must be given to a servant' (*panis, et disciplina, et opus servo*). But biblical authority is not alone in the delineation of the objective of the book. Citing the pseudo-Aristotelian *Oeconomica*, Benci writes:

> These same obligations that the *Ecclesiasticus*, inspired by the Holy Spirit, had found for the masters, Aristotle had discovered himself in the light of natural reason. When he enumerates the necessary instructions to the householders for the good administration of their houses, and reaches the issue of the masterly conduct of the servants, he says that the master owes them three things, work, sustenance and punishment: and that all three are equally necessary for him to achieve completely what he must do as a master. Because to sustain the servant without giving him occupation and punishment, when he deserves them, only makes him obstinate and rebellious; and to order him to work and punish him thereafter, not giving him any sustenance, is a violent and tyrannical thing (*tria vero cum sint opus, cibus et castigatio; cibus quidem sine castigatione et opera petulantem reddit; opus vero et castigatio sine cibo violenta res est*). Now combine both texts, the profane with the sacred; compare *panis* with *cibus*, *disciplina* with *castigatio*, and *opus* with *opus*: and you will see that either the Preacher (for *Ecclesiastiscus* also mean this) is a Philosopher to the divine, or that the Philosopher, for not being divine, is a Preacher.[15]

Here we have an explicit synthesis of classical thought and biblical tradition. Although the Ecclesiasticus supplies the conceptual triad from which Benci would lecture on the government of slaves, it is the Greek philosopher who explains the Christian ideas, as is inferred from the literal transcription of a passage of the *Oeconomica*, in its Latin version. The terminological comparison between the Latin texts of the Vulgate and of the *Oeconomica* has a clear objective: it demonstrates that the combination of terms reveals a universal truth, because it emanates not only from Scriptures but also from the main classical authority in the opinion of the Scholastic: Aristotle.

[14] Benci 1977 (1705): 49–50. The analysis of the writings of Benci and Antonil relies upon Marquese 1999: 57–85.

[15] Benci 1977 (1705): 51–2.

The further content of the *Christian Economy*, based upon other classical and Christian authors, follows the structure delineated in the text above: the first speech treats the provision of material sustenance, the second treats religious indoctrination, the third treats the punishments given to slaves, and the fourth speech treats slave labour. Obviously, what Benci understands as discipline – the evangelization of the slaves in the Christian faith – is something very different from what the classical sources meant by it. In the second speech, following the counter-reformation precepts, Benci postulates instruction in the Christian doctrine, the use of the sacraments, and the example of a good life as instruments for slave control.

Moreover, by choosing the pseudo-Aristotelian *Oeconomica*, Benci has opted for a particular household ideology. Why did he not choose Aristotle's *Politics* – which contains the most articulate discussion on slavery in the ancient world – or the *Oeconomicus* of Xenophon, one of the few remnants of ancient literature on the household? The fundamental difference of the pseudo-Aristotelian *Oeconomica* with both these works helps us to understand the reasons for its appropriation by Benci.

Central to the thought of Aristotle is the polis, the city-state. His discussion of the household (*oikos*) is just a preamble to a broader discussion about the character of the city. In Aristotle's words:

> Thus also the city-state is prior in nature to the household and to each of us individually (*kai proteron de tei phusei polis e oikos kai hekastos hemon estin*). For the whole must necessarily be prior to the part; . . . And now that it is clear what are the component parts of the state, we have first of all to discuss household management; for every state is composed of households. Household management falls into departments corresponding to the parts of which the household in its turn is composed; and the household in its perfect form consists of slaves and freemen. (Arist., *Politics* 1.1253a19; 1253b1)[16]

In Aristotle's view, as the households were the smallest parts from which the polis was constituted, it was their ability to be self-sustaining that made them key to the functioning of the polis. The ownership of property, here including the slaves, the independence it provided its members, and the owner's role in administering and defending his possessions constituted the foundation of the polis.

Also in Xenophon's *Oeconomicus* – a Socratic dialogue written in the fourth century BC – the discussion of the household is intimately linked to a discussion about citizenship. Summing up his arguments, Socrates says to Critobulus, his interlocutor:

[16] All translations of the Greek and Roman authors in this chapter are taken from the Loeb series.

Well now, we thought that estate management (*oikonomia*) is the name of a branch of knowledge, and this knowledge appeared to be that by which men can increase estates, and an estate appeared to be identical with the total of one's property, and we said that property is that which is useful for supplying a livelihood, and useful things turned out to be all those things that one knows how to use ... Moreover, since the crops grow and the cattle on a farm graze outside the walls, husbandry (*georgia*) seemed to us to help in some measure to make the workers valiant. And so this way of making a living appeared to be held in the highest estimation by our states, because it seems to turn out the best citizens and most loyal to the community. (Xen., *Oeconomicus* 6.4; 8–10)

However, we can see a shift in this doctrine of the centrality of the polis already in the works of Theophrastus, who took over the leadership of the Peripatetics when Aristotle left Athens in 323–322 BC, and in the pseudo-Aristotelian *Oeconomica*, as well as later in the *Epitome of Peripatetic Ethics and Politics* preserved in Stobaeus' *Florilegia*, written by the emperor Augustus' court philosopher, Arius Didymus, whose ideas on the household and polis testify to the modifications of Aristotle's theory of the state which were circulating in the first century BC and the first century AD.[17]

The authorship of the first book of the pseudo-Aristotelian *Oeconomica* – with which we are here concerned – is uncertain: perhaps it was written by Theophrastus or by one of his pupils. Although it apparently resembles, in its contents, the Aristotelian *Politics* and Xenophon's *Oeconomicus*, there are significant differences. Its author reaffirms the idea that the household is part of the city ([Arist.] *Oeconomica* 1343a15), but in the subsequent discussion the polis is no longer mentioned. With regard to Xenophon, we observe the same contrast. As Hans Klees has pointed out, Xenophon's *Oeconomicus* and the Peripatetic *Oeconomica* differ substantially since in the latter the consequences of the private economies for the political community are hardly touched upon.[18] When the *Epitome of Peripatetic Ethics and Politics* was written, such a perspective was already consolidated. In it, we see downplayed the Aristotelian family hierarchy and emphasis placed instead on the mutuality of the relationship between husband and wife. When the nature of the polis changed in the post-Alexander world, characterized by the pre-eminence of the Hellenistic kingdoms and of imperial Rome, so did the nature of the household. The diminution of the independence of the polis corresponded to a privatization of the household.[19]

[17] Nagle 2002: 198–9. [18] Klees 1975: 97. [19] Nagle 2002: 222.

This ideological framework that emphasized the privatization of the household suited very well the objectives of Benci. Ultimately, his proposals for the government of slaves – reduction of the working time, improvement of the material well-being, religious indoctrination for obedience, fair application of punishment – were based upon the principle of the reciprocal obligations between masters and slaves. The Jesuit intended to reach the Christian conscience of slaves and masters by implanting the ideal of Christian patriarchalism. Benci had in mind exclusively the master–slave relationships inside the household; he was not interested in discussing the political and economic features of the household. Thus, he selected those classical authors who proposed precepts according to which to deal with the slaves meant to preserve the domestic order, as was the case of the pseudo-Aristotelian *Oeconomica*.

This was not the case with Antonil, who advocated a less religious view of slave management and focused upon the broader economic context of Portuguese America. Although Antonil adopted precepts contained in the pseudo-Aristotelian *Oeconomica*, as well as in Xenophon's writings, he did not restrict himself to these works. Because of the character of the theme under scrutiny, the functioning of a unit of production – the *engenho* (sugar plantation) – that involved labour division, Antonil had to appeal to the Latin agronomists.

João Antônio Andreoni was an Italian Jesuit long established in Bahia. Between 1693 and 1698, he wrote an agronomic treatise on the culture of sugarcane and its manufacture in light of his direct observations at the 'Sergipe do Conde' plantation, owned by the Society of Jesus. In the first decade of the eighteenth century, he wrote three more treatises, on tobacco, gold mines, and livestock. He published the four treatises in 1711, with the title *Culture and Opulence of Brazil*, under the pseudonym of André João Antonil.[20]

The government of slaves was examined in the first treatise of the work, in the part dedicated to the manufacture of sugar. In the preface to this part, Antonil clarified his two great objectives. In the first instance, he intended to treat sugar, and not the recently discovered gold mines, as the most important product of the Portuguese empire. Secondly, he intended to offer a guide of 'practical information' to those who wished to run an *engenho*.[21] So, Antonil had both a broader objective related to the colony as

[20] The best edition is the one by Andrée Mansuy Diniz Silva; see Antonil 2001 (1711).

[21] Antonil 2001 (1711): 67.

a whole and a more specific one, related to the administration of sugar plantations.

Unlike Benci, Antonil did not mention the classical authors he consulted, and, therefore, in his work there are no nominal references to Xenophon, Pseudo-Aristotle, Cato, Varro or Columella. However, his dependence on the Greco-Roman writings on household and husbandry is clearly revealed by the way he organized the part dedicated to the sugar plantation, as well as by the issues he selects. In book I, which deals with the role of the master in the administration of the estate, the Jesuit discussed the following points: the choice of the appropriate lands, the relationship between the master and the neighbouring cane farmers, the choice between free and servile labour and the government of the household. In book II he described the techniques for proper cultivation of the sugarcane and the functioning of the sugar mill. Finally, in book III, he examined in detail the packaging of the sugar and its sale to the Portuguese market. In sum, Antonil structured the first part of his treaty analysing three aspects: land, men/equipment, and the making of the sugar.

Such structure resembles that of the Roman agricultural manuals, as can be seen in Varro's division of the subject:

> the chief divisions of agriculture are four in number. [. . .] First, a knowledge of the farm, comprising the nature of the soil and its constituents; second, the equipment needed for the operation of the farm in question; third, the operations to be carried out on the place in the way of tilling; and fourth, the proper season for each of these operations (Varro, *Res Rusticae* I, 5, 3)

Yet, the most striking similarities between the Jesuit and the ancient authors are those related to slave labour.

Antonil analysed the government of slaves in detail in two chapters of the first book. In chapter 5, he specified the tasks that needed to be carried out by the different types of overseers. In his view, the authority that the master conferred upon the chief overseer should be very well calculated:

> I say that this authority must be very orderly and dependent, and not absolute, in a way that the inferiors are subordinated to the superiors, and all of them to the master whom they serve. The slaves must be persuaded that the overseer has sufficient power to command them and to reprimand and punish them when necessary; however, the slaves also must know that they can appeal to the master who will attend to them with due justice.[22]

[22] Antonil 2001 (1711): 82–3.

The primary function of the overseer was to preserve order among the slaves, and this could only be achieved if the slaves recognized his authority over them. According to Antonil, if this did not happen, the slave could ultimately complain to the master about the grievances caused by the overseer. In this sense, the master remained the supreme arbitrator in relation to his human property, having under control all his subordinates – overseers and slaves – by means of the proper distribution of justice.

In writing his advice, Antonil was merely following prescriptions given by the Latin agronomists: the chief overseer of Antonil, the 'feitor-mor', corresponds exactly to the *vilicus*, a central figure in the treatises of Cato, Varro, and Columella.[23] To Cato (Cato, 5.1.2), the *vilicus* must settle disputes among the slaves and, if anyone commits an offence, he must punish him properly and in proportion to the fault. He also must see that the servants are well provided for and he must keep them busy with their work. In Varro's and Columella's works the same advice is present. Both authors highlight the importance of the overseers' authority. Varro says that they are not to be allowed to control their men with whips, but rather with words (Varro, *Res Rusticae* 1.17.5). Columella states that the overseer 'will have to observe those principles which are difficult to maintain in larger spheres of government, namely, not to deal either too cruelly or too leniently with those set under him' (Columella, 11.1.25).

In a passage very similar to the one by Antonil, Columella observes that, as the slaves are 'liable to a greater number of people, such as overseers, taskmasters, and jailers, they are the more liable to unjust punishment'; therefore, the master 'should give them frequent opportunities for making complaint against those persons who treat them cruelly or dishonestly' (Columella, 1.8.17–18). According to this model of slave government, the *pater familias* is responsible for dealing with the conflicts that may arise within the household because of the unequal status of the slaves in the *villa*. Having delegated administrative powers to the *vilicus*, the proprietor has to check if his orders are being carried out by means of a balance between rewards and punishments. Columella is here in accord with the ideas expressed by Seneca, another ancient author who was well known to the Jesuits. Benci frequently cites Seneca when he admonishes the masters not to be violent with the slaves, while Antonil adopts a Senecan tone in reminding the masters to control their vengeful impetus before punishing their slaves;[24] such ideas were expressed by the Roman philosopher in his

[23] Sergeenko 1986: 191–207; and Martin 1974: 267–97. [24] Antonil 2001 (1711): 83.

treatises on anger (*De Ira*) and clemency (*De Clementia*), and in the Letter 47 to Lucilius.

The other chapter of *Culture and Opulence* related to the government of slaves is the most important in this part of the work. Entitled 'How the master must behave with his slaves', the chapter prescribes the norms for the correct command of servants. Antonil firstly deals with the current practices of the masters in Brazil. Alleging moral principles, he criticizes the masters for not giving its due importance to the Christian indoctrination of the slaves. Antonil also censures the masters because they do not supply enough food to the slaves and they do not allow them to cultivate their own land on Sundays and during holidays. Instead, the masters simply force the slaves to work hard on a daily basis. According to Antonil, such behaviour by the master class only increases the possibility of flight and rebellion. Therefore, if the master

> behaves with the slaves as a father, giving them enough food and clothes, and some rest in the work, he will also be able to behave like a master afterwards, and the slaves, being convinced of the faults that they have committed, will not complain when receiving mercifully their fair and deserved punishment.[25]

In this connection, we also read in Antonil that the masters should allow the slaves' festivities, acting with liberality and giving them rewards for their continuous work.[26]

With the exception of the references to religious indoctrination, these precepts are derived from the Greco-Roman ideas of slavery. Like Benci, Antonil follows the pseudo-Aristotelian *Oeconomica*, in whose text we read that

> we may apportion to our slaves (1) work, (2) chastisement, and (3) food. If men are given food, but no chastisement nor any work, they become insolent. If they are made to work, and are chastised, but stinted of their food, such treatment is oppressive, and saps their strength. ([Arist.] *Oeconomica* 1344a35)

In stating that the Brazilian slaveowners must behave with liberality towards their slaves, Antonil follows Varro, according to whom the slaves

> are made to take more interest in their work by being treated more liberally in respect either of food, or of more clothing, or of exemption from work, or permission to graze some cattle of their own on the farm, or other things of this kind; so that, if some unusually heavy task is imposed, or punishment inflicted on them in some way, their loyalty and kindly feeling to the master may be restored by the consolation derived from such measures. (Varro, *Res Rusticae* 1.17.4ff.)

[25] Antonil 2001 (1711): 90–8. [26] Antonil 2001 (1711): 97–8.

Antonil's perspective on the government of slaves differs in some important aspects from that of Jorge Benci. Although both appealed to the biblical discourse of reciprocal obligations between masters and slaves, Antonil advocated a view that, in many respects, was secular, in contrast to the profoundly religious perspective adopted by Benci. Yet, both agreed on a relevant point: they tried to reconcile classical and Christian traditions, therefore interpreting modern slavery through the prism of ancient ideology.

MODERN SLAVERY AND ANCIENT IDEOLOGY

The resurgence of slavery in the modern world was due to historical processes substantially different from those that characterized the ancient world. Modern colonial slave societies were products of the expansion of the capitalist world since the fifteenth century, and were located at the periphery of the economic system.[27] In Greece and Rome, slavery was the main permanent labour in the rural and urban environments located at the core of those societies. There is yet another significant difference, concerning the slaves' origins. Unlike the ancient world, where enslavement took place within the very society that used the slaves – even if some slaves were also captured in the bordering areas of the empire, as in the wars carried on by Rome – in modern slavery, there was an early division between areas of slave production (Americas) and areas of slave reproduction (Africa). This latter region was constantly plundered of its human resources by the transatlantic slave trade. Consequently, modern slavery also acquired a racial character, as a result of the capture of blacks in Africa.

However, emphasis on the differences between ancient and modern slavery does not necessarily imply that there were no continuities between both systems. These show in the residual presence of slaves in European societies during the Middle Ages, as well as in the Roman legal codes on slavery, which supplied the juridical structure for the making of slavery in the Americas. Above all, though, it is the classical ideas of slavery and their role in the intellectual attitudes to black slavery that must be mentioned.

Certain elements of the ancient ideology of slavery were given particular consideration in the making of the ideology of the master class in the New World. First, as Keith Bradley has remarked for the Roman case, the master–slave relationship was just one of a sequence of asymmetrical relationships in society, according to an idea that traditional social

[27] See Wallerstein 1981; see also Schiavone 1999.

bonds, all dependent upon injunction and deference, served to perpetuate the established order of society.[28] Second, slavery was an essential part in any household since the house and household had a direct bearing on a man's standing and prestige. The Greek *oikos* included, together with the family, also the land, the dwellings, the warehouses, and the graves. Moreover, it included also the slaves and the instruments used to toil the land. And it was the *kurios*, the head of the household, who had supreme power, at least in theory, over all these elements.[29]

Equally, Richard Saller has observed that, when a Roman spoke of his *domus*, 'it is often impossible to discover whether he meant his physical house or the family and servants in it over whom he exercised *potestas* or *dominium*'.[30] Third, and as a result of the previous issues, ancient ideology was based on patriarchy,[31] even if in practice certain ideals attached to family life worked to counterbalance the power of the head of the household.[32] The foremost image of the *pater familias* that the Romans had in mind was that of an estate owner. To praise a Roman by calling him *bonus pater familias* was to credit him with responsible management of his property, including the slaves.[33] This is particularly visible in the Roman agricultural manuals, and this is also the view that pervades the Greek writings on economics.

These were precisely the points that interested the Jesuits in their formulation of an ethic for the Brazilian master class. Benci and Antonil tried to revive, from a Christian point of view, the image of the ancient head of the household (*kurios/pater familias*) in the European colonial world. That ideology, for instance, was compatible with the wider political project of the Society of Jesus. In comparison with the other European religious orders that wrote on the government of slaves in the transition from the seventeenth to the eighteenth centuries, the Jesuits were the only ones who elaborated an organic image of the patriarchal master. Such systematization was partly due to their political weight in the Portuguese empire, in clear contrast with the relatively little importance of the Anglicans and Dominicans in the English and French colonies.

Although endorsing the Portuguese imperial plan, the Jesuits carried on their own projects to guide colonial Christendom based upon the political ideas propagated by the Second Scholastic. For our purposes, their interpretation of the theory of indirect power, initially formulated by Francisco de Vitória and later developed by Francisco Suárez, is of special relevance.

[28] Bradley 1994: 4–5. [29] Jones 1984. [30] Saller 1984: 347. [31] Strasburger 1990: 19.
[32] Lassen 1997: 107. [33] Saller 1999: 191–2.

These theologians considered as quite distinct the spheres of ecclesiastical authority and of secular authority; therefore, they inferred that it was not possible for the Pope to exercise a direct coercive power over the secular Republics. However, in the case of religious issues, temporal power should submit itself to spiritual power. When crucial spiritual problems were to be faced, the Pope – or his representatives – should exercise his indirect power over the temporal authorities.[34]

Already in the sixteenth century, the theory of indirect power had been applied to Portuguese America, especially by Manuel da Nóbrega, as a result of the improper conduct of the settlers as well as of the secular clergy. The Jesuits – with the approval of the Crown – were to act for the political and moral protection of colonial society.[35] Benci and Antonil simply applied the theory of indirect power to a context in which the Society of Jesus was being heavily criticized by the settlers and metropolitan agents. From the end of the sixteenth century, there was a consensus among the Jesuits that the economic and religious foundations of Portuguese America rested on slavery, which allowed blacks to be rescued from paganism in Africa and evangelized in America.[36] What Benci and Antonil argued in their texts was that Luso-Brazilian masters did not know how to govern the slaves because they had moved away from Christian patriarchalism. Thus, the answer to such a problem should be sought in the ideal of the patriarchal master that the Jesuits formulated by combining the Christian and Greco-Roman traditions.

Though this combination did not occur in other parts of the colonial world, it already had been well established in Benci's and Antonil's land of origin since the Renaissance. For instance, we could relate this intellectual trend to the so-called *villeggiatura* literature that emerged in Italy, especially in Venice, during the sixteenth century, as a result of a process of formation of a new landowning class that displaced the old feudal aristocracy. To legitimate its status, this class promoted a literary genre that combined the *rei rusticae scriptores*, and their eulogy of agriculture, with humanist and Christian contents. For instance, in Alvise Cornaro, *Discorsi intorno alla vita sobria* (1583–95) and Vincenzo Scamozzi, *Idea dell'Architettura Universale* (1615), the biblical and the classical authorities appear side by side: Xenophon, Plato, Cicero, Pliny, and Ovid on one hand, and Hiob and Noah on the other, are taken as examples for the *Sancta Rusticitas*.[37]

[34] See Skinner 1978: 451–7; and Torgal 1982: 13–20. [35] See Zeron 1998: 72–4.
[36] See Alencastro 2000. [37] Bentmann and Müller 1990: 395–9.

Yet, the Jesuit revival of the ancient ideology of household and husbandry also points to a broader context of the history of the ideology of slavery. As Joseph Miller has argued, before the eighteenth century – when capitalism, civil society, and human rights created an antislavery attitude – slavery was embedded in ideologies of the family based upon a strong paternal authority, which in turn gave absolute power to the masters over their slaves. Private morality, not public ideologies, influenced the master–slave relationships.[38] The Jesuits established in Portuguese America continued to apply to the modern world an ancient ethic that appeared increasingly anachronistic.

Already at the beginning of the eighteenth century, another ideological framework suited to deal with the functioning of slavery was emerging. Individualism broke the set of reciprocal relationships that was crucial to the ancient ideology. The classical and Christian images of the patriarch were abandoned. Slaveholders began to be seen differently in the treatises on slave management. They now resembled the modern entrepreneur, an economic agent who should act rationally to achieve his material objectives.[39] Perhaps the best example of this rupture is Samuel Martin's *An Essay on Plantership*, one of the most popular West Indian agricultural manuals in the second half of the eighteenth century.[40]

Martin's intellectual attitude, completely in tune with the ethos of improvement advocated by the 'new husbandry' – whose intellectual foundations rested on the political economy's analytical categories of labour and production[41] – is synthesized in the title of his book. The author uses a neologism that had been created in the first years of English colonization of the Caribbean to characterize the status of a planter. Martin, however, gave a new meaning to the term. 'By plantership', he wrote, 'I understand the art of managing a sugar plantation to the best advantage, so as to make it produce the most, both in quantity and quality.'[42] In this new approach to the issues of agriculture and slavery, the moral tone of the classical and Christian sources could be of little help. The *auctoritas historiae* was no longer taken into account.

[38] Miller 2002a: 114–15.

[39] On the modern concept of *entrepreneur* see Vérin 1982: 121–74. On treatises on slave management, see Marquese 2004.

[40] There were at least nine editions of Martin's work. For details see Sheridan 1960: 126–39.

[41] Tribe 1978. [42] Martin 1767: 1.

PART IV

Exiting Slave Systems

CHAPTER 9

Processes of exiting the slave systems: a typology

*Olivier Pétré-Grenouilleau**

Comparative typology may be useful as a heuristic tool, not as an objective in itself. Indeed, to focus on constants can lead to fixing the features underlined by the observer and thereafter to masking the forces, the agents and the processes at work behind the repetitions or the deviations, processes which evidently participate in the 'fabrication' of history. Slavery, properly speaking, will be our subject. Other modes of dependence (e.g. collective dependence in antiquity, serfdom, etc.), as well as debt bondage, will be excluded.

Firstly, I will analyse the processes leading to what I propose to call 'systemic exits' from slavery, that is to say types of individual or collective deliverance, which do not call into question the equilibrium of a given slave system, while they may even sometimes reinforce it. Then, I will look at how the slaves, through modes of resistance, participated in the process of deliverance from slavery – a type of process, whose nature (systemic or not) will have to be defined. Finally, I will focus on two phenomena, which both led to the non-systemic deliverance from slavery: on one hand, the case of slave systems that seem to have slowly 'declined' before vanishing almost completely;[1] on the other hand, that of systems abolished as a result of specific measures or decisions.

1 SYSTEMIC EXITS

Although numerous, systemic exits refer to specific individuals and do not call into question the very nature of a slave system. On the contrary, they

* I would like to thank here Jacques Annequin (Besançon), historian of the ancient Greek world and Roger Botte (CNRS), Africanist, for having read and commented on a first version of this work. It goes without saying that its imperfections can only be attributed to its author. For a comparative study of the end of slavery and of dependence, see Weiler 2003.

[1] I use the expression 'seems to decline' because the idea of 'decline' is nowadays largely called into question as far as slavery in Roman antiquity is concerned.

can favour its reproduction, as Claude Meillassoux defined this term in his *Anthropology of Slavery*:[2]

> The majority of slavery theories are based upon the master-slave relationship, as it is expressed in terms of 'property'. They establish it as the first and foremost relation in order to describe the phenomenon of slavery in its totality . . . However, in order to conceive slavery as a system . . . there has to be a *continuity* in slavery relations, thus these relations have to be *organically and institutionally reproduced*, in a way that they preserve the socio-political organization of slavery; therefore, the social groups have to be placed in a specific and constantly renewed relation of exploitation and domination.[3]

With regard to our subject, we may distinguish two kinds of reproduction: the purely demographical one and the social or statutory one which favour the reproduction of a given slave system and not only that of individuals reduced to slavery. These two types are evidently related, though not in a mechanical way. The study of the systemic exits underlines this paradox. In this case, some slaves can leave the system and, thus, cause a problem in terms of demographic reproduction. But they may also constitute an advantage for the reproduction of the slave system as a whole.

The example of enfranchisement

Systemic exits refer both to enfranchisement and to customs, such as the adoption of a slave or the marriage between a master and a female slave,[4] which are related to it, since enfranchisement usually precedes or validates them. We also know that enfranchisement, in ancient Greece, seems to be as old as slavery itself.[5] But what is enfranchisement? According to a juridical approach, it is an immediate liberation unilaterally decided by the master, or a gift offered by him to his slave. Both these aspects are open to question. They probably reflect more the official view of enfranchisement, that of the master, than the reality.

Far from being a gift, freedom could be bought by the slave, especially in the Greco-Roman world, but also in modern colonial America and in

[2] Meillassoux's definition remains debatable. Putting the accent on two factors only – war and market (slaves being 'mainly renovated by *acquisition*'; see Meillassoux 1991: 327) – it seems to have completely excluded the possibility of reproduction by natural expansion which has sometimes been effective, as in the Old South of the United States of America during the first half of the nineteenth century and in Brazil's Minas Gerais during the late eighteenth century; see Bergad 1999. To a lesser degree, such reproduction has also been observed in sub-Saharan Africa, especially in the case of the royal slaves. See Harms 1981; and Manning 1990; see also Meillassoux 1983.

[3] Meillassoux 1991: 73.

[4] The contrary seems to have always been rare and very badly perceived.

[5] The synthesis in Calderini 1908 has not been replaced yet.

pre-colonial sub-Saharan Africa.[6] Freedom was also granted partly on account of the slave's actions, whether they were directed against his master – who may have decided to enfranchise him in order to get rid of him – or destined to gain his sympathy. In all these cases enfranchisement was the result of constant negotiations between the slave and the master, not just the consequence of a unilateral action.[7] So, from the master's viewpoint, we can say that enfranchisement refers only to consented and/or authorized exits.

Speaking about negotiation also implies the presence of duration and process, and not immediacy. The process is sometimes detectable for historians, especially when enfranchisement, although never an automatic consequence, was the culmination of a series of more or less precise steps. According to Meillassoux,[8] two steps could precede the act of manumission: change from the condition of *mansé* slave and change from the condition of *casatus* slave.

The *mansé* slave was the one who, while remaining completely under the authority of his master ('slave of labour'), had been granted time to use for the production of part of his subsistence. I am not really sure that, generally speaking, the type of the *mansé* slave has to be interpreted as a step in the process of enfranchisement: firstly because of its frequency and its expansion in modern colonial America, where the permission given by the masters to the slaves to cultivate a little parcel of land for themselves was not linked to the process of enfranchisement; secondly because of its relatively regulative character in the Black Muslim world;[9] thirdly, and above all, because the *mansé* slave was probably more related to a type of work exploitation than to a step toward liberty, as it was probably the case in antiquity.[10] I would add – because I think that slavery can not be

[6] Roger Botte tells me that contractual enfranchisement was exceptional in sub-Saharan Africa, but took place in societies ruled by Muslim law; according to Botte, on a more general level, the possibility of redemption constituted 'a general condition of slave systems' (Botte, personal communication).

[7] This leads to an issue that has become the object of an important and autonomous research field within the study of slavery in colonial America: the phenomenon of the *agency*, that is to say of the role played by the slaves themselves as agents in the slave system.

[8] For this question and the subsequent discussion, see Meillassoux 1991: 117–31.

[9] According to Roger Botte, Muslim law 'defines quite strictly the time left to the slave to produce part of his subsistence, at least a whole day, plus the time – morning or evening – not included in the day of labour for the master' (Botte, personal communication).

[10] At that time, the forms of servile labour were numerous, varying from that of slaves living among the free population (*khoris oikountes* in Athens), working as artisans and paying a rent to their master, to that of slaves rented to private individuals for a *misthos* paid to the owner and as part of the slave's nutrition. We know that, in ancient Rome, Pliny the Younger knew very well how to combine different systems of rural labour in order to manage his lands.

totally explicable in terms of economic relations – that the phenomenon of the *mansé* slave could also be linked to strategies of domination – since leaving the slave a certain degree of autonomy could contribute to the reduction of tensions – and demographic reproduction by offering the slave the possibility of maintaining a family.

The case of the *casatus* slave is more interesting for our purpose. According to Meillassoux, 'dispensed from cultivating the fields of the master', the *casatus* is 'responsible for the cultivation of a parcel of land' and 'has the obligation to return to the master a fixed part of the annual product'. Hence, the slave pays 'an in-kind fee and no longer a work-fee'. This condition is often related to the slave's marriage or to his/her life in a couple.[11] The *casati* slaves could sometimes redeem themselves with the help of savings. In Africa, entire villages of *casati* slaves existed. Sometimes located in remote or unsafe areas, they could serve political and military purposes, especially along frontier zones. In the case of the Mauritanian and Tuareg societies their location was determined by the water resources and so by the isohyets curve and the distribution of swamps. The *casati* slave villages were the norm there. While the nomads moved to the north, sometimes hundreds of kilometres away, where they stayed during several months, the sedentary slaves became responsible for the production of goods.[12]

Was it the same elsewhere? Yes and no. No, because we do not find the same procedures in other periods and areas. Yes, because, even if the forms are different, the main principle of 'setting up' a slave seems to have been 'very widely spread', according to Alain Testart.[13] Semi-autonomous slave villages never existed in colonial America, probably because the practice of the *mansé* slave – that is the one who could live as one of a couple and cultivate for himself/herself a small patch of land – was already the norm there.[14] In America, what could be perhaps more linked to the condition of the African *casatus* slave was the skilled slave. Hired by his master, he could gain a certain degree of autonomy, have access to monetary economy, and

[11] Meillassoux 1991: 118. I am not sure that living as a couple can be interpreted as a step towards enfranchisement. It was frequent both in colonial America and antiquity but this had no consequence on enfranchisement. The shepherd slaves, relatively autonomous, were undoubtedly the first to have a family. When it comes to the *vilicus*, who was placed at the head of the *familia rustica*, he lived with a *vilica*. But this was in part in order to ensure his continuous presence in the estate and his surveillance work both outdoors (*vilicus*) and indoors (*vilica*). Once more, this was a strategy benefiting the master and not necessarily a step towards enfranchisement.

[12] Botte, personal communication. [13] Testart 2001: 35–6.

[14] The commercial culture of exportation can also explain why '*casage*' and direct control were related here, while they were often disassociated in sub-Saharan Africa.

sometimes retrieve his liberty. The 'phenomenon of setting up a slave', remarks Alain Testart, can also be found in Asia, 'in particular in the *hill tribes* of Burma'.[15] One could establish an analogy with the situation of the *servus casatus* of the late Roman empire, as well as with that of the slaves in ancient Greece who were set up as little artisans or merchants.

Exits are often useful and controlled

The step or steps that led to liberty were never totally irreversible. Meillassoux observes that the *casati* slaves were recruited mostly 'among the slaves born in captivity'. But he adds that the master could always decide to allow the '*casage*' of slaves acquired by purchase, as well as to sell a *casatus* slave. Every privilege was 'granted arbitrarily'. The exit signal originated in the slavery institution itself. Therefore, it is not surprising that enfranchisement was rarely a gratuitous act.

In his study on slavery in ancient Greece, Yvon Garlan observes that, usually, the deliverance price corresponded to at least the market value of the slave. Its amount could be deducted from the slave's savings, lent by the master or advanced by an association of private individuals. With reference to Spanish colonial America from the sixteenth to the eighteenth centuries, Jean-Pierre Tardieu observes that enfranchisement was often officially linked to Christian love and charity. But this did not keep the masters and their heirs from protecting their interests, when elderly slaves, considered useless, were enfranchised or when the enfranchisement documents were conceded for a high price or included restrictive clauses safeguarding the owners' interest (as in 66 to 75 per cent of the enfranchisement documents). All things considered, enfranchisement for Tardieu was above all a 'commercial act' and very rarely a 'generous act'.[16]

We should also add that emancipation rarely brings about a total and immediate elimination of the dependence bonds. The emancipated slave remains for a variable length of time under the authority of his old master. The important comparative study conducted by Orlando Patterson[17] shows that this phenomenon is frequently attested in all periods and places.

In Greece, the following clauses intended to restrict the liberty of the newly enfranchised slaves arose as time went on: the need to have a patron or *prostates* – usually the former master or his heir – and the obligation to fulfil certain duties to him (*paramone* contract). The enfranchised slave could have had the obligation to remain in the house or city of his former

[15] Testart 2001: 35–6. [16] Tardieu 1982: 341–64, esp. 342 and 348. [17] Patterson 1982.

master, to accomplish numerous tasks, to follow him, take care of him, pay him an agreed sum of money, or even provide him with children. In case he/she failed to accomplish these duties, he/she ran the risk of being beaten up, whipped, put in irons and lent to a third party; he/she even ran the risk of having the act of enfranchisement annulled.

According to Yvon Garlan, the enfranchised slave's liberty has always been limited by analogous obligations. The only explanation for the multiplication of the *paramone* contracts at a later period would be the fact that it became necessary to formalize all these constraints, especially because the Roman occupation may have made it easier for the former slaves to escape.[18] Let us also add that, just like the *metics*, the enfranchised slaves did not enjoy civil rights; consequently, they were excluded from politics, were not allowed to possess land in Attica or to take out a mortgage loan. They had to pay a personal and small monthly tax, called *metoikion*. Since the middle of the fifth century BC the children coming from the union of an enfranchised slave and a citizen were also deprived of civil rights.[19]

The systematic analysis of a large number of ancient authors, thanks to a thematic index compiled at ISTA (Institute of Ancient Sciences and Techniques) in Besançon, confirms that in Roman antiquity some forms of dependence persisted after the act of enfranchisement. It is well known that the Roman *manumissio* gave the former slave a free status. However, he was called *libertus*, *libertinus*, that is to say 'newly free' and not *ingenuus*, free since birth. He also owed respect (*obsequium*) to his former master as well as certain services (*operae*). Unlike the clients (who were free men non-integrated into the *familia*), the dependence of the enfranchised slave on his former master was obligatory and highly codified. It is true that, in contrast to the Greek system, the Roman enfranchised slave could become a citizen. However, Yvon Garlan claims that this is a lame comparison. The *civitas Romana* offered only civil rights (as for metics in Athens) to those who enjoyed neither riches nor influence and very little real political power, unlike the Greek *politeia*. So, the Romans could show themselves more generous towards their enfranchised slaves at a very small cost.[20]

18 Garlan 1995: 83–7. For Yvon Garlan, the *paramone* contract allowed the masters to officially assert their rights on their enfranchised slaves. According to Alain Testart, *paramone* concerned the free men held as hostages. These two positions are not necessarily contradictory. Effectively, Testart is only interested in one kind of *paramone*, 'the *paramone* for debts, attested in the Hellenistic world, although not with certainty in ancient Greece'; see Testart 2001: 158.

19 This type of alliance was prohibited later under penalty of reduction to slavery. The examples of the bankers Pasion and Phormion, who both became citizens at the end of their lives, should not deceive us. This privilege of *ateleia* (exemption from the *metoikion*) was extremely rare; see Garlan 1995: 89.

20 Garlan 1995: 89.

Furthermore, there are plenty of texts that confess the contempt of the *ingenui* for the newly emancipated. Therefore, the slave stigma was usually not erased during the first generation, either by enfranchisement or by access to citizenship.

Regarding Black Africa, Meillassoux wrote that 'even if the slave condition has been abolished nowadays on a juridical level, the slaves' state remains identical: they conserve the stigma of servitude; the masters claim the right to be informed of their possessions; they are affected by the same prejudices as before and access to free women is still denied to men. They are not allowed to establish bonds of kinship with the free, the only kind of kinship that can lead to citizenship.'[21] According to Roger Botte, the stigma of past servitude, whilst always visible, varies considerably. It depends on the former status of the slaves (labour slaves, 'royal' slaves, etc.), as well as on the organization of dependent relations among the free. Since the notion of individual liberty is something relative in sub-Saharan Africa, the enfranchised slaves could only become a new *collective* entity, and so only pass from a clearly identified status to another one of the same collective nature – from the status of *abd* to that of *harratin* in Mauritania. As a result, the groups of enfranchised slaves had a tendency to form separate 'ethnic groups', even though *a priori* they do not present any of the characteristics of such a group. This led to the perpetuation of the servile stigma, similarly to the stigma attached to the free coloured population in the Americas.[22]

The reality of enfranchisement questioned

Since enfranchisement is ratified by law (either written law or common law) and since juridical decisions are usually final and irrevocable, enfranchisement is sometimes perceived as a definite break with the former servile state. In addition, since nowadays we conceive the notion of liberty as a concept opposite to that of servitude and/or dependence, one can be tempted to consider enfranchisement as a total and definite rupture not only with slavery but also with relations of dependence. The above examples, though, indicate that enfranchisement leads rather to a transformation of the dependence bond, than to its complete elimination. Its nature can change, depending on the place or the period examined. But, generally speaking, a form of dependence always remains. In other words, even if it

[21] Meillassoux 1991: 121. [22] Botte, personal communication.

validates a break with the world of slavery, the emancipation act signifies *only* a transition towards unconditional liberty. So, according to Claude Meillassoux, one may have to establish a clear distinction between two terms often used as synonyms: enfranchisement and manumission. 'Enfranchisement, in the literal sense of the term', he has written, is a process 'by which a slave acquires all the privileges of the free, including the *honour* attached to this status, and thus he achieves the *effacement* and oblivion of his origins.'[23]

This restrictive definition can be explained by the nature of the societies studied by Meillassoux, that is to say the great diversity of African slave systems. Some researchers have interpreted this diversity as synonymous of a 'soft' African slavery. It is an error, according to Meillassoux and Botte.[24] The diversity of African slave situations also resulted in the moderation of internal tensions, thus reinforcing the slave system as a whole. It is why, for Meillassoux, absolute enfranchisement – which implies the *effacement* of servile origins[25]– is very rare in sub-Saharan Africa (as well as in the Muslim world[26]). This way of seeing things may seem limited, particularly to the ancient slavery specialists and to those who work on slavery in colonial America. It would practically mean that true enfranchisement never really existed.

[23] Meillassoux 2001: 121. Nowadays, in Burkina Faso the descendant of a slave can often be denied the possibility of marrying an *ingenuus*; see Bazemo 2004. In Mauritania, slaves who had been enfranchised generations ago have yet to be considered *ingenui*. According to Botte, 'through the refusal of miscegenation, it is less the access to women that is sanctioned than the possibility of an opening towards a new status: this *jus sanguinis* allows to reproduce the inequalities of birth and prohibits contesting them'; see Botte 2001: 10, 12. Here, 'assimilation is an illusion'; see Botte 2001: 25. The *effacement* of origins depends to a large degree on gender. It is accelerated in the case of a female slave who, after becoming married to the master, gives him children: the children are free in all aspects. In Fouta-Djallon, it was in fashion, among the ruling families, that the mother of the leader would have been of servile origin; see Botte 2005.

[24] This is an idea that Meillassoux opposed. For him, 'labour slaves', represented 'the great majority' of African slaves. They are synonymous with 'integral exploitation': 'the slaves cultivate the lands of the masters and accomplish all the tasks that they are charged with (domestic, construction, transportation tasks, etc.), and without time limitation'; see Meillassoux 1991: 117–18. This concerns West Africa in the second half of the nineteenth century. Roger Botte told me that during that period the conditions of slavery in Africa were more rigorous than in the United States during the same period (Botte, personal communication).

[25] According to Meillassoux, 'any *public* ceremony called "enfranchisement ceremony" is not a veritable one' in Sahelian Africa; 'it does not deliver its beneficiary from the servile stain' but 'affirms it in the eyes of everybody' (see Meillassoux 1991: 122). Consequently, in order to be efficient, enfranchisement has to be kept practically a secret between the former master and the enfranchised slave, a secret which facilitates the perpetration of the dependence bonds.

[26] What Islam proposes on the matter of 'enfranchisement' is nothing more than an emancipation either onerous or gratuitous; see Meillassoux 1991: 120. On this subject, interpretations are numerous and often divergent.

On the systemic character of these exits

All these types of exits fulfilled the objectives of preservation and reproduction of the slave system. The 'chosen ones to be free' were either somewhat difficult slaves, or slaves that had grown to be less useful and, thus, easy to be separated from, or else, they were slaves that had become closer to the masters; this closeness might have resulted from their functions – if they surrounded the master – or from the colour of their skin (thus, according to Frédéric Régent, at the end of the eighteenth century, in Guadeloupe, the fairer the slave's complexion, the more chance he/she had to be enfranchised[27]), or even from the simple fact that the enfranchised was a child resulting from the union of the master with a slave. In his study of Spanish colonial America, Jean-Pierre Tardieu observes that enfranchisement was only granted 'to those who could represent a serious danger to the system's stability, that is to say those whom the everyday contact with the master was bound to make conscious of the injustice they were suffering ...[28] In this sense enfranchisement is nothing but a subtler subordination or even a veritable bribery'.[29]

This is why the slaves born in the master's 'house' (second generation slaves), independently of period or place, usually were more likely to be freed. In Spanish America and in colonial Brazil, this was also the case of the city slaves and women. It was the same in ancient Rome, with the *familia urbana* and the salaried slaves (*servi cum peculio*). Interested enfranchisement also concerned slaves performing qualifying or qualified functions, i.e. slaves (enfranchised or not) functioning as businessmen, administrators, or 'managers' in antiquity. As slaves, they possibly gained relative autonomy and the means to buy out their freedom. After being enfranchised, they started working independently; sometimes they were more productive than before, while they remained useful to their previous masters.[30]

In conclusion, exits through enfranchisement, marriage, or adoption are clearly systemic, for at least four reasons:

1. They do not contest the existence of the slave system: the decision comes from the master, it is controlled by him, and often it is to his advantage. The rupture of the master–slave bond is compensated by the durable

[27] Régent 2004.

[28] Perhaps it is on this account that we find so many *casati* slaves in sub-Saharan Africa; the distance from the master could constitute a means to avoid this realization.

[29] Tardieu 1982: 341–4, esp. 360.

[30] About interested enfranchisements, see Youni 2005: 183–95.

preservation of some forms of dependence, which can be as precise and/ or regulated as slavery itself. Emancipations are individual, or they only concern small groups of slaves belonging to the same master; this is the case, for instance, of slaves liberated at the death of their master.

2. These exits allow the slave system to be rid of the less useful elements or the ones that are more difficult to subjugate. This way, these exits contribute to moderate the internal tensions inherent in every slave system. Moreover, the exits of undesirable elements are often compensated quite easily by the arrival of new slaves, easier to subjugate.
3. These exits do not call into question the equilibrium of the slave society: the rupture introduced by the enfranchisement often leads to a more or less long transitional period, allowing the whole society to integrate the newly liberated. The available material supports the hypothesis of a relatively low percentage of liberated slaves in comparison with the total servile population. This allows the master to control more effectively and sometimes to integrate the enfranchised slaves; and, in any case, it keeps enfranchisement from constituting a threat to the equilibrium of a given slave society.

   Regarding Black Africa, for instance, Meillassoux remarked that the manumitted slaves have always represented a small percentage of the total enslaved population. In Gumbu in 1965, there were 1,040 *saarido* (slaves born in captivity) and only 53 manumitted slaves.[31] In the Roman Republic, the percentage of the enfranchised (*libertini*), calculated in an indirect way, seems to have been more important, this is what we may assume if we take into consideration the problems caused by their significant representation in the electorate. However, we are uncertain about their exact numbers (possibly between 10 and 50 per cent of the political body) and this is an exceptional case. Indeed, according to Jean-Christophe Dumont, one of the purposes of enfranchising and naturalizing the enfranchised slaves was to compensate for the effects of the depopulation of the free men in Italy. At that time slaves constituted maybe 32 per cent of the total population.[32]
4. Besides, if we compared different slave systems, we would notice that, beyond their numerous and obvious differences, all of them found means of auto-regulation. This means that, within them, a more 'liberal' element was always compensated by the presence of a more constraining one, which thus restored the equilibrium.

In Republican Rome, enfranchisement and naturalization could have been relatively important in the context of the depopulation of the free adult male population. However, as Yvon Garlan has remarked (see above),

[31] Meillassoux 1991: 121. [32] Dumont 1987: 57–77. See also Harris 1999: 62–75; Scheidel 1997: 156–69.

the political consequences were not as significant as in ancient Greece. We should also add that, according to Dumont, enfranchised slaves were mostly artisans and merchants working in urban areas.[33] Secondly, they belonged to the *familiae urbanae*, and thus they were servants. Rural slaves constituted the 'large majority of slaves', and, among them, there was only one *vilicus* – the person who kept the accounts for his master – for twelve to sixteen other slaves. In conclusion, these enfranchisements useful to Roman masters mainly concerned slaves who could be more easily integrated into the social and economic status quo.

This kind of balance between 'liberal' and 'constraining' factors may also be found in colonial America. Enfranchisements seem to have been numerous in the Spanish colonies, but they were followed (and so regulated) by a relatively long period of dependence. Conversely, in the ante-bellum American South, enfranchised slaves immediately enjoyed a relative autonomy with regard to their former masters, but enfranchisements were not numerous and the enfranchised usually remained poor and marginalized. Generally speaking, in colonial America, enfranchisement led to a more radical rupture of the dependence forms between master and former slave than in pre-colonial sub-Saharan Africa. The difference between the two societies could be explained by their different perceptions of the concepts of dependence, liberties, and Liberty. Besides, the 'racialization' of slavery in the Americas (a type of slavery almost entirely restricted to blacks) gave the stigma of the slave an almost indelible character. Since integration was here more problematic,[34] enfranchisement did not threaten the homogeneity of the society of the free. Less dangerous, enfranchisement could lead to a more definite rupture with the world of servitude and dependence than in other places.

Another example of this 'equilibrium' is the fact that both in colonial America and in the Greco-Roman world – where the phenomenon was more frequent – women have been enfranchised to a greater extent than men,[35] perhaps because afterwards they usually remained more dependent than men and because they had no actual power in terms of social reproduction. In other words, their liberation was less dangerous for the slave system than that of men.

[33] Here, according to Dumont, 'two thirds of the slaves reaching the thirtieth year of age could be liberated'; see Dumont 1987: 66.

[34] In the post-bellum American South, the white community managed to keep the black population at a greater distance.

[35] This was not necessarily the case of pre-colonial Africa, where women played various important roles. In the Delphic Acts, the percentage of women among the enfranchised adults ranged from 59 per cent to 77 per cent between 201–153 BC and AD 48–100; see Garlan 1995: 87.

2 SLAVE RESISTANCE AND EXITS FROM THE SLAVE SYSTEMS

Could the different forms of slave resistance and opposition against the slave system lead to exits from it? And, if they could, were these exits of a systemic nature (as they have been defined above) or not?

From the myth of the docile slave to the cliché of the always rebellious slave

Slaveowners have often developed an ambiguous perception of slave resistance. Based upon an interpretation of Aristotle, a number of plantation owners considered their slaves as 'animate tools'. This was both a way to legitimize slavery and an act of faith in the inferiority of their slaves. But, this way of seeing things was every day contradicted by voluntary and organized acts of slave resistance. In order to circumvent the contradiction, plantation owners explained these acts advocating perceived natural defects of the slaves: they were described as inclined to cause trouble, to be inveterately indolent and prone to unpredictable reactions. Therefore, it was necessary to employ constraining methods to deal with them, as well as to take advantage of some of their supposed vices – for instance, it was a widespread opinion that black slaves were easily seduced by flattery or by trinkets. This type of reasoning allowed plantation owners to present slave resistance as one more 'proof' of their inferiority and of their 'animal' nature. Some masters in Muslim regions perceived slaves in a similar way.[36] In the ancient world it was also usual to enumerate the most generic defects accompanying the standard portrait of the slave.[37] Those defects – such as laziness, greed, inclination to robbery, drinking, and immoderate sex – were generally considered to be shared by both men and women.

What about the historians' viewpoint? In the United States, the study of slave resistance seems to have arisen in 1918 with the publication of *American Negro Slavery* by Ulrich B. Philips.[38] He presented an idyllic world of plantations: the masters were paternalistic, the slaves quiet. The typical

[36] 'The Negro likes his ease above all and he does not work unless he is absolutely forced to; in addition, he does not submit to this obligation but under the most severe control . . . Imprisonment is not a punishment that frightens them – all the contrary: a Negro will be very happy to pass some days in prison, protected from heat and dispensed from work. He will be able to sleep and dream at his ease; he will rest and recover his forces in order to continue the course of his crimes once he regains his liberty. Hence, prison would be for the Negro such a pleasant residence, that he would neglect nothing in order to deserve it as often as possible. In these conditions, there is unfortunately only one efficient way: the corporal corrections' (see Ruete 1991 (1888): 239). The context here is that of the plantations of Zanzibar during the second half of the nineteenth century.

[37] Annequin, personal communication. [38] Philips 1968 (1918).

slave, 'Sambo', was docile and irresponsible, loyal but lazy, humble but constantly inclined to lies and theft. In one word, thanks to slavery, African Americans could reach a level of civilization superior to that of their brothers in Africa. This racist interpretation, advanced by a man of the South, was in fashion until the 1950s. Phillips' interpretations were evidently erroneous but he had based his work on historical sources to a greater extent than the majority of his contemporaries. In 1943, Herbert Aptheker published his *American Negro Slave Revolts*, but Aptheker was a communist and, thereafter not really listened to.[39] In the 1930s the WPA Federal Workers' Project sponsored interviews with former slaves in different regions of the South, filling several volumes of material. Little by little, criticism arose against Philips' methods, based exclusively on the study of big plantations, not on the much more important small and medium farms. In 1946, Frank Tannenbaum's fundamental work was published and ten years later it was the turn of Kenneth Stampp's *The Peculiar Institution*.[40] Stampp argued that Blacks were nothing more and nothing less than white people with black skin. The ideas of docility of the slaves, of the inferiority of the African American people, and of an unprofitable slavery only considered as a means to achieve racial control, were all refuted.

Thereafter, attention was directed towards the slaves, more than towards the masters. Slaves were viewed as actors in their own drama, not as passive instruments. The 1970s were a turning-point. A shift in perspective had already taken place in 1968, when Eugene Genovese published his *The World the Slaveholders Made*. In 1974, his interest led him to release *Roll, Jordan, Roll: The World the Slaves Made* and, in 1979, his equally famous *From Rebellion to Revolution*.[41] So, the 1970s coincided with the moment when the idyllic image of the world of the plantation fell apart.

This growing interest in forms of slave resistance in modern and contemporary America could be explained as a result of: (a) the existence of a third world movement and Marxist historiography, both attached to the 'exploited' and their 'struggles'; (b) the new attention to the historical agents, rather than the 'structures'; and (c) the growing complexity of the works dedicated to the Atlantic world. Finally, the role the slaves played in their own liberation has been considerably rehabilitated in the last three decades. This seems only fair, since it is logical to think that their acts of resistance were endemic in the majority of the societies founded on constraints other than economic.[42] However, this movement of rehabilitation

[39] Aptheker 1943. [40] Tannenbaum 1946; Stampp 1956. [41] Genovese 1969, 1974, 1979.
[42] Garlan 1995: 193–4; on this point, the author refers particularly to Foucault 1985: 89.

sometimes had equally biased results: the myth of the docile slave gave place to the cliché of the always rebellious slave described as the sole actor of his/her liberation, an idea gradually revised over the last few years.

Resistance and resistances

But what is 'resistance'? Scholars generally pose two types: 'passive' resistance, showing through jobs badly executed, so-called 'belly strikes' (refusals to give birth), or even poisoning; and 'active' resistance, leading to escape (or *maroonage*), or revolt. It is obvious that the distinction between these two types of resistance is based neither on their supposed intensity, nor on their power of destruction. Otherwise, poisoning (of other slaves, of the flock, and sometimes of the masters) would be placed in the category of active resistance, while some acts of minor escape, that did not provoke more damage than occasional thefts, should be considered as belonging to the category of 'passive' resistance.

So, upon what is this distinction implicitly based? Apparently, on the opposition between a great number of individual acts of resistance within the context of a slave system ('passive' resistance) and more collective forms of struggle ('active' resistance) seemingly aimed at the slavery institution itself. The works of some authors, who have presented slave revolts as the 'first manifestation of the historical conflict between the rich and the poor', a kind of 'social revolution' conducted by a 'proletariat' whose study is the competence of historians of 'socialism,'[43] make us think that this distinction between passive and active resistance could also partially originate from a certain confusion between the history of slavery and that of the labour movement. The confusion is probably the consequence of the classic question of whether the character of every struggle – conducted by serfs in the Middle Ages, by European peasants in the seventeenth century, or by the instigators of the Paris Commune of 1870–71, etc. – is revolutionary or not. In all cases, violent, collective, and revolutionary forms of resistance are characterized as 'active'. In all cases they are also overestimated compared to all other forms, summarily classified as 'passive'.[44] We could reach the same conclusion from a number of studies about slave resistance in ancient times. They often establish an opposition between the figures of the *erro* – a person opposed to the system while

[43] Lengellé 1998: 43–5.

[44] Recently some authors partly constructed similar arguments. See Hahn 2003; and Franklin and Schweninger 1999.

fighting against it from within, such as a vagabond slave, who disobeys without breaking the bonds with the *domus* – and the *fugitives*, engaged, instead, in active resistance. Only the latter is described as going against the system. This can explain the efforts of the owners and public authorities to fight against a phenomenon considered particularly dangerous.

This definition of what is 'passive' and 'active' resistance does not seem to me to be functional in all cases. Effectively, it is sometimes just as dangerous for the equilibrium of a given system to be threatened from within, rather than from outside by fugitive slaves. On the other hand it is obvious that a large number of forms of resistance, especially those called 'passive', could harm the productivity of slave labour and, thus, raise real fears in the masters.[45] In the final analysis, whichever form of resistance we look at, all of them clearly manifest, if not a total rejection of the institution of slavery, at least the beginning of a liberation from the ideological fetters imposed by that institution. Thus, all of them should be studied with the same attention.

That said, many forms of resistance depicted as 'passive' never led directly to exits from the system, either individual or collective. In colonial America, it was the case of jobs badly executed, absenteeism, or brief escapes, 'belly strikes', self-mutilation – cutting the fingers off the right hand, a practice adopted by American slaves, so as not to be sold and thus separated from one's family – poisoning or even arson. On the other hand, some of these acts have lightened the burden of the slave system to make it more tolerable and thus slowed down or prevented harder forms of opposition. The plantation owners were fully conscious of this. It was in their interest to allow some latitude in the system; hence the variety of forms of control, going from the very cruel to others more or less paternalistic.[46]

Does this mean that the daily actions of the slaves could never lead to some kind of exit from the system? No; the conclusion is, rather, that the historian is deprived of relevant sources, unless he discovers unknown

[45] In the American South, the fear of arson prompted a number of planters to have the kitchens – where the servants worked and met – built outside, in a building separated from the Big House. Poisoning was also particularly feared in the Caribbean.

[46] According to Maurice Godelier, there 'is no consent without violence, even if the latter does no more than exist as a possibility. But it is equally vain to imagine a durable period of domination and oppression that would be founded on pure violence and terror or on a total consent of all the members of the society. These are borderline cases, whose only true base in the historical evolution is ephemeral or transitory.' See Godelier 1977: 51. In Greek antiquity, the aspect of 'play' in the system could be enhanced through veritable carnival ceremonies of social inversion, in which the slaves appeared as the protagonists, according to Yvon Garlan. 'Such rituals', as Garlan remarks, referring to Emmanuel Le Roy Ladurie's *Carnaval de Romans*, 'only affirm the momentary inversion . . . in order to deny it best in the long run, in the regular social conditions . . . Inversion . . . is proved to be anti-revolutionary.' See Garlan 1995: 199–200.

biographical documents and has the possibility of studying former slaves' memoirs. As things stand, he can only presume that acts emanating from the *agency* of the slaves prompted or impelled the masters to act on their enfranchisement. However, in the majority of cases this cannot be proven. We can only think that the *agency* of the slaves was able to lead some of them towards enfranchisement, as the outcome of a long and always uncertain process. By doing so, the slave acts forwarded the either authorized or/and consented systemic exits. More visible and then more studied are the links between slave revolts and exits from slave systems.

Revolts and exits from the slave systems

Revolts, or attempted revolts, are apparently numerous in the case of colonial America. Nelly Schmidt has made an interesting list of them in her last book.[47] However, this list concerns the totality of the American continent during several centuries. It includes revolts of various extents – from minor localized movements to the major one in Saint Domingue, starting from 1791. Taking a detached view of things, we realize that revolts of a certain importance – since they called the slave system into question – are only few. The majority allowed the escape of only a small number of persons[48] – a phenomenon that, from our point of view, could be classified as 'gained systemic exits' (as compared to the authorized and/or consented exits). Even if, according to Plato, every slave could always be tempted to rebel,[49] resistance did not necessarily take the form of revolt. According to Keith Bradley,[50] revolt is an exceptional occurrence. Slaves at all times have always preferred less dangerous means either to escape from the slave system or to reconcile with it.

With regard to ancient Greece, we can only count two real slave insurrections in Yvon Garlan's *Les esclaves*.[51] The first broke out between

[47] Schmidt 2005: 357–60.

[48] We exclude from the present study the helot revolts. Effectively, they evoke less the kind of slavery examined here than what Yvon Garlan has called 'intra-communal servitudes'. Revolts of this kind, far from being permanent, belong almost all to a relatively limited period of Spartan history and seem to concern less the Laconian helots than the Messenian helots. We have also excluded the movements through which slaves have struggled against authority in the interest of a faction of citizens or against a hostile power at the instigation of the state authorities. See Garlan 1995: 191, 177.

[49] Cited in Dumont 1987: 29.

[50] Bradley 1989.

[51] Garlan 1995: 184. We do not count the revolt of the slaves in Syracuse in 415–413 BC, since it was known to a compiler in late antiquity called Polyaenus, but ignored by Thucydides. It is also possible that the slaves' commander, Sosistratus, was a citizen of high rank, aspiring to tyranny or partisan of the Athenians (see Garlan 1995: 181). So, if true, the revolt was probably part of a general movement during which slaves were used by the elites.

133 and 129 BC at the news of the victories won by the Sicilian slaves against the Roman legions. More than a thousand slaves seem to have revolted in Attica and elsewhere, such as Delos. The second revolt concerns chained slaves in the mines of Attica. It occurred during the second slave revolt of Sicily (104–100 BC). Rome saw three important slave wars, considering their duration, the mobilized forces, and their consequences. There were two revolts in Sicily (140/132 and 104/100 BC), which resulted in the creation by the slaves of a relatively stable state, lasting for some years, and the revolt of Spartacus, which seemed to threaten Rome (73/71 BC).[52] The Republic was shaken on those occasions. On the contrary the empire never witnessed a large scale slave revolt. By way of explanation, Moses Finley affirms that the great majority of slaves in antiquity were reconciled with their condition, either passively and against their will or by adopting a blend of the two attitudes. 'Besides, which other way could the slaves adopt in order to survive, if not compromise and accommodation? And, from the owners' point of view, in which other way would the whole system, and thus society, have been able to survive?'[53]

It is logical to assume that this prudent position was also adopted by the majority of slaves in the Americas. Otherwise, how should we explain the valid argument advanced by David Brion Davis that slaves 'have been so productive' and 'contributed to such an economic development'?[54] Finley remarks that, on a total of approximately 250 registered slave revolts in the history of the United States, the most important of them remained a purely local affair, which did not implicate more than a few hundred people for some months and whose fights did not last longer than three days. In conclusion, despite the significant concentration of slaves, there were relatively few very important revolts in America.[55]

The same situation is attested in the Middle Ages. In late antiquity, there were outbreaks of rural revolts (not just slave revolts), as in the case of the Bagaudes' movements. *Circa* 770, the kingdom of Asturias and Leon was shaken by a slave revolt. In Wales, the Viking incursions especially in the ninth century lead to an outbreak of similar troubles.[56]

Comparing serf revolts with slave revolts of pre-colonial Africa, Meillassoux has observed that the former were numerous, while the slaves

[52] Other revolts, less important, that are worth mentioning, include occupations of Rome's Capitol by revolted slaves (501, 460 and 419 BC), a revolt of 3,000 slaves enrolled in order to reinforce the fleet during the First Punic War (260 BC), the revolt of Setia (198 BC), the revolt of Etruria (196 BC), and that of Apulia (185 BC).

[53] Finley 1998: 155–6; with regard to Rome, see Dumont 1987: 165.

[54] Davis 2000: 452–66, esp. 465.

[55] Finley 1998: 153.

[56] On all these questions, see Dockès 1979.

revolted rarely. This did not happen because the slave system was 'milder' in the first case, but because it is in the nature of a slave system to block the crystallization of class conscience.[57] This is certainly related to the subtle character of the forms of alienation of the slaves in pre-colonial sub-Saharan Africa – subtler than the clear distinction between black slaves and white masters in the Americas. Among other factors that stood in the way of collective revolts, the emphasis should be put on issues such as the extent of the ideology defending slavery – 'embraced by everybody' in west Africa, according to Roger Botte – the heterogeneity of slaves,[58] or the fact that the masters in Muslim societies were supposed to possess a certain number of magical religious powers. This latter factor facilitated the task of domination of the slaves, who were pagans, while at the same time the masters let the slaves believe that their salvation in the other world depended exclusively on their obedience to them.[59]

I should add that the question of revolts in pre-colonial sub-Saharan Africa has not been extensively studied.[60] Bruce Mouser published a text on a revolt in the south of present-day Guinea in the second half of the nineteenth century. Roger Botte also carried out some research on a group of slaves (called Mikhiforés) who resisted attacks from their former masters for several years at the end of nineteenth century, in the area between Rio Pongo and Nunez, and who were known as Peuls of Fouta-Djallon. Addarahmane N'Gaide's attention was directed to the revolt of the Maccube of Fuladu (Senegal) who, while struggling for both their freedom and the emancipation of their masters, founded a state that they governed until the establishment of the 'colonial order' (1870–1903).[61] However, there is still a lot to be done. Unlike the case of the Americas, no real interest has been manifested for the acts of resistance and the role of the *agency* of the slaves in relation to internal forms of slavery. So, maybe we underestimate the real extent and the importance that these acts of resistance had in the past, though nowadays it would be more clearly detectable.[62]

[57] Meillassoux 1991: 93. Yvon Garlan underlines also that chattel slaves rarely rebelled and that helots were more tempted to; see Garlan 1995: 191.

[58] Twenty-seven different ethnic groups only for Fouta-Djallon, even if some of them were only marginally represented; see Botte 1994: 109–36.

[59] Roger Botte tells me the idea was so powerful that it is still shared nowadays by a number of slaves in Mauritania, Nigeria, and North Cameroon. This religious factor explains why colonial abolitions or those decreed by the governments are not considered legitimate by a part of the servile class. Here, enfranchisement is not valid if it is not pronounced by the master (Botte, personal communication).

[60] Historians have attempted to study revolts that occurred before embarkation on the slave-trade ships, but not those related to intra-African slavery.

[61] See Mouser, Botte and N'Gaide 1999.

[62] See on this subject, Botte 2005.

A typology of revolts according to their context

Generally speaking, whatever the place, we could distinguish three different contexts or periods that favoured revolts. The first seems to have corresponded to the times either following the establishment of a slave system or its quick expansion. For example, its expansion in the colonial Americas covers an extensive period of time, depending on the region, from the sixteenth century, as in Brazil, and the end of the eighteenth century, as in the British island of St Kitts, until the nineteenth century, as with the rise and transformation of slavery in Cuba. In this context, it is common to witness the outburst of sporadic, but still numerous revolts. The 770 revolt in the kingdom of Asturias and Leon, which followed the reinforcement of the slave system in the region, could also be classified in this category.

Another category of slave revolts often coincides with a moment in which a slave system seems to be threatened, either because it appears to be slowly 'declining', as at the end of the Roman empire, or because new forces are opposed to it, as in the case of the complex relations between colonization and endogenous slavery in sub-Saharan Africa at the end of the nineteenth century,[63] or finally because all the conditions point toward an imminent abolition of slavery. According to Monica Schuler, this was the case with the abolitionist movement which, by making people hope for a reform and/or the destruction of the slave system, favoured the revolts of the Akan populations in the British colonies in the nineteenth century.[64]

[63] Paul Lovejoy and Martin Klein have argued in favour of the unusual and at times violent importance of runaway slaves in pre-colonial West Africa, upon the arrival of the colonizers, who, it was thought, were going to abolish slavery. Thereby, these movements of the population anticipate the end of slavery, rather than produce it (see Lovejoy and Hogendorn 1993). We have to note, however, that the colonial French and English authorities did everything they could to prevent or at least reduce the number of runaways. Sometimes, it was also the masters who moved, to reach new unoccupied regions and, thus, maintain their control on their slaves, as in the case of the nomads Peuls of Waalo and of Dimar after 1882.

[64] According to Schuler, it is mainly from the abolition of the slave trade by England and its ensuing tenacious efforts to achieve its abolition in other countries that originated a change in the nature of revolts. Until then, and since the very beginning of the seventeenth century, revolts aimed at the conquest of autonomous territories, which would allow some of the slaves to escape the slave system. After 1808, the acts of resistance were destined to facilitate and accelerate the end of the slave system – an aim at which both the abolitionist circles and the British Crown were working simultaneously; see Schuler 1973: 373–86. Some also have insisted on the importance of the events in Saint Domingue and the proclamation of a black Republic in Haiti in 1804. Although the importance of this event was considerable, as far as Latin America is concerned, the example of Haiti seems to have mostly frightened the Creoles, who were essential actors in the process of decolonization. Francisco Miranda wrote the following words in 1798: 'it is said that, at this moment, Santa Fé, Caracas, Mexico and even Chile are preparing an insurrection . . . Let God not allow these beautiful countries

A third category of period favourable for the emergence of slave revolts can be detected, besides the two types mentioned above. These are the periods of great turmoil in history, leading to the downfall of the established order, as in the case of the Viking invasions of the ninth century. A more recent example is the one of the divisions between the white 'masters' and the emergence of an international abolitionist movement at the end of the eighteenth century, with the great wave of the Atlantic revolutionary movements started in the thirteen American colonies influencing continental Europe.

Evidently, we can discern some connections between these three categories of periods. The importance of the two revolts of Sicily and that of Spartacus lies in the concomitance of two phenomena. One of them is connected with the rapid increase in the number of slaves, often first generation – thus, slaves who had known freedom – coming from various remote regions (the majority of those slaves came from allied nations), accustomed to fight and then able to profit from any occasion. This came about at a time when Republican Rome was growing into a true slave society, a fact that caused tension or even changes in the master–slave relationships.[65] In this case, we note a combination of elements of the first category of periods with some extremely favourable conditions that belong to the third category of periods, and specifically a time of great economic, social, and political instability marked by numerous conflicts, mostly civil wars.[66]

Therefore, no matter what place or time, there are only a few really important revolts to look at. All of them except one – the revolt of Saint Domingue that led to the establishment of the Haitian Republic in 1804 – failed; this was the case of the one led by Spartacus and also of that of the Zendj, the black slaves in the southern area of Iraq, who rebelled in the ninth century AD.[67] In conclusion, large-scale slave revolts have only gone as far as shaking the slave systems, as in the case of the servile revolts in the Dutch Suriname after 1772. Apart from the unique case of Saint Domingue – a case which, deservedly belongs to the category of greatest

to become a theatre of blood and crimes, like Saint-Domingue, under the pretext of establishing Liberty; I would rather see them remain one more century, if that is what it takes, under the stupid and barbaric Spanish domination'; see Bohorquez 2003: 228.

65 Dumont insists on the idea of a kind of transgression of rules and habits by the new masters: all slaves were automatically marked, not only those who had opposed the master, as seems to have been the habit before; repression was without reason, illegal reduction to servitude increased (see Dumont 1987: 240–8, 301–4). Keith R. Bradley is of the same opinion and adds that, due to a disorder in the habits concerning enfranchisement, the hope of liberation had become more improbable (see Bradley 1989: 128–9). Thereby, classic means of attenuation of tensions declined at the very moment when Rome was strongly affirming itself as a slave society. All this could result only in revolts.

66 On this subject, see Bradley 1989, 1988: 369–76; and Dumont 1987.

67 See Popovic 1998.

unrests in history – they did not lead to anything more than gained systemic exits for those who were not killed or captured in the process.

This does not mean, though, that they did not have major consequences. For example, the revolt of the Zendj in southern Iraq may have failed, but thereafter there was no other attempt to re-establish such massive slave concentrations in the region. Another example is that of the slave revolts in Republican Rome, which seem to have induced the elites to allow greater latitude to the system. Even if they did not treat their slaves in a better way, at least the Roman elites made efforts to regulate the master–slave relationship.[68] These ways, those revolts allowed future slaves to experience their state of servitude in a different way. This was not necessarily a harmful process for the slave system – all the contrary since the reduction of its inherent tensions allowed it to go on.

The definitive escape, or 'great maroonage*'*

What about the definitive way of escaping a slave system, something called 'great *maroonage*' in the case of colonial America? These slaves are called *marrons* in the French colonies, *maroons* in the British ones, *cimarrones* and *palenques* in the Spanish-speaking areas, *quilombos* and *mocambos* in Brazil. We need to distinguish between the small-scale escapes, which corresponded to absenteeism, or a temporary running away which lasted a few hours or days, and the big escape. The latter was definitive and often led to the formation of groups or even whole communities of fugitive slaves.

Mostly in the colonies of '*terra firma*', vast zones of difficult access (such as Guyana and Brazil), as well as in border areas between colonies under different authorities,[69] durable societies of fugitives were likely to be founded. Indeed, in order to survive, these had to be situated in zones of difficult access, such as the jungles of Guyana, the isolated swamps in the South of the United States, or even 'hole areas' – regions of limestone wells and deep gorges found in Jamaica. The natural features were reinforced by

[68] At least, this is what we deduce from the already cited works by Bradley and Dumont (see n. 65, above). According to the latter, 'we can observe a continuity in the argumentation of the period around 130 BC and the attitude of the Empire, and the Roman masters, sufficiently marked by the revolts, did not wait until the imperial period in order to understand that at least their interest, well thought of, incited them to a certain humanity towards the slaves' (see Dumont 1987: 306).

[69] This is the case of the area called 'the Land of the Cape North', on the Eastern fringes of the Brazilian Guinea; see Gomes 2002: 469–98. It is a zone of changing frontiers, the object of constant disputes being at the crossroad of English, French, Dutch and Spanish interests, especially during the second half of the eighteenth century. Thus, fugitive slaves were a chronic problem for plantation owners in this area.

making treacherous paths scattered with traps or leading to moving sand, or by building villages surrounded by palisades – from where the Spanish term *palenque* derives – as well as by a solid mastery of guerrilla techniques, which disconcerted Europeans accustomed to more conventional tactics. Cities could also offer the slaves the chance to elude their pursuers by disappearing into the crowd – this was especially the case of skilled slaves, desirous of mingling with the population of free coloureds. Finally, the so-called 'sea fugitives' used ships in order to cross one or more international borders. Escape percentages were high in Dutch Suriname, in Jamaica, and to a lesser extent, in Saint Domingue, in Martinique, and in Guadeloupe, and also in the eastern part of Cuba especially at the beginning of the nineteenth century. In the United States, the phenomenon of 'great *maroonage*' was smaller in extent and remained quite marginal.[70]

We have at our disposal only little information on runaway slaves in the ancient world.[71] However, Yvon Garlan estimates that it would be reasonable to presume that running away, just like numerous acts of resistance on a daily basis – i.e. 'passive resistance' for researchers working on the modern period – was a permanent temptation. This would explain, as he observes, the frequent praise of the *paramonimos* slave – the slave 'willing to stay' – as opposed to the *drapetes* – the fugitive slave. Also, Egyptian papyri regarding Zenon's correspondence refer to attempts at running away, but rather conducted by two or three slaves together than individually.[72] As it is related by Yvon Garlan, the slave revolt in the island of Chios during the first half of the third century BC[73] bears a notable resemblance to the resistance movements related to *maroon* societies in the modern period.

In the Middle Ages, the slaves expressed their wish for liberty mostly by escape, at a time when immense forests offered numerous areas of refuge. This is how certain woods, swamps, and wastelands were developed and gained value. In addition, increased needs in manpower allowed some of the fugitive slaves to be hired as free workers elsewhere; this was especially the case in Italy and Spain between the second half of the seventh and the beginning of the eighth centuries, after the plague had led to a reduction of the active population.

[70] During the period preceding the American Civil War (1861–5), even though slave escapes were very well organized and facilitated by the network of the 'underground railroad', only about 2,000 slaves a year managed to move to the North; see Hesseltine 1960.

[71] 'We still lack a synthesis on runaway slaves in the Greek world'; see Garlan 1995: 194.

[72] Garlan 1995: 194. On the question of social banditry, see Hobsbawm 1969 and 1959.

[73] Garlan 1995: 181–3.

At all times, many slaves escaped from slavery thanks to *maroonage*. These exits were usually by individuals or by small groups. They did not call into question the slave system as a whole. We could even think that they relieved it by allowing it to rid of the less docile slaves. *Maroonage*, when it led to the escape of the more restless slaves, was sometimes a factor that helped reduce the danger of large-scale revolts. We could categorize these sorts of systemic exits as seized, conquered, or swept.

It is true that, in the long run, these exits could lead to the foundation of large fugitive slave communities that were capable of organizing themselves, holding entire regions and, thus, maintaining their independence,[74] sometimes for a long time – for several generations or even centuries. Robert L. Paquette has remarked that, in the Americas, plantation owners feared the communities of fugitive slaves far more than they feared revolts.[75] But even if these communities defied the slave system, they did not necessarily threaten it. In fact, in the colonial Americas, these societies had to come to terms with it, since they needed the outside world in order to secure their supplies of a number of products, and also of women. Even if war was frequent between the plantation owners and these communities, as in Dutch Surinam in the eighteenth century, sometimes the two also cooperated. This was the case of the 'blue Negroes' of Jamaica, who helped the British to repress slave revolts in exchange for their guaranteed autonomy.[76] The situation of the fugitive slaves in the mountainous zones of Chios, under the command of a leader called Drimakos, seems to have been similar. These ex-slaves established a community or even a state, whose relative continuity was officially ensured in return for playing a role in preventing other slaves from escaping.[77]

Finally, we come across a number of cases of former slaves, either fugitives or rebels, who became slaveowners themselves. This poses the problem of the existence, or invention, of alternatives to slavery. We have to be careful not to confuse slave resistance with the ideology of the western antislavery movements. There could be some links between these two processes, but they were also different. Thus, in general, we can say that, unfortunately, revolts and acts of resistance have mostly led to systemic exits.

[74] In the ancient times, the *fugitivi* could threaten the system from outside by forming bands or by associating with groups of bandits (the association *fugitivus-latro*). For Black Africa, see the case of Mikhiforés in Mouser *et al.* 1999.

[75] Paquette 1998: 334–44.

[76] On all these questions, see, for the colonial Americas, Price 1973, 1979; and Heuman 1986.

[77] Garlan 1995: 181–3.

3 'NATURAL' EXITS AND IMPOSED EXITS

Since slave systems excelled at perpetuating themselves, true exits from them took two courses. Chronologically speaking, the first was that of an apparent 'decline', as if, by slowly dying a 'sweet death', the slave system could disappear in an almost 'natural' way.

Exits by 'long' decline

The best-known, and maybe unique, example of this course is that followed by the Roman slave system, which was more or less replaced by serfdom.[78] Authors disagree on the reasons for its decline. In the nineteenth century, emphasis was often placed, especially by Henri Wallon,[79] upon cultural and/or ideological aspects, such as the role played by Christianity in the decline and humanization of slavery. Later on, from Joseph Vogt to Peter Garnsey and from Moses Finley to Alain Testart,[80] this role was revised or even criticized. Nowadays, the accent is put more on the adaptability of the slavery institution to a new religious ideology, which sometimes provided it with the necessary arguments. On one hand, Paul urged slaves to obey their masters and masters to treat their slaves well. On the other hand, Augustin, in the fifth century AD, introduced a whole new doctrine by presenting slavery as a punishment for the sins of men. The Church also had interests in slaveownership. Even if it favoured enfranchisement for the laity, it did not adopt this practice itself. Hence, the majority of authors nowadays cite a great number of factors in order to explain the regression of slavery,[81] while they also underline the diversity of modes of evolution over time and space.

78 We should note that, given the hiatus between these two forms of dependence, serfdom cannot be considered as a simple continuation of slavery. After appearing mainly in the ninth century, serfdom began to lose importance from the thirteenth century, with the exception of England, and hardly resisted, in western Europe, the crisis at the end of the Middle Ages. Hence, its history appears much shorter than that of slavery. Nevertheless, the issue of the links between medieval serfdom and the 'second serfdom' in eastern Europe would deserve to be more studied.

79 Wallon 1988 (1847). 80 Garnsey 1996; Testart 2001; Finley 1998.

81 At first, the Church tended to fight against the enslavement, through capture of 'true' Christians – meaning the non-orthodox – even if it legitimized slavery. Then, around the year 1000, various factors played their part in its decline. These factors included technical progress (evidenced by the use of hydraulic power in mills and by better yokes), economic development during the eighth and ninth centuries, and thus land reclamations and manpower mobility, and the disintegration of state structures – which earlier could have favoured the control of massive slavery – at the advantage of a seigneurial system.

If we pause to look at these apparently 'decentralized' points for our subject, it is because they underline that there is nothing 'natural' in the supposed extinction of ancient slavery. The very idea of slavery's slow 'decline' is nowadays out of date. The same can be said about the connected concept of the 'decline' of the late Roman empire.[82] We now know that this period was marked by profound social and economic changes and by a transformation in the relations of domination, all things leading to the development of relations of dependence either renewed or built afresh. This theory of transformations and evolution (and not of decline) coincides with what we have learnt about the history of medieval slavery.

Indeed, instead of regressing, slavery recovered new strength in the fifth century. The barbaric kingdoms that succeeded Rome were slave states. According to Pierre Bonnassie, in the two centuries that followed, slavery reached its zenith in Europe.[83] The laws passed during that time classify *servus* and *ancilla* as livestock. They formally prohibit any union between slaves and free. Apart from field slaves, who were the majority, we should take into account the specialized slaves: guards, swineherds, hunters, millers, jewellers, goldsmiths, blacksmiths, domestic servants, or attendants of the royal palace. Those may have been persons born in slavery but also persons recently reduced into slavery. Effectively, the omnipresent threat and practice of war was in those times considered to be an enterprise based on pillage and people-hunting. Other routes to enslavement included judicial sentences, famine, kidnapping, and sale of children. Later on, the constitution of the Carolingian empire gave new impulse to slavery.[84]

Slavery, which was close to disappearing in certain regions around the year AD 1000, persisted until the end of the Middle Ages in Mediterranean Europe.[85] It was sometimes based on domestic and artisan slaves, because of commercial development, in Italy, Spain and Portugal. There were also networks for the importation of captives that supplied the Mediterranean regions with slave manpower. The victims of this type of slavery were mainly Muslims, Jews, and Orthodox Christians – or Slavs, Greeks, and Bulgarians. According to Jacques Heers, 'condemned and persecuted by the very Church of the Orient', captured and then 'sold to the Italians, Bulgarians appeared' at that time 'in great number in the markets of the West' constituting 'a non-negligible part of the slave population especially

[82] On this issue, as well as ancient slavery in general, Andreau and Descat 2006 is indispensable. This important book was published just as I finished this chapter.

[83] Bonnassie 1985: 307–43. [84] Bonnassie 1985; Bloch 1947: 30–45, 161–70.

[85] Heers 1981; Verlinden 1955–77; Stella 2000; Vincent and Stella 1996: 289–300; Rotman 2004.

in the years 1200 and 1300'.[86] Greek men and women were also enslaved in great numbers. Moreover, one should add to the regular imports the occasional captures of Catalans, Genovese, and Venetians by hunters and slave traders, either during military or piracy operations. Even subjected regions continued to be exploited in this way under the pretext that schismatics – considered as heretics – could make fine slaves. Sometimes Italians, Castillans, and Catalans went as far as buying slaves from the Turks, their enemies. The Spanish and Italians were thus implicated in a large-scale slave trade for at least three centuries.

On the whole, in the Middle Ages, slavery networks either persisted or were reactivated and, in certain Mediterranean regions, such as Sicily, slavery continued until well into the early modern period. This raises a question posed first by Charles Verlinden,[87] but subsequently studied only scantily:[88] was there a possible 'transfer' of methods or practices relating to slavery between the medieval Mediterranean and the colonial Americas in the early modern period – perhaps one with the intermediate step of the introduction of slavery in Atlantic islands, such as Madeira or Sao Tomé?[89] Indeed, a number of troubling facts can be observed, such as the role of Italian merchants in the Iberian slave trade networks,[90] at a time when African slaves began to be used for the first time after the conquest of Constantinople by the Turks, as a result of the reduction in European access to the market of Slavic slaves. We should add that, in Iberian America, the enslavement of indigenous people happened very quickly, whereas in the colonies kept by northern European powers, such as France, the United Provinces, and England, there was an initial system of employment of white workers under contract before the implementation of African slavery. The explanation of this phenomenon relates in part to differences in the regional density of indigenous populations. However, we cannot exclude the possibility that other factors, in particular earlier practices, could also have played a significant role.

[86] Heers 1981: 67, 71. [87] See Verlinden 1949: 113–53, 1951: 217–36. [88] See Phillips 1985.

[89] This point is now taken for granted in some important studies, such as Davis 2006; Blackburn 1997; and Curtin 1990. I think, nevertheless, that this issue would merit more specific and detailed research so as to point out resemblances and differences.

[90] In 1460 Antonio di Noli, 'river captain of Genoa', was granted by the king of Portugal the authorization to introduce African slaves into the islands of Capo Verde to grow sugar. Between 1489 and 1497, a Florentine, Cesare de Barchi, sold in Valencia more than 2,000 African slaves. After the fall of Constantinople, Bartolomeo Marchionni, another Florentine, settled in Lisbon. He invested in the sugar plantations of Madeira and also obtained the authorization by the king of Portugal to trade in slaves (see Drescher and Engerman 1998).

All in all, we can argue in favour of two ways of looking at the problem of the gradual extinction of ancient slavery. On one hand, its decline was neither 'natural', nor regular. On the other hand, it was neither total nor definitive. It happened, at times, that a slave system that had seemed to disappear gradually left behind more than just traces, while it gave birth to other forms of slavery. The fact that a slave system can convert itself, rather than simply allowing itself to disappear, has been brilliantly demonstrated in the work of Youval Rotman on Byzantium.[91] Apparently, the only means to get rid of slavery once and for all seems to have been its abolition. This is, in fact, what happened in the nineteenth and twentieth centuries as a result of the emergence of an international abolitionist movement, whose origins, however, may be traced in the distant past.

Abolitionism: radical projects, practical reforms

It would be outside the scope of the present chapter to examine the debates on the origins and modalities of the emergence of the abolitionist movement, as it appeared at the end of the eighteenth century. It is sufficient to say that it resulted from the emergence of a philosophical and political movement, a humanitarian and/or religious trend, and a utilitarian pragmatism related to the beginnings of political economy.[92] From then on, the problem was no longer that of liberating a certain number of slaves through enfranchisement or emancipation; instead it became imperative to put an end to the slave system as such. Hence, the abolitionist movement was new in the history of humanity and a radically innovative departure altogether. In antiquity, slavery had been objects of debates and its legitimacy questioned. An original natural law had even been invented, ignoring slavery and opposed to it. However, nobody ever thought of abolishing it or of abrogating it through a substantive law.[93]

The radical character of the abolitionist project was reinforced by the historical context in which it developed. The abolitionist movement was consolidated at the same moment the colonial system reached its height. For a long time, the prevailing idea was that the colonial system was in decline at the end of the eighteenth century. The colonial world, victim of an inherent dialectic contradiction, was perceived as following the same direction as the economy of the *ancien régime*, which was also considered to be in 'crisis'. Such a view of things confirmed the Marxist idea of a critical

[91] Rotman 2004. [92] These issues are developed in Pétré-Grenouilleau 2004.
[93] Annequin, personal communication.

transition from 'feudalism' to 'capitalism'. The great French economic historian Ernest Labrousse defended that idea in one of his famous works. The work of Ragatz and, above all, that of Eric Williams – who later became the first Prime Minister of the islands of Trinidad and Tobago – contributed in spreading this idea about the colonial world.[94] The theory[95] was revised to a great extent by the works of Seymour Drescher,[96] who reversed the thesis of the decline of the colonial economy. We now know that, at the end of eighteenth century, the slave based world of the plantations was not condemned to decline. Its productivity and profitability were supposed to improve. The phenomenal rise of sugar trade in the Caribbean did not obstruct the equally spectacular progress of the, until then, less-developed production of cocoa and coffee; hence, the unprecedented increase in the Atlantic slave trade. About 855,000 slaves arrived in the Americas between 1701 and 1720; then, 926,000 between 1721 and 1740; 1,197,000 between 1741 and 1760; 1,309,000 between 1761 and 1780; 1,440,000 between 1781 and 1800.[97]

The prosperity and economic efficiency of the slave-based plantation system, the rise of the slave trade, and the reinforcement of the exclusion systems based on colour in the Antilles as well as in some European metropoleis indicate that the world the abolitionists intended to reform was far from being on the defensive by the end of the eighteenth century. The majority of the other emancipation movements that occurred in the same period – emancipation of peasants in Europe, and of Jews and

[94] On one side, the alleged decline of the British colonial system following the Seven Years War (1756–63) and the loss of the Thirteen American Colonies (1783) could no longer have justified the continuation of the English slave trade. On the other hand, the latter seemed to have become an obstacle for British industrial development. The prices of the colonial products were, in fact, expensive, whereas the mercantile system of exclusivity, on which the colonial world was founded, proved to be contrary to the interests of a newly born industrial capitalism more inclined to free exchange. In other words, having grown to be an obstacle for the British economy, the slave trade no longer had reason to exist in a colonial world that had been restricted and was in crisis. See Labrousse 1990 (1945); Ragatz 1971 (1928); and Williams 1944.

[95] On the French side of this merchant world and crisis theory, see Pétré-Grenouilleau 1997: 126–45.

[96] In Drescher 1977, Seymour Drescher demonstrated that, around 1804–6, the English slave system in the West Indies reached its height. Hence, by stimulating British foreign trade, it supported an economy threatened with suffocation by the Napoleonic Wars and the introduction of the continental blockade. In addition, we know now that the English slave trade reached its peak between 1794 and 1805; this makes it difficult to believe that hard-pressed planters would have massively invested in the purchase of new slaves. Drescher 2002 completes and corroborates this hypothesis. It shows how English abolitionists realized progressively that the slave system was economically viable, that the abolition of slavery was not necessarily a good affair for England, and that their arguments, founded on the virtues of free labour, were becoming invalidated by the hard evidence of the facts.

[97] The figures are in Klein 1999: 210.

indigenous people in Spanish America – was presented and/or appeared to be facilitating, encouraging, or completing a modernization process useful to the interests of the state as well as to some members of the elite. The situation regarding the abolition of the slave trade and slavery in the colonial societies that depended closely on such institutions was, in fact, entirely different, since these societies were productive, efficient and, in this sense, modern.[98] This is the reason why the abolitionist movement was, in all ways, radical.

However, the abolitionists of the eighteenth century did not demand the immediate breakdown of the slave system. Among the multiple and complex propositions formulated in that period, the one brought forward by the Marquis de Condorcet introduced a plan for escalating enfranchisements according to age, gender, and the role fulfilled in the plantation, so as to put an end to the slave system after a transitory period of about seventy-seven years. Some other abolitionists wished to awaken the slaves' interest in agriculture, so to gradually transform them into free farmers. Abolitionists also wished to put an end to the slave trade, and thus to the commerce that supplied the slave economies with captives, so as to progressively oblige the slave system to reform itself. Tactically, this attitude also avoided a direct confrontation with the plantation owners.

The study of the abolitionists' arguments confirms this moderation. At the end of the eighteenth century, some of them, for the sole purpose of prompting a reaction in their society, brought forward the image of a black Spartacus, but this was only a virtual threat reflecting the literary metaphor of a sleeping volcano. The abolitionists never wished for a slave revolt to happen. Their aim was a progressive abolition, so to guarantee social peace. In practice, they did not incite revolts or any other acts of resistance. One of the most famous visual documents related to abolitionism shows a black person on his knees imploring humanity with the following slogan: 'Am I not a Man and a Brother?' During the nineteenth century, official paintings representing abolition insisted on the theme of the gift – from the nation or from the Republic – and on that of redemption achieved thanks to the power and high ideals of the white people. So, in this sense, there is nothing really subversive about such representations.[99]

Various explanations could be proposed to explain the abolitionists' pragmatism. First of all, the continuous efficiency and the growth of the slave economy led to moderate action. On the other hand, the

[98] See Mintz 1996: 1–21. [99] On these issues see Smalls 1998: 65–76.

ideas that resulted in the political revolutions of the end of the eighteenth century were profoundly reformist in their origins. We should also add a fundamental principle, in agreement with the central tenets of both Enlightenment philosophy and the bourgeois revolutions of the end of the eighteenth century: the respect for the right to property. In the light of the importance of this right, how could it be possible that the masters liberated all their slaves immediately and without compensation? Finally, let us not forget that even the more fervent abolitionists did not think that the slaves were mature enough for freedom. This was not due to their intrinsic inferiority – as was argued by the apologists of slavery – but to the slave status resulting in the brutalization of human beings (according to the environmentalist thesis).[100] Thus, it was considered necessary to exit the slave system in a way that would serve both the interests of the slaves, since to enfranchise them right away was perceived as a way of abandoning them to themselves, and the need to keep social peace. Finally, we should not ignore the fact that the enlightened individuals who lived at the end of the eighteenth century, influenced by their classical education, might have been tempted to reproduce in a rational and regulated way the process of the slow 'decline' of ancient slavery.

The reformist programme advanced by the abolitionists was globally observed. Everywhere, except in Saint Domingue, the abolition of the slave trade preceded that of slavery.[101] The masters were sometimes compensated. The English put into practice a transitory system called *apprenticeship* that lasted for five to seven years, from emancipation until the very end of slavery. In France and Brazil, the dilemma between 'gradualism' and 'immediatism', which reflected the wish to put an end to slavery right away, was more acute. In neither case, though, was radical 'immediatism' put

[100] For a number of enlightened *philosophes*, there was no contradiction between, on one hand, the attachment to the principles of natural law and of unity of humankind and, on the other hand, the idea of gradual abolition of slavery; especially because they were sensible to the concept of evolutionism. 'The rights of men', according to Condorcet, 'result uniquely from the fact that they are sensible beings, *susceptible to acquire* moral ideas and to reason based on these ideas'; see Condorcet 1781. He also observed that, in this way 'there are some natural rights from which very young children, as well as imbeciles and crazy men, are excluded. In the same way, if . . . on account of the brutalization caused by slavery . . . the slaves of the European colonies became incapable of fulfilling the functions of free men', we have to 'treat them as those men whom misfortune or illness have deprived of part of their faculties, to whom we cannot allow the full exercise of their rights, without exposing them to the risk of harming others or even themselves, and who need not only the protection of the law, but also the care of humanity'; Condorcet quoted in Dubois 1998: 174–5.

[101] The British abolished the slave trade in 1807 and slavery in their colonies in 1833. In France, laws against the trade were passed in 1818, 1827, and 1831, before the definitive abolition of slavery in 1848.

into practice before the years immediately preceding the definitive abolition of slavery. So, globally, the process employed was based on reforms. In the majority of cases, abolition was acquired following legislative procedures and states *imposed* abolition upon slaveowners. A typology of these procedures can be established, according to a dialectic schema, that of the 'inside' and the 'outside'.[102]

In the first instance, the abolitionist movement and the state moved from *outside* the slave system and acted forcing societies based on slavery to change. This was the case of the English (1833), of the French (1848)[103] and of other European colonial powers. It was also the case of the USA shortly after the mid-nineteenth century, when the victorious North forced the defeated South to abandon the slave system at the end of the American Civil War. Abolition was imposed from outside the slave system also in sub-Saharan Africa after its colonization by the Europeans. Slavery had been considerably reinforced there during the second half of the nineteenth century. One of the arguments used to justify colonization had been the struggle against slavery.[104] The colonizers worked in this direction, though not without ambiguities; this was so because, on one hand, they needed the support of the local elites, still depending on slavery, and, on the other hand, because they themselves resorted largely to what was called 'forced labour'.

Latin America (Brazil excepted) presents a second case. Having acquired their independence during the first half of the nineteenth century, the countries of the Latin American continent often opted for an *internal* abolition of slavery without excessive external pressure. This procedure was facilitated by the fact that slavery had been less important there than in the US South and the Caribbean and by the fact that it was already in decline by the end of the eighteenth century. So, in a way, abolition in Latin America validated a phenomenon already in progress, by making it official. This allows us to presume that several interesting comparisons could be made between this case and that of the 'decline' of ancient slavery. The example of Iran[105] demonstrates that abolition could also be

[102] This typology does not take into account the Arab world. Here, there was no western style abolitionist movement; see Pétré-Grenouilleau 2004: 287–92, 302–8. Nevertheless, sometimes abolition took an official character, both political and legislative, as in the case of Iran; see Mirzai 2004.

[103] The 1794 abolition was part of a different historical context – that of the French Revolution, of the revolt of Saint Domingue, and of the war with England – and did not include compensation to the masters.

[104] See, in particular, Renault 1971.

[105] See Mirzai 2004.

implemented from within the slave system, independently from the western world.

A third case, in between the ones cited above, is that of Brazil and Cuba, which also obtained independence in the course of the nineteenth century. Abolition put an end to a slave system still vigorous, which in both countries had been reinforced and modernized during the second half of the century. In this case, abolition was the result of *internal* as well as *external* phenomena, such as British pressure in the case of Brazil and Spanish and American pressure in the case of Cuba.

CONCLUSION

To conclude, we can distinguish three processes of exit from slavery:

(1) The process wished for and/or consented by the masters, or even grasped, seized or conquered by the slaves – a process in which systemic exits were, by far, the majority. In most cases, these actually facilitated the reproduction of the slave system as a whole.

(2) The process favoured by the evolution of global society, one entailing a slow 'decline' of the slave system, which did not necessarily lead to the total eradication of the practices related to slavery, in the absence of abolitionist legislation. The reverse is also true: without the evolution of global society, abolitionist measures were not sufficient.

(3) In the ultimate analysis, only a combination of the evolution of global society with the implementation of abolitionist measures seems to have allowed the creation of the conditions necessary to put a true end to any slave system.

CHAPTER 10

Emancipation schemes: different ways of ending slavery

*Stanley Engerman**

I

There is some general agreement among scholars about the conditions under which slavery has existed, particularly in large-scale slave societies as in the ones in the Americas. In the analysis of such slave societies, economic surpluses play a major role, and variants of the Domar–Nieboer[1] argument that related slavery to a high ratio of land to labour have been frequently resorted to. If some scepticism about this argument exists today, certainly it was one often used by many contemporaries in describing the rise and fall of slavery and the new forms of labour control that replaced it. Correspondingly, discussions of the expected ending of slavery were frequently based on arguments positing a declining ratio of land to labour. Expectations of the reported successes (or lack of them) of the transition to free labour were also related to the relative amounts of land and labour. The rise and fall of smaller-scale slave societies was often explained by economic elements, although various social and political factors may have had a major influence in some of these cases.[2] Slavery, in those societies with written documents, was generally dealt with through extensive law codes, often with thorough details and broad coverage. These laws provided the fundamental basis for the control of slave labourers, as well as imposing limits on the masters and non-slaveholding free people. Such laws influenced, among other things, the treatment given to slaves, the limits on the ability of free individuals to attract slaves away from their owners, and the right of slaves to be manumitted.

Manumission meant the freeing of individuals and families. This was sometimes a gift freely granted, sometimes more the grant of a right to purchase oneself at the market price or other agreed upon price. These

* This chapter was written while a Fellow at the W. E. B. Du Bois Institute for African and African American Research, Harvard University.

[1] See Domar 1970 : 18–32; and Nieboer 1971 (1910): 417–27. [2] See Engerman 1973 : 43–65.

could be based on an immediate transaction or, as in the Spanish and other cases of *coartación*, a contract allowing for periodic payments for a period of time until payment was complete and full freedom achieved.[3] Manumissions did not lead to the ending of the system of slavery, since, even where most practised, the numbers were generally quite small. Moreover, manumission was regarded as consistent with, if not a contribution to, the long-term survival of slavery. The right of manumission could serve as an incentive to slave labour or else as a safety valve for the oppressiveness of the system.[4] While there were some concerns about the rights of the manumitted and free blacks, and of their relations with former masters and the overall society, the problems of adjustment to freedom by those freed by manumission were not considered a major issue.

The problem of the emancipation of an entire slave population is, however, a considerably more complex problem than manumission, particularly in societies with a relatively large slave population. With the numbers involved, there is a need for concern with the economics and politics of the overall transition from a slave to a free society. Planning this transition was seldom, however, a legislative matter discussed until the very end of slavery. The lead time of legislation over the period of emancipation was quite small, and there had generally been little prior attention given to any long-range planning for freedom.

2

Emancipation may be the result of a voluntary set of agreements among slaveowners, presumably at a time when slavery has become unprofitable and slaves are not able to provide any economic gains. Historically, there are relatively few such cases at least in modern times. Moses Finley[5] presents this argument to describe the transition from Roman slavery, while a similar pattern possibly occurred in medieval Scandinavia.[6] The possibility of this occurrence explaining slavery's decline also featured in US debates in the 1850s, which forecast the ending of slavery occurring as a

[3] On manumission in Cuba, see, most recently, Bergad *et al.* 1995; and Fuente 2006. As part of the plans for amelioration in 1824, the British proposed a system of compulsory manumission, under which slaves could petition to be freed at an agreed-upon price; see Green 1976: 104–7. This was not adopted by all colonies initially, but in 1829 it was imposed on all crown colonies by an Order in Council. A case of compulsory manumission in Trinidad under this proposal is discussed in Engerman 2002: 273–302.

[4] The incentive argument of manumission can be found as far back as in such Greek writers on slavery as [Aristotle], *Oeconomica*, and Xenophon, *Conversation of Socrates*.

[5] Finley 1998 (1980): 191–227. [6] See Karras 1988: 82.

result of the increased ratio of labour to land and the consequent decline in price of slaves. Abraham Lincoln, among others, argued that slaveowners would be willing to voluntarily free slaves when they increased in numbers sufficiently to drive the price of slaves to zero.[7] Despite these predictions, this did not occur, perhaps because not enough time was allowed to pass to achieve this end.[8]

An unusual case of uncompensated, non-legislated, emancipation of serfs occurred in England in the aftermath of the Black Death.[9] The labour shortage faced by landowners, due to a population decline of over 25 per cent, led to a breakdown of the cartel protecting ownership rights, and competitive bidding for labour led to the freeing of the serfs as a means of attracting them to new locations. That a labour shortage need not lead to the freeing of coerced labour is reflected in the different adjustment to the Black Death in eastern Europe. There, serfdom became more strictly enforced, again because labour had become more valuable. The nature of the political and economic systems differed in these two cases, leading to these conflicting outcomes.[10]

There was an important scenario, based on the ending of the slave trade hopefully leading to voluntary slave emancipation, which was frequently discussed before the mid-nineteenth century. In most cases, legislation was passed that ended the international slave trade at least a decade or two before slavery itself was ended. It seemed easier to attack the slave trade and the movement across long distances, than slavery where it existed, in part because all the problems related to dealing with freed slaves were not present. It was anticipated that the end of the slave trade would lead to the ending of slavery within some short (or long) time period because of the adjustments made by slaveowners to the ending of the trade and the absence of new slave imports.

[7] See Fehrenbacher 1989a: 514–15, 677–8, 807–11. Stephen Douglas pointed out that one implication of Lincoln's argument was that it would, in effect, end slavery by 'extinguishing the [N]egro race', by having the slaves 'starve to death' as their productivity fell; see Fehrenbacher 1989a: 753. Even during the Civil War Lincoln argued for gradual and compensated slave emancipation, with a policy of colonization. There was compensated manumission in Washington in 1862, but at below market prices. The *Emancipation Proclamation*, however, provided for immediate and uncompensated emancipation of southern slaves; see again Fehrenbacher 1989b: 276–8, 307–17, 340–3, 406–15, and 671–2. Lincoln's argument for compensation to end slavery and the war was based on a comparison of the costs of emancipation with the financial costs of the war.

[8] See Engerman 2005: 15–30. [9] See Hilton 1969.

[10] On this contrast, based on the power of the crown vis-à-vis the nobles and the peasants, see Blum 1957: 807–36. The different possible outcomes to labour scarcity are discussed also in the United States, with northern political and economic equality contrasted with southern slavery, the regional differences being based also on the nature of climate and crops.

Thus, the ending of the British slave trade was projected by the abolitionist William Wilberforce[11] to lead to the ending of slavery within about two centuries. This ending could take place, it was argued at the time, because of either the continued population decline and ultimate disappearance of slavery in the British West Indies or, conversely, because of the increased value of slaves, which would lead to better care, treatment, and incentives, until basically the slaves would be regarded as free workers. Lincoln[12] had argued that with the early ending of the slave trade, the Founding Fathers expected to usher in the ending of slavery, because of population increases and lowered prices. This expectation was, however, offset by the invention of the cotton gin and southern territorial expansion. In none of the New World examples, as well as in most other cases, however, did the end of the slave trade lead directly to the subsequent ending of slavery, although the ending of the slave trade almost always preceded the ending of slavery.

In the USA and elsewhere, most emancipations occurred as a result of political and legislative actions, laws passed against the wishes of slaveowners or as a result of political and economic debates and arguments between slaveowners and others. This legislation seldom could be attributed to the economic failure of the slave system and, indeed, conflicts reflect more the success than the difficulties of the slave economy. This legislation took a number of different forms, with quite different impacts on the economic position of the slaveowners, the slaves, and the free population.

3

Two basic questions characterized the emancipation debates. First, should the freeing of slaves be immediate or gradual? Second, should emancipation be uncompensated or compensated; and, if compensated, who should be given the compensation, the slave or the slaveowner?

Most cases of immediate emancipation were the result of legislative or legal decisions. Compensation to the owner could be paid in the form of cash or bonds, or else working time, while the slave could conceivably be given land or cash. Forms of gradual emancipation, such as the law of the 'free womb', provided compensation to slaveowners by increasing the number of years the slaves and their offspring worked for the master after

[11] Wilberforce 1807. [12] Fehrenbacher 1989a: 514–15, 677–8, 809–11.

the decision to emancipate them.[13] In some cases, however, this period of compelled apprenticeship was ended early and all slaves were freed. In some cases compensation for the slaves would be paid to slaveowners. In other cases of gradual emancipation, additional years of labour from slaves were provided for by setting the date of emancipation in some future year.

Some types of emancipation included both cash payments and labour time. The British colonies' emancipation schemes involved a payment in cash plus an expected four to six years of slave apprenticeship. Emancipation was, however, granted immediately by two British colonies, Bermuda and Antigua. Planters in Antigua argued that the island's high population density meant that labourers would indeed remain on plantations even without legal coercion, since adequate coercion would be provided by demographic forces.[14] Planters in Antigua and Bermuda did receive cash payments as did the other British slaveowners but they did not worry about the expected complications concerning labour from the ex-slave apprentices. In some, but not all, cases, emancipation was granted without slaveowner compensation in the form of labour time but slaveowners did receive their compensation in the form of payments in cash.

There were some nations in the Americas which implemented policies of immediate emancipation, such as Haiti, the USA, Mexico, Central America, and Santo Domingo, as well as the French, Swedish, and Danish West Indies, and two of the US northern states. In these cases, emancipation was immediate and often compensation was paid. Historically, however, most emancipation schemes followed some variant of gradual emancipation. In these cases, slaves, in effect, paid for at least some of the costs of their emancipation by labouring for their owners.[15] The Danes had introduced a free womb emancipation scheme in 1847 but in 1848, as a result of slave protests, emancipation was made immediate.[16]

Two unusual cases of emancipation, immediate and uncompensated, were Haiti and the United States. In the United States, emancipation was due to federal legislation, but made possible by the outcome of the Civil War. Wartime hostilities (as well as the high value of slaves) made any discussion of compensation to the losers rather doubtful. The other unusual case of immediate emancipation was that of Haiti, where it was

[13] Those born after the specified date were legally considered to be not slaves, but apprentices.
[14] See Engerman 1982: 191–220; and Green 1976: 124–5.
[15] For details, see Dorijay 2003; Engerman 1995: 223–41; Fogel and Engerman 1974a; H. Klein 1986; M. Klein 2002; Rout 1976; Zilversmit 1967; and Ziskind 1993.
[16] Cochin 1863a: 389–94.

the result of a slave revolution that was ultimately successful in giving slaves freedom in an independent nation.[17]

4

It might seem obvious that, given the 'sin' involved in slave ownership, the best resolution should have been immediate emancipation with compensation provided to slaves for their having been exploited, their labour expropriated, and forced to suffer the theft of their bodies and the loss of their freedom.[18] Yet that was not the way that slavery and serfdom were usually ended. There were several related arguments made to support the process of gradual emancipation. By continuing the period of labour coercion and economic returns to the owner, the cost of emancipation was reduced and shifted from the taxpayers or the slaveowners to the slaves themselves. Also, in regard to working and labour considerations, it was claimed there was a need for slaves to be educated into freedom and free labour to eradicate the problems created by the pernicious effects of enslavement.

The basic argument for gradual emancipation was presented by French philosophers even before the emancipation debates emerged concerning New World slavery. Both Jean Bodin[19] and the Marquis de Condercet[20] argued that, if slavery was as destructive to the slaves as was claimed by antislavery advocates, any immediate emancipation could not be successful, since the freed people would not be able to take advantage of their freedom. A gradual process could be useful to educate the slaves in necessary work habits and desired models of reasonable living and, thus, provide a higher probability of long-run success from emancipation. Such arguments were made in subsequent years by many others, including antislavery advocates and black writers, who had to deal with the full implications of their antislavery argument in regard to the psychological costs of enslavement.[21]

Gradual emancipation could, however, take different forms and its duration could vary quite significantly. One basic form of gradual emancipation was the British scheme of apprenticeship, the outlines of which were followed three decades later by the Dutch, who introduced an even longer period of tied labour. The British system entailed cash

[17] Leyburn 1941; Dubois 2004a, and 2004b.
[18] See, among others, Cuguano 1999 (1787): 57, 59; Hopkins 1776; and Cochin 1863b: 109–10.
[19] Bodin 1962 (1606): 45–6. [20] Condorcet 1781.
[21] See, for example, Cuguano 1999 (1787): 57, 59, 98–9; Benezet 1771; Rush 1773; Hopkins 1776; and the various early US arguments in Adams 1908: 91, 171, 173–6, 202–4.

compensation for slaveowners, based upon a fraction of the slave's market prices between 1823 and 1830, plus a provision for a period of tied labour. The slaves, now legally called apprentices, were required to remain at work for their former owners, for some four to six years, depending on their occupation (then shortened to four years for all).

Apprenticeship presumably provided more favourable living arrangements than slavery, as well as established improved working conditions. The process of apprenticeship was monitored by a set of appointed stipendiary magistrates, originally established in an attempt to equalize the bargaining powers of ex-slaves and former owners. Labour in the period of apprenticeship yielded financial gains to the landowners, and it is estimated that four years of apprenticeship yielded an income of roughly one-half the price of a slave before emancipation. Since the cash compensation paid equalled approximately another half of the slave prices in the 1823–30 period, slaveowners received almost full compensation for their slaves in the British cases.[22]

While agreeing with the need for apprenticeship, as in the British case, Alexis de Tocqueville[23] in his discussion of the prospective French abolition was concerned about the negative psychological impact upon ex-slaves of remaining at work for former masters. He advocated a form of state socialism for plantation ownership, so to avoid this problem. This was, however, not attempted and the link of ex-slave to ex-master persisted wherever apprenticeship schemes were introduced.

Another approach to gradual emancipation was to set a date a number of years in the future at which all slavery would end. This resembles the apprenticeship scheme, except that during the intervening years the enslaved were still legally considered slaves, whereas apprentices were considered legally free. As with apprenticeship, these additional years of legally coerced labour reduced the loss to the slaveowner, with the payment being made, in effect, by the slave.[24]

5

The most frequent form of emancipation was a variant of what was called, in the Brazilian case, the law of the 'free womb',[25] apparently first utilized

[22] Fogel and Engerman 1974b: 377–401. [23] Tocqueville 1840.

[24] The State of New York passed a law of the 'free womb' in 1799, but, in 1817, legislated an end to all slavery, to take place in 1827.

[25] See Conrad 1972.

in the northern US states between 1780 and 1804. Children born to slave mothers after a certain date were to be considered free but were treated as apprentices, subject to their staying with the mother's owner and working for the owner for a specific period of years. No person who was a slave at the date of legislation was freed by this act and slaves presumably were to remain such until they died. In a number of cases these slaves were freed by some subsequent legislation or constitutional decisions, as in some of the northern states of the United States, Cuba, and Brazil, but there were cases such as Pennsylvania,[26] which never legally ended their slavery by legislative action. The children born after the legislation was passed – Cuba set a date of two years before the passage of its legislation – worked for their mothers' owners for somewhere between fifteen and thirty years.

As St George Tucker[27] pointed out, the choice of age was based on some economic calculations regarding the length of time it would take for the children to produce enough to cover the discounted cost of rearing them.[28] This, in effect, meant that the slaveowner would have only a minimal loss on a slave – the owner would pay rearing costs but was given the right to use the labour for a sufficient period of time to recoup them. The source of the slaveowner's returns was the slave's labour, while the taxpayers bore no financial burden. This policy, in which the deferred grant of freedom to the slaves effectively cost nothing to taxpayers, presumably made this form of emancipation a more acceptable policy.[29]

The net outcome of this policy was that those enslaved before the legislation was enforced would be slaves until they died, not benefiting directly from the emancipation laws. The children born after the passage of the legislation would be legally free, but subject to coercive working conditions for, depending on the area, up to more than two decades. This was presumably a period of learning how to survive and maybe even prosper under freedom, after it was achieved. When emancipation was legally immediate, as it was to be later in Africa, it often neither contained a necessary action by the state freeing the slave nor specified any enforcement mechanism, so that the achievement of freedom required some legal or other direct action to be brought by the enslaved.

[26] See Nash and Soderlund 1991. [27] Tucker 1970 (1796).

[28] There were earlier statements of this argument, for example in Hutcheson 1968 (1755). See also Dillwyn 1773: 270–8; Baldwin and Edwards Jr 1773; Hart 1775; Green 1779.

[29] See Zilversmit 1967; and Fogel and Engerman 1974b: 377–401.

6

The examination of whether compensation was or was not to be paid and to whom points to certain key philosophical differences between the present and the past. Today we are concerned with the payment of reparations to the descendants of former slaves (to compensate them for crimes committed against them under slavery) as well as the continuing economic costs of their exploitation, resulting from the earlier enslavement.[30] 'Slavery is theft' meant that those bearing the costs deserve payment for their sufferings. The descendants of the owners were presumably the most qualified to make good these payments and, as former slaveowners, they had no claim on society's resources. This was not the same as the view held before the end of the nineteenth century. Then, when slavery was being ended by legislation, there was a firm belief in the property rights of slaveowners and, thus, the requirement that they be compensated, as were owners of any asset, to offset the costs of any action which confiscated their legally owned property. Since slaves at that time were accepted as a legitimate form of property, the state recognized its obligation to compensate those slaveowners who lost their property by slave emancipation. There might have been legitimate disputes about the specifics of determining the prices of slaves to be used for compensation and also about whether the compensation should be paid in cash or securities. However, the general point was that there was a perceived need for payment of compensation of slaveowners for their loss of property.[31]

In no case of slave emancipation, immediate or gradual, were the slaves offered any compensation in the form of cash, bonds, or land. No 'forty acres and a mule' were provided to US slaves nor were any equivalent benefits given to slaves elsewhere. This lack of compensation paid to freed labour also characterized the ending of serfdom in nineteenth-century Europe.[32] Compensation was generally allowed to landowners, in cash or land. In some cases, payments were made by the state and, in others, payments made by the ex-serfs in the form of labour time or by cash payments, sometimes considered as a means to purchase land from their landlords.[33] These arrangements under serfdom could lead to unexpected

[30] For a late-nineteenth century advocacy of reparations linked to the government payment of pensions to injured Civil War veterans, see Berry 2005; see also Bittker 1973; and Robinson 1970.

[31] Toqueville had suggested that the British emancipation scheme should have delayed the ability of the ex-slaves to purchase land, thus creating a wage labour force; see Tocqueville 1843.

[32] See Blum 1978. [33] See Field 1976; Kingston-Mann 1999; and Kolchin 1987.

consequences, since it is claimed that in Russia the compulsory purchase of land by ex-serfs was at above market price,[34] adding to the costs of emancipation. Land purchases by ex-slaves in most societies were permitted after emancipation; but this required the use of funds that the slaves had acquired, either under slavery or afterwards, and was not a gift from the state or the slaveowners.

Compensation paid to the owners of slaves was to cover the losses in value of their assets. Compensation could take the form of payments of cash or of bonds, or else in the form of labour time, by an extension of the time spent in coerced labour. Most provisions for ending slavery (and serfdom) also allowed the slaveowners to maintain their property in land and capital, thus reducing their overall losses and, with difficulties for slaves to acquire land, permitting the emergence of free wage labour agriculture where slavery had previously existed. While the reduction of the effective labour input with emancipation led to some probable fall in land values, the slaveowners did remain landowners, and the ex-slaves were unable to get their own land, at first, and they needed to acquire sufficient assets to purchase their withdrawal from the wage labour force.

The payment of compensation did not mean that the slaveowners would be granted 100 per cent of the value of the slaves at the time of emancipation. Given the conflict of interest between those desiring to free slaves and those owning slaves, the precise amount of payment would depend upon the outcome of a political bargaining process, so to reach an agreement on a mutually acceptable amount. There were also some complications in calculating the specific amounts, even with some agreement on general principles regarding compensation. The precise number of years chosen to determine the proper value of slaves, the impact of the age–sex composition of the slave population, and the allowances to be made for skills and for handicaps which influenced prices, all would affect the magnitude of compensation and its distribution among slaveowners. The evaluation of the slaves was not always used to set the amount of compensation but rather to allocate among the individual slaveowners the total amount of payments that the legislators decreed.

In the case of British emancipation, there was yet another political matter to be settled by the British government in its planning. Those islands with low slave prices, the result of high population densities, argued, with what they regarded as appropriate moral concerns, that payments should be made per slave – i.e. based on the number of slaves owned,

[34] Domar 1989: 429–39.

not on slave prices.[35] Not only did payment per slave seem more consistent with the moral arguments for abolition, but to have done otherwise would have meant to penalize those areas that had provided good care for slaves, leading to higher population growth and, thus, to lower slave prices. Nevertheless, the distribution among slaveholders under most compensation schemes was based upon the relative prices of slaves, not the number of those freed. Differentials per island were also implemented by the French and the Dutch, based on relative slave prices by area. The costs of these government schemes were generally borne by the taxpayers, although there was a proposal (not adopted) by the Dutch to have the ex-slaves reimburse the costs of their freedom out of subsequent earnings.[36]

7

Even emancipation by the law of the 'free womb', which, in effect, entailed a large compensation paid for by the slaves, still meant generally less than 100 per cent compensation. There was no loss to the slaveowner on those already enslaved, since their legal status had not changed. Although the time specified was intended to cover the costs of raising children, owners were not allowed those returns produced by slaves in their twenties and afterwards, earnings that provided the incomes to justify positive prices for slaves.

Thus, the value of the after-born was less than if slavery had continued through the slave's entire lifespan. This meant, also, that there was some reduction in the value of childbearing females among those enslaved. Nevertheless, given the long time periods involved before such returns would occur, the loss to slaveowners would be quite small.[37]

8

The most important cases in which cash compensation was paid – some also with an apprenticeship period – concerned efforts made by European nations in the 1830s, 1840s, and 1860s to end slavery in their Caribbean colonies. The British legislation of 1833, after debates on whether providing slaveowners loans or grants, as well as on the amounts involved, provided

35 See Engerman 1982: 191–220, and 1984: 133–50.

36 Kuitenbrouwer 1995: 67–88. The Dutch legislation of 1863 also included provisions to encourage immigration of labour, as well as permitting apprentices some choice of residence and occupation, provided that they did work; see Cochin 1863b: 221–35.

37 See Fogel and Engerman 1974a: 59–106, 153–5.

for cash payments to be made on the basis of an allocation of slave prices on each island in the years 1823 to 1830.[38] Payments to slaveowners were made in cash out of the British budget, with the funds raised by an expansion of the public debt. Schemes similar in some ways to aspects of the British compensation pattern were implemented by the French, Swedish, Danish, and Dutch. In the cases of the French and Dutch, this came after extended debates on the overall policy and procedures to be adopted.

In the British case, the cash payments were about 45 per cent of the value of slaves in the period 1823–30. This was about the same ratio estimated for the French Caribbean colonies, where the distribution was based on sale values for 1825–34, a period of prosperity.[39] In the British slave colonies, however, there was some earlier decline of prices, beginning with the expanded antislavery activity of the 1820s, which raised some possibility that emancipation might be inevitable. In none of these cases, however, did payments account for a large share of the overall budget of the government, let alone of national income.[40]

As noted above, there were two particularly unusual cases regarding compensation. The slaves of Saint Domingue achieved their freedom and won complete control of their nation as a result of their successful revolution. Whites lost their slaves, their lands, and often their lives. The complaints of white survivors about their expropriation did not lead to any financial settlement, at first, but these expropriations did play a role in leading to a limitation of Haiti's political and economic contacts with the rest of the American and European worlds. Nevertheless, when, a quarter of a century later in 1825, Haiti wanted to resume trade relations with France, the French demanded that compensation be paid for the slaves freed, as a precondition for any trade agreement.[41] The Haitian government agreed to a sum to be paid over future years, and with some periodic delays and reductions, they succeeded in the accomplishment. Thus, after a prolonged period, the government of the ex-slaves of Haiti was required to pay compensation to their former French owners. While the money did go to France, it is not yet certain that it went as payment to the actual former slaveowners or to their families.[42]

[38] See Drescher 2002. [39] See Fogel and Engerman 1974b: 377–401; and Cochin 1863a: 143–50.

[40] See Cochin 1863a: 150–3; and Fogel and Engerman 1974b: 377–401.

[41] Apparently the compensation claimed (and received) was based on the expected profits of Haitian trade, and the length of time of the revolutionary warfare between the French and the slaves, and not on the specifics of any slave evaluations; see Rotberg 1971: 66–7, 86.

[42] See Rotberg 1971.

The USA was one of the few examples of slave emancipation without any form of compensation being paid, although such schemes had been discussed before the Civil War.[43] 'Free womb' policies, such as those used by the northern states prior to 1804, were infrequently discussed at the national level, nor were there many proposals that cash or bonds be paid to free the slaves. The problem was that the prices and the numbers of slaves in the mid-nineteenth century was quite high, and the use of cash payments or the annual interest costs on bonds to emancipate slaves would have required a large increase in the size of the federal debt and the federal budget. A large tax increase to pay slaveowners was not politically feasible and presumably the main alternatives were either to await a sharp decline in slave prices or to implement non-economic, political or military measures to lower the value of slaves or, at least, the prices that slaveowners would accept to free the slaves.

After the US slave emancipation, there were cases of emancipation without financial compensation in the remaining two slave powers in the Americas, Cuba and Brazil. Both initiated the process of emancipation by introducing a law of the 'free womb' and nearly two decades later ended slavery with no financial compensation paid. In none of these cases of emancipation was land given to ex-slaves, and the 'forty acres and a mule' desired by US slaves did not materialize there or anywhere else, whatever the expected economic or political effects might have been.[44]

9

The early ending of the slave trade in England led to some legal debates about the need to compensate slave traders for the losses imposed when a government's long-sanctioned and, indeed, frequently encouraged activity was suddenly declared illegal. The traders commented that they had entered into this activity in the past because of government approval and encouragement, and that, to the extent that it required specialized equipment not utilizable for other purposes, there would be costs occurring once its termination took place. The traders petitioned parliament without success, since it was argued that to provide payments for such adjustments would reduce the government's ability to introduce any desirable social changes. Thus, the bulk of slave traders suffered capital losses when the slave trade closed.

[43] Fladeland 1976: 169–86.

[44] For a discussion of southern post-bellum land policy and of the believed promised 'forty acres and a mule', see Oubre 1978.

There was some compensation paid, however, but only to those vessels that were already at sea when the new legislation was passed.[45] Other early variants of payments made of losses include refunds agreed between nations for expected losses from ending the slave trade. In 1817, Britain gave a 'bribe' of £400,000 to Spain and a smaller amount to Portugal to entice them to cut off part of their slave trading.[46] And, at about this same time, the British paid an indemnity to US slaveowners for slaves removed during the War of 1812, recognizing differential slave prices in different states.[47] After the Revolutionary War, however, there was no agreed-upon plan for compensation to be paid for losses to American slaveowners.[48]

10

The concern with the nature of the transition from slavery to freedom often led to a gradual process of emancipation, within which slaves and masters would presumably have opportunities to adapt to the new institutional arrangements. In some cases, the government provided agents to deal with labourers and landowners in order to influence subsequent bargaining and decisions. The British introduced a system of stipendiary magistrates in their colonies, while the Freedmen's Bureau in the US South was intended to accomplish similar purposes. The balance of political and economic power remained, however, with the former masters, who generally received compensation when slaves were freed and were able to keep their land and capital. The British legislation to control labour in the colonies was based on the long-standing *Master and Servant Acts*, which did not distinguish black ex-slaves from British white labour. Indeed, much of the British debate about the expectations from ex-slave labour was based on the general effects of land–labour ratios, not on race or prior legal status.[49]

Without being granted land-ownership in those locations where they had been slaves, the ex-slaves had several sets of options. These depended on the related issues of land availability and the land–labour ratio. One possibility would be to remain in agriculture in the location where they were, renting or, if possible, purchasing land or, by working for landowners (perhaps their former owners), entering the free agricultural wage labour force. Or, if free land at other locations was available, they could purchase

[45] See Porter 1970. [46] Eltis 1987: 106–11, 142–4. [47] Bemis 1965: 168, 175–6.

[48] See Robinson 1970: 347–53, and Bemis 1965: 70–2. Throughout the ante-bellum period, when slaves were transported or executed after being convicted of crimes, the state often paid some compensation to the slaveowners.

[49] See Engerman 1984: 133–50.

land, as some did, and move into these areas and begin small-scale agriculture on their own, with possibly lower incomes than if they had kept at plantation labour.

II

In describing the economic outcomes of emancipation, the issues of gradual versus immediate, and of the nature and magnitude of compensation, seem less important than did the regional land–labour ratios and the ability of ex-slaves to avoid wage labour. Thus, all the British colonies received compensation and all had apprenticeships available when ending slavery. However, three quite different patterns emerged. Barbados and Antigua had high population densities and were able to maintain the plantation system in the absence of free land for the ex-slaves to move to. As noted, this was known to Antiguan planters who avoided apprenticeship since workers had nowhere to move to. Initially Barbados kept the plantation system intact by preventing emigration of the population. Jamaica and several other colonies with less productive soils saw labour move to avoid plantation regions, but with a large and long-lasting output decline. In Trinidad and British Guiana, with much excess land, ex-slaves left the plantations, but some twenty years after emancipation imports of indentured labour from India and elsewhere were legalized, permitting a major expansion in sugar production on plantations.[50]

These were only some of the areas that received indentured labour in the aftermath of slave emancipation or, once indentured labour became acceptable, in the absence of prior enslaved populations, e.g., Fiji and Australia. Indentured labour generally lasted less than one-half century; it was ended by the areas which provided the indentures – unlike the ending of the international movements of slave labour by the recipient countries – and was not followed by compensation paid to anyone when the system ended.

In the US South, Cuba, and Brazil, slave labour was replaced by white labour – southern European immigrants in Cuba and Brazil, with subsidized transportation and relocation costs, and white southern farmers in the USA. These adjustments were permitted by the adoption of new or existing technologies that allowed production of sugar, coffee, and cotton to take place on units smaller than plantations, albeit probably at higher costs than with the plantation means of production. These new working arrangements

[50] Northrup 1995.

were acceptable to white labourers, who would always have avoided plantation labour. The French and Dutch West Indies also drew upon indentured labour from India plus, in the Dutch case, Java, to meet work demands.[51] In many cases, therefore, ex-slaves were able to move into new areas of their home countries and to avoid plantation work or labour, but this did not guarantee their high productivity or enhanced consumption.

12

Fundamental to the process of abolition were two sets of beliefs, which today we often find difficult to reconcile.[52] One was the desire to end slavery to provide freedom to all members of the population. The anti-slavery movement attracted many members and achieved considerable success – though some might claim it was still somewhat limited – in what was, historically, a relatively short time. But also, there was a great belief in the importance of maintaining property rights, including those of slaveowners.

The process of emancipation was often gradual; many slaveowners were granted compensation and none of the other assets of slaveowners were taken away from them as part of the settlement. Political power remained with the existing governments, except in Haiti, and subsequent legislation often was to benefit ex-slaveowners, not ex-slaves. So, despite the moral attack and its success, slave (and serf) emancipation can be seen as a rather conservative and limited reform, one generally paid for by either those freed or by other members of society.

APPENDIX

Table 10.1 *The timing of the ending of the slave trade and slavery*[a] *(from Engerman 1995)*

	Ending of slave trade	Ending of slavery
Denmark	1803	1848
England	1808	1834
United States	1808	1865
Netherlands	1814	1863
France	1815	1848[b]
Brazil	1830	1888

[51] See again Northrup 1995: 16–42.
[52] On the debates about emancipation and its timing, see Davis 1984.

Table 10.1 (*cont.*)

Spain (Cuba)	1835	1886
Sweden	1794?	1847

[a] Dating the ending of the slave trade is, for several areas, (the French West Indies, Brazil, and Cuba) rather difficult, given the lag between the date of signing international treaties pledging to end the slave trade, the date of the legislation ending the slave trade, and then the date of actual enforcement of these laws that effectively ended slave imports. Thus dating the ending of the slave trade by the dates of the last sets of slave shipments would give France 1831; Brazil, 1852; and Cuba, 1867.
[b] Haiti, by 1804, is a special case.

Table 10.2 *Slavery laws in the northern United States*

	Law of free birth	Law or provision ending slavery
Pennsylvania	1780	–
Rhode Island	1784	1842
Connecticut	1784	1848
New York	1799	1817 (to be ended 1827)
New Jersey	1804	1846

Table 10.3 *Slavery laws in Spanish America*

	Law of free birth	Law or provision ending slavery
Argentina	1813	1853
Peru	1821	1854
Ecuador	1821	1851
Colombia	1821	1851
Venezuela	1821	1854
Uruguay	1825	1853
Boliva	1831	1861
Paraguay	1842	1869

Table 10.4 *Slavery laws in the Spanish Caribbean and Brazil*

	Law of free birth	Law or provision ending slavery
Puerto Rico	1870	1873
Cuba	1870	1886
Brazil	1871	1888

Table 10.5 *Emancipation of serfs in Europe*

Period	Number of decrees
1771–1800	5 (including Denmark and France)
1801–20	11
1821–30	0
1831–40	5 (all in 1831 and 1832)
1841–50	13 (mostly German states)
1851–64	4

Source: Blum 1978: 356

PART V

Slavery and unfree labour, ancient and modern

CHAPTER 11

Spartiates, helots and the direction of the agrarian economy: toward an understanding of helotage in comparative perspective

Stephen Hodkinson

The subject of my study is the system of helotage within the ancient Greek polis of Sparta.[1] A fundamental feature of Spartan society was that the Spartiate citizens lived as rentier landowners supported economically by a servile population, the helots, who worked their estates. The Spartiates inhabited a cluster of villages within the region of Lakonia, towards the northern end of the Eurotas valley.[2] Their landholdings, in contrast, were much more extensive. At the peak of their power, from *c.* 600 BC to 370 BC, when Spartan territory covered the entire southern Peloponnese, the Spartiates' estates farmed by helot cultivators were spread across both its main regions: their 'home' region of Lakonia and the neighbouring region of Messenia to the west, occupying overall perhaps some 1,400 km^2 out of a total geographical area of 8,500 km^2. After Sparta's loss of Messenia in 370 BC, the helots of Lakonia continued to be the predominant labour force on citizen estates in the region until at least the second century BC.[3]

Modern thought has often followed ancient Greek and Roman sources in portraying Sparta as an exceptional society, somewhat different from other Greek poleis, and indeed from most other civilized human societies. In recent years my work has increasingly been concerned with

1 I am grateful to Sue Alcock, Richard Catling, and Nino Luraghi for allowing me to read their important forthcoming work in advance of publication, to Peter Gatrell for advice on comparative reading on Russian serfdom, and to the participants in the Harvard conference on *Helots and their Masters* in March 2001 for their supportive reception of the original version of this chapter. This chapter was written during my tenure of an award under the Research Leave scheme of the UK Arts and Humanities Research Board and was originally published as Hodkinson 2003. It is re-published here with light modifications.

2 The geographical term 'Lakonia' is not contemporary, but (as the name of the modern administrative unit based on Sparta) is commonly used in modern scholarship to denote the eastern part of Spartan territory.

3 The figure of 1,400 km^2 derives from the calculations in Hodkinson 2000: 131–45. On the end of helotage, Ducat 1990: 193–9.

deconstructing that image as it relates to Greek antiquity, exploring the complex manner in which Spartan institutions and practices were frequently both distinctive and yet reflected, and sometimes even exemplified, trends observable elsewhere in the Greek world. For the study of helotage, the value of examining Spartan institutions in broader Greek context is demonstrated in a recent essay by Hans van Wees, which views the helots as the most prominent example of a range of Greek populations enslaved by wars of conquest in the archaic period.[4] This chapter is designed to develop such a comparative approach one stage further by extending it beyond the ancient Greek world, by exploring some ways in which the operation of helotage may profitably be studied against the backdrop of systems of unfree labour in other historical times and places from antiquity to the modern world. It aims to ask: in what ways might the history and sociology of other systems of unfree labour help to illuminate the character of helotage and of relations between the helots and their masters? Given, in particular, the paucity of the ancient evidence for helot–Spartiate relations – the lack of historical detail highlighted recently by Susan Alcock[5] – to what extent can comparative study help us to map out some plausible broad contours for the operation of helotage, even if much of the detailed topography must necessarily remain obscure? For the purposes of this investigation I shall focus on Spartiate–helot relationships within the key area of the agrarian economy.

COMPARATIVE APPROACHES

As has been emphasized in a number of studies, such as Mark Golden's salutary article on the uses of cross-cultural comparison in ancient social history,[6] the enterprise of comparative history, and especially the methodology of comparison between unfree labour in antiquity and in more recent periods, is by no means straightforward. Some remarks are therefore appropriate by way of introduction to the comparative approach taken in my discussion.

I will start by indicating one kind of comparative approach which is *not* particularly fruitful for my purposes, an approach that I would broadly characterize as 'globalizing'. The prime example is the longstanding debate about how the helots should be defined in terms of modern legal or sociological definitions of servile status. There has been considerable debate, in particular, about whether helotage should be categorized as a

[4] Van Wees 2003. [5] Alcock 2003: 3–5. [6] Golden 1992: 309–31.

form of slavery or a form of serfdom – with the modern definition of serfdom in Article 1 of the UN Supplementary Convention of 1956 being invoked by Geoffrey de Ste Croix as alleged proof of the helots' classification as 'state serfs'.[7] It is not my intention to dismiss entirely the exercise of definition; but the problem with such definitions for the purpose of comparative study is that they have only limited value in illuminating the actual operation and condition of helotage.[8] The restricted range of categories (slavery-serfdom-debt bondage or slavery-serfdom-wage labour) employed in most modern classificatory schemes means that some considerable compression of actuality is inherent in the very act of classification.[9] Even Ste Croix – in the midst of a long discussion of the classification of different types of unfree labour – concedes that, 'Actually, we know of no precise parallels to the condition of the Helots . . . and a certain amount of oversimplification is involved by forcing it into any general category.'[10] Moreover, even if the classification of helots were unproblematic, status is on its own a poor guide to economic and social reality.[11] As many students of slavery and serfdom have emphasized, persons of identical servile status can enjoy vastly different lifestyles or socio-economic conditions, even within a single society, let alone between different societies.[12]

[7] Classification of helotage as a form of slavery: e.g. Oliva 1971: 'undeveloped slavery'; Lotze 1959: 'Kollektivsklaverei'. Definition as 'state serfs': e.g. Ste Croix 1983 (1981): 147, 149; Cartledge 1987: 172, 1988: 33–41, esp. 39. Ste Croix's invocation (Ste Croix 1983 [1981]: 135–6) of the 1956 *UN Supplementary Convention on the Abolition of Slavery, the Slave Trade and Practices similar to Slavery* is followed by Cartledge in both works cited. For criticism of the definition of helots as serfs, see Finley 1999 (1973): 65, with 189 n. 5. Other classifications have been suggested, such as 'intercommunal servitude' (see Garlan 1988: 93–8).

[8] Note Ducat's criticism of the similar approach of the ancient sources: 'leur façon de réfléchir était le plus souvent globalisante, et visait beaucoup plus à définir un esclavage de type hilotique qu'à dresser le catalogue des spécificités de chacun des statuts relevant de ce type'; see Ducat 1994: 116.

[9] The statement in Greenidge 1958: 24, quoted approvingly by Ste Croix, that serfdom 'is a status intermediate between slavery and complete freedom' reads uncannily like Aristophanes of Byzantium's inadequate classification of the helots, Penestai, and a number of other groups as 'between free people and slaves' (*apud* Pollux, *Onomasticon* 3.83).

[10] Ste Croix 1983 [1981]: 149. Despite this admission, he then continues, 'but for convenience I shall treat them as the "State serfs" they undoubtedly were' – a dogmatic approach that reads like classification for its own sake.

[11] Cf. the comments in Biezunska-Malowist and Malowist 1989: 17–31, esp. 18–19; and in Bush 1996b: 1, 16–17. Cf. also Finley's criticism of the consequences of modern attempts at classification: 'So the helots become serfs and the slaves with a *peculium* are discussed in the first instance as slaves, when, economically and in terms of the structure and functioning of society, they were mostly self-employed craftsmen, pawnbrokers, moneylenders and shopkeepers'; see Finley 1999 (1973): 65.

[12] A few, very selective examples: by ancient historians, Bradley 1987: 15–16; Finley 1999 (1973): 64–5; by students of modern servile systems, Bush 1996c: 119–224; Hoch 1996: 311–22, esp. 320; and the title of Lovejoy 2000b [1983]. Cf. the remarks in Annequin 1985: 639–72, esp. 664, on the heterogeneity of historical forms of slavery.

Conversely, there is often considerable overlap between the practical conditions of different categories of unfree labour, especially between different societies.[13] Within the realm of the agrarian economy, various forms of coerced labour have been exploited by ruling elites for both subsistence and market-orientated farming. The character of relationships between landowners and these different unfree labour forces is often affected by common variables; and, although examination of these variables may frequently reveal key differences between different forms of exploitation, at other times comparable conditions can be seen to apply. For example, as we shall see in more detail below, one important variable in many systems of unfree labour is the extent of labour obligations owed to the landowner. On this subject one can legitimately draw a contrast between most systems of serfdom – in which serfs typically exercised some control over their labour, working only part-time for their lords with several days a week to farm their own lands – and some systems of agrarian slavery, in which the slaves worked full-time for their masters, being allocated little more than garden plots and little time to cultivate them. In other slave systems, however, such as in pre-colonial West Africa and in much of the Caribbean, the slaves' access to land and to time for its cultivation was often far closer to that enjoyed by most serfs.[14] The existence of common variables and, in certain circumstances, of overlapping conditions applying to different categories of unfree labour reinforces my argument that legal or sociological classification is not a fruitful starting-point for the comparative study of Spartiate–helot agrarian relations. As Michael Bush has observed, summarizing the conclusions of a recent comparative volume on serfdom and slavery: 'Both serfdom and slavery were defined by law . . . But what does this reveal about their true nature? . . . The conclusion is: very little . . . the character and condition of both were determined in reality by a wide range of other factors.'[15]

In contrast to the unhelpfulness of globalizing approaches, a more promising comparative approach to an understanding of helotage is, I suggest, through the investigation of *specific* aspects or problems which can legitimately be viewed in broader historical perspective. A good example of such a 'specific' comparative approach is Paul Cartledge's article 'Rebels and *Sambos* in classical Greece: a comparative view',[16] in which he

[13] Engerman 1996: 18–41, esp. 19–21.

[14] Smith 1955; Hill 1985: 33–50, esp. 37–8; Lovejoy 2000b [1983]: 187–8; Kolchin 1993: 153.

[15] Bush 1996b: 1. [16] Cartledge 2001 [1985].

successfully employed comparative insights from Eugene Genovese's study of slave revolts, *From Rebellion to Revolution*,[17] to explain the capacity of the Messenian helots to revolt, in contrast to chattel slaves elsewhere in Greece. Similarly, my comparative chapter takes as its subject another major aspect of helotage: the character of Spartiate–helot relationships within the agrarian economies of Lakonia and Messenia during their respective periods of domination by Sparta. Its specific focus is the social relations of production between Spartiates and helots, especially the degree of Spartiate direction of helot farming and the implications for the helots' experience of servitude.

In line with my criticisms of the limitations of classificatory approaches to the comparative study of helotage, my study will purposely draw upon insights from diverse systems and types of unfree agrarian labour at different historical times and places. In this study, I will concentrate mainly upon three major agrarian servile systems from the modern world: serfdom in rural Russia; slavery in the US South; and slavery in pre-colonial Africa. I shall also refer, at appropriate points, to contemporary servile populations from Greek antiquity, especially the Penestai of Thessaly; and on occasion to certain systems of dependent agrarian labour in which the exploited labour force is legally free.[18] My study will focus upon certain key variables which have been shown to possess widespread significance for the character of social relations of production across these different types and systems of agrarian labour. The patterns and conclusions indicated, both positively and negatively, by comparative study of these variables will be used as context for assessing the limited and partial ancient literary and archaeological evidence, for drawing out implications, and for suggesting fresh insights into the nature of Spartiate–helot agrarian relations. On occasion, where there is a sufficient degree of similarity to conditions in another servile system, those correspondences will be used to supplement the

[17] Genovese 1979.

[18] Pertinent comparisons between free and unfree agrarian populations are appropriate on occasions when their conditions of exploitation are affected by similar variables. There have also often been respects regarding the practical conditions of agrarian life in which 'he [the serf] closely resembled the free peasant' (Bush 1996c: 206) or in which 'the difference between slave and free was only one of degree' (Klein and Lovejoy 1979: 181–212, esp. 188). For a defence against criticisms (Cartledge 1993: 127–36, esp. 132; Cartledge 1998: 4–24, esp. 13) of my previous study (Hodkinson 1992: 123–34), in which I illuminated Spartiate–helot sharecropping arrangements through comparative evidence for systems of dependent tenancy, see now Hodkinson 2000: 116–17; cf. also Alcock 2002b: 199 n. 9. Attested within systems of servile labour (e.g. Smith 1954: 38), as well as within those involving legally 'free' tenants, sharecropping is a good example of a topic for which comparative study embracing systems of both free and unfree dependent labour is highly appropriate.

exiguous ancient evidence by developing, with all due caution, plausible hypotheses regarding the character of helot servitude.[19]

The scope of my approach, consequently, differs from the kind of cross-cultural comparison currently most favoured by anthropologists: namely, comparison within a region or culture area. It also differs in scope from the approach adopted in many previous comparative studies by historians of ancient slavery, certainly in those focused upon agrarian labour, which have most frequently restricted their comparisons to ancient chattel-slave systems judged to have operated through modes of exploitation directly comparable with the slave systems of the modern New World.[20] My focus on diverse examples of servile exploitation also necessarily implies the illumination of helotage by means of difference as well as by similarity. In terms of method, my approach shares something in common with each of the three types of comparative history identified in an influential article by Skocpol and Somers[21] – macro-causal analysis; parallel demonstration of theory; and contrast of contexts – though it also differs from each in certain important respects. It shares with macro-causal analysis the method of breaking individual cases down into sets of variables and an interest in generalization, though not its use of quantitative techniques or its de-emphasis upon specificity. Although not aimed at the demonstration of theory, my approach shares an interest in extracting parallel insights, where appropriate, from diverse historical cases. It also shares – as noted above – an awareness of contrast and difference between specific historical cases, although it does not eschew the formulation of explanatory generalizations through comparative analysis.

In his article on the methodology of comparative approaches to the history of slavery, Jacques Annequin has posed the question: 'une réflexion comparative doit-elle se fonder sur des ressemblances factuelles ou sur des convergences de problématiques?'[22] Although not impervious to the value, in appropriate context, of factual resemblances between helotage and other systems of unfree agrarian labour, the primary concentration of my own 'réflexion comparative' will be upon 'des convergences de problématiques',

[19] For both these sources of comparative insight, see, briefly, Annequin 1985: 640; and also the comments in Golden 1992: 311: 'Of course, reports on other cultures cannot in themselves replace missing data from Greece and Rome, but they can be very useful all the same in . . . developing hypotheses, in identifying patterns from scattered scraps, in refuting generalisations.'

[20] Cf. Martin 1980: 161–75; Biezunska-Malowist and Malowist 1989: 18, 23. Cf. also the works cited by Golden 1992: 312, n. 9.

[21] See Skocpol and Somers 1980.

[22] Annequin 1985: 641–2.

the issues and variables common to diverse systems of exploitation which permit pertinent comparative study across historical time and space.

THE AGRARIAN ECONOMY: SOCIAL RELATIONS OF PRODUCTION AND THE HELOT EXPERIENCE

One of the main puzzles concerning helot farming, and indeed of helot life more generally, is how it actually worked on the ground. It is clear that, from the viewpoint of the Spartiate masters, the essential function of the vast majority of the helot population was to cultivate the Spartiates' landholdings and to deliver sufficient produce to enable them to sustain their position as a *rentier* citizen elite with a near full-time devotion to civic affairs. What is less clear, however, is the extent to which Spartiate masters took steps to intervene actively in directing and controlling the process of agricultural production or, alternatively, left the practical planning and management of farming to the helots themselves. The question of the control of helot labour, of the social relations of production between Spartiates and helots, is important for our understanding of more than just helot agriculture, since comparative evidence suggests that the location of control over the productive process will have had a potentially profound effect on the fundamental conditions of helot life, including the nature of local helot communities.[23] The issues concerned are ones currently under debate in the study of diverse servile systems in human history, as scholars have become increasingly sensitive to the capacities of unfree peoples to develop, within their experience of servitude, various forms of (semi-)autonomous activity, organization, and culture.[24]

Direct insight from the ancient sources into Spartiate intervention in the agricultural process is confined to one brief passage in Xenophon's account of the conspiracy of Kinadon around 398 BC (*Hell.* 3.3.5). Kinadon is depicted as taking a potential recruit to the conspiracy out from the streets of Sparta to the Spartiates' estates, where he pointed out on each estate a single enemy, the master, surrounded by many potential allies to the conspiracy. The implication is that helots who farmed estates close to Sparta may have experienced a fair degree of intervention and direction from their Spartiate masters. This single episode, located at a particular

[23] See the comments in Cooper 1979: 103–25, in the context of African slavery.

[24] E.g. Hoch 1986: 91–159, 1996: 311–22; Kolchin 1987: 195–357, 1993: 133–68; Moon 1999: 156–281. In studies of US slavery the debate was sparked off by Stanley Elkins' controversial thesis (see Elkins 1959) regarding the 'Sambo' character of black slaves.

historical moment, is, however, a slender basis upon which to found an overall judgment regarding agrarian life throughout the entire 1,400 km^2 of helot-farmed territory within Lakonia and Messenia over a period of several centuries.

Indeed, comparative evidence from various types of agricultural labour systems suggests that, even within a common framework of exploitation, we should expect considerable variation in the degree of Spartiate intervention. For example, M. G. Smith's study of the system of slavery maintained by the Fulani aristocracy of Zaria province (northern Nigeria) around 1900 notes different levels of intervention; in some cases, slaves farmed their owner's fields through communal work under a slave overseer, whilst in other cases the slaves enjoyed desultory supervision, as long as they performed the required labour or provided rent in kind.[25] Similar variations in the degrees of autonomy permitted to slave cultivators have been noted within slavery in Thailand.[26] James Scott's classic study of peasant rebellions and subsistence in Southeast Asia also identified a spectrum of landlord–cultivator relationships, ranging from those in which there was a considerable degree of landlord involvement in agricultural decision making, and in provision of seed and necessary equipment, to relationships in which the landlord provided nothing beyond the land and a demand for rent.[27] Such variations in the degree of intervention by master or landowner, observed in diverse systems of dependent labour exploitation, have been found to correlate with a number of key variables. Although none, on its own, is necessarily decisive, collectively they constitute a set of interacting contributory factors that are worth examining in an attempt to illuminate the social relations of production between Spartiates and helots.

THE CHARACTER OF ECONOMIC EXPLOITATION

One relevant factor is the character of the economic exploitation of the dependent farming population, the nature of the obligations demanded by the master or landowner. Historically, there have been two main methods of exploitation. One method has been to demand labour services, with the cultivators being compelled to spend much of their time working the owner's landholdings. Often under this arrangement, the cultivators have been allocated some (varying) amount of land for their own use. The other method has been for the owner to require the payment of dues, with the

[25] Smith 1955: 103–4. [26] Turton 1980: 251–92, esp. 278–9. [27] Scott 1976: 174–6.

farming population being compelled to render tribute in kind (or, increasingly in the modern world, in cash) from the produce of the owner's estates. Comparative evidence indicates that obligations in the form of dues are typically associated with lower levels of intervention than when labour services are required.[28] Within modern Russian serfdom, for example, 'labour obligations (*barshchina*) required much greater supervision than dues (*obrok*) paid two or three times a year'.[29] Similarly, as Paul Lovejoy has noted, the system of plantation slavery practised in the Savanna region of Africa in the nineteenth century 'included a variety of work regimes and management strategies', ranging from cases in which slaves provided labour services, working 'in a regimented fashion on the fields of the master under an overseer' to less regimented arrangements in which 'slaves lived in their own villages and were subject to fixed payments'.[30] Although the associations are not hard and fast, and there can be other factors involved, the requirement for labour services tends to correlate with a higher, and the demand for dues with a lower, degree of production for the market.[31]

Our evidence for helotage suggests that the Spartiates extracted dues in kind rather than labour services.[32] This would fit well with the basic aims of agrarian production in Lakonia and Messenia. Although we should not think of Spartiates as completely divorced from market production, the primary function of their comparatively modest-sized landholdings – with a mean size of a mere 20 ha per citizen household – was to provide the subsistence needs of Spartiate families and the mess contributions required of their adult males.[33] This intimation that the subsistence-orientated aims of production favoured a lesser degree of Spartiate intervention is reinforced by comparison with the comparable contemporary servile population of the Penestai in Thessaly. In contrast to the helots, who delivered produce to their Spartiate masters, the large numbers of Penestai who worked the extensive landholdings of the wealthiest Thessalian aristocratic families appear to have lived under conditions of greater control in which they themselves were the recipients of monthly handouts from their

[28] Cf. Bush 1996c: 213–15. [29] Moon 1999: 205; cf. Kolchin 1987: 63–4.

[30] Lovejoy 2000b [1983]: 212; cf. Mason 1973: 453–71, esp. 465–6.

[31] Cooper 1979: 115; Kolchin 1987: 65; Moon 1999: 70–1.

[32] Ancient evidence: Tyrtaeus fr. 6, West; Myron, *FGrH* 106F 2, *apud* Athen. 657d; *Instituta Laconica* no. 41, *apud* Plut. *Mor.* 239e; Plut. *Lyc.* 8.4; 24.3 (probably also *Instituta Laconica* no. 22, *apud* Plut. *Mor.* 238e–f; Heracleides Lembus fr. 373.12, Dilts = Aristotelian *Lac. Pol.* fr. 611.12, Rose). Modern discussion: Hodkinson 1992, 2000: 85–90, 125–7.

[33] On the character of Spartiate agricultural production and the size of estates, Hodkinson 2000: 132–5, 382–5.

owners.[34] As Moon has pointed out,[35] this latter system represents the logical extreme of a system of labour obligations, as is indicated by its similarity to the monthly distributions of rations to slaves mentioned in Hesiod's *Works and Days* (line 767).

However, we should be careful not to exaggerate the lack of intervention implied by the nature of the helots' obligations. As the quotation above from Paul Lovejoy indicates, the dues required in the cases cited in the previous paragraph were in the form of fixed payments. The nature of the payments made by the helots is a matter of controversy. Later sources write of a fixed payment, but these references almost certainly relate to new conditions introduced by the third-century revolution. In archaic and classical times the helots' dues were probably organized on a sharecropping basis, comprising a proportional share of the produce.[36] This arrangement would have provided a greater incentive for Spartiate masters to intervene in helot farming, since they would gain directly from any consequent increase in agricultural production. This incentive may have been intensified by the fact that Spartiates themselves were compelled, on pain of loss of citizenship, to make monthly contributions of specified foodstuffs (barley flour, wine, cheese, and figs) to their common messes. Consequently, they had to ensure that helot farming arrangements were geared towards the production of sufficient quantities of these particular foodstuffs, although the need for special pressure on this point would have been lessened by the fact that the foodstuffs in question were mainly staples required anyway by the helots for their own subsistence.

RELATIONSHIP TO THE LAND

Another relevant factor is the relationship of the farming population to the landholdings they worked, the extent to which they enjoyed practical fixity of tenure, whether *de iure* or simply *de facto*. This factor is clearly directly connected to the capacity of the master or landowner to intervene in the agricultural process by moving his labour force around to suit his interests. Here the practices of certain landowners with regard to peasant sharecropping tenants are particularly instructive. In the region of Tuscany in post-unification Italy, for example, tenants' rights were weak. The

[34] Theocritus 16.34–5; Scholion (*Oxoniensis Bodleianus Holkhamensis* 88) on Aristoph. *Wasps* 1274; *Etymologicum Gudianum*, s.v. Heilotes, as interpreted in Ducat 1994: 46–8, 90–1. The evidence of Theocritus appears to derive from that of Simonides at the end of the sixth century. For the different picture presented by the third-century writer Archemachus, see below.

[35] Moon 1999: 73. [36] Hodkinson 1992, 2000: 125–31.

landlord's control was ensured by terms of contract which specified that the labour capacity and subsistence needs of the tenant's family should match the size and labour requirements of the holding. To achieve this balance landlords were able to disperse members of their tenants' families elsewhere or order the adoption of living-in help, could give or withhold permission for marriage, and could vet the appointment of new household heads.[37] Such a high level of intervention in the (dis)placement of the agricultural labour force is also common in systems of slave labour. The potential of the master to separate slave families – man from woman, children from parents – has often been noted as the most poignant example of the potential powerlessness of slaves to ensure some element of continuity in their position.[38] Within the plantation slavery of the ante-bellum US South, for example, children could be taken away into domestic service, and slaves of all ages were frequently sold, hired, or loaned to other owners, or moved to other plantations. It has been estimated that, due largely to the strength of the interregional slave trade, 'in the upper South about one first marriage in three was broken by forced separation and close to half of all children were separated from at least one parent'.[39] The fact that a common occasion of sale was the death of the owner highlights the fundamental insecurity of the slave's link to the land that he/she cultivated.

Such an extreme degree of insecurity has not, however, been universal, even for slaves. In the lower US South, for example, although owners' rights were no less strong, in practice slaves experienced much less disruption than in the upper South, owing to the region's position as net importer of slaves.[40] Within other servile systems the security of farmers' attachment to the land has been increased by other factors. For example, within the Islamic society of the north African Savanna, although masters retained the legal right of sale, in practice public opinion against the sale of those born into slavery or living *en famille* exercised considerable restraint on their actions.[41]

Similarly, within Russian serfdom, noble landowners had by the early eighteenth century acquired the legal right to move their serfs between estates, convert them to domestic duties, and even buy and sell them

[37] Gill 1983: 146–69, esp. 147. [38] E.g. Bradley 1987: 52–70.

[39] Kolchin 1993: 125–6, drawing upon the work of Tadman 1989. [40] Kolchin 1993: 126.

[41] Hill 1985: 37–8; Lovejoy 2000b [1983]: 13. Cooper 1979: 118–19, argues that the lower frequency of sales of second-generation slaves was also a reflection of a different balance of power vis-à-vis their masters in comparison with first-generation slaves.

separately from the land;[42] and a few landowners did exercise these rights. On most estates, however, decisions regarding the relationship of serf households to the land were shared between the landowner's estate manager or steward and serf functionaries elected by their own village communes.[43] The outcome was a generic fixity of tenure at communal level, although there was a tendency towards greater instability of tenure at the level of individual households. The essence of Russian serfdom was that the serfs were peasants legally bound to the land. Commune members were secure, as a collectivity, from arbitrary removal from the local farming territory. However, since many communes were collectively responsible for meeting the demands of the landowner for labour services or dues, they themselves frequently intervened to ensure that the amount of land farmed by their member households matched their size and economic potential. Allocations of land were made to newly formed households and to those increasing in size, if necessary by taking land off households that had become smaller. Many communes also practised a periodic redistribution of land to take account of changes in household size. The instability of tenure potentially generated by these practices was, however, limited by the prevailing 'complex household' structure of most serf households (embracing an 'extended family' of two or more related married couples or a married couple with their children and one or more other relatives), especially those practising *post-mortem* division of inheritance, which helped to smooth out fluctuations in the size of each of its constituent nuclear families.

When we turn to applying these comparative considerations to the case of helotage, we encounter several points of uncertainty. There is no direct literary evidence for the nature of the helots' relationship to the landholdings they worked. The nearest piece of evidence is a passage from the geographer Strabo,[44] reporting a statement by the fourth-century historian Ephorus that 'it was not permitted for the holder [of helots] either to liberate them or to sell them outside the boundaries'. This statement raises several issues whose discussion lies beyond the scope of this chapter.[45] The essential question, however, is whether the fact that Ephorus mentions only the prohibition of sale outside Spartan territory can be interpreted as

[42] Moon 1999: 67.

[43] The following discussion is based on Moon 1999: 156–80, 199–236. Although he prefers the term 'seigniorial peasants' to the traditional term 'serfs', I have retained the latter usage, partly because of its familiarity to non-specialists, partly due to the absence of an obvious substitute for the noun 'serfdom'.

[44] Strabo, *Geography* 8.5.4.

[45] For fuller discussion, see Hodkinson 2000: 117–19.

signifying that internal sales were permitted.[46] There is currently disagreement on this point.[47] However, even a scholar like Jean Ducat,[48] who advocates the permissibility of private internal sales, envisages that they normally took place when landholdings underwent a change of Spartiate owner, so that the helots would remain attached to the land they already farmed. A new Spartiate landowner would surely often want to retain the intimate knowledge which resident helot farmers possessed about the local agricultural terrain, with its diverse microclimates and specialized ecological niches.[49] Hence, even if internal sale were permissible, it would not necessarily be incompatible with the possibility that many helots possessed effective fixity of tenure.

Sale, however, was not the only means by which Spartiate masters may potentially have intervened in the disposition of their helot labour force. By analogy with both American slavery and Russian serfdom, young helots may have been taken off the land into personal and domestic service. We have particular evidence for the important roles played by male helot servants as batmen on campaign and by helot female domestics as wet-nurses of Spartiate children and as sexual partners of Spartiate citizens; sons produced through such liaisons were accorded an honourable place in Spartan society and may have added to the prestige of the citizen household.[50] However, we have no evidence about whether or to what extent the supply of personal and domestic servants was drawn from the helot agricultural population.

Another, potentially more significant, form of intervention was through Spartiate masters' redeployment of their helot workforce. A certain basic level of redeployment may have been necessary as a normal response to regular ongoing fluctuations, such as the changing requirements of agricultural exploitation, the varying demands of Spartiate households, and the diverse demographic histories of helot families. In addition, however, we need to consider the impact of more fundamental, long-term changes, which we are now for the first time beginning to perceive through the

[46] I interpret the 'boundaries' in the passage as a reference to the boundaries of Spartan territory, rather than to the boundaries of individual landholdings as suggested in MacDowell 1986: 35.

[47] For two different recent interpretations, Hodkinson 2000: 119 (Ephorus' text is inconclusive); Luraghi 2002a: 227–48, esp. 228–9 (the text proves the permissibility of internal sales).

[48] Ducat 1990: 21–2.

[49] Cf. the reported comments of the wealthy Roman senator Publius Volusius, who declared 'that estate most fortunate which had as tenants natives of the place, and held them, by reason of long association, even from the cradle, as if born on their father's own property' (Columella, *De Re Rustica* 1.7.3).

[50] Hodkinson 1997: 45–71, esp. 46–55; Hodkinson 2000: 336–7.

results of recent intensive archaeological survey. The *Laconia Survey* conducted by the British School at Athens, a survey of some 70 km^2 of mainly arid, marginal hill territory immediately to the east and north-east of Sparta, has revealed a story of major changes in the area's settlement patterns during the archaic and classical periods.[51] Following a total absence of settlements in previous periods, the sixth century (and especially the half-century between *c.* 550 and 500 BC) witnessed a relatively rapid phase of rural colonization in a pattern of widespread settlement dispersion, involving the foundation of a minimum of eighty-seven sites, mainly of small and medium size from farmsteads to hamlets. Then, within a short period from *c.* 450 BC onwards, there was further radical change: a sharp reduction in the number of sites (from 87 to 46), involving a marked discontinuity in site occupation and a permanent desertion of many of the smallest farmstead sites, along with a proportionate increase in medium-sized sites, especially in the number of hamlets. This growth and subsequent decline in numbers of settlements have been interpreted as signifying an initial intensification of agricultural exploitation of this previously marginal area through the location of farms close to areas of cultivation, followed by subsequent retraction due to a combination of land failure and concentration of land-ownership.

The socio-economic implications of these significant changes are, unfortunately, obscured by uncertainty over the status of the inhabitants of most of the survey area. Plausible cases can be made for viewing them either as helots working Spartiate farms or as *perioikoi* working the land on their own account or with slave labour. It seems certain, however, that most of the western sector of the survey area, closest to Sparta itself, was Spartiate owned – especially the area embracing the low hills and spurs along the eastern edge of the Eurotas valley from the confluence of the Rivers Eurotas and Kelephina to the state sanctuary of the Menelaion. Within this particular area, there was an initial foundation of sixteen sites in the sixth century, comprising thirteen small farmsteads (0.01–0.14 ha) and three somewhat larger sites (0.15–0.30 ha). In the later fifth-century decline, the total number of settlements was reduced to ten. Only six of the thirteen original small farmsteads and one of the larger sites continued in occupation; three new small farmsteads were also founded. More detailed analysis of these specific changes lies beyond the scope of this chapter, but the general implications are clear. The initial wave of colonization must have entailed Spartiate masters moving their helots into new settlements to

[51] The following discussion is based upon Catling 2002: 151–256.

facilitate the new or more intensive cultivation of nearby land. Equally significantly, the subsequent decline and readjustments must have involved the removal of some helot households from the landholdings they had formerly worked and the resettlement of others in different locations. In some cases, of course, removal or resettlement may have occurred at times when a helot household was becoming unviable anyway due to agricultural failure; but it is unlikely that such major changes could have been effected with no element of arbitrary Spartiate intervention or untimely disruption of helot life.

THE FORMATION OF THE AGRARIAN ECONOMY

The evidence just considered comes, as already indicated, from one small area of Spartiate territory and raises again the question whether we can extrapolate the evidence from an area close to Sparta to other areas for which we lack similarly detailed published survey evidence. Here comparative evidence might once again hope to offer some illumination. In general, it seems that the extent of the masters' or landowners' intervention to control the location and disposition of their dependent labour force is often related to the degree to which they themselves were responsible for forming the fundamental elements of the agrarian economy. In Russia, the considerable extent of local self-determination had its roots in the fact that 'serfdom and the other means by which the "ruling groups" exploited the peasantry were superimposed on a peasant society and economy which already existed. The ruling and landowning elites were not primarily responsible for creating the main productive units in Russia's rural economy.'[52] In contrast, the US plantation system, in which masters exercised strong control over the disposition of their slaves, was the creation of the white masters themselves, and in many states had initially been operated using mainly white indentured servants before the large-scale importation of black slaves.[53] The situation revealed by the *Laconia Survey* is clearly more similar to that of the US plantation system, in the sense that the local agrarian economy was one created by Spartiate landowners themselves. However, the means by which Spartan domination and helotization were established over more distant areas of Lakonia, and the consequent implications for the formation of their local economies, are unclear.[54]

[52] Moon 1999: 66. [53] Elkins 1959: 37–40; Kolchin 1993: 8–13.

[54] The divergent accounts in classical and later sources are of little historical value: evidence in Cartledge 2001 [1979]: 348–9; discussion in Luraghi 2003.

The case of Messenia might seem, at first sight, more straightforward. A fragment from the late seventh-century Spartan poet Tyrtaeus (fr. 5, West) depicts the Spartans as having gained control of Messene two generations previously through act of conquest.[55] Thucydides (1.101) presents a similar picture in his statement that the majority of helots who revolted in 464 were descendants of the 'old Messenians' who had been enslaved in the past. To this evidence we may add another fragment of Tyrtaeus (fr. 23, West), which seems to mention the Messenians as a unified group engaged in military conflict with the Spartans, and also references in later sources to a Second Messenian War (in effect, an abortive revolt from Spartan control) during Tyrtaios' own lifetime.[56] The impression given by this evidence is of a coherent local population which retained its integrity even after its initial conquest – a population whose agricultural practice may not have been massively disrupted by the Spartan conquest. As I recently suggested, 'after their conquest most Messenian working farmers presumably became servile cultivators of the same fields they had farmed before the conquest'.[57]

Although I am not convinced by every aspect of recent revisionist interpretations of the origins and development of helotage,[58] I would now present a less-simple, more nuanced, picture of the formation of the Messenian agrarian economy under Spartiate rule. I would retain the concept of a mass enslavement of the pre-existing population following a military conquest of Messene, as described by Tyrtaeus. His reference to the enemy fleeing the mountain range of Ithome and abandoning their rich farmlands should not be interpreted as signifying a mass desertion of the conquered region. Tyrtaeus is surely referring to a wealthy elite such as the one that dominated warfare and landholding in most contemporary Greek communities, including Sparta itself.[59] Their flight would not have involved the mass of the farming population, which was subjected to the servitude described in other surviving fragments of his poetry (frs. 6–7, West).

Doubt has been expressed about the feasibility of such a mass enslavement, in light of Orlando Patterson's comparative study, which highlights

[55] The phrase 'fathers of our fathers' may of course have a generic rather than specific temporal reference, but this does not affect Tyrtaeus' location of the conquest in time past.

[56] The first attested reference to the Second Messenian War probably derives from Ephorus (cf. Diod. 15.66).

[57] Hodkinson, 2000: 119. [58] Luraghi 2002a, 2003.

[59] For what it is worth, Pausanias' account of the episode (4.14.1) states that leading Messenians with foreign *proxeniai* fled abroad, whilst the mass of the populace returned home as before.

'a strong tendency on the part of a conquering group not to enslave a conquered population en masse and in situ' and observes that such attempts 'were almost always disastrous failures'.[60] In particular, it has been argued that, 'a formerly independent group, with a full social structure and its own ruling elites, cannot be reduced to slavery without huge bloodshed'.[61] However, as the evidence of Tyrtaeus suggests, the local population subjugated by Sparta was one already deprived of its full social structure by the flight of its ruling elite, a factor that would have considerably facilitated the initial act of enslavement.[62] Moreover, modern doubters of the basic feasibility of a mass enslavement of a pre-existing population in Greek antiquity should not forget that it was deemed feasible by intelligent later commentators like Thucydides and Theopompus, who also ascribed the Thessalians' domination over the Penestai to the same mechanism.[63] Indeed, the Spartans were only one of many archaic Greek poleis who enslaved neighbouring populations through wars of conquest.[64] Several of these mass enslavements were comparatively short lived; but others, such as the servile systems of Messenia, Thessaly, and Crete, lasted for several centuries.[65] Early Greek practice is not exceptional. As Van Wees has demonstrated, there are considerable parallels with the Spanish conquests in Central and South America and their subsequent exploitation of the native Indian population. The Spanish system of exploitation lasted for over a century and declined, not because of native revolts, but owing to economic changes introduced by the Spanish themselves, along with the decimation of the native labour force through imported diseases.[66]

That said, I would accept that the process of forming the new agrarian regime within the conquered territory of Messene will have been less straightforward and entailed a greater degree of Spartiate manipulation than the simple superimposition of exploitation on top of existing structures suggested by the statement in my earlier study. One symptomatic indication is the discontinuous character of the region's settlement history in Geometric and archaic times.[67] Moreover, I would agree with the

[60] Patterson 1982: 110. [61] Luraghi 2002a: 237.

[62] That, even so, there remained considerable ethnic solidarity and resistance – as Patterson's thesis would suggest – is shown by Tyrtaeus' reference (fr. 23, West) to further conflict involving the Messenians (even if one dismisses the later sources' picture of a full-scale Second Messenian War).

[63] Theopompus, *FGrH* 115 F122, *apud* Athen. 265b–c.

[64] Van Wees 2003.

[65] On Thessaly and Crete, van Wees 2003: 53–61, with references to specialist studies.

[66] Van Wees 2003: 66–71, with references to specialist studies.

[67] Davis *et al.* 1997: 391–494, esp. 452; Alcock *et al.* 2005: 158–72, citing both the detailed results of the *Pylos Regional Archaeological Project* and the earlier *University of Minnesota Messenia Expedition.*

revisionist argument on two important points: first, that the Spartan conquest of 'Messene' mentioned by Tyrtaios probably related to the settlement at the foot of Mt Ithome and its adjacent territory in eastern Messenia, rather than to any wider geographical area; and, secondly, that it is unlikely that the entire region which later became Messenia had been united before the Spartan conquest, especially as the discontinuities in site occupation mentioned above go back to the pre-conquest period.[68] Exactly when and how the remainder of the region came under Spartiate control is not precisely known. But in these circumstances it seems that, within a framework of potential intra-regional variations, we should expect some degree of scope for the incoming Spartiates actively to mould local agrarian economies. Some support for this probability may be found in preliminary indications from archaeological survey of an increase in settlements in Messenia in the archaic period in comparison with the Geometric period and of a pattern of nucleated settlement under Spartan rule that contrasts with contemporary patterns elsewhere in Greece.[69]

GEOGRAPHICAL DISTANCE, SUPERVISION AND ABSENTEEISM

We should not imagine, however, that the modalities through which helotage was set in place necessarily exercised a determining impact on Spartiate–helot relations throughout the entire period of Spartan domination. For example, the economic framework of plantation slavery in most regions of Africa was – as in the USA – a creation of the slaveowners themselves, using newly enslaved imported labour which was typically subjected to close supervision. However, in certain circumstances established second-generation slave villages could become subject to less intervention and gradually assume greater self-direction of their agricultural labour.[70] In assessing the development of helotage, we need to give consideration to two further interrelated variables which comparative evidence suggests may have had an important influence. In this section I shall examine the question of geographical distance between owner and cultivator; in the following section, the pattern of residence of the unfree population.

[68] Luraghi 2002b; cf. the abandonment of Nichoria around the mid-eighth century, McDonald, Coulson and Rosser 1983.

[69] McDonald and Hope Simpson 1972: 117–47, esp. 144; Davis *et al.* 1997: 455–6; Alcock 2002b: 185–99.

[70] Klein and Lovejoy 1979: 184–7; Lovejoy 2000b [1983]: 213.

The issue of geographical distance has already been implicitly posed by the fact that both the literary evidence of Xenophon and the archaeological evidence of the *Laconia Survey* suggest a considerable degree of Spartiate intervention in those areas closest to Sparta itself. To what extent should we expect similar levels of intervention further afield? Comparative evidence from a variety of servile systems suggests that the presence or absence of the master or owner can exercise a considerable influence upon the level of landowner intervention. Within Russian serfdom, for example, there was a marked difference between estates held by petty squires, who normally resided on their estates and ran their domains themselves, giving village communes and their peasant officials little independence, and estates in the hands of the most important noblemen, who were typically absentee landowners on state service in Moscow or in the army. Some absentee landowners did attempt to make use of stewards to impose an authoritarian regime. But on most such estates the management of agricultural production was in practice a shared enterprise between, on the one hand, the landlord's stewards or estate managers and, on the other, household patriarchs and peasant functionaries elected by the communes, which in most cases were based upon village communities.[71] The difficulties that absentee landowners often had (or thought they had) in ensuring that their stewards – who were themselves normally serfs – performed their duties properly further diminished their capacity for effective intervention. One notable sign of these differential degrees of intervention was that resident landowners almost universally demanded labour services, whereas absentee owners 'often preferred to leave their serfs on obrok [dues] rather than worry about the supervisory abilities of their stewards'.[72]

As Peter Kolchin's comparative study of American slavery and Russian serfdom has noted, the great majority of US slaves – in contrast to their Russian serf counterparts – had resident masters, who managed their plantations directly, usually without even an overseer, and on smaller farms personally directed their labour and even worked alongside the slaves.[73] Under these conditions slave independence of action was severely restricted. Nevertheless, there were exceptional areas, most notably the ante-bellum South Carolina low country, in which absenteeism was common among wealthy slaveowners, who often resided in the town of Charleston rather than on their estates. Some, though not all, absentee landowners appointed a white steward as supervisor; but the key figure in

[71] Kolchin 1987: 200–1. [72] Kolchin 1987: 58–65 (quotation from 64–5), 87–9; Moon 1999: 202–5.
[73] Kolchin 1987: 59–61, 65–8, 1993: 93–132.

directing work on many estates was usually a black 'driver', himself a slave. Hand-in-hand with a lower degree of direct owner intervention went a more moderate version of labour services: the so-called 'task' system, according to which slaves were assigned given tasks and could cease work for the day on their completion. Within a more flexible, self-managed work regime, slaves were able to devote more time to working for themselves and to accumulate small amounts of property.[74] The huge difference which the presence or absence of the slave owner can have on the character of farming operations is also emphasized by the Roman agricultural writer Columella. He strongly advocated the advantages of farming nearby estates through slave labour working under close supervision by the owner. In contrast, he recommended turning over to tenant farmers distant estates 'which it is not easy for the owner to visit', due to the difficulty of controlling the activities of slaves, even when there was a slave overseer.[75]

In the above cases we have been dealing with a relatively sharp dichotomy between the owner's residence on the estate and his absenteeism in a distant town or on state service. As Orlando Patterson[76] points out, however, we should distinguish between such full-scale absenteeism and the simple 'living apart' of the master class, as is illustrated by the case of slavery in nineteenth-century, pre-colonial Africa. In various regions of the continent, particular economic and political conditions following the decline of the European slave trade led to the widespread growth of a system of agricultural slavery geared to market production whose most common shared characteristic was the establishment of plantations grouped around the towns.[77] Under this system, residential arrangements of both slaves and masters were varied.[78] On smaller plantations groups of slaves were often housed in a separate section within the compound of the master's family, and owner and slaves worked the fields side by side. On somewhat larger plantations (over about twenty slaves), the owner's family might live apart from their slaves, though at not any great distance; under these circumstances relatively close supervision was still feasible. The largest plantations of several hundred or more slaves often involved

[74] Morgan 1983: 83–141; Kolchin 1993: 31–2. [75] Columella, *De Re Rustica* 1.7.5–7.

[76] Patterson 1982: 180–1.

[77] The economic and political conditions, the prevalence of plantation slavery, and its physical manifestations are sketched in Lovejoy 1979: 1267–92, esp. 1267–71, and outlined more broadly in Lovejoy 2000b [1983]: 165–251.

[78] The varied nature of these arrangements is indicated by the semantic range of local terms (such as *rinji* and *gandu*) used to describe larger plantations within the Sokoto Caliphate in Islamic West Africa. These terms could embrace slaves living in the same compound as the master's family through to separate slave villages (see Lovejoy 1979: 1279–80).

separate slave villages, located at a variety of distances from the town, from the immediate suburbs up to a radius of 30 km or more. Given the range of distances involved, the degree of separateness between master and slaves and the extent of intervention from the master varied considerably. Some owners of large plantations, such as government officials, military personnel, and merchants resident in the towns, were absentees who relied upon slave overseers. In other cases, however, the plantations might be managed by junior members of the master's lineage.

Within one of the most-studied regions, the nineteenth-century Sokoto Caliphate in Islamic West Africa, larger slaveowners appear in general to have been able to maintain a relatively strict and closely defined regime of labour services, in which the slaves were organized in gangs farming the masters' fields, although they also possessed their own plots which they were allocated time to cultivate. However, within one region of the Caliphate – that of Nupe in the Bida emirate – the slave villages, which comprised homogeneous populations of captives taken from other areas of Nupe and located together according to ethnic group, enjoyed considerably less intervention, in spite of their relatively recent foundation, organizing their own labour regime under village headmen and periodically remitting agricultural tribute.[79] In other regions of West Africa too, such as among the Sherbro of Sierra Leone, 'the slave villages being spatially peripheral to the master's household, slaves were often so little supervised'.[80]

How might these comparative insights illuminate Spartiate–helot relations? The Spartiates all resided in the cluster of villages that constituted Sparta itself. As regards their holdings in the Sparta valley and neighbouring areas, the distinction drawn above between genuine absenteeism and simple 'living apart', along with the example of the closely regulated 'suburban' West African slave villages, reinforces the impression we have already gained from both the literary and the archaeological evidence: namely, that, even if there was a residential separation between the Spartiate masters and their helots, the minimal distance between them would not have posed any great barrier to a high degree of intervention in helot farming. Such intervention would have been facilitated by the fact that one of these Spartiate villages, Amyklai, was located in the very centre of the valley, 5 km south of the main cluster. A further indication of

[79] Lovejoy 1978: 341–68, 1979: 1267–92, esp. 1280–6, 2000b [1983]: 196–9, 205–6, 212–16; Mason 1973: 465–6.

[80] MacCormack 1977: 181–203, esp. 198.

Spartiate intervention is the finding of the *Laconia Survey* that the pottery assemblage of most of the settlements in its western sector close to Sparta lacked evidence of storage vessels, suggesting that their agricultural produce was taken for storage to Sparta itself.[81] In several respects, Spartiate management of their estates in the Sparta valley and its environs appears similar to the level of intervention ascribed to the Athenian landowner Ischomachus in Xenophon's *Oeconomicus*.[82] Ischomachus and his wife reside in a town house, where the agricultural produce is stored;[83] but whenever he has no pressing business in town he walks out to his slave-worked farm, where he superintends all the details of the work and implements improvements in method.[84]

Many Spartiate estates, however, lay some considerable distance from Sparta. Thucydides (4.3) estimated that Pylos on the coast of western Messenia was 'about 400 stades from Sparta', approximately 70 km.[85] Even the eastern Messenian plains were some 40 km distant and parts of the Helos valley in southern Lakonia some 30 km.[86] The impression given by literary sources which describe the Spartiate lifestyle, such as Xenophon's *Polity of the Lacedaemonians* and Plutarch's *Life of Lycurgus*, is that Spartiate life entailed a male citizen's more-or-less continuous presence in or around Sparta itself, so that he would be available for civic duties and especially for the evening meal at his mess group, attendance at which was compulsory except if delayed by sacrifice or hunting.[87] In contrast, other evidence suggests that periods of individual absence from Sparta were not uncommon: for example, Spartiates are attested as travelling abroad to visit foreign guest-friends and to worship or compete in games at foreign sanctuaries.[88] It is possible therefore that citizens could periodically obtain leave to visit their distant estates. However, since the estates of many Spartiates, and especially the wealthy, were probably fragmented into smaller holdings scattered throughout Lakonia and Messenia, it is unlikely that most male citizen landowners would be able to obtain long enough leave to visit each of their holdings with sufficient regularity to sustain an effective degree of personal intervention. Nor is it easy to imagine that most members of the other major set of landowners,

[81] Catling 2002: 195–6. [82] Xenophon, *Oeconomicus* 7.29–21.12. [83] Ibid. 9.2–10.

[84] Ibid. 11.14–18; cf. 21.10. [85] Cf. Hornblower 1996: 154.

[86] I have suggested elsewhere that the Spartiates may have held estates even further south in Lakonia, in the plain of Molaoi some 50 km distant (see Hodkinson 2000: 141).

[87] Plutarch, *Lycurgus* 12.2.

[88] Cf. Hodkinson 1999: 147–87, esp. 160–76, 2000: 174–5; 294–8; 307–23; 337–52.

Spartiate women, had the time or opportunity to make such wide-ranging personal visits, given their attested household responsibilities in Sparta.[89] Hence, as far as their more distant estates were concerned, the probability is that most Spartiate landowners were effectively absentees.[90]

The obvious question is how absentee Spartiate citizens could ensure the effective management of their distant estates. The comparative evidence considered above suggests that the most common method by which absentee landowners have exploited distant servile agrarian populations is through the agency of individuals drawn from the servile population itself in each locality: serf stewards and communal officials within Russian serfdom; black drivers in low country South Carolina; slave overseers or village headmen within the slave villages of pre-colonial Africa. Similarly, it is *a priori* probable that absentee Spartiate landowners drew upon the services of certain individual helots in the management of their holdings – and not only of their holdings in distant Messenia. Even in the case of estates within the Sparta valley, the Spartiate owner could not be continuously present due to his civic duties, and there will have also been shorter periods when large numbers of owners were unavoidably absent on

[89] Plato, *Laws* 805e; Xenophon, *Polity of the Lacedaemonians* 1.9. Of course, many estates would also be held by minors, both male and female, who were tied to Sparta during their public upbringing; but I take it that responsibility for management lay in the hands of their adult guardians.

[90] See below for discussion of the large inhabited building discovered at Kopanaki in the Soulima valley. It has been interpreted as the home of a Spartiate landlord with his helots living in attendance (Kaltsas 1983: 207–37; cf. Harrison and Spencer 1998: 147–62, esp. 162). As indicated below, however, our knowledge of the surrounding settlement pattern is currently insufficient to sustain this conclusion. Moreover, even if the building were the centre of a Spartiate estate, it would not necessarily imply the physical presence of the Spartiate owner. A further piece of evidence is Xenophon's account of the conspiracy of Cinadon, which includes a reference (*Hellenica* 3.3.8) to 'Lacedaemonians [probably Spartiates] both older and younger', who had visited perioikic Aulon – possibly located in the Soulima valley (Roebuck 1941: 25–6; Lazenby and Hope Simpson 1972: 81–99, esp. 98, n. 101, though there is some uncertainty whether the name signifies a town or a region: Cartledge 2001 [1979]: 274). Aulon is said to be a place where there were helots, whom Cinadon was ordered to arrest, along with certain of its citizens. The circumstances in which both Spartiates and helots were present in Aulon are, however, unclear. It could be a matter of citizens supervising distant estates: it is not impossible that Spartiates owned land near to perioikic settlements, in which helot farmers also resided. However, the order to arrest Aulonitai and helots could equally indicate that we are dealing with helot fugitives and *perioikoi* harbouring them, and that the visiting Spartiates were on official business (Cartledge 2001 [1979]: 274–5; Lazenby 1997: 437–47, esp. 445). This interpretation is strengthened by the fact that the word Xenophon uses to describe the younger Spartiate visitors, *neoteroi*, is the same used in the previous sentence to refer to young men from the elite military squad of *hippeis* who were sent with Cinadon on his mission. Other interpretations of the episode have been suggested by other scholars, such as that the helots were farming perioikic estates or serving a Spartiate garrison (cf. Lazenby 1997: 445). Overall, the context of the episode is too unclear to serve as the basis for any interpretations about the direction of Aulon's agrarian economy.

military campaigns.[91] So too, even under the comparatively strict supervisory regime described in Xenophon's *Oeconomicus*, Ischomachus put his farms in the management of slave bailiffs at times when he was not personally present.[92]

There is, in fact, a piece of evidence which can enable us to identify, at least by their generic name, the helots who probably acted as managing agents on behalf of Spartiate landowners. A gloss which survives from Hesychius' lexicon of rare words refers to the '*mnōionomoi*: leaders of the helots'.[93] Drawing upon the evidence of the poem of Hybrias,[94] Jean Ducat has concluded that the *mnōia* was a group of slaves living and working on an estate.[95] On this interpretation, the *mnōionomoi* can be viewed as leading men drawn from the helots themselves, men who exercised supervision and control over the persons in their *mnōia*, and through whom a Spartiate owner would be likely to work. The extant version of Hesychius' text is too brief to indicate any distinctions between the roles played by helot *mnōionomoi* in different geographical locations. In view of the comparative evidence considered above, however, we should expect that differences in levels of Spartiate supervision dictated by geographical distance will have led to considerable variations in the degree of responsibility for agricultural management possessed by different *mnōionomoi*. Xenophon's Ischomachus, whom we have compared to owners of estates in the Sparta valley, given his ability to walk to his farms, was able to exert a strict regime of supervision and correction over his slave bailiff.[96] Such close supervision would not have been feasible further afield. It is possible (though by no means certain) that, in order to monitor the activities of *mnōionomoi* on their distant estates, some wealthy Spartiates may have appointed outside agents, most plausibly, perhaps, drawn from among the *perioikoi*: men with functions comparable to those of estate managers within Russian serfdom, appointed by

[91] During the period of Sparta's overseas empire in the late fifth and early fourth centuries, a sizeable number of prominent Spartiates spent substantial periods – sometimes several years – away from Spartan territory (Hodkinson 1993: 146–76, esp. 153–7).

[92] *Oeconomicus* 12.2.

[93] Hesychius' lexicon, which probably dates to the fifth century AD but drew upon much earlier specialist lexica, focused on rare words in poetry and in Greek dialects. It survives only in a severely abridged form, in which the original lexicon has been reduced to a mere glossary (*Oxford Classical Dictionary*[3], 701–2). The extant text, μονομοιτῶν Εἱλώτων ἄρχοντες (μ1626, ed. Latte, ii.676) has been plausibly emended in Wilamowitz-Moellendorf 1924: 249–73, esp. 273 to read μνῳονόμοι τῶν Εἱλώτων ἄρχοντες. Quite apart from the explanatory gloss, the term *mnōionomoi* itself implies a controlling and supervisory role, just as the *paidonomos* had charge of and responsibility for the youths in the Spartiate upbringing (Xenophon, *Polity of the Lacedaemonians* 2–4).

[94] *Apud* Athenaeus, *Deipnosophistae* 695f–696a. [95] Ducat 1990: 63, 74.

[96] Xenophon, *Oeconomicus* 12.2–14.10; cf. 20.16–20; 21.9.

landowners to exercise a general supervision over their dispersed holdings. However, the Russian experience[97] suggests that, even had such a practice been employed, the outcome of such supervision would normally have been a shared responsibility which left plenty of initiative for the *mnōionomos*.

In the absence of the Spartiate owner, how far then might the responsibilities of helot *mnōionomoi* extend? Was their management limited to strictly agricultural matters, such as ensuring the availability of the appropriate equipment, seed and animals, supervising the input of labour, determining the mix of crops to be grown, deciding the timing of sowing and harvest, and ensuring delivery of the owner's share of the produce? Or did it extend to more 'structural' responsibilities, such as ensuring that the level of available labour matched the size of the holding and the owner's requirements for produce: responsibilities which might have involved (re)distributing cultivation rights between households or exerting influence over key life decisions affecting the growth or diminution of helot families? The possibility of such an extended role raises questions regarding the capacity in which the *mnōionomos* performed his role. Clearly, he was in one sense an overseer accepted, if not appointed, by the Spartiate owner; but did his position also reflect, as Ducat[98] has suggested, the structure of the local helot community? Ducat terms the *mnōionomoi* 'des chefs coutumiers'; I would think particularly of the heads of larger and more important helot households.

RESIDENCE AND HELOT COMMUNITIES

The proposition that the persons chosen as *mnōionomoi* may have emerged from the structure of local helot society also raises the question whether their roles were confined to individual Spartiate estates or may have had a wider communal aspect. Despite Ducat's understandable linkage of the *mnōia* to a group of helots working a Spartiate estate, the term itself is unspecific in reference and could equally refer to a broader grouping of helots. In approaching this question, it is relevant to examine the issue of helot residence patterns. The comparative material considered above suggests that a relatively high degree of local, communal self-direction of agricultural production may be particularly associated with a nucleated settlement pattern, as in the case of the village communities of Russian serfs and certain groups of African slaves.

This association does appear to apply, both positively and negatively, in the case of helotage. We have already seen that the *Laconia Survey* area

[97] Moon 1999: 202–3. [98] Ducat 1990: 63.

adjacent to Sparta itself was one of dispersed, small-scale settlements. Although both archaeological and literary evidence is limited, current indications are that the Sparta plain too contained no sizeable settlements beyond the Spartiate villages and that the helot cultivators were dispersed in a mixture of isolated farmsteads and hamlets.[99] In short, those helot farmers under the closest degree of supervision by their Spartiate masters were settled in a pattern of residence less conducive to collective coordination of agricultural production by the helots themselves.

We are sadly ill informed about residential patterns in other helotized areas of Lakonia. As regards distant Messenia, however, the indications are that settlement patterns were considerably more nucleated than in the areas of Lakonia closest to Sparta. These differential patterns can be seen most clearly through comparison of the results of the *Laconia Survey* with those of the *Pylos Regional Archaeological Project (PRAP)*, which has recently surveyed an area of western Messenia whose distance from any definitely attested perioikic settlements suggests that 'there is no overwhelming reason to envisage the residents . . . as anything but of helot status'.[100] Whereas the *Laconia Survey* discovered 87 late archaic and 46 classical sites within the 70 km^2 of its survey area, the 40 km^2 of western Messenia surveyed by *PRAP* produced a mere five definite archaic and four definite classical sites.[101] The principal settlement in the area (named by the survey team 'IO4, Romanou *Romanou*') was marked by a sherd scatter of some 18–22 ha in the archaic period and some 14–27 ha in classical times,[102] compared with a mere 3 ha and 6 ha for the largest sites in the *Laconia Survey* (the perioikic village of Sellasia and the fort of Agios Konstantinos). It was clearly a sizeable conglomeration with a population size well into four figures.[103] Moreover, in both the archaic and classical periods the second largest site within the survey area (a different site in each period) lay close by, a mere 1.5 km distant. In the classical period these are the only securely attested places of permanent habitation in the entire survey area.[104] Although a complete picture of habitation within the region is obscured by the fact that the various sectors within the *PRAP* survey area are not contiguous, the survey results indicate an indisputable pattern of residential concentration.

[99] Catling 2002: 232–3. [100] Alcock 2002b: 193.

[101] Alcock *et al.* 2005: 163–9, partly superseding Alcock 2002b: 193–5. [102] Alcock *et al.* 2005: 166.

[103] Population densities for unwalled settlements of some 100–125 persons respectively per ha, which have been suggested by other intensive surveys (Catling 2002: 205–6; Jameson, Runnels, and Van Andel 1994: 545) would give it a population of some 1,800–2,750 persons in the archaic period and some 1,400–3,375 in the classical.

[104] Of the other two sites, one is probably a shrine; the other is attested by only three sherds and may be a seasonal dwelling or a place of 'off-site' rural activity (Alcock 2002b: 195; Alcock *et al.* 2005: 168).

Further indications of this pattern have emerged from other, less intensive surveys. The mean size of archaic sites reported by the *University of Minnesota Messenia Expedition*, whose survey area covered the whole of Messenia (and more), has been calculated at approximately 3 ha, often taken as denoting hamlets or villages and equivalent to the sherd scatter from the village of Sellasia, at the top end of the range of habitations in the *Laconia Survey*.[105] Conversely, survey of the 'Five Rivers' area by the Gulf of Messenia revealed no evidence of dispersed habitation in farmsteads in the archaic and classical periods, in contrast to the Hellenistic period.[106] As Richard Catling has recently commented, in comparing the settlement patterns of Lakonian and Messenian helots, 'a clear distinction begins to emerge in the way these two groups were distributed in the landscape and presumably in the way that the regions were farmed'.[107]

Not that settlement patterns were necessarily uniform throughout Messenia. One indication of diversity is the eleven-room building (about 30 × 17 m) built around a central courtyard, with thick walls suggestive of a second storey, which was uncovered by rescue excavation in the modern village of Kopanaki in the Soulima valley.[108] This impressively large structure, whose broad assemblage of domestic pottery including storage facilities marks it clearly as a habitation site, has been interpreted – along with an apparently similar building about 9 km ESE down the valley, near the village of Vasiliko – as evidence of 'a plantation-like sort of settlement, with big and isolated buildings forming the centre of large landholdings'.[109] Although so precise a conclusion seems premature, given our ignorance – in the absence of intensive field survey – of settlement patterns in the region of each building,[110] their monumental character does suggest a different kind of settlement from those discussed above. Nevertheless, the

105 Alcock 2002b: 191; Alcock *et al.* 2005: 159. For the classical/Hellenistic periods, the mean size of *UMME* sites was 2.2 ha (Alcock *et al.* 2005: 162); but the historical implications are obscured by the expedition's acknowledged difficulty in differentiating sherds of the two periods.

106 Lukermann and Moody 1978: 78–112, esp. 99; cf. Harrison and Spencer 1998: 160–1.

107 Catling 2002: 253. 108 Kaltsas 1983: 207–37. 109 Luraghi 2002a: 232.

110 Interpretation of what little evidence does exist is hampered by uncertainty over the period of occupation of the building at Kopanaki. The excavator dated it from the second half of the sixth century to the first quarter of the fifth; but Richard Catling (see Catling 1996: 33–89, esp. 34, n. 12) has argued that the building's pottery assemblage should be downdated to the second half of the fifth century (perhaps *c.* 450–425). Classical sherds have been noted at two nearby locations: (i) 1 km ENE, on the summit of Stylari hill (see McDonald and Rapp 1972: 298: Register A no. 233); (ii) 1.5 km W, at one of the tholos tombs at Ano Kopanaki, Akourthi (ibid. no. 234), which constitutes possible evidence of tomb cult (cf. Alcock 1991: 465 no. 23; Antonaccio 1995: 85–7). On the building at Vasiliko, see Valmin 1941: 59–76; and Pikoulas 1984: 177–84. The dating of its sherds and inscriptions to the late sixth and early fifth centuries is somewhat generic and beset with some uncertainties: cf. Valmin 1941: 66, 70 n. 1, 73; and Jeffery 1990: 203, n. 2.

picture here too seems to be of a population concentrated rather than spread thinly across the landscape.

The concentration of the Messenian helot population into nucleated rather than dispersed settlements was probably an important factor in ensuring the capacity of helot *mnōionomoi* to act effectively as local coordinators of agricultural production. It also makes more plausible the possibility that the *mnōionomoi* may have operated at a broader communal level, perhaps even at the level of a large village like 'IO4 Romanou *Romanou*', where they might in effect have been village leaders comprising the more important household heads. Unfortunately, we have no direct evidence for the nature of helot household structures. I have suggested elsewhere that, as part of a strategy to even out some of the above fluctuations and divergences, helot households may have taken the form of co-residential multiple family households.[111] Under such arrangements, the heads of large households would have been notable figures, men of some authority in the wider community. This suggestion, however, must necessarily remain hypothetical.

Whatever the structure of helot households, in considering the kinds of roles that village leaders could have played, we can turn for potential illumination to the best attested case for comparison, namely, the officials of Russian serf communes, who played an important mediating role between absentee landowners and the local serf community. David Moon[112] has noted that, 'communes were the basic institutions of local government in Russian villages . . . guided by state decrees and landowners' instructions, as well as the peasants' unwritten customary law . . . Communal officials were responsible for a wide range of village affairs, including day-to-day administration, sharing out and collecting the obligations communities owed to their landowners and the state, and distributing the village's arable land between households. Communes directed the village economy, especially the three-field system of crop rotation.'

Of course, in the absence of hard information, we cannot simply transfer the capacities of Russian commune officials onto Messenian helot *mnōionomoi*. We saw earlier that, whereas in Russia serfdom was superimposed on a pre-existing peasant society, there is room for debate about the relative contributions made by the incoming Spartiates and the local farming population to the formation of the Messenian agrarian economy under Spartan rule. Nevertheless, as already noted, the examples of many second-generation African slave villages indicate how even initially disparate groups of slaves transplanted into new territory can, within a context of

[111] Hodkinson 2000: 125, 386–7. [112] Moon 1999: 199.

village residence and landowner absenteeism, come to assume greater self-direction of the agrarian economy. In particular, the aforementioned case of Nupe slave villages, which comprised ethnically homogeneous groups of captives taken from other parts of Nupe territory, shows how the development of semi-autonomous agricultural production can be powerfully facilitated when the servile population shares a common ethnic identity – as was increasingly the case in fifth-century Messenia, whether founded in a longstanding collective identity or spurred by the development of a secondary ethnic consciousness under the common conditions of servitude imposed by Spartan rule.[113] The example of the Russian serf commune, consequently, constitutes an appropriate comparison to think with.

We can reasonably hypothesize that the experience of shared residence will have led many Messenian helot village communities to undertake a number of communal functions. Like any human community, helot villages will have needed to establish mechanisms for regulating antisocial behaviour, maintaining internal law and order, and administering social sanctions. The village was also no doubt the place where helot households working on different estates would interact socially and intermarry. Although evidence from the *PRAP* survey shows that Messenian settlement patterns under Spartan rule were not unchanging, the pre-eminence of the village 'IO4 Romanou *Romanou*' throughout the archaic and classical periods also suggests a significant degree of permanence and continuity, especially in comparison with the situation within the area of the *Laconia Survey*. Recent research has shown how, even among the fragile servile communities on US slave plantations, physically separated from one another and constantly vulnerable to disruption by their masters, there still existed 'extended kinship networks among slaves, who often exhibited impressive awareness of and attachments to more distant familial relations'.[114] Hence, we should expect some meaningful level of kinship relations and community within helot settlements – even among the dispersed, less permanent and more tightly supervised settlements close to Sparta.

We can get some sense of the decision-making capabilities of helot communities in both Lakonia and Messenia in the Spartans' infamous appeal to the helots 'to pick out those of their number who claimed to have most distinguished themselves in the wars'.[115] Even helot communities in

[113] Luraghi 2002a: 238–40. [114] Kolchin 1993: 140.

[115] Thucydides 4.80. 'Infamous' because the Spartans subsequently put all those selected to death. This is not the place to enter into the recent debate about the historical authenticity of the episode. At the very least, Thucydides and his source(s) believed the helots capable of such communal decision-making.

Lakonia possessed, at the very least, effective channels of internal communication, as was demonstrated in 371 when, despite Sparta itself being under siege, a Spartan call for volunteers was disseminated so effectively that more than 6,000 Lakonian helots came forward to enlist.[116] Under the more favourable and enduring conditions of Messenian helot villages, we should expect a particularly solid network of kinship relations and community; and with it a strong sense of a shared past and an attachment to place which could have served as the basis for the development of communal institutions. Some indication of the sense of attachment that some Messenian communities had to their territory and their past is evident in the 'social memories' recently explored by Susan Alcock,[117] in particular through the evidence for local tomb cults, which indicate the operation of some level of communal organization for the commemoration of the 'heroes' of the past buried in monumental Bronze Age tombs.[118] The existence of these local cults in archaic and classical Messenia is an especially notable sign of communal identity, in that comparable tomb cults are considerably less present in other regions of archaic and classical Greece, and are almost totally absent from the helotized parts of Lakonia.[119]

In these circumstances, we should give serious consideration to the possibility that some helot village communities may have taken on a role in the management of agricultural labour and in the fulfilment of the obligations towards the Spartiate landowners whose estates were cultivated by their inhabitants. There is a hint in the case of the Penestai of Thessaly that the obligations of some of their servile communities were organized on a communal level. As Jean Ducat[120] has noted, the term *syntaxeis*, by which Archemachus of Euboea[121] refers to the dues owed by Penestai to their masters, may carry the connotation of dues rendered collectively rather than individually by each servile household.[122] However, the parallel with the Messenian helots is not exact, in that the very large numbers of Penestai

[116] Xenophon, *Hellenica* 6.5.28–9. [117] Alcock 2002a: 32–75.

[118] On Messenian tomb cult, see esp. Alcock 1991: 132–75; Antonaccio 1995: 70–102. The spread of these cults throughout diverse parts of Messenia suggests that they cannot be ascribed exclusively to Messenian *perioikoi*.

[119] Antonaccio 1995: 69–70. [120] Ducat 1994: 90–1. [121] *Apud* Athenaeus, *Deipnosophistae* 264a–b.

[122] Ducat squares this evidence with the evidence cited earlier of Penestai being paid monthly rations by suggesting that the difference reflects either the distinction between Penestai directly attached to the master's 'palace' and those located in more distant and independent situations, or a distinction between the archaic period when the power of the Thessalian aristocracy was in full flower and later periods when its weakening in the face of the development of poleis had led to a modification in the Penestai's terms of servitude (Ducat 1994: 91; cf. 118–19).

held by the wealthiest Thessalians probably meant that the servile inhabitants of certain Penestic villages, like the serfs of most Russian communes, all owed their obligations to a single master;[123] in these circumstances a collective responsibility for dues would make perfect sense. Although individual wealthy Spartiates reportedly possessed holdings of helots which far exceeded private holdings of slaves in contemporary Athens,[124] it is doubtful whether any were sufficiently large as to encompass an entire village.[125] Hence communal responsibility for dues would have involved coordinating payments of produce to a number of different Spartiate owners; if so, this would have entailed a very significant level of communality indeed.

LEADERSHIP AND POLITICS

The crucial point that, for all their common residence, different helot households would have been working on different plots of land for different masters, subject to a range of variations in their treatment and therefore to different perceptions of their personal requirements and needs, is a useful reminder that even among the most unified human societies there is a point at which impulses towards communal behaviour hit the buffer of household self-interest. Recent research has demonstrated that even the Russian commune, so often idealized as a model of social cooperation and egalitarianism, was itself a hive of village politics dominated by household patriarchs or by factions of wealthier peasants whose power was based on kinship and patronage. In a spirit of collusion between household heads, communal officials, and the landowner's bailiff, local village elites 'used the power entrusted to them by landowners to oppress and exploit other

123 Ducat 1994: 88–9. As he points out, the fact that Menon of Pharsalus could equip 300 of his Penestai as troops (Dem. 23.199) implies that his total holdings ran well into four figures.

124 [Plato], *Alcibiades I* 122d.

125 I have suggested (Hodkinson 2000: 385–8) that an 'ordinary' Spartiate estate of just over 18 ha might have sustained about five helot families and that the average landholding of wealthy Spartiates may have been roughly two and a half times as large at about 45 ha. If we assume, *exempli gratia*, that the wealthiest non-royal Spartiate (I purposely exclude the kings) might have held double that amount, some 90 ha, his estates might have sustained some twenty-five helot families, or a total population of about 125 helots. Even if all his landholdings were concentrated in one place, on the estimates of village population density of some 100–125 persons per ha referred to above (n. 103), this would imply only a very modest settlement of hardly more than a hectare in extent. In reality, however, most Spartiate estates were probably fragmented into a number of different holdings. If one were to adopt the comparatively low figures for the total helot population proposed in Figueira (2003) and Scheidel (2003), the likelihood of the inhabitants of a sizeable helot village belonging to a single Spartiate would be even more remote.

peasants in pursuit of their own interests'.[126] We are not of course able to determine the extent to which helot leaders such as the *mnōionomoi* were able to engage in similar exploitative behaviour over their fellow helots. However, the existence of comparable underlying conditions of economic and social inequality is clearly evident. As in other societies – such as low country South Carolina[127] – in which unfree farming populations have enjoyed a certain level of independence, helots were able to accumulate not insignificant amounts of moveable property. The ancient sources depict helots engaging in private sales,[128] insuring their boats, and expecting to receive rewards of silver.[129] In the late third century no fewer than 6,000 Lakonian helots were each able to accumulate the sum of five Attic minas (500 drachmas) with which to purchase their freedom.[130] This property accumulation was doubtless rooted in the system of sharecropping, which created possibilities for households enjoying a high ratio of labourers to household size to gain some benefit from agricultural surpluses that they produced.

A necessary consequence of private property accumulation was economic differentiation. In addition to temporary economic differences between helot households deriving from the normal fluctuations of household life cycles, more enduring differentiation will have resulted from divergent demographic histories and consequent differences in household size. Studies of pre-industrial agrarian societies have often noted positive correlations between household size and levels of wealth.[131] The potential for considerable economic differentiation among a helot-like servile population is suggested by the claim of Archemachus of Euboea (in the passage cited above) that many Penestai were wealthier than their Thessalian masters.[132] The presence of differential prosperity amongst a rural population under Spartiate rule has now been documented archaeologically through the wide variations in ceramic assemblages at different sites within the area of the *Laconia Survey*.[133] Within Messenia, archaeological indications of socio-economic differentiation and the exercise of social control may be present in the evidence for the phenomenon of tomb cult mentioned above. Several recent studies of tomb cults have observed that, while

[126] Moon 1999: 230–6 (quotation at 231); Hoch 1996. Cf. the detailed case studies of Hoch 1986; Melton 1993: 559–85.

[127] Morgan 1983: 120–2. [128] Herodotus 9.80. [129] Thucydides 4.26.

[130] Plutarch, *Cleomenes* 23.1. [131] Shanin 1972: 63–8.

[132] As Ducat 1994: 15 notes, the statement is a 'paradoxe banal' and is doubtless exaggerated, but makes sense only in the context of economic differentiation among the servile population.

[133] Catling 2002: 193–5.

they are in one sense a sign of community solidarity, they could also be used to proclaim the superiority of leading families who claimed to trace their pedigrees back to the heroic age, and in particular to the 'ancestor' commemorated in the cult.[134]

Excavated finds from the best published example of Messenian tomb cult – that at Tholos F at Nichoria in the Five Rivers region, which dates to the later fifth and early fourth century – suggest that the horizons of some of the cult participants were more than purely Messenian: of twenty-three recorded items of fine ware, at least thirteen (56 per cent), have been identified as either imported items or local imitations of foreign work, with especial links to Olympia and Attica.[135] Moreover, finds of *pithoi* and *amphorae* suggest that the cult's administration included the storage of foodstuffs and liquids for communal dining, a vehicle by which leading helots could perhaps articulate their leadership through the extraction of surplus produce from their own or others' holdings. Thus the administration of tomb cult brings us back to the organization of agricultural production and to the authority over other helots which the *mnoionomoi*, 'the leaders of the helots', may have exercised through their supervision and direction of the agrarian economy. As Jacques Annequin[136] has justly remarked, 'Surveiller c'est exercer un pouvoir'.

Other than the tantalizing hints provided by tomb cult, our ignorance of so many of the details of helot society generally prevents us from detecting historical episodes in which more prominent helot households used their position for their own self-advancement at the expense of their fellow helots. One set of episodes in which such personal self-advancement can clearly be seen, however, is the positive response given by several thousand helots, from 424 BC onwards, to Spartan calls for military recruits, often in return for freedom from helot status.[137] Some of these former helot recruits were, indeed, placed on garrison service at Lepreon near the border of northern Messenia,[138] where one of their duties was presumably the capture of runaway helots. Given the evidence of differential status within helot communities and the hint of some communal role in the recruitment process, one wonders whether the composition of these groups of

[134] Morris 1988: 750–61, esp. 756–8; cf. Antonaccio 1995: 142, 257–68; Alcock 2002a: 18.

[135] These are my own calculations from the finds published in Coulson and Wilkie 1983: 332–50. Cf. also Antonaccio 1995: 90–3, although it is unclear how her interpretation that the tomb was reused as a rural or pastoral shelter accords with the presence of fine tableware.

[136] Annequin 1985: 647.

[137] E.g. Thucydides 4.80; 5.67; 7.19; 8.5; Xenophon, *Hellenica* 3.1.4; 3.4.2; 6.5.28. Cf. Ducat 1990: 159–66; Hunt 1998: esp. 53–62; 170–5.

[138] Thucydides 5.34.

manumitted helots was skewed towards members of the more prominent households. To what extent was the acceptability, indeed desirability, to many helots of military service in Sparta's armies rooted in the social relations of production between helot *mnoionomoi* and their Spartiate masters, in the process of privileged collaboration practised by the *mnoionomoi* in the management of Spartiate estates?

In raising this particular question, of course, we are led logically on to the broader, political question that lies at the heart of modern debates about helot–Spartiate relationships: how, in the face of occasional widespread revolt, the minority elite group of Spartiates, largely confined to Sparta itself, maintained effective control for several centuries over the much larger servile helot population spread around their large and often distant territory. The particular insight to emerge from this chapter is, I suggest, that the issue of Spartiate collective political management stands parallel to, and may have been interlocked with, the issue of individual Spartiate management of agricultural estates. If the relations of privileged collaboration established in the agrarian sphere between Spartiate masters and the *mnoionomoi* reinforced the authority of wealthy helot households, the influence exercised by those prominent helots within their own communities may in turn have contributed towards the maintenance of order and the stifling, for the most part, of protest against Spartan rule.

CONCLUSIONS AND PROSPECTS

The substantive part of this chapter began by asking how helot farming actually worked on the ground, in particular to what extent it was directed by intervention from Spartiate owners, and what the implications were for the fundamental conditions of helot life, including the nature of local helot communities. In addressing these questions, I have attempted to examine certain key variables and general insights suggested by comparative evidence from other systems of unfree agrarian labour, as a means of providing context to and extracting maximum value from the limited ancient literary and archaeological evidence. The first variable to be examined, the nature of helot obligations, was one which took a common form throughout the helotized regions of Spartiate territory: the payment of dues in kind through a sharecropping arrangement. Comparative evidence indicated that the payment of dues was typically correlated with a lesser degree of direct intervention by the owner, although the use of sharecropping may have provided a somewhat greater incentive for such intervention than if the dues had been fixed. The next issue examined was whether helots enjoyed practical fixity of tenure on the land. The ancient evidence regarding the sale of helots proved to be somewhat ambiguous; but the changing agrarian settlement patterns close to Sparta revealed by the *Laconia Survey* suggested that in this region Spartiate owners actively settled their helots onto new agricultural land and subsequently re-settled them when conditions deteriorated.

This insight prompted investigation of the underlying issue of responsibility for the formation of the agrarian economy, which comparative study suggested was an important initial influence upon the dominant group's capacity to intervene in agricultural production. It was concluded that, in contrast to the *Laconia Survey* area, Sparta's acquisition of control over eastern Messenia involved the incorporation of a pre-existing farming population within its own territory, although there was probably some scope for the incoming Spartiates to mould local agrarian structures. From here, the observation, derived again from comparative evidence, that subsequent developments in agrarian structures could sometimes override initial patterns of exploitation led to examination of two interrelated variables which have frequently been noted as exercising a significant influence upon social relations of production: geographical distance and patterns of residence among the unfree population. The first of these was, by definition, a factor differentiating different regions of Spartiate territory. Comparative material indicated that the high degree of Spartiate intervention in areas of Lakonia close to Sparta would not have been feasible in regions further afield where, as absentee landowners, Spartiates would have had to manage their estates through helot overseers, such as the *mnoionomoi*, the 'leaders of the helots'. This distinction according to geographical distance was seen to correlate with a marked difference between the dispersed settlement pattern of areas close to Sparta and the prevailing pattern of nucleated residence in Messenia. This latter pattern would have created greater potential scope for the development of communal identity and institutions in the context of village residence. Prompted by comparative evidence, however, it was noted that inequalities among the helots may have led to the domination of communal activities by wealthier households who, through their collaboration with Spartiate landowners, could gain private advantage which gave them a vested interest in the maintenance of Spartan rule.

Through use of the comparative method we have been able to reach a deeper understanding, not only of the relationships between Spartiate landowners and their unfree labour force in the operation of the agrarian economy, but also of the implications for certain aspects of helot society, such as their experience of leadership and community. Indeed, the insights of this chapter regarding the social relations of production between Spartiates and helots could be profitably extended into a more in-depth examination of relations of patronage and of the potential use of helots as a source of socio-political influence. A number of other aspects of helotage, some of them briefly touched on in this chapter – aspects such as the use of helots (or ex-helots) in warfare, their employment in domestic service, helot property ownership, and religious practice – could also be fruitfully explored in the context of other systems of unfree labour, drawing upon a wider range of societies, and in greater depth, than in this initial study. For the present, however, this chapter has indicated how the practice of comparative history can illuminate the relationship between the helots and their masters to a greater degree than is possible through exclusive reliance on the exiguous data from the ancient world.

Bibliography

Acklen, J. A. S. (1856) 'Rules in the management of a Southern estate', *De Bow's Review* 21: 617–20.

Adams, A. D. (1908) *The Neglected Period of Anti-Slavery in America (1808–1831)*. Cambridge, MA.

Agresti, A. (1996) *Introduction to Categorical Data Analysis*. New York.

Alcock, S. E. (1991) 'Tomb cult and the post-classical polis', *American Journal of Archaeology* 95: 447–67.

(2002a) *Archaeologies of the Greek Past: Memories, Monuments and Landscapes*. Cambridge.

(2002b) 'A simple case of exploitation? The helots of Messenia', in *Money, Labour and Land in Ancient Greece: Approaches to the Economies of Ancient Greece*, ed. P. Cartledge, E. Cohen and L. Foxhall. London and New York: 185–99.

(2003) 'Researching the helots: details, methodologies, agencies', in Luraghi and Alcock 2003: 3–9.

Alcock, S. E. *et al.* (2005) 'Pylos regional archaeological project. Part VII: Historical Messenia, Geometric through late Roman', *Hesperia* 74: 147–209.

Alencastro, L. F. de (2000) *O Trato dos Viventes. Formação do Brasil no Atlântico Sul, séculos XVI–XVII*. São Paulo.

Ameling, W. (1988) 'Landwirtschaft und Sklaverei im klassischen Attika', *Historische Zeitschrift* 266: 281–315.

Amigues, S. (2003) 'Le crible à ivraie d'Aristophane fr. 497K–A', *Revue de Philologie* 77: 17–22.

Andreau, J. and Descat, R. (2006) *Esclaves en Grèce et à Rome*. Paris.

Annequin, J. (1985) 'Comparatisme/comparaisons: ressemblances et hétérogénéité des formes d'exploitation esclavagistes – quelques réflexions', *Dialogues d'Histoire Ancienne* 11: 639–72.

Anon. (1849) 'Rules on the plantation', *Southern Cultivator* 7: 103, reprinted in Breeden 1980: 82–3.

Anon. Mississippi Planter (1851) 'Management of negroes upon Southern estates', *De Bow's Review* 10: 621–7.

Anon. Small Farmer (1851) 'Management of negroes', *De Bow's Review* 11: 369–72.

Antonaccio, C. (1995) *An Archaeology of Ancestors: Tomb Cult and Hero Cult in Early Greece*. Lanham.

Antonil, A. J. (2001 [1711]) *Cultura e Opulência do Brasil por suas Drogas e Minas*. Lisboa.

Aoki, M. (2001) *Toward a Comparative Institutional Analysis*. Cambridge, MA.

Aptheker, H. (1943) *American Negro Slave Revolts*. New York.

Arango y Parreño, F. (1952 [1791]) 'Representación hecha a S. M. con motivo de la sublevación de los esclavos en los dominios de la Isla de Santo Domingo', in Arango y Parreño, *Obras de D. Francisco de Arango y Parreño*. La Habana: vol. I: 111–12.

(1952 [1792]) 'Discurso sobre la agricultura de La Habana y medios de fomentarla', in F. Arango y Parreño, *Obras de D. Francisco de Arango y Parreño*. La Habana: vol. I: 115–62.

(1952 [1811]) 'Representación de la Ciudad de la Habana a las Cortes, el 20 de julio de 1811' in Arango y Parreño, *Obras de D. Francisco de Arango y Parreño*. La Habana: vol. II: 145–89.

Armitage, D. and Braddick, J. M. (eds.) (2002) *The British Atlantic World, 1500–1800*. New York.

Arthur, M. (1984) 'Early Greece: The origins of the western attitude toward women', in *Women in the Ancient World: The Arethusa Papers*, ed. J. Peradotto and J. P. Sullivan. Albany: 23–5.

Assunção, P. de (2004) *Negócios Jesuíticos. O Cotidiano da Administração dos Bens Divinos*. São Paulo.

Athanassakis, A. N. (ed.) (2004) *Hesiod's Works and Days and Theogony*. Baltimore.

Auden, D. (1996) *The Making of an Enterprise: The Society of Jesus in Portugal, Its Empire and Beyond, 1540–1750*. Stanford.

Aufhauser, R. K. (1974) 'Slavery and technological change', *Journal of Economic History* 34: 36–50.

Austin, M. M. and Vidal-Naquet, P. (1977) *Economic and Social History of Ancient Greece*. London.

Ayalon, D. (1951) *L'Esclavavage du Mamelouk*. Jerusalem.

Backhaus, Wilhelm (1989) '*Servi vincti*', *Klio* 71: 321–9.

Bagnall, R. S., Frier, B. W. and Rutherford, I. C. (1997) *The Census Register P. Oxy. 984: The Reverse of Pindar's Paeans*. Brussels.

Baier, S. and Lovejoy, P. (1977) 'The Tuareg of the central Sudan', in *Slavery in Africa: Historical and Anthropological Perspectives*, ed. S. Myers and I. Kopytoff. Madison: 391–411.

Baks, C. J., Breman, C. and Noolj, A. T. (1966) 'Slavery as a system of production in tribal societies', *Bijdrgen tot de Taal-, Land – en Volkenkunde* 122: 90–109.

Baldwin, E. and Edwards, J. Jr (1773) 'Some observations on the enslavement of negroes', *The Connecticut Journal and the New Haven Post*, 8 October, 15 October, 17 December, 31 December, reprinted in Bruns 1977: 293–302.

Ball, E. (1998) *Slaves in the Family*. New York.

Ball, L. F. (2003) *The Domus Aurea and the Roman Architectural Revolution*. Cambridge.

Barickman, B. J. (1998) *A Bahian Counterpoint: Sugar, Tobacco, Cassava, and Slavery in the Recôncavo, 1780–1860*. Stanford.

Bartens, A. (1996) *Der kreolische Raum: Geschichte und Gegenwart.* Helsinki.
Barzel, Y. (1977) 'An economic analysis of slavery', *Journal of Law and Economics* 20: 87–110.
Bazemo, M. (2004) 'Captivité et esclavage dans les anciens pays du Burkina Faso. Pérennité et mutations : analyse du fonctionnement'. Doctoral thesis, University of Besançon.
Bell, M. (1994) *Le ravitaillement en blé de Rome et des centres urbains des débuts de la république jusqu'au Haut Empire.* Rome.
Belote, J. and Belote, L. S. (1984) 'Suffer the little children: death, autonomy, and responsibility in a changing "low technology" environment', *Science, Technology and Human Values* 9: 35–48.
Bemis, S. F. (1965) *A Diplomatic History of the United States.* New York.
Benci, J. (1977 [1705]) *Economia Cristã dos Senhores no Governo dos Escravos.* São Paulo.
Benezet, A. (1771) *Some Historical Accounts of Guinea*, reprinted in Bruns 1977: 145–84.
Bentmann, R. and Müller, M. (1990) 'Die Villa als Herrschaftsarchitektur: Versuch einer kunst- und sozialgeschichtlichen Analyse', in *Die römische Villa*, ed. F. Reutti. Darmstadt: 389–435.
Bergad, L. W. (1990) *Cuban Rural Society in the Nineteenth Century: The Social and Economic History of Monoculture in Matanzas.* Princeton.
(1996) 'After the mining boom: demographic and economic aspects of slavery in Mariana, Minas Gerais, 1750–1818', *Latin American Research Review* 31: 67–97.
(1999) *The Demographic and Economic History of Slavery in Minas Gerais, Brazil, 1720–1880.* Cambridge.
(2004) 'American slave markets during the 1850s: slave price rises in the United States, Cuba, and Brazil in comparative perspective', in *Slavery in the Development of the Americas*, ed. David Eltis *et al.* Cambridge: 219–35.
Bergad, L. W. *et al.* (1995) *The Cuban Slave Market 1790–1880.* Cambridge.
Berlin, I. (1980) 'Time, space, and the evolution of Afro-American society on British mainland North America', *American Historical Review* 85: 44–78.
(1998) *Many Thousands Gone: The First Two Centuries of Slavery in North America.* Cambridge, MA.
(2003) *Generations of Captivity: A History of African-American Slaves.* Cambridge, MA.
Berlin, I. and Morgan, P. D. (eds.) (1993) *Cultivation and Culture: Labor and the Shaping of Slave Life in the Americas.* Charlottesville.
Bernus, E. and Bernus, S. (1975) 'L'evolution de la condition servile chez les Touregs saheliens', in *L'esclavage en Afrique Precoloniale*, ed. C. Meillassoux. Paris: 27–47.
Berry, M. F. (2005) *My Face is Black is True: Callie House and the Struggle for Ex-slave Reparations.* New York.
Bethell, L. (1970) *The Abolition of the Brazilian Slave Trade: Brazil and the Slave Question (1807–1869).* Cambridge.

Bezis-Selfa, J. (1999) 'A tale of two ironworks: slavery, free labor, work, and resistance in the early Republic', *William & Mary Quarterly* 56: 677–700.

Biezunska-Malowist, I. and Malowist, M. (1989) 'L'esclavage antique et moderne: les possibilités de recherches comparées', in *Mélanges Pierre Lévêque, 2: Anthropologie et Société*, ed. M.-M. Mactoux and E. Geny. Paris, 17–31.

Biot, E. (1840) *De l'abolition de l'esclavage ancien de Occident*. Paris.

Bittker, B. I. (1973) *The Case for Black Reparations*. New York.

Blackburn, R. (1997) *The Making of New World Slavery. From the Baroque to the Modern 1492–1800*. London.

Blassingame, J. W. (1979) *The Slave Community: Plantation Life in the Antebellum South*. New York, 2nd edn.

Bloch, M. (1928) 'Pour une histoire comparée des sociétés européennes', *Revue de synthèse historique* 46: 15–50.

(1947) 'Comment et pourquoi finit l'esclavage antique', *Annales: Economies Sociétés Civilisations* 2: 30–45, 161–70.

(1975 [1932]) *Feudal Society*. London.

Blum, J. (1957) 'The rise of serfdom in eastern Europe', *American Historical Review* 62: 807–36.

(1978) *The End of the Old Order in Rural Europe*. Princeton.

Blunt, T. E. (1847) 'Rules for the government of overseers', *Southern Cultivator* 5: 61–2, reprinted in Breeden 1980: 82.

Boardman, J. and Vaphopoulou-Richardson, C. E. (eds.) (1986) *Chios: A Conference at the Homereion in Chios 1984*. Oxford.

Bodin, J. (1962 [1606]) *The Six Bookes of a Commonwealth*. Cambridge, MA.

Bohorquez, C. (2003) 'L'ambivalente présence d'Haïti dans l'indépendance du Venezuela', *Outre-Mers* 340–1: 227–40.

Bonnassie, P. (1985) 'Survie et extinction du régime esclavagiste dans l'Occident du Haut Moyen Age', *Cahiers de civilisation médiévale* 38: 307–43.

(1991) *From Slavery to Feudalism in South-Western Europe*. Cambridge.

Boserup, E. (1970) *Women's Role in Economic Development*. London.

(1997) 'The economics of polygyny', in *Perspectives on Africa: A Reader in Culture, History and Representation*, ed. R. R. Grinker and C. Steiner. Cambridge, MA, 506–17.

Botte, R. (1994) 'Stigmates sociaux et discriminations religieuses : l'ancienne classe servile au Fuuta Jaloo', *Cahiers d'Études Africaines* 133–5: 109–36.

(2001) *L'ombre portée de l'esclavage: aratars contemporains de l'oppression sociale*. Paris.

(ed.) (2005) 'Esclavage moderne ou modernité de l'esclavage ?', *Cahiers d'Études Africaines* 179–80.

Bowman, S. D. (1993) *Masters and Lords: Mid-Nineteenth-Century U.S. Planters and Prussian Junkers*. New York.

Bradley, K. (1987) *Slaves and Masters in the Roman Empire: A Study in Social Control*. New York.

(1988) 'The Roman slave wars 140–70 BC: a comparative perspective', in *Forms of Control and Subordination in Antiquity*, ed. T. Yuge and M. Doi. Leiden.

(1989) *Slavery and Rebellion in the Roman World 140 B.C.–70 B.C.* Bloomington.
(1994) *Slavery and Society at Rome*. New York.
(2004) 'On captives under the Principate', *Phoenix* 58: 298–318.
Braudel, F. (1975 [1949]) *The Mediterranean and the Mediterranean World in the Age of Philip II*. London.
Breeden, J. O. (ed.) (1980) *Advice Among Masters: The Ideal in Slave Management in the Old South*. Westport.
Breen, T. and Innes, S. (1980) *'Myne Owne Ground': Race and Freedom on Virginia's Eastern Shore, 1640–1676*. New York.
Brito, L. M. (1986) 'Los barracones de esclavos en la antigua región de Cienfuegos', *Islas* 85: 74–103.
Broadhead, S. H. (1983) 'Slave wives, free sisters: Bakongo women and slavery c. 1700–1850', in *Women and Slavery in Africa*, ed. C. C. Robertson and M. A. Klein. Madison: 160–81.
Brooks, G. E. (1994) *Landlords and Strangers: Ecology, Society and Trade in Western Africa, 1000–1630*. Boulder.
Brown C. L. and Morgan, P. D. (eds.) (2006) *Arming Slaves: From Classical Times to the Modern Age*. New Haven.
Brown, V. (2003) 'Spiritual terror and sacred authority in Jamaican slave society', *Slavery and Abolition* 24: 24–53.
Bruns, R. (1977) *Am I Not a Man and a Brother: The Antislavery Crusade of Revolutionary America, 1688–1788*. New York.
Brunt, P. A. (1971) *Italian Manpower*. Oxford.
(1987) *Italian Manpower 225 B.C. – A. D. 14*. Oxford, 2nd edn.
Buckland, W. W. (1908) *The Roman Law of Slavery*. Cambridge.
Burton, M. and White, D. R. (1984) 'Sexual division of labor in agriculture', *American Anthropologist* 86: 568–83.
Burton, M., Brudner, L. and White, D. R. (1977) 'A model of the sexual division of labor', *American Ethnologist* 4: 227–51.
Bush, M. L. (ed.) (1996a) *Serfdom and Slavery: Studies in Legal Bondage*. London.
(1996b) 'Introduction', in Bush 1996a: 1–17.
(1996c) 'Serfdom in medieval and modern Europe: a comparison', in Bush 1996a: 199–224.
(2002) *Servitude in Modern Times*. Cambridge.
Calderini, A. (1908) *La manomissione e la condizione dei liberti in Grecia*. Milan.
Callahan, W. J. (1967) 'La propaganda, la sedición y la revolución francesa en la capitanía general de Venezuela, 1786–1796', *Boletín Histórico* 14: 177–205.
Campbell, G., Miers, S. and Miller, J. C. (2005) 'Introduction', *Slavery and Abolition* 26: 163–82.
Campuzano, L. (2004) *En torno a las Antillas hispánicas. Ensayos en homenaje al profesor Paul Estrade*. Puerto del Rosario.
Canarella, G. and Tomaske, J. A. (1975) 'The optimal utilization of slaves', *Journal of Economic History* 35: 621–9.
Carandini, A. (1988) *Schiavi in Italia: gli strumenti pensanti dei Romani fra tarda Repubblica a medio Impero*. Rome.

Carlton, D. and Coclanis, P. A. (2003) *The South, the Nation, and the World: Perspectives on Southern Economic Development*. Charlottesville.

Cartledge, P. (1985) 'Rebels and *Sambos* in classical Greece: a comparative view', in *Crux: Essays Presented to G. E. M. de Ste. Croix on his 75th Birthday*, ed. P. A. Cartledge and F. D. Harvey. London: 16–46.

(1987) *Agesilaos and the Crisis of Sparta*. London.

(1988) 'Serfdom in classical Greece', in *Slavery and Other Forms of Unfree Labour*, ed. L. Archer. London: 33–41.

(1993) 'Classical Greek agriculture: recent work and alternative views', *Journal of Peasant Studies* 21: 127–36.

(1998) 'The economy (economies) of ancient Greece', *Dialogos* 5: 4–24.

(2001 [1979]) *Sparta and Lakonia: A Regional History, 1300–362 BC*. London; 2nd edn.

(2001 [1985]) 'Rebels and *Sambos* in classical Greece: a comparative view', in *Spartan Reflections*. London: 127–52. Originally published in *Crux: Essays presented to G. E. M. de Ste Croix on his 75th Birthday*, ed. P. Cartledge and F. D. Harvey. Exeter: 16–46.

(2001) 'The political economy of Greek slavery', in *Money, Labour and Land: Approaches to the Economies of Ancient Greece*, ed. P. Cartledge, E. E. Cohen and L. Foxhall. London: 156–66.

(2002) 'Greek civilisation and slavery', In *Classics in Progress: Essays on Ancient Greece and Rome*, ed. T. P. Wiseman. Oxford: 247–62.

Carvalho, M. J. M. De (1998) *Liberdade: rotinas e rupturas do escravismo. Recife – 1822–1850*. Recife.

Cassagnac, B. A. G. De (1842–4) *Voyage aux Antilles Françaises, Anglaises, Danoises, Espagnoles* (2 vols.). Paris.

Castro, A. B. de (1976) 'Escravos e senhores nos engenhos do Brasil'. Ph.D. thesis, State University of Campinas.

Catling, R. W. V. (1996) 'The archaic and classical pottery', in *Continuity and Change in a Greek Rural Landscape. The Laconia Survey, II: Archaeological Data*, ed. W. Cavanagh, J. Crouwel, R. W. V. Catling and G. Shipley. London: 33–89.

(2002) 'The early Iron Age to the Classical periods (*c*. 1050–323 BC)', in W. G. Cavanagh *et al.* 2002: 151–256.

Cauna, J. (1994) 'Les diasporas des anciens colons de Saint-Domingue: le cas de la Jamaïque', *Revue Française d'Histoire d'Outre-Mer* 81: 333–59.

Cavanagh, W. G. *et al.* (2002) *Continuity and Change in a Greek Rural Landscape*. London.

Chalhoub, S. (1989) 'Slaves, freemen, and the politics of freedom in Brazil', *Slavery & Abolition* 10: 64–84.

Chambers, D. (1997) '"My own nation": Igbo exiles in the diaspora', *Slavery and Abolition* 18: 72–97.

(2002) 'The significance of Igbo in the light of Biafra slave-trade: a rejoinder to Northrup's "Myth Igbo"', *Slavery and Abolition* 23: 101–20.

Clendinnen, I. (1991) *Aztecs: An Interpretation*. Cambridge.

Cochin, A. (1863a) *The Results of Emancipation*. Boston.
(1863b) *The Results of Slavery*. Boston.

Cohen, D. and O' Connor, M. (eds.) (2004) *Comparison and History: Europe in Cross-National Perspective*. London.

Cohen, E. E. (1992) *Athenian Economy and Society: A Banking Perspective*. Princeton.

Collins, R. (1854) 'Essay on the treatment and management of slaves', *Southern Cultivator* 12: 205–6, reprinted in Breeden 1980: 17–27.

Condorcet, M. de. (1781) 'Reflections on black slavery', reprinted in Williams 1999: 308–16.

Conrad, R. E. (1972) *The Destruction of Brazilian Slavery, 1850–1888*. Berkeley.

Cooper, F. (1979) 'The problem of slavery in African studies', *Journal of African History* 20: 103–25.

Coronil, F. (1995) 'Transculturation and the politics of theory: countering the center, Cuban counterpoint' in *Cuban Counterpoint. Tobacco and Sugar*, ed. F. Ortiz. Durham: IX–LVI.

Coulson, W. D. E. and Wilkie, N. (1983) 'Archaic to Roman times: the site and environs', in McDonald, Coulson and Rosser 1983: 332–50.

Craton, M. (1997) *Empire, Enslavement and Freedom in the Caribbean*. Kingston.

Crone, P. (1980) *Slaves On Horses*. New York.

Crosby, A. W. (1994) *Germs, Seeds and Animals: Studies in Ecological History*. London.

Cuguano, Q. O. (1999 [1787]) *Thoughts and Sentiments on the Evil of Slavery*. Harmondsworth.

Cuomo, S. (2002) 'The machine and the city: Hero of Alexandria's *Belopoeica*', in *Science and Mathematics in Ancient Greek Culture*, ed. C. J. Tuplin and T. E. Rihll. Oxford: 165–77.

Curtin, P. (1990) *The Rise and Fall of the Plantation Complex: Essays in Atlantic History*. New York.

Curtin, P. D. (1975) *Economic Change in Precolonial Africa: Senegambia in the Era of the Slave Trade*. Madison.

Curtis, R. I. (2001) *Ancient Food Technology*. Leiden.

Curto, J. and Lovejoy, P. (eds.) (2004) *Enslaving Connections: Changing Cultures of Africa and Brazil during the Era of Slavery*. New York.

Dal Lago, E. (2005) *Agrarian Elites: American Slaveholders and Southern Italian Landowners, 1815–1861*. Baton Rouge.

David, P. A. (2001) 'Path dependence, its critics and the quest for "historical economics"', in *Evolution and Path Dependence in Economic Ideas: Past and Present*, ed. P. Garrouste and S. Ioannides. Cheltenham: 15–40.

Davis, D. B. (1966) *The Problem of Slavery in Western Culture*. New York.
(1975) *The Problem of Slavery in the Age of Revolutions, 1770–1823*. New Haven.
(1984) *Slavery and Human Progress*. New York.
(2000) 'Looking at slavery from broader perspectives', *American Historical Review* 105: 452–66.
(2006) *Inhuman Bondage: The Rise and Fall of Slavery in the New World*. New York.

Davis, J. L. *et al.* (1997) 'The Pylos regional archaeological project. Part I: overview and the archaeological survey', *Hesperia* 66: 391–494.

De Long, J. B. (1992) 'Productivity growth and machinery investment: a long-run look 1870–1980', *Journal of Economic History* 52: 307–24.

Dean, W. (1976) *Rio Claro: A Brazilian Plantation System, 1820–1920*. Stanford.

Debien, G. and Wright, P. (1975) 'Les colons de Saint-Domingue passés à la Jamaïque, 1792–1835', *Bulletin de la Societé d'Histoire de la Guadeloupe* 26: 3–216.

Degler, C. N. (1971) *Neither Black nor White: Slavery and Race Relations in Brazil and the United States*. New York.

Del Priore, M. and Gomes, F. D. S. (eds.) (2003) *Os senhores dos rios*. Rio de Janeiro.

Delfino, S. and Gillespie, M. (eds.) (2005) *Global Perspectives on Industrial Transformation in the American South*. Columbia.

Desch-Obi, T. J. (2000) *Engolo: Combat Traditions and African Diaspora*. Los Angeles.

Dew, C. B. (1966) *Ironmaker to the Confederacy*. New Haven.

(1994) *Bond of Iron: Masters and Slaves at Buffalo Forge*. New York.

Dew, T. R. (1832) 'Abolition of Negro slavery', *American Quarterly Review* 12, reprinted in Faust 1981: 21–77.

Díaz Soler, L. M. (1965) *Historia de la esclavitud negra en Puerto Rico*. Puerto Rico.

Díaz, M. E. (2001) *The Virgin, the King, and the Royal Slaves of El Cobre: Negotiating Freedom in Colonial Cuba, 1670–1780*. Stanford.

Dillwyn, W. (1773) *Brief Considerations on Slavery*, in *Am I Not a Man and a Brother*, reprinted in Bruns 1977: 270–8.

Dockès, P. (1979) *La libération médiévale*. Paris.

Domar, E. (1970) 'The causes of slavery or serfdom', *Journal of Economic History* 30: 18–32.

(1989) 'Were Russian serfs overcharged for their land in 1861? The history of one historical table', in *Agrarian Organization in the Century of Industrialization: Europe, Russia and North America*, ed. G. Grantham and C. Leonard. Greenwich: 429–39.

Dorijay, M. (ed.) (2003) *The Abolitions of Slavery: From Léger Félicité Sonthonax to Victor Schoelcher, 1793, 1794, 1848*. Paris.

Dorsey, J. C. (2003) *Slave Traffic in the Age of Abolition: Puerto Rico, West Africa, and the Non-Hispanic Caribbean, 1815–1859*. Gainesville.

Drescher, S. (1977) *Econocide: Economic Development and the Abolition of the British Slave Trade*. Pittsburgh.

(1988) 'Brazilian abolition in comparative perspective', *Hispanic American Historical Review* 68: 429–60.

(1999) *From Slavery to Freedom: Comparative Studies in the Rise and Fall of Atlantic Slavery*. New York.

(2002) *The Mighty Experiment: Free Labor versus Slavery in British Emancipation*. New York.

(2004) 'White Atlantic? The choice for African slave labor in the plantation Americas', in Eltis *et al.* 2004: 31–69.

Drescher, S. and Engerman, S. L. (eds.) (1998) *Historical Guide of World Slavery*. New York.

Dubois, L. (1998) *Les esclaves de la République*. Paris.

(2004a) *A Colony of Citizens: Revolution & Slave Emancipation in the French Caribbean, 1787–1804*. Chapel Hill.

(2004b) *Avengers of the New World: The Story of the Haitian Revolution*. Cambridge, MA.

Ducat, J. (1990) *Les Hilotes*. Paris.

(1994) *Les Pénestes de Thessalie*. Paris.

Dumont, J.-C. (1987) *Servus. Rome et l'esclavage sous la République*. Rome.

Dunaway, W. A. (2003) *Slavery in the American Mountain South*. New York.

Duncan-Jones, R. P. (1978) 'Two possible indices of the purchasing power of money in Greek and Roman antiquity', in *Les Dévaluations à Rome: époque républicaine et impériale*. Rome: 159–68.

Dusinberre, W. (1996) *'Them Dark Days': Slavery in the American Rice Swamps*. New York.

Earle, C. V. (1978) 'A staple interpretation of slavery and free labor', *Geographical Review* 68: 51–65.

Edelstein, L. (1967) *The Idea of Progress in Classical Antiquity*. Baltimore.

Edwards, B. H. (2003) *The Practice of Diaspora: Literature, Translation, and the Rise of Black Internationalism*. Cambridge, MA.

Eilers, C. (2002) *Roman Patrons of Greek Cities*. Oxford.

Eisenberg, J. (2000) *As Missões Jesuíticas e o Pensamento Político Moderno. Encontros Culturais, Aventuras Teóricas*. Belo Horizonte.

Elkins, S. (1959) *Slavery: A Problem in American Institutional and Intellectual Life*. Chicago.

Elliott, J. H. (2006) *Empires of the Atlantic World: Spain and Britain in the Americas*. New Haven.

Eltis, D. (1987) *Economic Growth and the Ending of the Transatlantic Slave Trade*. New York.

(2000) *The Rise of African Slavery in the Americas*. Cambridge.

Eltis, D. and Walvin, J. (1981) *The Abolition of the Atlantic Slave Trade: Origins and Effects in Europe, Africa, and the Americas*. Madison.

Eltis, D. *et al.* (eds.) (2004) *Slavery in the Development of the Americas*. New York.

Ember, M. (1974) 'Warfare, sex ratio, and polygyny', *Ethnology* 13: 197–206.

Engerman, S. L. (1973) 'Some considerations relating to property rights in man', *Journal of Economic History* 33: 43–65.

(1975) 'Comments on the study of race and slavery', in *Race and Slavery in the Western Hemisphere: Quantitative Studies*, ed. S. L. Engerman and E. D. Genovese. Princeton: 495–530.

(1982) 'Economic adjustments to emancipation in the United States and the British West Indies', *Journal of Interdisciplinary History* 12: 191–220.

(1984) 'Economic change and contract labor in the British Caribbean: the end of slavery and the adjustment to emancipation', *Explorations in Economic History* 21: 133–50.

(1986) 'Servants to slaves to servants: contract labour and European expansion', in *Colonization and Migration: Indentured Labour Before and after Slavery*, ed. P. C. Emmer. Dordrecht: 263–94.

(1995) 'Emancipations in comparative perspective. A long and wide view', in Oostindie. 1995: 223–41.

(1996) 'Slavery, serfdom and other forms of coerced labour: similarities and differences', in Bush 1996a: 18–41.

(ed.) (1999) *Terms of Labor: Slavery, Serfdom, and Free Labor*. Stanford.

(2002) 'Pricing freedom: evaluating the costs of emancipation and of freedom', in *Working Slavery, Pricing Freedom: Perspectives from the Caribbean, Africa, and the African Diaspora*, ed. V. Shepherd. Kingston: 273–302.

(2005) 'On the accuracy of some past and present forecasts', *IMF Staff Papers*, 52 (September 2005): 15–30.

Engerman, S. L. and Genovese E. D. (eds.) (1975) *Race and Slavery in the Western Hemisphere*. Princeton.

Engerman, S. L. and Higman, B. W. (1997) 'The demographic structure of the Caribbean slave societies in the eighteenth and nineteenth centuries', in *General History of the Caribbean*, ed. Alan Knight. London: vol. III: 47–57.

Epstein, S. R. (1998) 'Craft guilds, apprenticeship, and technological change in preindustrial Europe', *Journal of Economic History* 58: 684–713.

Etienne, R. (1978/9) 'Production vinicole et esclavage chez Columelle', *Index* 8: 206–13.

Evans, J. K. (1981) *War, Women and Children in Ancient Rome*. London.

Faak, M. (ed.) (1982) *Alexander von Humboldt: Lateinamerika am Vorabend der Unabhängigkeitsrevolution. Eine Anthologie von Impressionen und Urteilen aus den Reisetagebüchern*. Berlin.

(ed.) (1986/90) *Alexander von Humboldt: Reise auf dem Río Magdalena, durch die Anden und durch Mexico* (2 vols.). Berlin.

(ed.) (2000) *Alexander von Humboldt: Reise durch Venezuela. Auswahl aus den amerikanischen Reisetagebüchern*. Berlin.

Falola, T. and Childs, M. (eds.) (2004) *The Yoruba Diaspora in the Atlantic World*. Bloomington.

Faust, D. G. (ed.) (1981) *The Ideology of Slavery: Pro-Slavery Thought in the Antebellum South, 1830–1860*. Baton Rouge.

(1982) *James Henry Hammond and the Old South: A Design for Mastery*. Baton Rouge.

Fehrenbacher, D. E. (ed.) (1989a) *Abraham Lincoln: Speeches and Writings, 1832–1858*. New York.

(ed.) (1989b) *Abraham Lincoln: Speeches and Writings, 1859–1865*. New York.

Fenoaltea, S. (1984) 'Slavery and supervision in comparative perspective: a model', *Journal of Economic History* 44: 635–68.

Ferlini, V. L. A. (1988) *Terra, Trabalho e Poder. O mundo dos engenhos no Nordeste colonial*. São Paulo.

Ferrer, A. (2003a) 'Noticias de Haití en Cuba', *Revista de Indias* 63: 675–93.

(2003b) 'La société esclavagiste cubaine et la révolution haïtienne', *Annales HSS* 58: 333–56.

Fick, C. A. (1998) 'Dilemmas of emancipation: from the Saint Domingue insurrections of 1791 to the emerging Haitian state', *History Workshop Journal* 46: 1–15.

Fick, C. E. (2000) 'The Saint-Domingue slave insurrection of 1791: a socio-political and cultural analysis', in *Caribbean Slavery in the Atlantic World: A Student Reader*, ed. V. A. Shepherd and H. Beckles. Princeton: 961–82.

Field, D. (1976) *The End of Serfdom: Nobility and Bureaucracy in Russia, 1855–1861*. Cambridge, MA.

Figueira, T. J. (1981) *Aegina: Society and Politics*. New York.

(2003) 'The demography of the Spartan helots', in Luraghi and Alcock 2003: 193–239.

Findlay, R. (1975) 'Slavery, incentives, and manumission: a theoretical model', *Journal of Political Economy* 83: 923–34.

Fine, J. A. (1983) *The Ancient Greeks: A Critical History*. Cambridge, MA.

Finkelman, P. and Miller, J. C. (eds.) (1998) *Macmillan Encyclopedia of World Slavery*, vols. I–II. New York.

Finley, M. I. (1959) 'Was Greek civilization based on slave labour?', *Historia* 8: 145–64.

(1960) 'Was Greek civilization based on slave labor?', in *Slavery in Classical Antiquity*, ed. M. I. Finley. Cambridge: 141–54.

(1968) 'Slavery', in *International Encyclopedia of the Social Sciences*, ed. D. L. Sills. New York, vol. XIV: 307–13.

(1979) *The World of Odysseus*. London.

(1981) *Economy and Society in Ancient Greece*. London.

(1998 [1980]) *Ancient Slavery and Modern Ideology*. Princeton, 2nd edn.

(1999 [1973]) *The Ancient Economy*. Berkeley.

Fisher, N. R. E. (1993) *Slavery in Classical Greece*. London.

Fitzhugh, G. (1854) *Sociology for the South*. Richmond.

Fitzhugh, G. (1988 [1857]) *Cannibals All! Or Slaves without Masters*. Cambridge.

Fladeland, B. (1976) 'Compensated emancipation: a rejected alternative', *Journal of Southern History* 42: 169–86.

Fogel, R. W. (1989) *Without Consent or Contract: The Rise and Fall of American Slavery*. New York.

Fogel, R. W. and Engerman, S. L. (1974a) *Time on the Cross: The Economics of American Negro Slavery*. New York.

Fogel, R. W. and Engerman, S. L. (1974b) 'Philanthropy at bargain prices: notes on the economics of gradual emancipation', *Journal of Legal Studies* 3: 377–401.

Follett, R. J. (2005) *The Sugar Masters: Planters and Slaves in Louisiana's Cane World, 1820–1860*. Baton Rouge.

Foner, E. (1983) *Nothing but Freedom: Emancipation and its Consequences*. Baton Rouge.

Foner, L. and Genovese, E. D. (eds.) (1969) *Slavery in the New World: A Reader in Comparative History*. Englewood Cliffs.

Forbes, C. A. (1955) 'The education and training of slaves in antiquity', *Transactions of the American Philological Association* 86: 321–60.

Foucault, M. (1985) *Discipline and Punish: The Birth of Prison*. London.

Fox-Genovese, E. and Genovese, E. D. (1983) *The Fruits of Merchant Capital: Slavery and Bourgeois Property in the Rise and Expansion of Capitalism*. New York.

(2005) *The Mind of the Master Class: History and Faith in the Southern Slaveholders' Worldview*. New York.

Foxhall, L. (1990) 'The dependent tenant: land leasing and labour in Italy and Greece', *Journal of Roman Studies* 80: 97–114.

(1993) 'Oil extracting and processing equipment in classical Athens', in *La production du vin et de l'huile en Méditerranée*, ed. M.-C. Amouretti and J.-P. Brun. Paris: 183–99.

(2001) 'Access to resources in classical Greece: the egalitarianism of the Greek polis in practice', in *Money, Labour and Land in Ancient Greece*, ed. P. Cartledge, E. Cohen and L. Foxhall. London: 209–20.

Foy, D. and Nenna, M.-D. (2003) *Echanges et commerce du verre dans le monde antique*. Montagnac.

Fraginals, M. M. (1978) *El Ingenio. Complejo económico social cubano del azúcar* (3 vols.). La Habana.

(1983) *La historia como arma y otros estudios sobre esclavos, ingenios y plantaciones*. Barcelona.

(1986) 'Peculiaridades de la esclavitud en Cuba', *Islas* 85: 3–12.

Frankfort, T. (1959) 'Les classes serviles en Étrurie', *Latomus* 18: 3–22.

Franklin (1844) 'Overseers', *Carolina Planter* 1: 25–6.

Franklin, J. H. and Schweninger, L. (1999) *Runaway Slaves: Rebels on the Plantation*. New York.

Fredrickson, G. (1981) *White Supremacy: A Comparative Study of the United States and South Africa*. New York.

Freehling, W. W. (1994) *The Reintegration of American History: Slavery and the Civil War*. New York.

Freitag, U. (2005) 'Translokalität als ein Zugang zur Geschichte globaler Verflechtungen'. [http://geschichte-transnational.clio-online.net/forum/2005-06-001]

Freyre, G. (1946 [1933]) *The Masters and the Slaves: A Study in the Development of Brazilian Civilization*. New York.

Frier, B. W. (2000) 'Demography', in *Cambridge Ancient History*, vol. XI, ed. A. K. Bowman, P. Garnsey and D. Rathbone. Cambridge, 2nd edn: 787–816.

(2001) 'More is worse: some observations on the population of the Roman empire', in *Debating Roman Demography*, ed. W. Scheidel. Leiden: 139–59.

Fuente, A. de la (2004a) 'Slave law and claims-making in Cuba: the Tannenbaum debate revisited', *Law and History Review* 22: 339–69.

(2004b) 'Sugar and slavery in early colonial Cuba', in *Tropical Babylons*, ed. S. B. Schwartz. Chapel Hill: 115–57.

(ed.)(2004c) 'Su "único derecho": los esclavos y la ley', *Debate y Perspectivas: Cuadernos de Historia y Ciencias Sociales* 4.

(2006) 'Slaves and the creation of rights in Cuba: *Coartación* and *Papel*'. Unpublished paper presented at the University of Pittsburgh.

Gage, R. G. (1857) 'Plantation hygiene', *Farmer and Planter* 8: 25–31, reprinted in Breeden 1980: 132–3.

Galbraith, J. K. (1984) *The Anatomy of Power*. London.

Gallenga, A. C. N. (1873) *The Pearl of the Antilles*. London.

Games, A. (2006) 'Atlantic history: definitions, challenges, opportunities', *American Historical Review* 111: 741–57.

Gareth, A. (2005) *Labour, Land and Capital in Ghana: From Slavery to Free Labor in Asante, 1807–1956*. Rochester.

Garlan, Y. (1988) *Slavery in Ancient Greece*. Ithaca.

(1995) *Les esclaves en Grèce ancienne*. Paris.

Garnsey, P. (1988) *Famine and Food Supply in the Greco-Roman World*. Cambridge.

(1996) *Ideas of Slavery from Aristotle to Augustine*. Cambridge.

(1998) *Cities, Peasants and Food in Classical Antiquity: Essays in Social and Economic History*, ed. with addenda W. Scheidel. Cambridge.

Garnsey, P. and Saller, R. (1987) *The Roman Empire: Economy, Society and Culture*. London.

Geggus, D. P. (1987) 'The enigma of Jamaica in the 1790s: new light on the causes of slave rebellions', *William and Mary Quarterly* 44: 274–99.

(1997) 'Slavery, war, and revolution in the Greater Caribbean, 1789–1815', in *A Turbulent Time: The French Revolution and the Greater Caribbean*, ed. D. B. Gaspar and D. P. Geggus. Bloomington: 1–50.

(ed.) (2001) *The Impact of the Haitian Revolution in the Atlantic World*, Columbia: University of South Carolina Press.

(2003) 'The influence of the Haitian revolution on Blacks in Latin America and the Caribbean', in *Blacks, Coloureds and National Identity in Nineteenth-Century Latin America*, ed. P. N. Naro. London: 38–59.

Genovese, E. D. (1965) *The Political Economy of Slavery: Studies in the Economy and Society of the Slave South*. New York.

(1969) *The World the Slaveholders Made: Three Essays in Interpretation*. New York.

(1974) *Roll, Jordan, Roll: The World that Slaves Made*. New York.

(1979) *From Rebellion to Revolution: Afro-American Slave Rebellions in the Making of the Modern World*. Baton Rouge.

(1992) 'Our family, white and black: family and household in the Southern slaveholders' world view', in *In Joy and in Sorrow: Women in the Victorian South*, ed. C. Bleser. New York: 69–87.

Gibbons, D. (2001) 'Shipwrecks and Hellenistic trade', in *Hellenistic Economies*, ed. Z. H. Archibald *et al.* London: 273–312.

Gill, D. (1983) 'Tuscan sharecropping in united Italy: the myth of class collaboration destroyed', *Journal of Peasant Studies* 10: 146–69.

Gilmore, A.-T. (ed.) (1978) *Revisiting Blassingame's The Slave Community: The Scholars Respond*. Westport.

Gilroy, P. (1993) *The Black Atlantic: Modernity and Double Consciousness*. London.

Glancey, J. A. (2002) *Slavery in Early Christianity*. New York.

Godelier, M. (1977) 'Infrastructure, société, histoire', *Dialectiques* 21.

Golden, M. (1992) 'The uses of cross-cultural comparison in ancient social history', *Echos de Monde Classique/ Classical Views* 11: 309–31.

Goldschmidt, W. (1979) 'A general model of pastoral social systems', in *Pastoral Production and Society*, ed. L'equipe Ecologie et Anthropologie des Sociétés Pastorales. Cambridge: 15–27.

Gomes, F. D. S. (2002) 'A 'safe heaven': runaway slaves, Mocambos and borders in Colonial Amazonia, Brazil', *Hispanic American Historical Review* 3: 469–98.

Gomes, Flávio D. S. (1999) 'Fronteras e mocambos: o protesto negro na Guiana brasileira', in *Nas Terras do Cabo Norte. Fronteiras, colonização e escravidão na Guiana Brasileira – séculos VVIII/XIX*, ed. F. D. S. Gomes. Belém: 225–318.

(2003a) *Experiências atlânticas. Ensaios e pesquisas sobre a escravidão o pós-emancipação no Brasil.* Passo Fundo.

(2003b) 'Other Black Atlantic borders: escape routes, Mocambos, and fears of sedition in Brazil and French Guiana (eighteenth to nineteenth centuries)', *New West Indian Guide* 77: 253–87.

Gomez, M. A. (1998) *Exchanging our Country Marks: The Transformation of African Identities in the Colonial and Antebellum South*. Chapel Hill.

Gonzalez Ripoll, M.-D. *et al.* (eds.) (2005) *El rumor de Haiti en Cuba. Temor, raza y rebeldia, 1789–1844*. Madrid.

González-Ripoll Navarro, M.-D. (1999) *Cuba, la isla de los ensayos: cultura y sociedad, 1790–1815*. Madrid.

(2001) 'Vínculos y redes de poder entre Madrid y La Habana: Francisco de Arango y Parreño (1765–1837), ideólogo y mediador', *Revista de Indias* 61: 291–305.

(2002) 'Dos viajes, una intención: Francisco de Arango y Alejandro Olivan en Europa y las Antillas azucareras (1794 y 1829)', *Revista de Indias* 62: 85–101.

Goody, J. (1980) 'Slavery in time and space', in *Asian and African Systems of Slavery*, ed. J. L. Watson. Oxford: 16–42.

Goody, J. and Tambiah, S. J. (1973) *Bridewealth and Dowry*. New York.

Gordon, M. (1990) *Slavery in the Arab World*. New York.

Graham, R. (2004) 'Another middle passage? The internal slave trade in Brazil', in *The Chattel Principle: Internal Slave Trades in the Americas*, ed. Walter Johnson. New Haven: 291–324.

Green, J. (1779) *A Sermon Delivered at Hanover*, reprinted in Bruns 1977: 432–40.

Green, K. (2000) 'Technological innovation and economic progress in the ancient world: M. I. Finley reconsidered', *Economic History Review* 53: 29–59.

Green, W. A. (1976) *British Slave Emancipation: The Sugar Colonies and the Great Experiment, 1830–1865*. Oxford.

Greenidge, C. W. W. (1958) *Slavery*. London.

Greif, A. and Laitin, D. (1984) 'A theory of endogenous institutional change', *American Political Science Review* 98: 633–52.

Griffeth, R. (2002) 'The Hausa city-states from 1450 to 1804', in Hansen 2002c: 482–506.

Gunmere, R. M. (1963) *The American Colonial Mind and the Classical Tradition: Essays in Comparative Culture*. Cambridge, MA.

Hahn, S. (2003) *A Nation Under Our Feet: Black Political Struggles in the Rural South from Slavery to the Great Migration*. Cambridge, MA.

Hall, G. M. (1971) *Social Control in Slave Plantation Societies: A Comparison of St. Domingue and Cuba*. Baltimore.

(1972) *Social Control in Slave Plantation Societies: A Comparison of Saint Domingue and Cuba*. Baton Rouge.

(2006) *Slavery and African Ethnicities in the Americas: Restoring the Links*. Chapel Hill.

Hammond, J. H. (1840–50) 'Governor Hammond's instructions to his Overseer', reprinted in Rose 1976: 345–54.

(1842) 'Letter to an English Abolitionist', reprinted in Faust 1981: 168–205.

Hanes, C. (1996) 'Turnover cost and the distribution of slave labor in Anglo-America', *Journal of Economic History* 56: 307–29.

Hannaford, I. (1996) *Race: The History of an Idea in the West*. Baltimore.

Hansen, M. H. (1985) *Demography and Democracy: The Number of Athenian Citizens in the Fourth Century BC*. Systime.

(1988) *Three Studies in Athenian Demography*. Copenhagen.

(2002a) 'The concepts of city-state and city-state culture', in Hansen 2002c: 11–34.

(2002b) 'Conclusion: the impact of city-state cultures on world history', in Hansen 2002c: 598–623.

(ed.) (2002c) *A Comparative Study of Thirty City-State Cultures: An Investigation Conducted by the Copenhagen Polis Centre*. Copenhagen.

Hanson, C. (1986) *Economia e Sociedade no Portugal Barroco, 1668–1703*. Lisboa.

Hanson, V. (1995) *The Other Greeks: Family Farm and the Agrarian Roots of Western Civilization*. New York.

Harms, R. (1981) *River of Wealth, River of Sorrow: The Central Zaire Basin in the Era of the Slave Trade and the Ivory Trade, 1500–1891*. New Haven.

Harris, E. M. (2002) 'Did Solon abolish debt-bondage?', *Classical Quarterly* 52: 415–30.

Harris. G. (1972) 'Taita bridewealth and affinal relationships', in *Marriage in Tribal Societies*, ed. M. Fortes. Cambridge: 55–87.

Harris, W. (1999) 'Demography, geography and the sources of Roman slaves', *Journal of Roman Studies* 89: 62–75.

(1971) *Rome in Etruria and Umbria*. Oxford.

(ed.) (2005) *Rethinking the Mediterranean*. Oxford.

Harrison, A. and Spencer, N. (1998) 'After the palace: the early "history" of Messenia', in *Sandy Pylos: An Archaeological History from Nestor to Navarino*, ed. J. L. Davis. Austin: 147–62.

Harrison, W. H. (1840) 'Stoves for negroes' dwellings', *Farmers' Register* 8: 212–13.

Hart, L. (1775) *Thoughts on Abolition*, reprinted in Bruns 1977: 365–76.

Hassig, R. (1988) *Aztec Warfare: Imperial Expansion and Political Control*. Norman.

Haverkamp, A. (1974) 'Zur Sklaverei in Genua während des 12. Jahrhunderts', in *Geschichte in der Gesellschaft*, ed. F. Prinz, F.-J. Schmale and F. Seibt. Stuttgart: 160–215.

Hazard, W. W. (1831) 'On the general management of Negroes', *The Southern Agriculturalist* 4: 350–4.

Heers, J. (1981) *Esclaves domestiques au Moyen Age dans le monde méditerranéen*. Paris.

Hegel. G. W. F. (1961 [1807]) *The Phenomenology of Mind*. London.

Hellie, R. (1982) *Slavery in Russia, 1450–1725*. Chicago.

Hesseltine, W. B. (1960) *The South in American History*. Englewood Cliffs, 2nd edn.

Heuman, G. (ed.) (1986) *Out of the House of Bondage: Runaways, Resistance and Maroonage in Africa and in the New World*. London.

Heywood, L. (ed.) (2002) *Central Africans and Cultural Transformations in the American Diaspora*. Cambridge and New York.

Hicks, J. (1969) *A Theory of Economic History*. Oxford.

Higman, B. W. (2002) 'Plantagensklaverei in Nord-Amerika und der Karibik', *Zeitschrift für Weltgeschichte* 3: 9–23.

Hill, P. (1976) 'From slavery to freedom: the case of farm slavery in Nigerian Hausaland', *Comparative Studies in Society and History* 18: 395–426.

(1985) 'Comparative west African farm-slavery systems (south of the Sahel) with special reference to Muslim Kano Emirate (N. Nigeria)', in *Slaves and Slavery in Muslim Africa, II: The Servile Estate*, ed. J. R. Willis. London: 33–50.

Hilton, R. (1969) *The Decline of Serfdom in Medieval England*. London.

Hobhouse. L. T. (1992) *The Material Culture and Social Institutions of the Simpler Peoples*. London.

Hobsbawm, E. J. (1959) *Primitive Rebels: Studies in Archaic Forms of Social Movement in the 19th and 20th Centuries*. Manchester.

(1969) *Bandits*. London.

Hoch, S. (1986) *Serfdom and Social Control in Russia: Petrovskoe, a Village in Tambov*. Chicago.

(1996) 'The serf economy and the social order in Russia', in Bush 1996a: 311–22.

Hodes, M. (2003) 'The mercurial nature and abiding power of race: a transnational family story', *American Historical Review* 108: 84–118.

Hodgson, M. C. S. and Burke III, E. (eds.) (1993) *Rethinking World History: Essays on Europe, Islam, and World History*. New York.

Hodkinson, S. (1992) 'Sharecropping and Sparta's economic exploitation of the helots', in *FILOLAKWN. Lakonian Studies in Honour of Hector Catling*, ed. J. M. Sanders. London: 123–34.

(1993) 'Warfare, wealth, and the crisis of Spartiate society', in *War and Society in the Greek World*, ed. J. Rich and G. Shipley. London: 146–76.

(1997) 'Servile and free dependants of the classical Spartan *oikos*', in *Schiavi e Dipendenti nell'Ambito dell'Oikos e della Familia*, ed. M. Moggi and G. Cordiano. Pisa: 45–71.

(1999) 'An agonistic culture? Athletic competition in archaic and classical Spartan society', in *Sparta: New Perspectives*, ed. S. Hodkinson and A. Powell. London: 147–87.

(2000) *Property and Wealth in Classical Sparta*. London.

(2003) 'Spartiates, Helots and the direction of the agrarian economy: towards an understanding of Helotage in comparative perspective', in Luraghi and Alcock 2003: 248–85.

Hogendorn, J. S. (1977) 'The economics of slave use on two plantations in the Zaria Emirate of the Sokoto Caliphate', *Journal of International African Historical Studies* 10: 369–83.

Holm, P. (1986) 'The slave trade of Dublin, ninth to twelfth centuries', *Peritia* 5: 317–45.

(2000) 'Viking Dublin and the city-state concept: parameters and significance of the Hiberno-Norse settlement', in Hansen 2000c: 251–62.

Holt, T. C. (1992) *The Problem of Freedom: Race, Labor, and Politics in Jamaica, 1832–1938*. Baltimore.

Hopkins, A. (ed.) (2002) *Globalization in World History*. New York.

Hopkins, K. (1978) *Conquerors and Slaves*. Cambridge.

(1995/6) 'Rome, taxes, rents and trade', *Kodai* 6/7: 41–75, reprinted in Scheidel and Von Reden 2002: 190–230.

Hopkins, S. (1776) *A Dialogue Concerning the Slavery of the Africans*, reprinted in Bruns 1977: 397–426.

Horden, P. and Purcell, N. (2000) *The Corrupting Sea: A Study of Mediterranean History*. Oxford.

(2006) 'The Mediterranean and the "New Thalassology"', *American Historical Review* 111: 722–40.

Hornblower, S. (ed.) (1996) *A Commentary on Thucydides, II: Books IV–V.24*. Oxford.

Howard, P. A. (1998) *Changing History: Afro-Cuban Cabildos and Societies of Color in the Nineteenth Century*. Baton Rouge.

Humboldt, A. von (1804) 'Isle de Cube', *Biblioteka Jagiellońska*. Krakow: 1159–61.

(1826a) 'Cuba-Werk', in *Alexander von Humboldt: Studienausgabe. Sieben Bände*, ed. H. Beck *et al.* (1992). Darmstadt: vol. III.

(1826b) *Essai Politique sur l'Ile de Cuba, avec une carte et un supplément qui renferme des considérations sur la population, la richesse territoriale et le commerce de l'Archipel des Antilles et de Colombia* (2 vols.). Paris.

Hunt, P. (1998) *Slaves, Warfare, and Ideology in the Greek Historians*. Cambridge.

Hutcheson, F. (1968 [1755]) *A System of Moral Philosophy*, vol. II. New York.

Irwin, J. (1988) 'Exploring the affinity of wheat and slavery in the Virginia Piedmont', *Explorations in Economic History* 25: 295–322.

Jacoby, H. G. (1995) 'The economics of polygyny in Sub-Saharan Africa: female productivity and the demand for wives in the Cote d'Ivoire', *Journal of Political Economy* 103: 938–71.

Jameson, M. H. (1992) 'Agricultural labor in ancient Greece', in *Agriculture in Ancient Greece*, ed. B. Wells. Stockholm: 135–46.

(2001) 'On Paul Cartledge, "The political economy of Greek slavery"', in *Money, Labour and Land*, ed. P. Cartledge, E. Cohen and L. Foxhall. London: 167–74.

Jameson, M. H. (1977) 'Agriculture and slavery in classical Athens', *Classical Journal* 73: 122–45.

Jameson, M. H., Runnels, C. N. and Van Andel, T. H. (1994) *A Greek Countryside: The Southern Argolid from Prehistory to the Present Day*. Stanford.

Jasny, N. (1950) 'The daily bread of the Ancient Greeks and Romans', *Osiris* 9: 227–53.

Jay, P. (ed.) (1973) *The Greek Anthology*. London.

Jeffery, L. H. (1990) *The Local Scripts of Archaic Greece*. Oxford, 2nd edn.

Jew, D. (1999) 'Food, Silver, Trade and Liturgies: Modeling the Athenian Economy'. M.Phil. thesis, Cambridge.

Johnson, W. (1999) *Soul by Soul: Life Inside the Antebellum Slave Market*. Cambridge, MA.

(2001) 'Time and revolution in African America: temporality and the history of Atlantic slavery', in *Rethinking American History in a Global Age*, ed. T. Bender. Berkeley: 148–67.

(2003) 'On agency', *Journal of Social History* 37: 113–24.

(ed.) (2004) *The Chattel Principle: Internal Slave Trades in the Americas*. New Haven.

Jok, M. J. (2001) *War and Slavery in the Sudan*. Philadelphia.

Jones, A. (1981) 'Theophile Conneau at Galinhas and New Sestos, 1836–1841: a comparison of the sources', *History in Africa* 8: 89–106.

Jones, A. H. M. (1956) 'Slavery in the ancient world', *Economic History Review* 9: 185–99.

Jones, J. (1985) *Labor of Love, Labor of Sorrow: Black Women, Work and the Family from Slavery to the Present*. New York.

Jones, N. T. Jr (1990) *Born a Child of Freedom, Yet a Slave: Mechanisms of Control and Strategies of Resistance in Antebellum South Carolina*. Hanover.

Jones, P. V. (ed.) (1984) *The World of Athens*. Cambridge.

Jongman, W. (2003) 'Slavery and the growth of Rome: the transformation of Italy in the second and first centuries BCE', in *Rome the Cosmopolis*, ed. C. Edwards and G. Woolf. Cambridge: 100–22.

Jumare, I. M. (1996) 'The ideology of slavery in the context of Islam and the Sokoto Jihad', *Islamic Quarterly* 40: 31–8.

Kaltsas, N. (1983) 'ἡ ἀρχαῖκη ὀικιά στõ κορανάκι τῆς μεσσηνιάς', 'Αρχαιολογικη 'Εφημερις: 207–37.

Karasch, M. (1987) *Slave Life in Rio de Janeiro 1808–1850*. New Jersey.

(2000) *A vida dos escravos no Rio de Janeiro (1808–1850)*. São Paulo.

Karras, R. M. (1988) *Slavery and Society in Medieval Scandinavia*. New Haven.

Kellenbenz, H. (1966) 'Deutsche Plantagenbesitzer und Kaufleute in Surinam vom Ende des 18. Jahrhunderts', *Jahrbuch für Geschichte von Staat, Wirtschaft und Gesellschaft Lateinamerikas* 3: 152–74.

Kilson, M. L. and Rotberg, R. I. (1986) *The African Diaspora*. Cambridge, MA.

Kingston-Mann, E. (1999) *In Search of the True West: Culture, Economics and Problems of Russian Development*. Princeton.

Kirschenbaum, A. (1987) *Sons, Slaves, and Freedmen in Roman Commerce*. Jerusalem.

Klees, H. (1975) *Herren und Sklaven: Die Sklaverei im oikonomischen und politischen Schriftum der Griechen in klassicher Zeit*. Wiesbaden.

(1998) *Sklavenleben im klassischen Griechenland*. Stuttgart.

Klein, H. (1967) *Slavery in the Americas: A Comparative Study of Virginia and Cuba*. Chicago.

(1986) *African Slavery in Latin America and the Caribbean*. New York.

(1994) 'Slavery, the international labour market and the emancipation of slaves in the nineteenth century', *Slavery & Abolition* 15: 197–220.

(1999) *The Atlantic Slave Trade*. New York.

(2002) 'El comercio atlántico de esclavos en el siglo XIX y el suministro de mano de obra a Cuba y Brasil', in *Azúcar y esclavitud en el final del trabajo forzado. Homenaje a M. Moreno Fraginals*, ed. J. A. Piqueras. México: 37–49.

Klein, M. A. (1983) 'Women in slavery in the Western Sudan', in *Women and Slavery in Africa*, ed. C. C. Robertson and M. A. Klein. Madison: 67–94.

(1998) *Slavery and Colonial Rule in French West Africa*. New York.

(2002) *Historical Dictionary of Slavery and Abolition*. Lanham.

Klein, M. and Lovejoy, P. E. (1979) 'Slavery in west Africa', in *The Uncommon Market: Essays in the Economic History of the Atlantic Slave Trade*, ed. H. A. Gemery and J. S. Hagendorn. New York: 181–212.

Kojeve. A. (1969) *Introduction to the Reading of Hegel*. New York.

Kolchin, P. (1987) *Unfree Labor: American Slavery and Russian Serfdom*. Cambridge, MA.

(1990) 'Some thoughts on emancipation in comparative perspective: Russia and the United States South', *Slavery & Abolition* 11: 351–67.

(1996) 'Some controversial questions concerning nineteenth-century emancipation from slavery and serfdom', in Bush 1996a: 42–67.

(1999) 'After serfdom: Russian emancipation in comparative perspective', in Engerman. 1999: 87–115.

(2000) 'The Big Picture: a comment on David Brion Davis' "Looking at slavery from broader perspectives"', *American Historical Review* 105: 467–71.

(2003a) *A Sphinx on the American Land: The Nineteenth-Century South in Comparative Perspective*. Baton Rouge.

(2003b) *American Slavery, 1619–1877*. New York, 2nd edn.

Kolendo, J. (1971) 'Les esclaves employés dans les vignobles de l'Italie antique', in *Acta Conventus Eirene XI*. Bratislave: 33–40.

Konetzke, R. (ed.) (1958–62) *Colección de Documentos para la Historia de la Formación Social de Hispanoamérica, 1493–1810*. Madrid: vol. III.

Korotayev, A. (2001) 'An apologia of George Peter Murdock. Division of Labor by gender and postmarital residence in cross-cultural perspective: A reconsideration', *World Cultures* 12: 179–203.

Koselleck, R. (1993) *Futuro Pasado: Para una Semántica de los Tiempos Históricos.* Barcelona.

Koshiba, L. (1988) 'A Honra e a Cobiça. Estudo sobre a Origem da Colonização'. Ph.D. thesis, University of São Paulo.

Kuethe, A. J. (1998) 'La fidelidad cubana durante la edad de las revoluciones', *Anuario de Estudios Americanos* 55: 209–20.

Kuitenbrouwer, M. (1995) 'The Dutch case of antislavery: late abolitions and elitist abolitionism', in Oostindie 1995: 67–88.

Kula, W. (1976 [1962]) *An Economic Theory of the Feudal System: Towards a Model of the Polish Economy, 1500–1800.* London.

Kyrtatas, D. J. (2001) 'Domination and exploitation', in *Money, Labour and Land*, ed. P. Cartledge, E. Cohen and L. Foxhall. London: 140–55.

La Fontaine, J. (1972) 'Gisu marriage and affinal relations' in *Marriage in Tribal Societies*, ed. Fortes. Cambridge: 88–120.

La Rosa Corzo, G. (2003) *Runaway Slave Settlements in Cuba: Resistance and Repression.* Chapel Hill.

Labrousse, E. (1990 [1945]) *La crise de l'économie française à la fin de l'Ancien Régime et au début de la Révolution.* Paris.

Lamounier, L. (1995) 'Early experiments with free labour & patterns of slave emancipation in Brazil & Cuba', in *From Chattel Slaves to Wage Slaves: The Dynamics of Labour Bargaining in the Americas*, ed. Mary Turner. London: 185–200.

Landers, J. G. (1999) *Black Society in Spanish Florida.* Urbana.

(2000a) 'Cimarrón ethnicity and cultural adaptation in the Spanish domains of the Circum-Caribbean, 1503–1763', in *Identity in the Shadow of Slavery*, ed. P. Lovejoy. London: 30–54.

(ed.) (2000b) *Colonial Plantations and Economy in Florida.* Gainesville.

Lara, S. H. (1996) 'Do singular ao plural: Palmares, Capitães-do-mato e o Governo dos Escravos', in *Liberdade por um Fio. História dos Quilombos no Brasil*, ed. J. J.Reis and F. dos S. Gomes. São Paulo: 81–109.

(ed.) (2000) *Legislação sobre Escravos Africanos na América Portuguesa*, in *Nuevas Aportaciones a la Historia Juridica de Iberoamerica.* Madrid.

Lassen, E. M. (1997) 'The Roman family: ideal and metaphor', in *Constructing Early Christian Families: Family as Social Reality and Metaphor*, ed. H. Moxnes. London: 103–20.

Law, R. (1997) 'Ethnicity and the slave trade: 'Lucumi' and 'Nago' as ethnonyms in West Africa', *History in Africa* 24: 205–19.

(2001) 'The evolution of the Brazilian community in Ouidah', *Slavery and Abolition* 22: 22–41.

Lazenby, J. F. (1997) 'The conspiracy of Kinadon reconsidered', *Athenaeum* 85: 437–47.

Lazenby, J. F. and Hope Simpson, R. (1972) 'Greco-Roman times: literary tradition and topographical commentary', in McDonald and Rapp 1972: 81–99.

Le Roy Ladurie, E. (1979) *Carnival in Romans.* New York.

Lee, O. (1857) 'The laborer, his rights and duties', *De Bow's Review* 22: 486–91.

Legare, J. D. (1833) 'Account of an agricultural excursion made into the South of Georgia in the winter of 1832', *The Southern Agriculturalist* 6: 359–416.

Legon, R. P. (1981) *Megara: The Political History of a Greek City-State to 338 B.C.* Ithaca.

Leitner, U. (2002) '"Anciennes folies neptuniennes!" about the rediscovered "Journal du Mexique à Veracruz" from the Mexican travel chronicles of Alexander von Humboldt', *International Review for Humboldtian Studies* 3. [www.uni-potsdam.de/u/romanistik/Humboldt]

(ed.) (2005) *Alexander von Humboldt: Von Mexiko-Stadt nach Veracruz. Tagebuch.* Berlin.

Lengellé, M. (1998) *L'esclavage.* Paris, 2nd edn.

Leveau, P. (1996) 'The Barbegal water mill in its environment', *Journal of Roman Archaeology* 9: 137–53.

Lewis, E. (1995) 'To turn as on a pivot: writing African Americans into a history of overlapping Diasporas', *American Historical Review* 100: 765–87.

Leyburn, J. G. (1941) *The Haitian People.* New Haven.

Lienhard, M. (2001) *Le discours des esclaves de l'Afrique à l'Amérique latine (Kongo, Angola, Brésil, Caraïbes).* Paris.

Lind, M. D. (2002) 'Mixtec city-states and Mixtec city-state culture', in Hansen 2002c: 567–80.

Linebaugh, P. and Rediker, M. (2000) *The Many-Headed Hydra: Sailors, Slaves, Commoners, and the Hidden History of the Revolutionary Atlantic.* Boston.

Long, P. O. (1991) 'Invention, authorship, "intellectual property" and the origin of patents', *Technology and Culture* 32: 846–84.

Loomis, W. T. (1998) *Wages, Welfare Costs and Inflation in Classical Athens.* Ann Arbor.

Lotze, D. (1959) *METAXU ELEUQEPWN KAI DOULWN: Studien zur Rechtsstellung unfreier Landbevölkerung in Griechenland bis zum 4. Jahrhundert v. Chr.* Berlin.

Lovejoy, P. E. (1978) 'Plantations in the economy of the Sokoto Caliphate', *Journal of African History* 19: 341–68.

(1979) 'The characteristics of plantations in the nineteenth-century Sokoto caliphate (Islamic West Africa)', *American Historical Review* 84: 1267–92.

(1981) 'Slavery in the Sokoto caliphate', in *The Ideology of Slavery in Africa*, ed. P. E. Lovejoy. London: 201–43.

(1997) 'Biography as source material: towards a biographical archive of enslaved Africans', in *Source Material for Studying the Slave Trade and the African Diaspora*, ed. R. Law. Stirling: 119–40.

(2000a) 'Identifying enslaved Africans in the African Diaspora' in *Identity in the Shadow of Slavery*, ed. P. Lovejoy. London: 1–29.

(2000b [1983]) *Transformations in Slavery: A History of Slavery in Africa.* Cambridge, 2nd edn.

(2004a) 'Muslim freedmen in the Atlantic World: images of manumission and self-redemption', in *Slavery on the Frontiers of Islam*, ed. P. Lovejoy. Princeton: 233–62.

(2004b) 'Slavery, the Bilād al-Sūdān, and the frontiers of the African Diaspora', in *Slavery on the Frontiers of Islam*, ed. P. Lovejoy. Princeton: 1–29.

(2004c) 'The Yoruba factor in the Trans-Atlantic slave trade', in *The Yoruba Diaspora in the Atlantic World*, ed. T. Falola and M. Childs. Bloomington: 40–55.

(2005) *Slavery, Commerce and Production in the Sokoto Caliphate of West Africa*. Trenton.

Lovejoy, P. and Hogendorn, J. (1993) *Slow Death for Slavery: The Course of Abolition in Northern Nigeria, 1897–1936*. Cambridge.

Lovejoy, P. and Law, R. (1997) 'The changing dimensions of African history: Reappropriating the Diaspora', in *Rethinking African History*, ed. S. McGrath *et al.* Edinburgh: 181–200.

Lovejoy, P. and Trotman, D. V. (2002) *Trans-Atlantic Dimensions of Ethnicity in the African Diaspora*. London.

Lukermann, F. E. and Moody, J. (1978) 'Nichoria and vicinity: settlement and circulation', in *Excavations in Nichoria in Southwest Greece I: Site, Environs and Techniques*, ed. G. Rapp, Jr and S. Aschenbrenner. Minneapolis: 78–112.

Luraghi, N. (2002a) 'Helotic slavery reconsidered', in *Sparta: Beyond the Mirage*, ed. A. Powell and S. Hodkinson. London: 227–48.

(2002b) 'Becoming Messenian' *Journal of Hellenic Studies* 122: 45–69.

(2003) 'The imaginary conquest of the helots', in Luraghi and Alcock 2003: 109–41.

Luraghi, N. and Alcock, S. (eds.) (2003) *Helots and their Masters in Laconia and Messenia: Histories, Ideologies, Structures*, Cambridge, MA.

MacCormack, C. P. (1977) 'Wono: institutionalised dependency in Sherbro descent groups (Sierra Leone)', in *Slavery in Africa: Historical and Anthropological Perspectives*, ed. S. Myers and I. Kopytoff. Madison: 181–203.

(1983) 'Slaves, slave owners and slave dealers: Sherbro coast and hinterland', in *Women and Slavery in Africa*, ed. C. C. Robertson and M. A. Klein. Madison: 271–94.

MacDowell, D. M. (1986) *Spartan Law*. Edinburgh.

MacMullen, R. (1987) 'Late Roman slavery', *Historia* 36: 359–82.

Madden, R. (1849) *The Island of Cuba: Its Resources, Progress, etc., in Relation Especially to the Influence of its Prosperity on the Interests of the British West India Colonies*. London.

Malanima, P. (1988) *I piedi di legno. Una macchina alle origini dell'industria medievale*. Milan.

Mann, K. (2001) 'Shifting paradigms in the study of the African diaspora and of Atlantic history and culture', *Slavery and Abolition* 22: 3–21.

Mann, M. (2003) 'Die Mär von der freien Lohnarbeit. Menschenhandel und erzwungene Arbeit in der Neuzeit. Ein einleitender Essay', in *Menschenhandel und unfreie Arbeit*, ed. M. Mann. Leipzig: 7–22.

Manning, P. (1990) *Slavery and African Life: Occidental Oriental and African Slave Trades*. Cambridge.

Marcílio, M. L. (1987) 'The population of colonial Brazil', in *The Cambridge History of Latin America*, ed. Leslie Bethell. Cambridge: vol. II: 37–63.

Marmon, S. E. (1999) 'Domestic slavery in the Mamluk Empire: a preliminary sketch', in *Slavery in the Islamic Middle East*, ed. S. E. Marmon. Princeton: 1–24.

Marquese, R. de Bivar. (1999) *Administração & Escravidão: Idéias sobre a Gestão da Agricultura Escravista Brasileira*. São Paulo.

(2004) *Feitores do Corpo, Missionários da Mente. Senhores, Letrados e o Controle dos Escravos nas Américas, c.1660–1860*. São Paulo.

Marte, R. (1989) *Cuba y la República Dominicana. Transición económica en el Cariba del siglo XIX*. Santo Domingo.

Martin, R. (1974) 'Familia rustica: les esclaves chez les agronomes latins', *Annales Littéraires de l'Université de Besançon* 163: 267–97.

(1980) 'Du nouveau monde au monde antique: quelques problèmes de l'esclavage rural', *Ktema* 5: 161–75.

Martin, S. (1767) *An Essay on Plantership*. Antigua.

Martínez-Fernández, L. (2002) *Protestantism and Political Conflict in the Nineteenth-Century Hispanic Caribbean*. New Brunswick.

Marx, A. W. (1998) *Making Race and Nation: A Comparison of South Africa, the United States, and Brazil*. Cambridge.

Marx, Karl (1999 [1867–95]) *The Capital*. New York.

Mason, M. (1973) 'Captive and client labour and the economy of the Bida Emirate, 1857–1901', *Journal of African History* 14: 453–71.

Matory, J. L. (1999) 'The English professors of Brazil: on the diasporic roots of the Yorùbá nation', *Comparative Studies in Society and History* 41: 72–103.

Matsuda, M. K. (2006) 'The Pacific', *American Historical Review* 111: 758–80.

Mattingly, D. and Salmon, J. T. (eds.) (2001) *Economies beyond Agriculture in the Classical World*. London.

Mattingly, D. J. (1993) 'Maximum figures and maximising strategies of oil production? Further thoughts on the processing capacity of Roman olive presses', in *La production du vin et de l'huile*, ed. M.-C. Amouretti and J.-P. Brun. Athens: 483–98.

Mattos de Castro, H. M. (1988) 'Beyond masters and slaves: subsistence agriculture as a survival strategy in Brazil during the second half of the nineteenth century', *Reseña Histórica Hispano Americana* 68: 461–89.

(1995) 'El color inexistente: Relaciones raciales y trabajo rural en Río de Janeiro tras la abolición de la esclavitud', *Historia Social* 22: 83–100.

Mauro, F. (1987) 'Political and economic structures of Empire, 1580–1750', in *Colonial Brazil*, ed. L. Bethell. Cambridge: 39–66.

May, R. E. (1973) *The Southern Dream of a Caribbean Empire, 1854–1861*. Baton Rouge.

(ed.) (1995) *The North, the South, and the Atlantic Rim*. West Lafayette.

Mayers, R. (ed.) (1984) *The Children of Pride: A True Story of Georgia and the Civil War*. New Haven.

McDonald, R. A. (1993) *The Economy and Material Culture of Slaves: Goods and Chattels on the Sugar Plantations of Jamaica and Louisiana*. Baton Rouge.

McDonald, W. A. and Hope Simpson, R. (1972) 'Archaeological exploration', in McDonald and Rapp 1972: 117–47.

McDonald, W. A. and Rapp, G. R. Jr (eds.) (1972) *The Minnesota Messenia Expedition: Reconstructing a Bronze Age Regional Environment*. Minneapolis.

McDonald, W. A., Coulson, W. D. E. and Rosser, J. (eds.) (1983) *Excavations at Nichoria in Southwest Greece, III: Dark Age and Byzantine Occupation*. Minneapolis.

Meadows, D. R. (2000) 'Engineering exiles social networks and the French Atlantic community, 1789–1899', *French Historical Studies* 23: 67–102.

Meillassoux, C. (ed.) (1975) *L'esclavage en Afrique Precoloniale*. Paris.

(1983) *Women and Slavery in Africa*. Madison.

(1991) *The Anthropology of Slavery: The Womb of Iron and Gold*. Chicago.

Mello, E. C. de (1998) *O Negócio do Brasil. Portugal, os Países Baixos e o Nordeste, 1641–1669*. Rio de Janeiro.

Melton, E. (1993) 'Household economies and communal conflicts on a Russian serf estate, 1800–1817', *Journal of Social History* 26: 559–85.

Menard, R. and Schwartz, S. B. (1993) 'Why African slavery? Labor force transitions in Brazil, Mexico and the Carolina Lowcountry', in *Slavery in the Americas*, ed. W. Binder. Erlangen: 89–114.

Metzler, J. (1975) 'Rational management, modern business practices, and economies of scale in the ante-bellum southern plantations', *Explorations in Economic History* 12: 123–50.

Middell, M. (2000) 'Kulturtransfer und Historische Komparatistik–Thesen zu ihrem Verhältnis', in *Kulturtransfer und Vergleich*, ed. M. Middell. Leipzig: 7–40.

Miller, J. C. (1988) *Way of Death: Merchant Capitalism and the Angolan Slave Trade, 1730–1830*. Madison.

(1997) 'O Atlântico escravista: açúcar, escravos, e engenhos', *Afro-Ásia* 19–20: 9–36.

(1999a) 'History and Africa/Africa and History', *American Historical Review* 104: 1–32.

(ed.) (1999b) *Slavery and Slaving in World History: A Bibliography* (2 vols.). Armonk.

(2002a) 'Stratégies de marginalité. Une approche historique de l'utilisation des êtres humains et des ideologies de l'esclavage: progéniture, piété, protection personelle et prestige – produit et profits des propriétaires', in *Déraison, esclavage et droit: les fondements idéologiques et juridiques de la traite négrière et de l'esclavage*, ed. I. C. Henriques and L. Sala-Molins. Paris: 105–60.

(2002b) 'The historical contexts of slavery in Europe', in *Slavery Across Time and Space: Studies in Slavery in Medieval Europe and Africa*, ed. P. O. Hernaes and T. Iversen. Trondheim: 1–57.

(2003a) 'Meanings of resistance in the various contexts of enslavement', Unpublished paper, Conference on 'Resistance and Accommodation', University of Nottingham, Institute for the Study of Slavery, 8–10 September 2003.

(2003b) 'Retention, re-invention, and remembering: restoring identities through enslavement in Africa and under slavery in Brazil', in *Enslaving*

Connections: Changing Cultures of Africa and Brazil during the Era of Slavery, ed. J. C. Curto and P. E. Lovejoy. Amherst: 81–121.

(2004a) 'Abolition as discourse: slavery as civic abomination', Unpublished paper, Conference on 'Discourse of Abolition', University of Nottingham, Institute for the Study of Slavery, 13–15 September, 2004.

(2004b) 'Africans' experiences of enslavement and colonialism in the Atlantic World', Unpublished plenary address, Symposium on 'Enslavement and Colonialism in the Atlantic World', Miami University, 2–3 April 2004.

(2004c) 'Slaving and colonialism', *Journal of Colonialism and Colonial History* 5. [http://muse.jhu.edu/journals/cch]

(2005) 'The integrities of history in Africa', Unpublished paper, University of Wisconsin, Madison, 11–13 March 2005.

(2007a) *Slavery*. Boston.

(2007b), 'Slavery', *Encyclopedia Britannica*. London.

(2007c) 'Introduction: females in slavery, facing freedom, owning women, and facing women others own. Women's experiences from Africa, the Indian Ocean world, and the early Atlantic' in *Women and Slavery*, eds. G. Campbell, S. Miers, and J. C. Miller. Athens, vol. 1.

Mintz, S. (1985) *Sweetness and Power: The Place of Sugar in Modern History*. New York.

(1996) 'Models of emancipation during the Age of Revolution', *Slavery and Abolition* 17: 1–21.

Mintz, S. W. and Price, R. (1992) *The Birth of African-American Culture: An Anthropological Perspective*. Boston.

Mirzai, B. (2004) 'Slavery, the abolition of the slave trade and the emancipation of slaves in Iran (1828–1928)'. Ph.D. thesis, York University.

Moheit, U. (ed.) (1993) *Humboldt: Briefe aus Amerika 1799–1804*. Berlin.

Mokyr, J. (1992) 'Technological inertia in economic history', *Journal of Economic History* 52: 325–38.

Moon, D. (1999) *The Russian Peasantry 1600–1930: The World the Peasants Made*. London.

Morgan, P. D. (1983) 'Black society in the Lowcountry, 1760–1810', in *Slavery and Freedom in the Age of the American Revolution*, ed. I. Berlin and R. Hoffman. Charlottesville: 83–141.

(1998) *Slave Counterpoint: Black Culture in the Eighteenth-Century Chesaspeake & Lowcountry*. Chapel Hill.

Morley, N. (1996) *Metropolis and Hinterland: The City of Rome and the Italian Economy 200 B.C. – A.D. 200*. Cambridge.

Mörner, M. (1992) 'Labor systems and patterns of social stratification in colonial America: North and South', in *Nord und Süd in Amerika. Gegensätze. Gemeinsamkeiten. Europäischer Hintergrund*, ed. W. Reinhard and P. Waldmann. Freiburg: vol. 1: 347–63.

(1993) 'African slavery in Spanish and Portuguese America: some remarks on historiography and the present state of research', in *Slavery in the Americas*, ed. W. Binder. Erlangen: 57–87.

Morris, I. (1988) 'Tomb cult and the "Greek Renaissance"', *Antiquity* 62: 750–61.
(2001) 'Hard surfaces', in *Money, Labour and Land*, ed. P. Cartledge, E. Cohen and L. Foxhall. London: 8–43.
(2004) 'Economic growth in ancient Greece', *Journal of Institutional and Theoretical Economics* 160: 709–42.
(2007) 'Early Iron Age Greece', in *The Cambridge Economic History of the Greco-Roman World*, ed. W. Scheidel, I. Morris and R. Saller. Cambridge: 211–41.
Morris, T. D. (1996) *Southern Slavery and the Law, 1619–1860*. Chapel Hill.
Moulier-Boutang, Y. (1998) *De l'esclavage au salariat. Économie historique de salariat bridé*. Paris.
Mouser, B. *et al.* (1999) 'Conquête de la liberté, mutations politiques, sociales et religieuses en haute Casamance. Les anciens Maccube du Fuladu', in *Figures Peules*, ed. R. Botte, J. Boutrais and J. Schmitz. Paris.
Mrozek, S. (1989) *Lohnarbeit im klassischen Altertum: Ein Beitrag zur Wirtschafts- und Sozialgeschichte*. Bonn.
Mullin, M. (1992) *Africa in America: Slave Acculturation and Resistance in the American South and the British Caribbean, 1736–1831*. Urbana.
Murdock, G. P. (2001) 'Division of labor by gender and postmarital residence in cross-cultural perspective: a reconsideration', *World Cultures* 12: 179–203.
Murdock, G. P. and Morrow, D. O. (1970) 'Subsistence economy and supportive practices: cross-cultural codes 1', *Ethnology* 9: 302–30.
Murdock, G. P. and Provost, C. (1973a) 'Factors in the division of labor by sex: a cross-cultural analysis', *Ethnology* 12: 203–25.
(1973b) 'Measurement of cultural complexity', *Ethnology* 12: 379–93.
Murdock, G. P. and White, D. R. (1969) 'Standard cross-cultural samples', *Ethnology* 8: 329–69.
Murray, O. (1993) *Early Greece*. London, 2nd edn.
Nagle, B. D. (2002) 'Aristotle and Arius Didymus on household and polis', *Rheinisches Museum für Philologie* 145: 198–223.
Naranjo Orovio, C. (1999) 'Humboldt y la isla de Cuba en el siglo XIX', in *Las flores del Paraíso*, ed. P. San Pío and M.-A. Puig-Samper. Barcelona: 121–38.
(2000) 'Humboldt en Cuba: reformismo y abolición', *Debate y perspectivas: Cuadernos de Historia y Ciencias Sociales* 1.
(2005) 'La amenaza haitiana, un miedo interesado : poder y fomento de la población blanca en Cuba', in *El rumor de Haiti en Cuba. Temor, raza y rebeldia, 1789–1844*, ed. M. Dolores Gonzalez Ripoll *et al.* Madrid: 101–78.
Naro, N. P. (ed.) (2003) *Blacks, Coloureds and National Identity in Nineteenth-Century Latin America*. London.
Naroll, R. (1965) 'Galton's problem: the logic of cross-cultural analysis', *Social Research* 32: 428–51.
(1968) 'Some thoughts on comparative method in cultural anthropology' in *Methodology in Social Research*, ed. H. M. Blalock and A. B. Blalock. New York: 236–77.
Nash, G. B. (1998) 'Reverberations of Haiti in the American North: black Saint Dominguans in Philadelphia', *Pennsylvania History* 65: 44–73.

Nash, G. B. and Soderlund, J. R. (1991) *Freedom by Degrees: Emancipation in Pennsylvania and its Aftermath*. New York.
Neeve, P. W. de (1984a) *Colonus: Private Farm-Tenancy in Roman Italy during the Republic and the Early Principate*. Amsterdam.
(1984b) *Peasants in Peril: Location and Economy in Italy in the Second Century BC*. Amsterdam.
Nieboer, H. J. (1971 [1910]) *Slavery as an Industrial System: Ethnological Research*. New York.
Northrup, D. (1995) *Indentured Labor in the Age of Imperialism, 1834–1922*. Cambridge.
(2000) 'Igbo and myth Igbo: culture and ethnicity in the Atlantic world, 1600–1850', *Slavery and Abolition* 21: 1–20.
O' Brien, M. (2004) *Conjectures of Order: Intellectual Life in the Old South* (2 vols.). Chapel Hill.
Oakes, J. (1982) *The Ruling Race: A History of American Slaveholders*. New York.
Oliva, P. (1971) *Sparta and her Social Problems*. Prague.
Olmsted, F. L. (1968 [1861]) *The Cotton Kingdom*. New York.
Oostindie, G. (ed.) (1995) *Fifty Years Later: Antislavery, Capitalism and Modernity in the Dutch Orbit*. Leiden.
Ortiz, F. (1906) *Los negros brujos (apuntes para un estudio de etnología criminal)*. Madrid.
(1916) *Hampa afro-cubana: Los negros esclavos. Estudio sociológico y de derecho público*. La Habana.
(1940a) *Contrapunteo cubano del tabaco y del azúcar (advertencia de sus contrastes agrarios, económicos, históricos y sociales, su etnografía y su transculturación)*. La Habana.
(1940b) 'El fenómeno social de la transculturación y su importancia en Cuba', *Revista Bimestre Cubana* 46: 273–8.
Ortmayr, N. (2004) 'Kulturpflanzen: Transfers und Ausbreitungsprozesse im 18. Jahrhundert', in *Vom Weltgeist beseelt. Globalgeschichte 1700–1815*, ed. M. Grandner and A. Komlosy. Vienna: 73–99.
Osborne, R. (1985) *Demos: The Discovery of Classical Attika*. Cambridge.
Osterhammel, J. (2003) 'Transferanalyse und Vergleich im Fernverhältnis', in *Vergleich und Transfer. Komparatistik in den Sozial-, Geschichts- und Kulturwissenschaften*, ed. H. Kaelble and J. Schriewer. Frankfurt am Main: 439–66.
Otterbein, K. F. (1970) *The Evolution of War: A Cross-Cultural Study*. New Haven.
Oubre, C. (1978) *Forty Acres and a Mule: The Freedmen's Bureau and Black Land Ownership*. Baton Rouge.
Pagden, A. (1982) *The Fall of Natural Man. The American Indian and the Origins of Comparative Ethnology*. Cambridge.
Paquette, R. (1997) 'Revolutionary Saint Domingue in the making of territorial Louisiana', in *A Turbulent Time: The French Revolution and the Greater Caribbean*, ed. D. B. Gaspar and D. P. Geggus. Bloomington: 204–25.
(1998) 'Revolts', in *A Historical Guide to World Slavery*, ed. S. Drescher and S. L. Engerman. New York: 334–44

Parra-Pérez, C. (1954–7) *Mariño y la independencia de Venezuela* (5 vols.). Madrid.
Patterson, O. (1967) *The Sociology of Slavery: Jamaica, 1655–1838*. London.
(1977) 'The structural origins of slavery: a critique of the Nieboer-Domar hypothesis', *Annals of the New York Academy of Sciences* 292: 12–34
(1979) 'Slavery and slave formations', *New Left Review* 117: 31–67.
(1981) 'Slavery', *Collier's Encyclopedia* 21: 71–6.
(1982) *Slavery and Social Death: A Comparative Study*. Cambridge, MA.
(1991) *Freedom: Freedom in the Making of Western Culture*. New York.
(2000) 'Codes from slavery and social death', in *Pre-Coded Variables for the Standard Cross-Cultural Sample*, ed. W. Divale. New York. [http://eclectic.ss.uci.edu/~drwhite/worldcul/SCCS2.pdf]
(2003) 'Reflections on slavery and freedom', in Luraghi and Alcock 2003: 289–309.
Paz, M. B. (2000) *La rebelión de esclavos de 1825 en Guamacaro*. Ciudad Habana.
Peacock, D. P. S. (1982) *Pottery in the Roman World*. New York.
Pearson, M. P. and Thorpe, I. J. N. (eds.) (2005) *Warfare, Violence and Slavery in Pre-History*. Oxford.
Peel, J. D. Y. (2002) 'Yoruba as a city-state culture', in Hansen 2002c: 507–17.
Pelteret, D. A. (2001) *Slavery in Early Medieval England from the Reign of Alfred until the Twelfth Century*. Woodbridge.
Pérez de la Riva, J. (1975) *El barracón y otros ensayos*. La Habana.
Pérez Jr, L. A. (ed.) (1992) *Slaves, Sugar, & Colonial Society: Travel Accounts of Cuba, 1801–1899*. Wilmington.
(1999) *On Becoming Cuban: Identity, Nationality, and Culture*. Chapel Hill.
(2001) *Winds of Change: Hurricanes & the Transformations of Nineteenth-Century Cuba*. Chapel Hill.
Pétré-Grenouilleau, O. (1997) *Les négoces maritimes français XVIIe–XXe siècles*. Paris.
(2004) *Les traites négrières. Essai d'histoire globale*. Paris.
Phillips, U. B. (1908) *A History of Transportation in the Eastern Cotton Belt to 1860*. New York.
(1963 [1929]) *Life and Labor in the Old South*. Boston.
(1968 [1918]) *American Negro Slavery: A Survey of the Supply, Employment and Control of Negro Labor as Determined by the Plantation Regime*. Baton Rouge.
Phillips, W. D. (1985) *Slavery from Roman Times to the Early Transatlantic Trade*. Minneapolis.
(1996) 'Continuity and change in Western slavery: ancient to modern times' in Bush 1996a: 71–88.
Picó, F. (1993) *Al filo del poder: subalternos y dominantes en Puerto Rico, 1739–1910*. Río Piedras, Puerto Rico.
Pikoulas, G. A. (1984) 'TO FULAKEION STO BASILIKO KAI H SHMASIA TOU GIA THN ISTORIKH TOPOGRAFIA THS PERIOCHS', in *PRAKTIKA B/ TOPIKOU SUNEDRIOU MESSHNIAKWN SPOUDWN*. Athens: 177–84.
Pitts, J. (ed.) (2003) *Writings on Slavery*. Baltimore.

Pocock, J. G. A. (1975) *The Machiavellian Moment: Florentine Political Thought and the Atlantic Republican Tradition*. Princeton.
Pollak-Eltz, A. (2000) *La esclavitud en Venezuela: un estudio histórico y cultural*. Caracas.
Popovic, A. (1998) *The Revolt of African Slaves in Iraq in the IIIrd–IXth Century*. Princeton.
Porter, D. H. (1970) *The Abolition of the Slave Trade in England, 1784–1807*. Hamden.
Portuondo, M. M., (2003) 'Plantation factories: science and technology in late-eighteenth-century Cuba', *Technology and Culture* 44: 231–57.
Price, R. (1973) *Maroon Society*. New York.
(ed.) (1979) *Maroon Societies: Rebel Slave Communities in the Americas*. Baltimore.
(2006) 'The miracle of Creolization', in *Afro-Atlantic Dialogues. Anthropology in the Diaspora*, ed. K. A. Yelvington. Oxford: 115–47.
Pryor, F. L. (1977) 'A comparative study of slave societies', *Journal of Comparative Economics* 1: 81–102.
Puig-Samper, M. Á. (2000) *Historia del Jardín Botánico de la Habana*. Aranjuez.
Queirós Mattoso, K. M. De (1988) *Família e sociedade na Bahia do século XIX*. São Paulo.
(1992) *Bahia, século XIX: uma província no Imperio*. Rio de Janeiro.
R. W. N. N. (1856) 'Negro cabins', *Southern Planter* 16: 121–2, reprinted in Breeden 1980: 129–32.
Ragatz, J. L. (1971) *The Fall of the Planter Class in the British Caribbean, 1763–1833: A Study in Social and Economic History*. New York.
Rahe, P. A. (1992) *Republics, Ancient and Modern: Classical Republicanism and the American Revolution*. Chapel Hill.
Régent, F. (2004) *Esclavage, métissage, liberté. La Révolution française en Guadeloupe, 1789–1802*. Paris.
Rehder, J. B. (1999) *Delta Sugar: Louisiana's Vanishing Plantation Landscape*. Chapel Hill.
Reid, A. (2002) '*Negeri*: the culture of Malay-speaking city-states of the fifteenth and sixteenth centuries', in Hansen 2002c: 431–43.
Reinhold, M. (1984) *Classica Americana: The Greek and Roman Heritage in the United States*. Detroit.
Reis, J. J. (2003) *Rebelião escrava no Brasil. A história do levante dos malê em 1835*. São Paulo.
Reis, J. J. and Gomes, F. D. S. (eds.) (1996) *Liberdade por um fio. História dos quilombos no Brasil*. São Paulo.
Renault, F. (1971) *Lavigerie, l'esclavage africain et l'Europe, 1868–1892*. Paris.
Richard, C. J. (1994) *The Founders and the Classics: Greece, Rome, and the American Enlightenment*. Cambridge.
Rihll, T. E. (1993) 'War, slavery and settlement in early Greece', in *War and Society in the Greek World*, ed. J. Rich and G. Shipley. London: 77–107.
(1996) 'The origin and establishment of Greek slavery', in Bush 1996a: 89–111.

(1999) 'Making money in classical Athens', in *Economies Beyond Agriculture*, eds. D. Mattingly and J. Salmon. London: 115–42.

Robertson, C. C. and Klein, M. A. (1983) 'Women's importance in African slave systems', in *Women and Slavery in Africa*, ed. C. C. Robertson and M. A. Klein. Madison: 3–25.

Robinson, D. L. (1970) *Slavery in the Structure of American Politics 1765–1820*. New York.

Rodriguez, J. P. (ed.) (1997) *Historical Encyclopedia of World Slavery*. Santa Barbara.

(ed.) (1999) *Chronology of World Slavery*. Santa Barbara.

Roebuck, C. (1986) 'Chios in the sixth century BC', in Boardman and Vaphopoulou-Richardson 1986: 81–8.

Roebuck, C. A. (1941) *A History of Messenia from 369 to 146 B.C.* Chicago.

Rogers, K. M. (1966) *The Troublesome Helpmate: A History of Misogyny in Literature*. Seattle.

Röhrig-Assunção, M. (1993) *Pflanzer, Sklaven und Kleinbauern in der brasilianischen Provinz Maranhão 1800–1850*. Frankfurt.

(2003) 'From slave to popular culture: the formation of Afro-Brazilian art forms in nineteenth-century Bahia and Rio de Janeiro', *Iberoamericana. América Latina – España – Portugal. Ensayos sobre letras, historia y sociedad. Notas. Reseñas iberoamericanas* 3: 159–76.

Röhrig-Assunção, M. and Zeuske, M. (1998) '"Race", ethnicity and social structure in nineteenth-century Brazil and Cuba', *Ibero-Amerikanisches Archiv. Zeitschrift für Sozialwissenschaften und Geschichte. Neue Folge* 24: 375–443.

Rose, W. L. (ed.) (1976) *A Documentary History of Slavery in North America*. New York.

(1982) *Slavery and Freedom*. New York.

Rosemond de Beauvallon, J.-B. (2002) *La isla de Cuba. Primera Parte: Viaje a la Habana, a las costas, al interior, a Santiago. Sociedad – Costumbres – Paisajes – Episodios*. Santiago de Cuba.

Rosenberg, N. (1976) *Perspectives on Technology*. Cambridge.

Rosivach, V. (1993) 'Agricultural slavery in the Northern colonies and in classical Athens: some comparisons', *Comparative Studies in Society and History* 35: 551–67.

Ross, F. A. (1857) *Slavery Ordained of God*. Philadelphia.

Rostovtzeff, M. (1957) *The Economic and Social History of the Roman Empire*. Oxford.

Rotberg, R. I. (1971) *Haiti: The Politics of Squalor*. Boston.

Rotman, Y. (2004) *Les esclaves et l'esclavage. De la Méditerranée antique à la Méditerranée médiévale VIe–XIe siècles*. Paris.

Rout, L. B. (1976) *The African Experience in Spanish America: 1502 to the Present Day*. Cambridge.

Rubin, V. and Tuden, A. (eds.) (1977) *Comparative Perspectives on Slavery in the New World Plantation Societies*. New York.

Ruete, E. (1991 [1888]) *Memoires d'une princesse arabe*. Paris.

Rush, B. (1773) *An Address to the Inhabitants*, reprinted in Bruns 1977: 224–31.
Russi, A. (1986) 'I pastori e l'esposizione degli infanti nella tarda legislazione imperiale e nei documenti epigrafici', *Mélanges de l'École Francaise de Rome* 98: 855–72.
Saco, A. (1961) *Colección de papeles científicos, históricos, políticos, y de otros ramos sobre la Isla de Cuba, ya publicados, ya inéditos, por Antonio Saco* (3 vols.). La Habana.
(1982 [1862–74]) *Acerca de la Esclavitud y su Historia*. La Habana.
Saint-Méry, M.-L.-É. M. De (1913) *Voyage aux Etats-Unis de l'Amérique, 1793–1798*. New Haven.
Sala-Molins, L. (1987) *Le Code Noir ou le calvaire de Canaan*. Paris.
Sallares, R. (2002) *Malaria and Rome: A History of Malaria in Ancient Italy*. Oxford.
Saller, R. P. (1982) *Personal Patronage under the Early Empire*. Cambridge.
(1984) '*Familia*, *domus*, and the Roman concept of the family', *Phoenix* 38: 336–55.
(1996) 'The hierarchical household in Roman society: a study of domestic slavery' in Bush 1996a: 112–29.
(1999) '*Pater familias*, *Mater familias*, and the gendered semantics of the Roman household', *Classical Philology* 94: 182–97.
(2002) 'Framing the debate over growth in the ancient economy', in Scheidel and von Reden 2002: 251–69.
Salman, M. (2001) *The Embarrassment of Slavery: Controversies over Bondage and Nationalism in the American Colonial Philippines*. Berkeley.
(2004) 'Resisting slavery in the Philippines: ambivalent domestication and the reversibility of comparisons', *Slavery and Abolition* 25: 30–47.
Salmon, J. B. (1984) *Wealthy Corinth: A History of the City to 338 BC*. Oxford.
Salzman, P. (ed.) (1971) 'Comparative studies of nomadism and pastoralism', *Anthropological Quarterly* 44.
(1979) 'Inequality and oppression in nomadic society', in *Pastoral Production and Society*, ed. Equipe Ecologie. Cambridge: 429–46.
San Miguel, P. L. (1997) *La isla imaginada: Historia, identidad y utopía en La Española*. San Juan – Santo Domingo.
Sardan, J.-P. O. de (1983) 'The Songhay-Zarma female slave: relations of production and ideological status', in *Women and Slavery in Africa*, ed. C. C. Robertson and M. A. Klein. Madison: 130–43.
Sarikakis, T. C. (1984) 'Commercial relations between Chios and other Greek cities in antiquity', in Boardman and Vaphopoulou-Richardson 1984: 121–31.
Sarracino, R. (1988) *Los que volvieron a Africa*. La Habana.
Sartorius, D. (2003) 'Conucos y subsistencia: el caso del ingenios Santa Rosalía', in *Espacios, silencios y los sentidos de la libertad: Cuba 1898–1912*, ed. F. Martínez Heredia *et al.* La Habana: 108–27.
Satchell, V. (2002) 'Innovations in sugar-cane mill technology in Jamaica 1760–1830', in *Working Slavery, Pricing Freedom*, ed. V. Shepherd. Abingdon: 93–111.

Saunders, A. C. de C. M. (1982) *A Social History of Black Slaves and Freedmen in Portugal, 1441–1555*. New York.

Scarano, F. A. (1984) *Sugar and Slavery in Puerto Rico: The Plantation Economy of Ponce, 1800–1850*. Madison.

Scarborough, W. K. (2003) *Masters of the Big House: Elite Slaveholders in the Antebellum South*. Baton Rouge.

Scheidel, W. (1989) 'Zur Lohnarbeit bei Columella', *Tyche* 4: 139–46.

(1994) 'Grain cultivation in the villa economy of Roman Italy', in *Land Use in the Roman Empire*, ed. J. Carlsen *et al.* Rome: 159–66.

(1996) *Measuring Sex, Age and Death in the Roman Empire: Explorations in Ancient Demography*. Ann Arbor.

(1997) 'Quantifying the sources of slaves in the early Roman empire', *Journal of Roman Studies* 87: 156–69.

(1998) 'Galley slaves' in Finkelman and Miller 1998, vol. I: 355–6.

(2001) 'The hireling and the slave: a transatlantic perspective', in *Money, Labour and Land*, eds. P. Cartledge, E. Cohen and L. Foxhall. London: 175–84.

(2003) 'Helot numbers: a simplified model', in Luraghi and Alcock 2003: 240–7.

(2004) 'Human mobility in Roman Italy, I: the free population', *Journal of Roman Studies* 94: 1–26.

(2005a) 'Human mobility in Roman Italy, II: the slave population', *Journal of Roman Studies* 95: 64–79.

(2005b) 'Real slave prices and the relative cost of slave labor in the Greco-Roman world', *Ancient Society* 35: 1–17.

(2006) 'The demography of Roman state formation in Italy', in *Herrschaft ohne Integration? Rom und Italien in republikanischer Zeit*, ed. M. Jehne and R. Pfeilschifter. Frankfurt: 207–26.

Scheidel, W. and Von Reden, S. (eds.) (2002) *The Ancient Economy*. London.

Schiavone, A. (1999) *La storia spezzata: Roma antica e Occidente moderno*. Rome-Bari.

Schmidt, N. (2005) *L'abolition de l'esclavage. Cinq siècles de combats XVIe–XXe siècle*. Paris.

Schmidt-Nowara, C. (1999) *Empire and Antislavery: Spain, Cuba, and Puerto Rico, 1833–1874*. Pittsburgh.

(2000) 'The end of slavery and the end of empire: slave emancipation in Cuba and Puerto Rico', *Slavery & Abolition* 21: 188–207.

Schmieder, U. (2003) *Geschlecht und Ethnizität in Lateinamerika im Spiegel von Reiseberichten: Mexiko, Brasilien und Kuba 1780–1880*. Stuttgart.

Schoelcher, V. von (1843) *Colonies étrangères et Haïti. Résulats de l'Émancipation Anglaise* (2 vols.). Paris.

Schuler, M. (1973) 'Akan slave rebellions in the British Caribbean', in *Caribbean Slave Society and Economy*, ed. H. Beckles. New York: 373–86.

Schumacher, L. (2001) *Sklaverei in der Antike*. Munich.

Schumpeter, J. (1994) *History of Economic Analysis*. London.

Schwartz, S. B. (1985) *Sugar Plantations in the Formation of Brazilian Society: Bahia, 1550–1850*. New York.

(1992) *Slaves, Peasants, and Rebels: Reconsidering Brazilian Slavery*. Urbana.
(2004a) 'A commonwealth within itself. The early Brazilian sugar industry, 1550–1670', in Schwartz 2004b: 158–200.
(ed.) (2004b) *Tropical Babylons: Sugar and the Making of the Atlantic World, 1450–1680*. Chapel Hill.

Scott, J. (1996) 'Crisscrossing empires: ships, sailors and resistance in the Lesser Antilles in the eighteenth century', in *The Lesser Antilles in the Age of European Expansion*, ed. R. L. Paquette and S. L. Engerman. Gainesville: 128–43.

Scott, J. C. (1976) *The Moral Economy of the Peasant: Rebellion and Subsistence in Southeast Asia*. New Haven.

Scott, R. (1987) 'Comparing emancipations: a review essay', *Journal of Social History* 20: 565–83.
(1994) 'Defining the boundaries of freedom in the world of cane: Cuba, Brazil, and Louisiana after emancipation', *American Historical Review* 99: 70–102.
(2001) 'Reclaiming Gregoria's mule: the meanings of freedom in the Arimao and Caunao valleys, Cienfuegos, Cuba, 1880–1899', *Past & Present* 170: 181–216.
(2002) 'The provincial archive as a place of memory: confronting oral and written sources on the role of former slaves in the Cuban war of independence (1895–98)', *New West Indian Guide* 76: 191–209.

Scott, R. and Zeuske, M. (2002) 'Property in writing, property on the ground: pigs, horses, land and citizenship in the aftermath of slavery, Cuba, 1880–1909', *Comparative Studies in Society and History* 44: 669–99.
(2004) 'Le "droit d'avoir des droits": l'oral et l'écrit dans les revendications legales des anciens esclaves à Cuba, 1872–1909', *Annales HSS* 3: 521–45.

Sellin, R. H. (1983) 'The large Roman water-mill at Barbegal', *History of Technology* 8: 91–109.

Sergeenko, M. E. (1986) 'Villicus', in *Schiavitù e produzione nella Roma repubblicana*, ed. I. B. Malowist. Rome: 191–207.

Shanin, T. (1972) *The Awkward Class*. Oxford.

Shaw, B. (1998a) 'A wolf by the ears' in Finley 1998 [1980]: 3–74.
(1998b) 'Introduction: the Roman slave wars and history', in *Spartacus and the Slave Wars*, ed. B. Shaw. New York: 1–30.

Sheridan, R. (1960) 'Samuel Martin, innovating sugar planter of Antigua, 1750–1776', *Agricultural History* 34: 126–39.

Shipley, G. (1987) *A History of Samos, 800–188 B.C.* Oxford.

Siegel, B. J. (1947) *Slavery during the Third Dynasty of Ur*. Menasha.

Sio, A. A. (1965) 'Interpretations of slavery: the slave status in the Americas', *Comparative Studies in Society and History* 7: 289–308.

Sivers, J. von (1861) *Cuba, Die Perle der Antillen. Reisedenkwürdigkeiten und Forschungen*. Leipzig.

Skinner, Q. (1978) *The Foundations of Modern Political Thought*. Cambridge.

Skocpol, T. and Somers, M. (1980) 'The use of comparative history in macrosocial inquiry', *Comparative Studies in Society and History* 22: 174–97.

Slenes, R. W. (1999) *Na senzala, uma flor: esperanças e recordações na formação da familia escrava, Brasil Sudeste, século XIX*. Rio de Janeiro.

(2004) 'The Brazilian internal slave trade, 1850–1888: regional economies, slave experience, and the politics of a peculiar market', in *The Chattel Principle: Internal Slave Trades in the Americas*, ed. W. Johnson. New Haven: 325–70.

Smalls, J. (1998) 'Art and illustration', in Drescher and Engerman: 65–76.

Smith, M. E. (2002) 'Aztec city-states', in Hansen 2002c: 581–95.

(2005) *The Aztecs*. Oxford, 2nd edn.

Smith, M. F. (1954) *Baba of Karo*. London.

Smith, M. G. (1955) *The Economy of Hausa Communities of Zaria*. London.

Smith, M. M. (1998) *Debating Slavery: Economy and Society in the Antebellum South*. New York.

Solow, B. (ed.) (1991) *Slavery and the Rise of the Atlantic System*. Cambridge, MA.: 43–61.

(ed.) (1993) *Slavery and the Rise of the Atlantic System*. New York.

Solow, B. and Engerman, S. L. (eds.) (1987) *British Capitalism and Caribbean Slavery: The Legacy of Eric Williams*. New York.

Solow, B. *et al.* (1987) 'Capitalism and slavery in the exceedingly long run', *Journal of Interdisciplinary History* 17: 711–37.

Soumonni, E. (2001) 'Some reflections on the Brazilian legacy in Dahomey', *Slavery and Abolition* 22: 61–71.

Spencer. H. (1893) *The Factors of Organic Evolution*. London.

Spurr, M. S. (1986) *Arable Cultivation in Roman Italy c. 200 B.C.–c. A. D.100*. London.

Stambaugh, J. E. (1988) *The Ancient Roman City*. Baltimore.

Stampp, K. (1956) *The Peculiar Institution: Slavery in the Antebellum American South*. New York.

Ste Croix, G. E. M. de (1983 [1981]) *The Class Struggle in the Ancient Greek World*. London.

Stein, S. J. (1985) *Vassouras: A Brazilian Coffee County, 1850–1900: The Roles of Planter and Slave in a Plantation Society*. Princeton.

Stella, A. (2000) *Histoires d'esclaves dans la péninsule ibérique*. Paris.

Stern, S. J. (1988) 'Feudalism, capitalism, and the world-system in the perspective of Latin America and the Caribbean', *American Historical Review* 93: 829–72.

Storey, G. (1997) 'The population of ancient Rome', *Antiquity* 71: 966–78.

Strasburger, H. (1990) *Zum antiken Gesellschaftsideal*, in *Studien zur Alten Geschichte*, vol. III. Hildesheim.

Strauss, B. (1996) 'The Athenian trireme, school of democracy', in *Demokratia: A Conversation on Democracies, Ancient and Modern*, ed. J. Ober and C. Hedrick. Princeton: 313–26.

Stringfellow, H. T. (1860) *Slavery: Its Origin, Nature and History Considered in the Light of Bible Teachings, Moral Justice and Political Wisdom*. Alexandria.

Strobel, M. (1983) 'Slavery and reproductive labor in Mombasa', in *Women and Slavery in Africa*, ed. C. C. Robertson and M. A. Klein. Madison: 111–29.

Tadman, M. (1989) *Speculators and Slaves: Masters, Traders, and Slaves in the Old South*. Madison.

(2000) 'The demographic coast of sugar: debates on slave societies and natural increase in the Americas', *American Historical Review* 105: 1534–75.

Tannenbaum, F. (1946) *Slave and Citizen: The Negro in the Americas*. New York.

Tardieu, J.-P. (1982) 'L'affranchissement des esclaves aux Amériques espagnoles XVIe–XVIIIe siècle', *Revue Historique* 268: 341–64.

Teitler, H. C. (1985) *Notarii and exceptores*. Amsterdam.

Temin, P. (2004) 'The labour market of the early Roman Empire', *Journal of Interdisciplinary History* 34: 513–38.

Terborg-Penn, R. *et al.* (eds.) (1987) *Women in Africa and the African Diaspora*. Washington, DC.

Testart, A. (2001) *L'esclave, la dette et le pouvoir. Études de sociologie comparative*. Paris.

Thornton, J. (1983) 'Sexual demography: the impact of the slave trade on family structure', in *Women and Slavery in Africa*, ed. C. C. Robertson and M. A. Klein. Madison: 39–48.

Thornton, J. K. (1991a) 'African dimensions of the Stono Rebellion', *American Historical Review* 96: 1101–13.

(1991b) 'African soldiers in the Haitian Revolution', *Journal of Caribbean History* 25: 58–80.

(1993) '"I am the subject of the King of Congo": African political ideology and the Haitian Revolution', *Journal of World History* 4: 181–214.

(1998) 'The Coromantees: an African cultural group in colonial North America and the Caribbean', *Journal of Caribbean History* 32: 161–78.

(2000) 'War, the state, and religious norms in "Coromantee" thought: the ideology of an African American nation', in *Possible Pasts: Becoming Colonial in Early America*, ed. R. B. St George. Ithaca: 181–200.

Thrasher, J. S. (ed.) (2001) Alexander von Humboldt, *The Island of Cuba: A Political Essay*. Princeton.

Thurston, T. and Miller, J. C. (2005) 'Slavery: annual biblographical supplement', *Slavery and Abolition* 26: 421–516.

Tocqueville, A. de. (1840) *Report Made to the Chamber of Deputies on Abolition of Slavery in the French Colonies, July 23, 1839*. Boston.

(1843) 'The emancipation of slaves', reprinted in Pitts 2003: 199–226.

Tod, M. (1901) 'Some unpublished catalogi paterarum argentearum', *Annual of the British School at Athens* 8: 197–230.

Tomich, D. W. (1988) 'The "second slavery": bonded labor and the transformations of the nineteenth-century world economy', in *Rethinking the Nineteenth Century: Contradictions and Movement*, ed. F. Ramírez. New York: 103–17.

(1990) *Slavery in the Circuit of Sugar: Martinique in the World Economy, 1830–1848*. Baltimore.

(1991) 'World slavery and Caribbean capitalism: the Cuban sugar industry, 1760–1868', *Theory and Society* 20: 297–319.

(1997) 'Spaces of slavery, times of freedom: rethinking Caribbean history in world perspective', *Comparative Studies of South Asia, Africa, and the Middle East* 57: 67–80.

(2003) 'The wealth of the empire: Francisco de Arango y Parreño, political economy, and the second slavery in Cuba', *Comparative Studies in Society and History* 45: 4–28.

(2004) *Through the Prism of Slavery: Labor, Capital, and World Economy*. Boulder.

Torgal, L. R. (1982) *Ideologia Política e Teoria do Estado na Restauração*. Coimbra.

Tourmagne, A. (1880) *Histoire de l'esclavage ancien et moderne*. Paris.

Townes, J. M. (1851) 'Management of negroes', *Southern Cultivator* 9: 87–8, reprinted in Breeden 1980: 258–9.

Tribe, K. (1978) *Land, Labour and Economic Discourse*. London.

Trouillot, M.-R. (1995) *Silencing the Past: Power and the Production of History*. Boston.

Troutman, P. (2000) 'Slave trade and sentiment in antebellum Virginia'. Ph.D. thesis, University of Virginia.

Tucker, S. G. (1970 [1796]) *A Dissertation on Slavery with a Proposal for the Gradual Abolition of it in the State of Virginia*. Westport.

Turley, D. (2000) *Slavery*. Oxford.

Turton, A. (1980) 'Thai institutions of slavery', in *African and Asian Systems of Slavery*, ed. J. L. Watson. Oxford: 251–92.

Vainfas, R. (1986) *Ideologia e Escravidão. Os Letrados e a Sociedade Escravista no Brasil Colonial*. Petrópolis.

(1996) 'Deus contra Palmares – Representações Senhoriais e Idéias Jesuíticas', in Reis and dos S. Gomes 1996: 60–80.

Valmin, N. (1941) 'Ein messenisches Kastell und die arkadische Grenzfrage', *Skrifter Utgivna av Svenska Institutet I Rom (Acta Instituti Romani Regni Sueciae) v, Opuscula Archaeologica* 2: 59–76.

Van der Linden, M. (2003) *Transnational Labour History: Explorations*. Aldershot.

Van Wees, H. (2003) 'Conquerors and serfs: wars of conquest and forced labour in archaic Greece', in Luraghi and Alcock 2003: 33–80.

Vaughn, J. (1977) 'Mafakur: a Limbic institution of the Margi', in *Slavery in Africa*, eds. Myers and Kopytoff. Madison.

Verger, P. (1968) *Flux et reflux de la traite des nègres entre le golfe de Bénin et Bahia de Todos dos Santos du XVIIe au XIXe siècle*. Paris.

Vérin, H. (1982) *Entrepreneurs, entreprise. Histoire d'une idée*. Paris.

Verlinden, C. (1949) 'Précédents et parallèles européens de l'esclavage colonial', *O Instituto* 113: 113–53.

(1951) 'Le problème de la continuité de l'histoire coloniale. De la colonisation médiévale à la colonisation moderne', *Revista de Indias* 11: 217–36.

(1955–77) *L'esclavage dans l'Europe médiévale* (2 vols.). Brugge.

Vidal Luna, F. and Klein, H. (2003) *Slavery and Economy of São Paulo 1750–1850*. Stanford.

Viecra, A. (2004) 'Sugar Islands: The sugar economy of Madeira and the Canaries, 1450–1650', in *Tropical Babylons: Sugar and the Making of the Atlantic World, 1450–1680*, ed. S. B. Schwartz. Chapel Hill: 42–84.

Vincent, B. and Stella, A. (1996) 'L'esclavage en Espagne à l'époque moderne : acquis et nouvelles orientations', in *Captius i esclaus a l'Antiguitat i al Mon Modern*, ed. M. Leon Sanchez and G. Lopez Nadal. Naples: 289–300.

Viotti da Costa, E. (1994) *Crowns of Glory, Tears of Blood: The Demerara Slave Rebellion of 1823*. New York.

Vries, J. de (1986) 'The population and economy of the preindustrial Netherlands', in *Population and Economy: Population and History from the Traditional to the Modern World*, ed. R. I. Rotberg and T. K. Rabb. Cambridge: 101–22.

Walker, D. (2004) *NO MORE, NO MORE: Slavery and Cultural Resistance in Havana and New Orleans*. Minneapolis.

Wallerstein, I. (1974) *The Modern World System, Vol. I: Capitalist Agriculture and the Origins of the European World-Economy in the Sixteenth Century*. New York.

(1974–1989) *The Modern World-System* (3 vols.). New York.

(1981) *The Modern World System, Vol. II: Mercantilism and the Consolidation of the European World-Economy, 1600–1750*. New York.

Wallon, H. (1988 [1847]) *Histoire de l'esclavage dans l'antiquité*. Paris.

Washington, A. (1907) *How Beauty was Saved*. New York.

Watson, A. (1977) *Society and Legal Change*. Edinburgh.

(1987) *Roman Slave Law*. Baltimore.

(1989) *Slave Laws in the Americas*. Athens, GA.

Watson, J. L. (1980) 'Slavery as an institution: open and closed systems', in *Asian and African Systems of Slavery*, ed. J. L. Watson. Berkeley: 1–15.

Weber, M. (1964 [1947]) *The Theory of Social and Economic Organization*. New York.

Weiler, I. (2003) *Die Beendigung des Sklavenstatus im Altertum: Ein Beitrag zur vergleichenden Sozialgeschichte*. Stuttgart.

Wergeland, A. M. (1916) *Slavery in Germanic Society during the Middle Ages*. Chicago.

Werner, M. and Zimmermann, B. (2003) 'Penser l'histoire croisée: entre empirie et reflexivité', *Annales HSS* 58: 36–77.

(2004) *De la comparaison à l'histoire croisée*. Paris.

Westenholz, A. (2002) 'The Sumerian city-state', in Hansen 2002c: 23–42.

Westermann, W. L. (1955) *The Slave Systems of Greek and Roman Antiquity*. Philadelphia.

(1968) 'Slavery and the elements of freedom in ancient Greece', in *Slavery in Classical Antiquity*, ed. M. I. Finley. Cambridge: 17–32.

Westermarck, E. (1906–8) *The Origin and Development of the Moral Ideas* (2 vols.). New York.

Weston, P. C. (1857) 'Rules on the rice estate of Plowden C. Weston', *De Bow's Review*, 22: 38–44.

Wheeler, V. (1974) 'Drums and guns: a cross cultural study of the nature of war'. Ph.D. thesis, University of Oregon.

White, A. (2003) 'The politics of "French Negroes" in the United States', *Historical Reflections* 29: 103–21.

Whitman, T. S. (1997) *The Price of Freedom*. Lexington.

Whittaker, C. R. (1987) 'Circe's pigs: from slavery to serfdom in the later Roman world', in *Classical Slavery*, ed. M. I. Finley. London: 88–122.

Wiedemann, T. (1981) *Greek and Roman Slavery*. London.

Wiedemann, T. and Gardner, J. (2002) *Representing the Body of the Slave*. London.

Wiencek, H. (1999) *The Hairstons: An American Family in Black and White*. New York.

Wigen, K. (2006) 'Introduction to the AHR forum: oceans of history', *American Historical Review* 111: 717–21.

Wikander, O. (ed.) (2000) *Handbook of Ancient Water Technology*. Leiden.

Wilamowitz-Moellendorf, U. von (1924) 'Lesefrüchte', *Hermes* 59: 249–73.

Wilberforce, W. (1807) *A Letter on the Abolition of the Slave Trade*. London.

Williams, E. (1964 [1944]) *Capitalism and Slavery*. London.

Williams, W. (ed.) (1999) *The Enlightenment*. Cambridge.

Willis, J. C. (1991) 'From the dictates of pride to the paths of righteousness: slave honour and Christianity in Antebellum Virginia', in *The Edge of the South: Life in 19th Century Virginia*, ed. E. Ayers and J. C. Willis. Charlottesville: 37–55.

Wilson, A. (2002) 'Machines, power and the ancient economy', *Journal of Roman Studies* 92: 1–32.

Wolf, E. (1982) *Europe and the People without History*. Berkeley.

Wood, E. M. (1983) 'Agricultural slavery in classical Athens', *American Journal of Ancient History* 8: 1–47.

Woodward, C. V. (ed.) (1981) *Mary Chesnut's Civil War*. New Haven.

(1985) 'History from slave sources', in *The Slave's Narrative*, ed. C. T. Davis and H. L. Gates Jr. New York: 48–59.

Wright, G. (1978) *The Political Economy of the Cotton South*. New York.

(2003) 'Slavery and American agricultural history', *Agricultural History* 77: 527–52.

Yacou, A. (1973) 'Santiago de Cuba a la hora de la revolución de Santo Domingo (1790–1804)', *Del Caribe* 26: 73–80.

(1986) 'El impacto incierto del abolicionismo inglés y francés en la isla de Cuba (1830–1850)', in *Esclavitud y derechos humanos. La lucha por la libertad del negro en el siglo XIX*, ed. F. de Solano and A. Guimerá. Madrid.

(1987) 'Reflexions comparées sur l'esclavage dans les Antilles françaises et espagnoles, à la veille de la Révolution française', in *L'Amérique espagnole á l'époque des lumières, Tradition – Innovation – Représentations*, ed. Groupe Interdisciplinaire de recherche et de Documentation sur l'Amérique Latine. Paris: 287–305.

(1996) 'La stratégie espagnole d'éradication de Saint-Domingue français, 1790–1804', in *L'Espace Caraïbe. Théâtre et Enjeu des Luttes Impériales (XVIe – XIXe siècle)*, ed. P. Butel and B. Lavallé. Bordeaux: 277–93.

Young, J. R. (1999) *Domesticating Slavery: The Master Class in Georgia and South Carolina, 1670–1837*. Chapel Hill.

Youni, M. (2005) 'Maîtres et esclaves en Macédoine hellénistique', in *Esclavage antique et discriminations socioculturelles*, ed. V. Anastasiadis. Bern: 183–95.

Zanetti Lecuona, O. and García Álvarez, A. (1987) *Caminos para el azúcar*. La Habana.

Zantwijk, R. Van. (1985) *The Aztec Arrangement: The Social History of Pre-Spanish Mexico*. Norman.

Zequeira, M. del C. B. (2003) *La otra familia. Parientes, redes y descendencia de los esclavos en Cuba*. La Habana.

Zeron, C. A. (1998) 'La Compagnie de Jésus et l'institution de l'esclavage au Brésil: les justifications d'ordre historique, théologique et juridique, et leur intégration par une mémoire historique (XVIe–XVIIe siècles)' Ph.D. thesis, École des Hautes Études en Sciences Sociales.

Zeuske, M. (1997) 'The Cimarrón in the archives: a re-reading of Miguel Barnet's biography of Esteban Montejo', *New West Indian Guide* 71: 65–279.

(2001a) '"Geschichtsschreiber von Amerika": Alexander von Humboldt, Kuba und die Humboldteanisierung Lateinamerikas', in *Humboldt in Amerika*, ed. M. Zeuske. Leipzig: 30–83.

(2001b) 'Humboldt, Historismus, Humboldteanisierung (Part 1)', *International Review for Humboldtian Studies* 2. [www.unipotsdam.de/u/romanistik/humboldt/hin/hin3.htm]

(2002a) 'Hidden markers, open secrets: on naming, race marking and race making in Cuba', *New West Indian Guide* 76: 235–66.

(2002b) 'Humboldt, Historismus, Humboldteanisierung (Part 2)', *International Review for Humboldtian Studies* 3. [www.unipotsdam.de/u/romanistik/humboldt/hin/hin4.htm]

(2003) '¿Humboldteanización del mundo occidental? La importancia del viaje de Humboldt para Europa y América Latina', *International Review for Humboldtian Studies* 4. [www.unipotsdam.de/u/romanistik/humboldt/hin/hin_6.htm]

(2004a) *Insel der Extreme. Kuba im 20. Jahrhundert*. Zürich.

(2004b) *Schwarze Karibik. Sklaven, Sklavereikultur und Emanzipation*. Zürich.

(2006a) 'Atlantik, Sklaven und Sklaverei – Elemente einer neuen Globalgeschichte', *Jahrbuch für Geschichte der Europäischen Expansion* 6: 9–44.

(2006b) *Sklaven und Sklaverei in den Welten des Atlantiks, 1400–1940. Umrisse, Anfänge, Akteure, Vergleichsfelder und Bibliografien*. Münster.

(2007) *Geschichte der Sklaven und der Sklaverei auf Kuba (1492–1973). Darstellung, Dokumente und Bilder*.

Zilsel, E. (2000 [1942]) 'The sociological roots of science', *Social Studies of Science* 30: 935–49.

Zilversmit, A. (1967) *The First Emancipation: The Abolition of Slavery in the North*. Chicago.

Ziskind, D. (1993) *Emancipation Acts: Quintessential Labor Laws*. Los Angeles.

Index